A Reader in Animation Studies

A Reader in Animation Studies

Edited by Jayne Pilling

John Libbey

LONDON · PARIS · ROME · SYDNEY

Illustration on the front cover: 'Vince in a tutu', animation cel from Joanna Quinn's film *Body Beautiful*. Still courtesy of artist and filmmaker Joanna Quinn.

National Library Cataloguing-in-Publication data:

A reader in animation studies

ISBN 1 86462 000 5

1. Animation (Cinematography). 2. Animated films. 3. Cartoonists.
   I. Pilling, Jayne.

741.58

Published by

John Libbey & Company Pty Ltd,
Level 10, 15–17 Young Street,
Sydney, NSW 2000, Australia.
Telephone +61 (0)2 9251 4099; facsimile +61 (0)2 9251 4428; e-mail jlsydney@mpx.com.au

John Libbey & Company Ltd, 13 Smiths Yard, Summerley Street, London SW18 4HR, England.
John Libbey Eurotext Ltd, 127 Avenue de la République, 92120 Montrouge, France.
John Libbey – C.I.C. s.r.l., via Lazzaro Spallanzani 11, 00161 Rome, Italy.

Printed in China

Contents

The Society for Animation Studies: A brief history

by Harvey Deneroff, Editor & Publisher, The Animation Report, *Canoga Park, California, the United States*

While I began the Society for Animation Studies (SAS) in Los Angeles in late 1987, I was an unemployed PhD and an adult child of an animator who had been harbouring a long-held frustration with the way the cinema studies establishment seemed to ignore animation. With no funds and lacking an academic affiliation, I nevertheless garnered immediate support from local universities and organisations, as well as a small cadre of academics, independent scholars and filmmakers who gladly agreed to serve on the SAS Steering Committee.

Armed with a grant from the Motion Picture Screen Cartoonists, IATSE Local 839 (it helped that I was their unofficial historian), a mailing was sent out, and memberships started coming in from the United States and Canada, as well as from Europe, Australia and New Zealand. The UCLA Animation Workshop (along with the UCLA Film & Television Archive) and Carleton University (with the Ottawa Animation Festival) put in bids to host the first SAS Conference, which took place in 1989 at UCLA. (Carleton hosted the 1990 conference.)

SAS, through its annual conferences and newsletter, has not only provided a focus for animation studies, but has led to papers and articles on animation appearing more regularly at academic conferences and scholarly journals. It also led to *Animation Journal,* the first juried publication in the field (founded by SAS member Maureen Furniss).

My current involvement with SAS has been rather minimal, preferring to allow my successors as president (William Moritz and Richard J. Leskosky) to ably manage the organisations on behalf of its members. Instead, I take pleasure in mining the friendships and knowledge acquired through my association with the Society in both my personal and professional life.

Introduction

Jayne Pilling

Over the past decade, animation seems finally to have emerged from its previously very marginalised status, both in terms of a growing adult audience for the very heterogenous range of films that come under the rubric 'animation' and in terms of academic study.

This explosion of interest reflects a growing recognition of animation as a medium that spans a far wider range of films than that of cartoons only for children.

The creation of a Society for Animation Studies (SAS) in 1988 is an indication of this changing attitude, and also a significant contributor to it. This book comprises a selection of papers presented at annual SAS conferences. However, 'animation studies' is still hardly established as an academic discipline. Consequently, a 'reader' might be considered a rather pre-emptive gesture in this instance and the conventional introduction to an academic reader (which usually seeks to place its contents in context through the critical and theoretical traditions in previous writings on the subject, and establishes a position or dialectic in relation to the latter), might seem inappropriate.

Nonetheless, 'Where can I find critical writing about animation?' and 'Why has there been so little written on the subject?' are recurrent questions from students and sometimes teachers on the multitude of courses that have begun to adress animation, whether as a component of film, media and popular culture studies, or those that are production-oriented with a critical studies element. It seems more useful, then, to use this introduction to look briefly at some of the reasons for animation's marginalisation, why this has changed in recent years, how this reflects in writing on the subject, and to touch on issues and problems raised in defining the area of animation studies itself.

Animation's rise in popularity

Several factors have contributed to the growing popularity of animation with adult audiences. The success of feature films such as *Who Killed Roger Rabbit?*, *The Nightmare Before Christmas*, the *Wallace & Gromit*[1] films or, in 'art-house' distribution, the films of Jan Svankmajer[2] and the Brothers Quay[3] are obvious examples of animation that have changed viewers' perceptions of the medium as one that is somehow intrinsically only appropriate for entertaining children to one of interest to adult audiences.

The 'movie brat' generation of Steven Spielberg and Joe Dante is vocal in proclaiming their love of Hollywood cartoons and many of their films abound with referential use of them – it is Spielberg who is godfather to *Roger Rabbit*. More recently, Tim Burton's films show similar – if stylistically and thematically wider – animation influences.[4] These are also contributory factors to the animated feature being seen as potentially viable with a hip, young adult audience. The re-emergence of Disney's animation features as a major commercial force, and the deliberate attempt to widen the films' market appeal beyond the traditional core target of the family with young children to an older, particularly adolescent/young adult audience, sees almost every major Hollywood studio rushing to set up an animated features division, for adult as well as family features.

Proliferating cable and satellite television channels demonstrate there is an audience for more innovative, adult-oriented cartoon series such as *The Simpsons*, *Ren & Stimpy*, and more recently, *Duckman* (admittedly more cult than mainstream); in the United Kingdom, Channel Four Television has commissioned series such as *Crapston Villas*, *Pond Life*, and another based on the Oscar-winning animated short *Bob's Birthday*.[5] Perhaps as significant to the development of an audience receptive to innovative animation is the way MTV has brought the work of many independent and more art-oriented animators to a wider audience through commissioning 'idents', thematic 'campaign' spots and occasional shorts. And, even though some people might deplore the techno-fetishistic tendencies associated with the phenomenon, the spectacular results due to developing computer technologies are generating new audience interest.

Animation festivals are currently mushrooming around the world and are accruing more diverse audiences; whereas in the past, the small number of dedicated festivals attracted mainly practitioners. In addition to showcasing new films, festivals also offer an opportunity to discover the enormous range and diversity of the medium's history, through retrospective and thematic programming. The market, however small, has grown: witness the number of art-house cinemas in the United States and Western Europe that have begun to screen whole programmes of short animation films, to appreciative audiences. Video and laserdisc distribution has allowed audiences greater access to, and possibilities for repeat viewing of, a wider range of material than that constrained by the economics of cinema and television distribution.

In the United Kingdom in particular, but also in some other countries, innovative and independent filmmakers are often commissioned to make animated advertising film. As with the example of MTV, television viewers are now used to seeing a far wider and more sophisticated range of animation styles and techniques than traditional cel-animated cartoons.[6]

The recent production boom has dramatically increased the demand for animation talent, and enabled more people who want to make it their profession to do so. Since animation is now seen to embrace a far greater range of styles, subjects and techniques than that of traditional commercial cartoon entertainment, it has also attracted a wider range of talent. Animation courses are proliferating all over Europe and the United States in response to this demand. And, while most courses are practical, they also demonstrate the need for students to learn something of the medium's history, to develop their visual vocabulary and critical awareness of it.

Yet a constant complaint of academics and of students in film, media and production courses is the relative paucity of critical and theoretical writing about animation. True, much has been published on Disney[7] – the man, the films, the cultural impact of an industrial phenomenon, while other cartoon studios from Hollywood's golden age have generated a number of historical and descriptive studies.[8] Nonetheless, the rich diversity of animation as an adult art form outside of the Hollywood classic cartoon remains relatively little known and even less studied – a state of affairs that reflects its commercial marginalisation.

It is worth remembering this critical disdain was not always so prevalent, at least not in Europe. The hot-house atmosphere of European and Russian modernism in the 1920s and early 1930s fostered collaboration and mutual inspiration between different art-forms, including film. Such films, animated shorts among them, were seen usually as shorts before features and discussed as part of that movement, the artistic avant-garde. Critical attention was given, for example, to the formal experiments of Hans Richter, Viking Eggeling and Oskar Fischinger in Germany; to the experimental work commissioned by the Post Office in Britain; to Bartosch's animated adaptation of the Franz Masereel's woodcut novel; along with films by Alexieff and Parker, early Jean Renoir, Painlevé and Ladislas Starewicz in France.[9]

If 'animation' tends to suggest 'cartoons for kiddies' this is clearly due, in great part, to Disney. Following Disney's audacious gamble on the animated feature film, animation became defined by the Disney model – that of the cartoon as child/family entertainment, and as such, a no-go area for most film critics and theorists other than as material for ideological/sociological analysis.

Short films generally have long been marginalised in terms of distribution and exhibition. Once cinemas abandoned the practice of supporting programmes to the feature film, to maximise revenue on more screenings of the latter, commercial production of animation shorts for adult cinema audiences became unviable. Around about the same time as this was happening, television was recycling (sometimes in 'censored for children' versions) Hollywood cartoons (and occasionally foreign animation, similarly adapted), which further defined the medium as only for children.

The issues of distribution and exhibition are important not only for what they tell us about film history, but also because it is clear that low visibility is a contributing factor to animation's marginalisation within film studies. After all, the institutionalised study of cinema is a relatively recent phenomenon.[10] As a developing academic area, film studies has an advantage in being able to assume a certain familiarity (at least until recently) with the 'text' in question, a shared (or at least a common) viewing experience. After all, movies are a mass medium. The same is true for media and pop culture studies. Limited distribution of animation means that no such assumptions of familiarity with a film under discussion could be made – with the obvious exception of Hollywood cartoons.

There was, no doubt, an element of snobbery to this critical disdain, underscored by the cartoon's association with comedy, itself a relatively under-theorised area of film studies.

The widespread use of animation for instructional films might also have contributed to its low status as an object of study.

While from the late 1950s onwards the development of *auteur* theory gave new intellectual status to the work of many Hollywood directors, and contributed to the rise of what came to be known as 'art' or *auteur* cinema, first in Europe, then around the world, a parallel development in animation (in East and Western Europe, Canada, and to a lesser degree in other Western countries) was largely ignored by the critical establishment. This seems all the more paradoxical since animation is often a form of cinema that often fulfills the criteria of art and *auteur*-ism in the most literal sense: a 'camera-stylo' *avant la lettre*.

Until recently, books available on animation[11] tended to fall into (all too few) categories: general historical surveys, which catalogue a small number of the great names and give brief descriptions of the films; studio histories, which have, for the most part, concentrated on the American cartoon studios (with Disney as market leader); 'how to' books of a technical nature for budding animators; books, small publications or anthologies on individual filmmakers; and the odd survey of a kind of animation defined by technique such as puppet animation. Inevitably, most of what has been published has concentrated on American, and mainly classic Hollywood, cartoons, given their familiarity to and popularity with a wide audience. Occasionally, a serious film magazine has devoted a special issue to animation such as the 1975 *Film Comment* issue on American cartoons. *Positif*, the French monthly, is rare among film magazines in giving animation screened at festivals consistent and serious critical attention.

Since the avant-garde has a tradition of critical exegesis of the 'artist-filmmaker', there is more critical–theoretical study of animation in the area of abstract and experimental or non-mainstream work,[12] found in issues of specialist film journals devoted to the avant-garde or theory[13] and occasional publications to accompany exhibitions at animation or other film festivals.[14]

The spate of publications on animation over the last two decades is indicative of the general groundswell of interest in the subject, and its publishing 'marketability'. It is significant that most of the books referred to above seem aimed at a readership that is not academic, but rather one with a particular interest in the subject. And, while the more obviously popular books are often rather lavish colour albums linked to the merchandising and memorabilia phenomenon spawned by the Hollywood studios, or used to promote a current release, they can contain useful information.

Problems of critical language

However, for most of what some call 'art animation' or 'personal filmmaking' that is aimed at adult audiences, there seems to be an even more intransigent problem at issue here: that of critical language.[15] Few film critics or theorists seem to feel equipped to deal with an aesthetic that often relates more to the graphic and plastic arts than to conventional film fiction narrative grounded in photo-realism and psychologism. When writing about live action, references to genre, shooting style, performance modes, lighting or editing can be used as shortcut descriptions or points of comparison, so that even if the reader hasn't seen the film under discussion, they can follow the writer's argument. Such descriptive analysis is more difficult with animation. And, since there are as many different kinds of films as there are visual artists, in this field it seems safer, for many, to plead a lack of ignorance about technique and context as a pretext for lack of a engagement.

Since so much 'art' animation is densely visual and often eschews linear narrative, it can be extremely difficult to describe and analyse because a reader's patience and overview would likely be lost in an exhaustive frame-by-frame description. A Hollywood cartoon is relatively easy to describe: the popping-out eyeballs of Tex Avery's wolf characters, for example, as opposed to a Russian animation using collage, cel and cut-out. Transformation is one of the qualities that animation can explore in ways that live action never could, and again, when it isn't done through graphic line in fairly obvious ways, it can be difficult to convey.

Is animation a misnomer?

The problems for a critical language for animation are further compounded by the enormous range that is produced.

Traditional animation tends to imply that it is a film that tells a story in moving drawings, is usually produced on cels and contains what has been called 'personality animation' with which the narrative's protagonists are imbued. And, while much model and plasticene animation is similarly narrative-driven and contains personality animation, the way it is filmed approximates far more closely to live action cinema than it does to any other form of animation. Then again, some animation is graphic art in motion: ranging from caricature to abstraction. Abstract animation might have more in common with formal experimentation in modern art and avant-garde film than with a gag or story-oriented animation. Heterogeneously found or constructed materials are used to radically different effect by filmmakers such as Svankmajer and the Brothers Quay. A filmmaker such as Patrick Bokanowski, who reworks live action frame by frame while sometimes incorporating other elements, is more likely to 'make sense' to someone with an interest and knowledge of avant-garde cinema – and indeed his films were often rejected by specialist festivals on the grounds of being 'not really animation'. The only consistent common factor to these disparate films is the fact they are all shot frame by frame.

There is no 'taxonomy' of animation styles on which writers can draw, never mind challenge or redraw. In informal discussion with other animation specialists about films, it is often the case that descriptions rely on a form of insiders' shorthand: 'very Zagreb' (which can indicate a visual style, but also an attitude); 'updated UPA'; or 'feels a bit National Film Boardish-ish'. But, there is no sustained attempt to develop a commonly agreed set of descriptive tools. Michael O'Pray[16] has suggested that 'emphasis on the means of representation being part of the representation itself seems central to much animation', which seems particularly true of self-consciously 'art'-oriented animators. Ironically, the art establishment has by and large shown equal lack of critical interest. The fact that many animation filmmakers are also practising artists would suggest that galleries, museums and the critical/promotional apparatus which surround them might have provided a site for reflection and stimulus for interest in this art-form, but this has happened to only a limited degree; perhaps this is related to the realities of the art-market – films are all too easily reproducible, which militates against the investment imperatives of the market.[17]

Perhaps the most significant factor militating against serious critical attention to animation within the rise of insitutionalised film studies is what David Bordwell has characterised as the 'Grand Theory', which dominated 'Anglo-American film studies during the 1970s '. . . as the indispensable frame of reference for understanding all filmic phenomena'.[18] This hugely influential movement made it difficult for those scholars or historians who did not subscribe to theory to gain a voice in the sometime Babel-like confusion of tongues. It also emphasised the fact that many forms of animation are recalcitrant to such approaches; in other words, some rather unconvincing attempts to graft existing film theory onto animation.[19]

Looking at how this situation has evolved, one might attribute this emergence of interest to the academic need to find new territories for its practitioners to explore. Less cynically, one might see changes over the last decade as having benefited from 'Post-Theory'[20] and this in turn has created an academic climate more receptive to a plurality of approaches that might make it easier for work on animation to develop.

SAS as a mirror to film, media and cultural studies

The predominant academic disciplines that inform papers presented at SAS conferences are the following:

- media and popular culture studies
- sociology
- film history (including the investigation of labour, technology and industrial practice)
- film theory, testing itself out (50 years after Eisenstein's writings on Mickey Mouse)
- feminist studies
- reception studies

(Although papers occasionally introduce approaches derived from art history and theory, anthropology and aesthetics, alongside others which emerge from reflections on a filmmaker's own practice, these tend to be in a minority.)

The main categories listed above parallel those found in film, media and cultural studies. The focus of so many SAS papers on Hollywood cartoons, while clearly related to their greater familiarity, seems also to reflect a shift in film studies into the areas of popular cultural and media studies. Issues of representation are recurrent concerns and lend themselves more readily to ideological analysis. Popular culture as fertile ground for critical commentary has contributed to, for example, the success of *The Simpsons* while the growing Western appetite for Japanese *manga* or *anime*, as well as the classic Hollywood cartoons, provide rich cultural studies material. Feminist studies are more receptive to a wider range of animation (i.e. non-Hollywood), probably because in the last twenty years such a lot of women animators have made their mark.

New computer technologies call into question the former distinctions between photographic realism and fantasy, the old Méliès/Lumière divide. Such ontological issues revive arguments about the very definition of animation,[21] as well as encourage academics with a science background into a field usually dominated by those from the arts and humanities.

The following list of topic areas from one year's 'call for papers' is instructive and indicative of the range and diversity of approaches; and also tell us something about the problems in defining 'animation studies':

- National cinemas
- Agendas of culture
- Ethnicity and diversity
- Globalisation of animation: industrial context
- Canon formations
- Modes of production: flipbooks, zoetropes, early cinema apparatus

- Commerce and art
- Analysis of individual films
- Animation theory
- Gender theory in relation to animation

At times, the wildly varying levels and types of discourse can be at once exhilarating, dizzying and deeply frustrating. Again, the question of the lack of common viewing experience compounds the difficulties of meshing and developing such heterogenous approaches, all of which tend to come equipped with their own tradition of critical terminology.

However, given the problems arising from critical language, definitions of animation itself and the marginalisation of non-mainstream animation, a number of books published in the last two years demonstrate how quickly the field of animation studies is developing and rising to meet such challenges.

Attempts to draw up a critical historic–aesthetic framework for popular American animation include Norman Klein's brilliant and ground-breaking work[22] as well as Raffaelli's provocative eschatological comparative analysis of Disney, Warner Brothers and Japanese animation[23] – subjects also examined, from rather different perspectives, in interesting work from Australia.[24]

Giannalberto Bendazzi's encyclopaedic *Cartoons: One Hundred Years of Cinema Animation*[25] covers all kinds of animation produced worldwide and has become the standard reference work. Indeed, it is the only one of its kind. It combines information and accessible critical commentary, taking 'a documentary, critical approach rather than an analysis of economic, industrial or political events' – although when appropriate such context is briefly sketched in – and aims to provide 'an interpretative introduction to filmmakers studied within their own single, specific cultures and inspirations, creative projects and ideas', within an art form that 'spans farce, tragedy, caricature, abstract art and Western and Eastern approaches'.[26]

A study of Czech surrealist artist and filmmaker Jan Svankmajer[27] can be found alongside others on Rosi, Loach and Jarman in a publishing series on 'directors . . . motivated by social, political or historical concerns, or working in opposition to conventional filmmaking systems and structures'. It might well be that Svankmajer figures in this series because, by moving into feature films, he is perceived to have joined the ranks of 'real' (i.e. live action) filmmakers;[28] nonetheless, the book's contributors, both Czech and Western authors, concentrate mainly on his short films.

Film studies' discovery of early cinema has also proved fruitful for animation studies, with Crafton's work in particular,[29] in which early animation is examined in a much wider historical context than is usually the case.

Some of the most interesting recent work to investigate critical and theoretical approaches has appeared in French and Italian publications.[30] One anthology of essays[31] concentrates on the use of sound and music in animation, drawing, in part, on Michel Chion's pioneering work on sound in live action cinema.[32] Indeed, it could be argued that sound has often played a more creative role in animation than it has in most live action. Jean Marcel's work[33] combines lively accessible writing with illuminating reflections on individual films that raise wider issues around line and movement, sound, corporeality, metaphor and metamorphosis in animation. Marcel's work is undeniably enriched by his knowledge of the 'other' cinema (i.e. live action), as is that of Joubert-

Laurencin.[34] While the latter is more academic and densely argued, his retrieval of Bazin's writings (among others) on the subject and his own detailed examination of a number of individual films is fascinating and thought-provoking. In addition, his extremely well-researched and annotated bibliographic sections are a contribution to the development of animation studies in themselves. Animation is the focus of interesting theoretical work in Russia, from the semiotic approach of Mikhail Yampolsky to the more humanist writings of Mikhail Gurevitch.[35] Once again, however, we have another 'language' problem, one that impedes the circulation of ideas – none of the books referred to, with the exception of Bendazzi's *Cartoons*, have been translated. One can only hope the gathering impetus of critical work on animation in the Anglo-American world will remedy this situation.

Although the range of serious books on animation was rather limited until recently, there has always been a wealth of written material outside of books, including work on many lesser-known aspects of animation. The problem was knowing how to find it. A very small number of specialists and aficionados might pass on information to one another, from all manner of obscure sources, but such networking all too often depends on chance encounters. The Internet has, in this respect, made an enormous difference. While much of the material on the Net maybe 'fanzine' in approach, its value as an information source is enhanced by the potential for dialogue between users. In addition, information in the American print magazines, for example, *The Animation Journal*[36] and the *Animation World Network Magazine*, accessible via their Website, provides a lively monthly forum on all aspects of animation internationally and has contributions from academics, industry figures and filmmakers.

This book aims to make available to a wider readership a selection of papers presented at the SAS conferences over the last five years. Most have remained unpublished, although some have appeared in specialist film journals. Any selection process is painful, but as should be clear from all of the above, it is also particularly problematic in this instance. Some conference papers are structured around audio-visual presentations, which are difficult to reproduce in purely written form, although an exception has been made where the visual references are quite easily accessible.[37] Others are more in the nature of 'work-in-progress'. A number of valuable papers on industrial/technological/labour history in relation to animation[38] warrant a book-length anthology with contextual linking material that is beyond the scope of the present volume.

An academic form of proportional representation in terms of subject matter across the totality of papers given at SAS conferences would reproduce the emphasis on American cartoons. The (relatively) European bias in this selection is therefore deliberate: to redress the balance, in terms of what is generally available. Close textual analyses and readings of individual films are privileged here since, in my view, this is an area of animation studies most urgently in need of development, given the issues around critical language already referred to. Although the films discussed might be unknown to some readers, they are all films that have been screened at most international festivals over the years, and many have been shown on United Kingdom television. Some are available on video cassette or laserdisc. Even to those unfamiliar with the films under discussion, I would hope that these essays might spark a desire to see them.

In order to give a more representative idea of the concerns of SAS conferences, and for intrinsic and historical interest, I have included a listing of *all* papers presented between 1989 and 1996. I hope that the selected papers, the bibliographies they contain, and the full list of papers presented, will at least stimulate further work in this new field of 'animation studies'.

Notes

1. Wallace and Gromit are the protagonists of the extremely popular plasticene animation films directed by Nick Park, of Aardman Animation Studios: *A Grand Day Out*, *The Wrong Trousers*, and *A Close Shave* which have gained three Academy Award nominations, with the two latter films winning the Award.

2. Svankmajer's short films are too numerous to mention here: the most well-known being *Dimensions of Dialogue*, which has won numerous awards at film festivals. They have enjoyed successful theatrical distribution in the United Kingdom, Germany and Austria, and to a more limited extent, the United States. More successful in terms of theatrical box-office, no doubt because they were feature films and hence more marketable, were *Alice* and *Faust*. See Michael O'Pray's and Paul Wells's essays in this volume for a more detailed discussion of Svankmajer.

3. The Brothers Quay, working in model animation, have an extensive filmography, and are perhaps best known for their award-winning *The Street of Crocodiles*. Again, their short films have had some success, in terms of theatrical distribution, in Japan, the United Kingdom and the United States. For a discussion of their work, see the essay in this volume by Steve Weiner.

4. The influence of pioneer model animator Ladislas Starewicz, whose most remarkable films were made between 1910 and the mid 1930s, can be clearly seen in *The Nightmare Before Christmas*. While the latter film was conceived by Tim Burton, who did many of the original sketches for the film, it's actual director Henry Selick has also talked in interviews of the influence of East European and experimental animation on his work. Michael Frierson has also written on other animation influences on Tim Burton in *Animation World Network Magazine*.

5. It is interesting to note that these three United Kingdom television animation series were originally inspired by short films madeby the respective filmmakers: Sarah Kennedy, Candy Guard, and Alison Snowden and David Fine.

6. The lucrative budgets allocated to the production of commercials have provided a living for many independent animators, which allows them to continue making their own films, as well as offering a form of subsidised research and development.

7. For a selective bibliography, see footnotes and references to Robin Allan's and other essays in this volume.

8. See especially J. Beck and W. Friedwald, *The Warner Brothers Cartoons* (New Jersey & London: Scarecrow Press, Inc., 1981), reprinted in a revised edition as *Looney Tunes and Merrie Melodies: A Complete Illustrated Guide to the Warner Bros Cartoons* (Henry Holt (1989) and L. Maltin, *Of Mice and Magic: A History of American Animated Cartoons* (New York: Plume, 1980)).

9. Such films were screened in England by the Film Society, a cultural force that brought the notion of film as art to the British intelligentsia.

10. See Mark Langer's essay in this volume.

11. Some examples: T. Sennett, *The Art of Hanna-Barbera* (New York, Viking Studio Books, 1989); ibid., *The Fleischer Story* (New York: Da Capo Press, 1988); R. Noake, *Animation: A Guide to Animated Film Techniques* (London & Sydney: Macdonald Orbis, 1988) (unusually for a book on technique, the author cunningly introduces notions of critical reading of individual films via the techniques discussed); J. Lenburg, *The Great Cartoon Directors* (Jefferson & London: Macfarland, 1983); Adamson, J. Tex Avery, King of the Cartoons, New York, Da Capo Press, 1975; A. Bastiancich (ed.), *Lotte Reiniger* (Turin: Assemblea Teatro/Compagnia del Bagatto, 1982); J. Pilling, (ed.), *Ladislas Starewiecz* (Edinburgh: Edinburgh International Film Festival, 1984). J. Beck (ed.), *The 50 Greatest Cartoons* (Atlanta: Turner Publishing, 1994); P. Brion, *Tex Avery: Les Dessins* (Paris: Editions Nathan Image, 1988).

12. R. Russett and C. Starr, *Experimental Animation* (New York: Van Nostrand Reinhold, 1976). Reprinted, in an expanded edition, subtitled *Origins of a New Art* (New York: Da Capo, 1988).

13. For example, in the United Kingdom, some issues of British journals *Screen*, *Undercut* and *Afterimage*.

14. For example: D. Curtis, *Robert Breer* (Cambridge, Cambridge Animation Festival, 1983); D. Curtis, *Len Lye* (Bristol Animation Festival, 1987).

15. For a pertinent discussion of critical/theoretical approaches to animation, see also M. O'Pray, 'The Animation Film', *Oxford Guide to Film Studies*, J.H.P.C. Gibson (ed.) (Oxford: OUP, 1997).

16. Ibid.

17. Although there a number of 'art galleries' that sell 'limited editions' of 'collectible' cel animation artwork, and this has become a quite lucrative business, this phenomenon is far removed from the role of traditional art galleries in promoting the work of individual artists. On the merchandising of 'artwork' relating to classic Hollywood cartoons, see M. Langer's essay in this volume.

18. D. Bordwell, in N. Carroll (ed.), *Post-Theory: Reconstructing Film Studies* (Madison: The University of Wisconsin Press, 1996).

19. A. Cholodenko (ed.), *The Illusion of Life* (Sydney: Power/Australian Film Commission, 1991).

20. D. Bordwell, in N. Carroll, op.cit.

21. See essays by Manovich and Denslow in this volume.

22. N.M. Klein, *Seven Minutes: The Life and Death of the American Cartoon* (London: Verso, 1993).

23. L. Raffaelli, *Le anime disegnate* (Rome: Castelvecchi, 1994). Now also available in French translation *Les Ames Dessinés* (Paris: Dreamland, 1996).

24. P. Brophy (ed.), *KABOOM! Explosive Animation from America and Japan* (Sydney, Museum of Contemporary Art, 1994).

25. G. Bendazzi, *Cartoons: One Hundred Years of Cinema Animation* (London: John Libbey , 1994).

26. Ibid., from the introduction.

27. P. Hames (ed.), *Dark Alchemy: The Films of Jan Svankmajer* (Trowbridge: Flicks Books, 1995).

28. Similarly, the Bergamo Film Festival, which, like most festivals, is live action feature-film oriented, and is particularly known for its retrospectives, decided to organise a homage to Svankmajer after discovering his most recent feature, *The Conspirators of Pleasure* (1996) and produced a publication to accompany the retrospective that covered all his films. See *Jan Svankmajer*, B. Fornara, F. Pitassio and A. Signorelli (eds) (Bergamo: Bergamo Film Meeting 1997).

29. D. Crafton, *Before Mickey: The Animated Film 1898–1928* (Cambridge–London: MIT, 1982). D. Crafton, *Emile Cohl, Caricature and Film* (New Jersey: Princeton, 1990).

30. For example, G. Bendazzi and G.B.G. Michelone (ed.), *Il Movimento Creato: Studi e documenti di ventisei saggisti sul cinema d'animazione* (Torino: Pluriverso, 1993). See the following footnotes for other references.

31. G. Bendazzi and G. Michelone (ed.) , *Coloriture: Voci, rumore, musiche nel cinema d'animazione* (Bologna: Pendragon, 1995).

32. M. Chion, *La Voix au Cinéma* (Paris: Editions de l'Etoile, 1982); M. Chion, *Le son au cinéma* (Paris: Cahiers du Cinéma, 1985); M. Chion, *La Toile Trouée: la parole au cinéma* (Paris: Editions de l'Etoile, 1988); M. Chion, *Audi-Vision: Sound on Screen* (New York & Chichester, West Sussex: Columbia University Press, 1994).

33. J. Marcel, *Le Langage des Lignes et autres essais sur le cinéma d'animation* (Québec: Cinéma Les 400 coups, 1995). See also his study on French-Canadian animation filmmaker Pierre Hébert, some of whose own reflections on animation are included, in J. Marcel, *Pierre Hébert, l'homme animé* (Québec: Cinéma Les 400 coups , 1996).

34. H. Joubert-Laurencin, *La Lettre Volante: quatre essais sur le cinéma d'animation* (Paris: Presses de la Sorbonne Nouvelle, 1997).

35. See list of SAS Conference Papers in this volume for English language work by Gurevitch.

36. Edited by Maureen Furniss: some SAS Conference papers have been published in this journal, and some, in revised versions, are included in this volume and are acknowledged, where applicable, although they are sometimes in a rather different 'edit' to that which appears here. In most cases, for the present publication, authors have been given the opportunity to revise their original presentation, and sometimes update their work in light of more recent research. The journal encourages contributions from scholars around the world.

37. See Simon Pummell' s essay in this volume.

38. See especially papers presented by M. Langer, R. Leskosky and H. Deneroff in the List of SAS Conference Papers in this volume.

1

What is animation and who needs to know?

An essay on definitions

Philip Kelly Denslow

There are many definitions of animation. The most obvious source of one, the *Webster* dictionary, says animation is:

a: a motion picture made by photographing successive positions of inanimate objects (as puppets or mechanical parts), b: Animated Cartoon, a motion picture made from a series of drawings simulating motion by means of slight progressive changes.

This is a fairly common understanding of the term animation, but it reflects a limited exposure to what the artform has to offer. Whether one agrees with it or not, the *Webster* definition is useful because one can learn something about who is doing the defining. In this case, the folks at G. & C. Merriam should be encouraged to attend an animation festival.

In the international animation community, many definitions have become established by various organisations and entities. We scholars, teachers and filmmakers would probably not be able to agree on a precise definition, but we would be able to compile a nice list of them. Definitions of animation vary from one another for many reasons, including historical development, production and marketing requirements, and aesthetic preferences.

The reason we are examining this issue is that no matter what definition you chose, it faces challenges from new developments in the technology used to produce and distribute animation. Is virtual reality a form of animation? Does computer-generated lifeform simulation qualify? What about the computerised recording of a mime's movements that are later attached to a character which is rendered a frame at a time? Do digital post-production techniques allowing for undetectable compositing and manipulation of live action scenes reduce the shooting of actors onto film to merely an image acquisition phase of the overall production? Is that production then in reality an animated film? Even a narrow definition of animation that excludes all but classic Disney character animation, and the consequent deification of gallery art from those films, is threatened by the computerised ink-and-paint process with its 'created cels' for the collector. All definitions of animation have to be re-thought in the context of changing technology.

The Association of International Film Animation (ASIFA) uses a definition that might be summed up as 'not live action'. This definition allows as many members as possible of the diverse international community of professionals, independents, amateurs, and audiences to participate. The purpose of organisations like ASIFA is to gain membership so as to sponsor activity. The more the merrier, as long as the identity of the group, the 'not live action' makers and fans, is not threatened. This bodes well for ASIFA's ability to absorb people interested in new technology, but the ASIFA sponsored festivals, like Annecy, will need to open new categories of competition if full inclusion is desired. ASIFA's name – the Association of International Film Animation (to crudely translate the French) – includes the technological restriction of the word film, which is becoming increasingly anachronistic as electronic and digital media replace chemical-based forms of production and distribution. For the audience, ASIFA's definition of animation is also becoming less useful as compositing techniques continue to improve, leaving less and less a margin of separation between the live action and the not-live action parts of a production.

Hollywood, or 'the industry' (by which I mean production companies that produce theatrical and television material in a factory-like method) has to define an animator by function. Union contracts, command hierarchy, and end-title credits all determine whether or not a worker is performing a task that is defined as animation. But when is an animator not an animator? The studio that produced the first seasons of *The Simpsons* television series declined to use the job title Animator as part of the process, preferring the term Character Layout for a worker that drew the key poses of a scene. Perhaps this was done to discourage ideas of grandeur and improved wages. The marketing of a studio's services can also influence the naming of that service. Computer-animation studios use the term Technical Director for the person who actually creates the animation on the computer system. Separating such people from the traditional studio animator because of the tools they use serves to highlight the uniqueness of the process for the benefit of clients, and could be a carry-over from the days when the systems used were too crude to create what could be marketed as animation. Most of these Technical Directors still think of themselves as animators, however.

Special Effects, a blurrily defined area of activity within a live action production, can include many methods that resemble animation in every way but by title. A feature film producer might feel more comfortable purchasing something with the name of special effects, which still sounds like filmmaking and whose name is not associated with cute forest creatures, as in animation. Nonetheless, such films as *Terminator 2* and *Death Becomes Her* are very much like *Tom and Jerry* cartoons, where animation is used to show a character being brutally clobbered and deformed, followed by the resumption of a normal appearance. In Hollywood, marketing or thinking about a film as animation automatically throws it into the sphere of influence of the Walt Disney Company. Disney, and now perhaps Turner's cartoon channel on cable, control how most audiences define animation. It is this perceived definition of audiences that studios gravitate toward or avoid when they choose whether or not to use the word animation to describe their product. In a happy merchandising frenzy, Disney markets collectible artwork from its current co-production with Pixar, a completely animated feature. Obviously Disney and now Turner have a vested interest in controlling the public's ideas about what animation is and who the public should look to as a source of it.

Academia uses definitions such as 'created performance', which are carefully worded to establish validity and secure resources for an animation program or class. These definitions function within an environment where animation is often an element that helps to flesh out a school's curriculum. If the animation faculty let their guard down and animation's definition as Film Art is diminished to the status of Cartoons in the minds of the other more numerous funds-hungry faculties, a program can gradually disappear through reallocation and reorganisation. Although academia has some need to maintain a stable definition of animation, this definition is usually adjusted to include anything on the technological horizon, other than that which might step on the toes of other curricular programs. The inclusion of advances in new technology within the purview of animation impresses departmental administrations. But, other areas of a school might also want to carry the new technology banner, leading to intense competition. Such hybrid courses as 'Digital Arts' or 'Multi Media' can sap resources that otherwise could have gone to support an animation program. Since donations are often the only way new equipment can be made available to students, it can be crucial for an animation program to publicise itself as the best repository for forward-thinking corporate support.

When considering the impact of new technology on our ideas about animation, it might be instructive to reflect on the changes already brought about by the use of electronic media in distribution. Over the last 40 years, animation has become a television mainstay, with studios gradually changing over to producing material primarily for home viewing – Disney being the most recent with their afternoon packages for syndication and the distribution of past works on videotape. Cartoons changed from adult theatrical throw-aways, requiring the constant generation of new product, to children's home toys requiring only a new generations of viewers. The placement of a somewhat permanent collection of animated videos in most households could tend to steer the development of innovative methods of production into ways of replicating those collections, spurred on by the economic advantages of having consumers buying everything all over again, with minimal cost to the producer. Witness the transition from analog to digital in the audio-recording market. Aesthetic innovation might be viewed by consumers and producers with suspicion, as it could be seen as posing a threat to the prior investment in products. This implies an ideology of tradition and a more rigid code of what passes for entertainment. Or, everyone will perhaps get sick of seeing over and over again the Disney (to pick on them again) catalogue, and there will be a great demand for something else.

Technology does hold out hope for independent artists to gain access to sophisticated tools as computers and digital reproduction become more and more economical. Visions of small-scale investment leading to large-scale access to markets using telecommunication networks, the aesthetic possibilities of replication and manipulation of existing or created material in the digital realm, and the popularisation of an animator's personal vision are all parts of an optimistic scenario. Although digital imagery is leading us to a preoccupation with the realistic representation of ideas, at the same time these images are less fixed and more malleable than ever before. The ability to edit, combine and reproduce animation or live action in undetectable ways not only blurs any distinctions between those elements, but also changes what value we can attach to it. The trade-off for cheap digital access to an audience via a Web page on the Internet, for example, is the difficulty in controlling ownership and collecting revenue. If there is no discernible difference between an original and a copy, even one many generations away from the first, can we still maintain our current ideas about copyright, royalties and artistic originality?

Is the determining factor for something to be considered animation the actual existence of separate frames? If a computer is dealing with separate images internally, but to the artist or viewer these frames are always seen as part of constant motion, can this still be animation? If it is easy to create quickly, will it be considered animation, or something else, such as electronic puppetry? Another determining factor is often the time needed to create it. How many animated films are touted as the product of many years of dedicated labour? Animators, and those who study animation, are usually fascinated with the processes involved. The definitions of animation usually incorporate some consideration of those processes. Those who make and study animation, whether it be traditional or computer based, are drawn to its requirements for obsessive, repetitive and socially isolated behavior. To turn to the *Webster* again, compulsion is defined as 'an irresistible impulse to perform an irrational act'. This could also serve as a definition of animation, for what is animation if not the desire to make real that which exists in the imagination?

In my own recent work, I have been experimenting with the idea of removing myself as much as possible from the creation of the animation. My goal is to see what happens when I allow a computer that has been configured as a filmmaking machine to make decisions regarding image, time and motion. Motivated by a combination of laziness and curiosity, my initial tests have been encouraging, because I enjoy watching the resulting animation. I bring this up here because I am also curious as to whether this animation is really animation or is it something else? My dilemma over the definition has to do with the concept at the heart of animation, that of bringing something to life. If a non-living thing creates something, is it brought to life? Did creation take place? If I set up a situation that allows this to happen, did I also then really create the film? How much credit do the developers of the hardware and software used by me deserve? Although I did put myself into the role of machine operator, since I had no idea beforehand how the animation would look or move, I hesitate to take too much credit.

With the future digitalisation of all media, all forms of production will perhaps be as much animation as anything else. The makers and studiers of live action film will face similar definitional dilemmas. On page nine of the catalogue titled *Motion Pictures from the Library of Congress Paper Print Collection 1894–1912* by Kemp R. Niver, UC Press, 1967, within the category of comedy, there is a short description of the film Animated Picture Studio, 1903, which notes: 'Before motion pictures got the name as such, they were called "animated" pictures.' We might realise this condition again.

2

'Reality' effects in computer animation

Lev Manovich

Giotto, the inventor of 3D

This is how Frederick Hartt, the author of a widely used textbook *Art. A History of Painting, Sculpture, Architecture* describes the importance of Giotto di Bondone, 'the first giant in the long history of Italian painting':

> In contemporary Italian eyes the step from Cimabue to Giotto was immense in that weight and mass, light and inward extension were suddenly introduced in a direct and convincing manner.[1]

> Giotto's miracle lay in being able to produce for the first time on a flat surface three-dimensional forms, which the French could achieve only in sculpture. For the first time since antiquity a painter has truly conquered solid form.[2]

When the students in an introductory art history survey course that uses Hartt's textbook were asked to compare Giotto and Cimabue, they described Giotto's achievements in a somewhat different language: 'Giotto first achieves strong 3D effect'; 'Cimabue is still 2D, while Giotto has much more of 3D'. I believe that they were referring to three-dimensional computer graphics imagery. For them it had already become the yardstick by which the realism of any visual representation is to be measured.

In his history of vision in the nineteenth century, Jonathan Crary suggested that the rapid development and diffusion of various computer graphics technologies in the 1980s constituted a 'transformation in the nature of visuality probably more profound that the break that separates medieval imagery from Renaissance perspective'.[3] Three-dimensional computer graphics is one of these technologies. Its ability to simulate three-dimensional images of both existent and imagined objects and environments has proven to be useful to education and advertising, business and the military, science and the entertainment industry. Usually, the viewer sees these simulated objects as images on a flat screen; however, new interfaces are being developed (e.g. virtual reality, computer holography) to enhance the illusion of their three-dimensional presence.

'Realism' is the concept that inevitably accompanies the development and assimilation of three-dimensional computer graphics. In media, trade publications and research papers, the history of technological innovation and research is presented as a progression toward realism – the ability to simulate any object in such a way that its computer image is indistinguishable from a photograph. At the same time, it is constantly pointed out that this realism is qualitatively different from the realism of optically based image technologies (e.g. photography and film), because the simulated reality is not indexically related to the existing world.

Despite this difference, the ability to generate three-dimensional stills does not represent a radical break in the history of visual representation of the multitude comparable to the achievements of Giotto. A Renaissance painting and a computer image employ the same technique (a set of consistent depth cues) to create an illusion of space, existent or imaginary. The real break is the introduction of a moving synthetic image – interactive three-dimensional computer graphics and computer animation. With these technologies, a viewer has an experience of moving around the simulated three-dimensional space – something one can't do with a painting.

In order to better understand the nature of 'realism' of the synthetic moving image, it is relevant to consider a contiguous practice of the moving image – the cinema. I will approach the problem of 'realism' in three-dimensional computer animation, starting with the arguments advanced in film theory in regard to cinematic realism. First, I review the key accounts which situate the realism of film in the histories of cinematic technology and style. The next section tests the models suggested in these accounts on the history of computer animation and computer graphics research. The third section shifts the emphasis by considering realism in computer animation as an effect of subject matter.

Technology and style in cinema

The idea of cinematic realism is first of all associated with André Bazin, for whom cinematic technology and style move toward a 'total and complete representation of reality'.[4] In 'The Myth of Total Cinema' Bazin claims that the idea of cinema existed long before the medium had actually appeared and that the development of cinema technology 'little by little made a reality out of original "myth" '.[5] In this account, the modern technology of cinema is a realisation of an ancient myth of mimesis, just as the development of aviation is a realisation of the myth of Icarus. In another influential essay, 'The Evolution of the Language of Cinema', Bazin reads the history of film style in similar teleological terms: the introduction of depth of field style in the end of 1930s and the subsequent innovations of Italian neo-realists in 1940s gradually bring a spectator 'into a relation with the image closer to that which he enjoys with reality'. The essays differ not only in that the first interprets film technology while the second concentrates on film style, but also in their distinct approaches to the problem of realism. In the first essay, realism stands for the approximation of phenomenological qualities of reality, 'the reconstruction of a perfect illusion of the outside world in sound, colour and relief'.[6] In the second essay, Bazin emphasises that a realistic representation should also approximate the perceptual and cognitive dynamics of natural vision. For Bazin, this dynamics involves the active exploration of visual reality. Consequently, he interprets the introduction of depth of field as a step toward realism, because now the viewer can freely explore the space of film image.[7]

Against Bazin's 'idealist' and evolutionary account, Jean-Louis Comolli proposes a 'materialist' and fundamentally non-linear reading of the history of cinematic technology and style. The cinema, Comolli tells us, 'is born immediately as a social machine . . . from the anticipation and confirmation of its social profitability; economic, ideological and symbolic'.[8] Comolli thus proposes to read history of cinema techniques as an intersection of technical, aesthetic, social and ideological determinations; however, his analyses clearly privilege an ideological function of the cinema. For Comolli, this function is the 'objective' duplication of the 'real' itself conceived as specular reflection.[9] Along with other representational cultural practices, cinema works to endlessly re-duplicate the visible thus sustaining the illusion that it is the phenomenal forms (such as the commodity form) that constitute the social 'real' – rather than 'invisible' to the eye relations of productions. To fulfil its function, cinema must maintain and constantly update its 'realism'. Comolli sketches this process using two alternative figures – addition and substitution.

In terms of technological developments, the history of realism in the cinema is one of additions. First, additions are necessary to maintain the process of disavowal, which for Comolli defines the nature of cinematic spectatorship.[10] Each new technological development (e.g. sound, panchromatic stock, colour) points to the viewers just how 'un-realistic' the previous image was and also reminds them that the present image, even though more realistic, will be superseded in the future – thus constantly sustaining the state of disavowal. Secondly, since cinema functions in a structure with other visual media, it has to keep up with their changing level of realism. For instance, by the 1920s the spread of photography with its finely gradated image made cinematic image seem harsh by comparison and the film industry was forced to change to the panchromatic stock to keep up with the standard of photographic realism.[11] This example is a good illustration of Comolli's reliance on Althusserian structuralist Marxism. Unprofitable economically for the film industry, this change is 'profitable' in more abstract terms for the social structure as a whole, helping to sustain the ideology of the real/visible.

In terms of cinematic style, the history of realism in cinema is one of the substitutions of cinematic techniques. For instance, while the change to panchromatic stock adds to the image quality, it leads to other losses. If earlier cinematic realism was maintained through the effects of depth, now 'depth (perspective) loses its importance in the production of "reality effects" in favour of shade, range, colour'.[12] So theorised, a realistic effect in the cinema appears as a constant sum in an equation with a few variables which change historically and have equal weight: if more shading or colour is 'put in', perspective can be 'taken out'. Comolli follows the same logic of substitution/subtraction in sketching the development of cinematic style in its first two decades: the early cinematographic image announces its realism through an abundance of moving figures and the use of deep focus; later these devices fade away and others, such as fictional logic, psychological characters and the coherent space–time of narration, take over.[13]

While for Bazin realism functions as an Idea (in a Hegelian sense), for Comolli it plays an ideological role (in a Marxist sense). For David Bordwell and Janet Staiger, realism in film is first of all connected with the industrial organisation of cinema. Put differently, Bazin draws the idea of realism from mythological utopian thinking. For him, realism is found in the space between reality and a transcendental spectator. Comolli sees it as an effect, produced between the image and the historical viewer and continuously sustained through the ideologically determined additions and substitutions of cinematic technologies and techniques. Bordwell and Staiger locate realism within the institutional discourses of film industries, implying that it is a rational and pragmatic tool in industrial competition.

Emphasising that cinema is an industry like any other, Bordwell and Staiger attribute the changes in cinematic technology to the factors shared by all modern industries – efficiency, product differentiation and maintenance of a standard of quality.[14] One of the advantages of adopting an industrial model is that it allows the authors to look at specific agents such as manufacturing and supplying firms and professional associations.[15] The latter are particularly important since it is in their discourses (conferences, trade meetings and publications) that the standards and goals of stylistic and technical innovations are articulated.

Bordwell and Staiger agree with Comolli that the development of cinematic technology is not linear; however, they claim that it is not random either, as the professional discourses articulate goals of the research and set the limits for permissible innovations.[16] According to Bordwell and Staiger, realism is one of these goals. They believe that such definition of a realism is specific to Hollywood:

> Showmanship, realism, invisibility: such cannons guided the SMPE [Society of Motion Picture Engineers] members toward understanding the acceptable and unacceptable choices in technical innovations and these too became teleological. In another industry, the engineer's goal might be an unbreakable glass or a lighter alloy. In the film industry, the goals were not only increased efficiency, economy and flexibility but also spectacle, concealment of artifice and what Goldsmith [1934 president of SMPE] called 'the production of an acceptance semblance of reality.[17]

Bordwell and Staiger are satisfied with Goldsmith's definition of realism as 'the production of an acceptance semblance of reality'. However, such general and transhistorical definition does not seem to have any specificity for Hollywood and thus can't really account for the direction of technological innovation. Moreover, although they claim to have successfully reduced realism to a rational and a functional notion, in fact they have not managed to eliminate Bazin's idealism. It reappears in the comparison between the goals of innovation in film and other industries. 'Lighter alloy' is used in aviation industry which can be thought of as the realisation of the myth of Icarus; and is there not something mythical and fairy tale-like about 'unbreakable glass' . . .

Technology and style in computer animation

How can these three influential accounts of cinematic realism be used to approach the problem of realism in computer animation? Bazin, Comolli, and Bordwell and Staiger present three different strategies, three different starting points. Bazin builds his argument by comparing the changing quality of the cinematic image with the phenomenological impression of visual reality. Comolli's analysis suggests a different strategy: to think of the history of computer graphics technologies and the changing stylistic conventions as a chain of substitutions functioning to sustain the reality effect for audiences. Finally, to follow Bordwell and Staiger's approach is to analyse the relationship between the character of realism in computer animation and the particular industrial organisation of the computer graphics industry. (For instance, we can ask how this character is affected by the cost difference between hardware and software development.) Further, we should pay attention to professional organisations in the field and their discourses which articulate the goals of research and where we might expect to find 'admonitions about the range and nature of *permissible* innovations'.[18]

I will try the three strategies in turn.

If we follow Bazin's approach and compare images drawn from the history of three-dimensional computer graphics with the visual perception of natural reality, his evolutionary narrative appears to be confirmed. Images progress towards the fuller and fuller illusion of reality: from wire-frame displays to smooth shadows, intricate textures, aerial perspective; from geometric shapes to moving animal and human figures; from Cimabue to Giotto to Leonardo and beyond. Bazin's idea that deep-focus cinematography allowed the spectator a more active position in relation to film image, thus bringing cinematic perception closer to real life perception, also finds a recent equivalent in interactive computer graphics, where the user can freely explore the virtual space of the display from different points of view. And with such extensions of computer graphics technology as virtual reality, the promise of Bazin's 'total realism' appears to be closer than ever, literally within arms reach of the virtual reality user.

The history of the style and technology of computer animation can also be seen in a different way. For example, Comolli reads the history of realistic media as a constant trade-off of codes, a chain of substitutions producing the reality effect for audiences, rather than as an asymptotic movement toward the axes labelled 'reality'. His interpretation of the history of film style is first of all supported by the shift he observes between the cinematic style of the 1900s and the 1920s, the example I have already mentioned. Early film announces its realism by excessive representations of deep space achieved through every possible means: deep focus, moving figures and frame compositions which emphasise the effect of linear perspective. In the 1920s, with the adaptation of panchromatic film stock, 'depth (perspective) loses its importance in the production of "reality effects" in favour of shade, range, colour'.[19] A similar trade-off of codes can be observed during the short history of commercial three-dimensional computer animation which begins around 1980. Initially, the single frames of animations were schematic; cartoon-like because the objects could only be rendered in wireframe or facet shaded form. Illusionism was limited to the indication of objects' volumes. To compensate for this limited illusionism of a single image, computer animations of the early 1980s ubiquitously showed deep space. This was done by emphasising linear perspective (mostly, through the excessive use of grids) and by building animations around rapid movement in depth in the direction perpendicular to the screen. Toward the end of the 1980s, with the commercial availability of such techniques as smooth shading, texture mapping and cast shadows, the individual frames of animations approached more closely the ideal of photo realism. At this time, the codes by which early animation signalled deep space started to disappear. In place of rapid in-depth movements and grids, animation began to feature lateral movements in shallow space.

The observed substitution of realistic codes in the history of computer animation seems to confirm Comolli's argument. The introduction of new illusionistic techniques dislodge old ones. Comolli explains this process of sustaining reality effect from the point of view of audiences. Following Bordwell and Staiger's approach, we can consider the same phenomenon from the producers' points of view. For the production companies, the constant substitution of codes is necessary to stay competitive.

As in every industry, the producers of computer animation stay competitive by differentiating their products. To attract clients, a company has to be able to offer some novel effects and techniques. But why do the old techniques disappear? The specificity of industrial organisation of the computer animation field is that it is driven by software innovation. (In this, the field is closer to the computer industry as a whole, rather than to film industry or graphic design.) New algorithms to produce new effects are constantly being developed. To stay competitive, a company has to quickly incorporate the new software into their offerings. The animations are designed to show off the latest algorithm. Correspondingly, the effects possible with older algorithms are featured less often – available to everybody else in the field, they no longer signal 'state of the art'. Thus, the trade-off of codes in the history of computer animation can be related to the competitive pressure to quickly utilise the latest achievements of software research.

While commercial companies employ programmers capable of adopting published algorithms for the production environment, the theoretical work of developing these algorithms mainly takes place in academic computer science departments and in research groups of top computer companies such as Apple or Silicon Graphics. To further pursue the question of realism we need to ask about the direction of this work. Do computer graphics researches share a common goal?

In analysing the same question for film industry, Bordwell and Staiger claim that realism 'was rationally adopted as an engineering aim'.[20] They attempt to discover the specificity of Hollywood's conception of realism in the discourses of the professional organisations such as SMPE.

For the computer graphics industry, the major professional organisation is SIGGRAPH (Special Interest Group on Computer Graphics of the Association for Computing Machinery). Its annual conventions, attended by tenths of thousands of delegates, combine a trade show, a festival of computer animation and a scientific conference where the best new research work is presented. The conferences also serve as the meeting place for the field's researchers, engineers and commercial designers. If the research has a common direction, we can expect to find its articulations in SIGGRAPH proceedings.

Indeed, a typical research paper includes a reference to realism as the goal of investigations in computer graphics field. For example, a 1987 paper presented by three highly recognised scientists offers this definition of realism:

> Reys is an image rendering system developed at Lucasfilm Ltd and currently in use at Pixar. In designing Reys, our goal was an architecture optimised for fast high-quality rendering of complex animated scenes. By fast we mean being able to compute a feature-length film in about a year; *high quality means virtually indistinguishable from live action motion picture photography; and complex means as visually rich as real scenes.*[21] (my emphasis)

In this definition, achieving synthetic realism means attaining two goals: the simulation of codes of traditional cinematography and the simulation of the perceptual properties of real life objects and environments.

The first goal, the simulation of cinematagraphic codes, was in principle solved early on as these codes are well defined and few in number. Every current professional computer animation system incorporates a virtual camera with a variable length lens, depth of field effect, motion blur and controllable lights.

The second goal, the simulation of 'real scenes', turned out to be more complex. The digital recreation of any object involves solving three separate problems: the representation of an object's shape, the effects of light on its surface and the pattern of movement. To have a general solution for each problem requires the exact simulation of underlying physical properties and processes. This is impossible because of the extreme mathematical complexity. For instance, to fully simulate the shape of a tree would involve mathematically 'growing' every leaf, every brunch, every piece of bark; and to fully simulate the colour of a tree's surface a programmer has to consider every other object in the scene, from grass to clouds to other trees. In practice, computer graphics researchers have resorted to solving particular local cases, developing a number of *unrelated* techniques for simulation of *some* kinds of shapes, materials and movements.

The result is a realism that is highly uneven. Of course, one may suggest that this is not an entirely new development and that it can already be observed in the history of twentieth-century optical and electronic representational technologies, which allows for a more precise rendering of certain features of visual reality at the expense of others. For instance, both colour film and colour television are utilised to assure an acceptable rendering of human flesh tones at the expense of other colours. However, the limitations of simulated realism are qualitatively different.

With optically-based representations, the camera records already existing reality. Everything that exists can be photographed. Camera artefacts such as depth of field, film grain, and the limited tonal range, affect the image as a whole. With three dimensional computer graphics, reality itself has to be constructed from scratch before it can be photographed by a virtual camera.

Therefore, the photo-realistic simulation of 'real scenes' is practically impossible because the techniques available to commercial animators only cover the particular phenomena of visual reality. For example, the animator using a particular software package can easily create a shape of human face, but not the hair; the materials such as plastic or metal but not cloth or leather; or the flight of a bird but not the jumps of a frog. The realism of computer animation is highly uneven, reflecting the range of problems that were addressed and solved.

What determines which particular problems received priority in research? To a large extent, this was determined by the needs of the early sponsors of this research – the Pentagon and Hollywood. I am not concerned here to trace fully the history of these sponsorships. What is important for my argument is that the requirements of military and entertainment applications determined the concentration of research to simulate the particular phenomena of visual reality such as landscapes and moving figures.

One of the original motivations behind the development of photo-realistic computer graphics was its application for flight simulators and other training technology.[22] And since simulators require synthetic landscapes, a lot of research went into the techniques to render clouds, rugged terrains, trees and aerial perspective. Thus, the work which led to the development of the famous technique to represent natural shapes (such as mountains) using fractal mathematics was undertaken at Boeing.[23] Other well-known algorithms to simulate natural scenes and clouds were developed by the researchers of Grumman Aerospace Corporation.[24] The latter technology was used for flight simulators and also was applied to pattern recognition research in target tracking by a missile.[25]

Another major sponsor was the entertainment industry, lured by the promise of lowering the costs of film and television production. In 1979, Lucasfilms, Ltd. (George Lucas's company) organised a computer animation research division. It hired the best computer scientists in the field to produce animations for special effects. The research for the effects in such films as *Star Trek II: The Wrath of Khan* and *Return of the Jedi* have led to the development of important algorithms which became widely used by others.[26]

Along with special effects, a lot of research activity has been dedicated to the development of moving humanoid figures and synthetic actors, since commercial film and video productions centre around characters. Significantly, the first time that computer animation was used in a feature film (*Looker*, 1980) was to create a three-dimensional model of an actress. One of the early attempts to simulate human facial expressions featured synthetic replicas of Marilyn Monroe and Humphrey Bogart.[27] In another acclaimed animation, produced by the Kleiser-Wolczak Construction Company in 1988, a synthetic human figure was humorously cast as Nestor Sextone, a candidate for the presidency in the Synthetic Actors Guild.

The task of creating fully synthetic human actors has turned out to be more complex than was originally anticipated. Researchers continue to work on this problem. For instance, the 1992 SIGGRAPH conference presented a session on 'Humans and Clothing' which featured such papers as 'Dressing Animated Synthetic Actors with Complex Deformable Clothes'[28] and 'A Simple Method for Extracting the Natural Beauty of Hair'.[29] Meanwhile, Hollywood has already created a new genre of films (*Terminator 2*, *Jurassic Park* and *Mask*) structured around 'the state of the art' in digital actor simulation. In computer graphics it is still easier to create the fantastic and extraordinary than to simulate ordinary human beings. Consequently, each of these films is centred around an extraordinary character consisting of a series of special effects – morphing into different shapes, exploding into particles and so on.

The icons of mimesis

While the privileging of certain areas in research can be attributed to the needs of the sponsors, other areas received consistent attention for a different reason. To support the idea of progress of computer graphics toward realism, researchers privilege particular subjects that culturally connote the mastery of mimetic representation.

Historically, the idea of mimesis has been connected with the success in illusionistic representation of certain subjects. The original episode in the history of Western painting is the story of the competition of Zeuxis and Parrhasiuss. The grapes painted by Zeuxis symbolise his skill to create living nature out of inanimate matter of paint. Further examples in the history of art include the celebration of the mimetic skill of those painters who were able to simulate another symbol of living nature – the human flesh.

While the painting tradition had its own iconography of subjects connoting mimesis, moving image media relies on a different set of subjects. Steven Neale describes how early film demonstrated its authenticity by representing moving nature:

> What was lacking [in photographs] was the wind, the very index of real, natural movement. Hence the obsessive contemporary fascination, not just with movement, not just with scale, but also with waves and sea spray, with smoke and spray.[30]

Computer graphics researchers resort to similar subjects to signify the realism of animation. 'Moving nature' presented at SIGGRAPH conferences have included animations of smoke, fire, sea waves and moving grass.[31] These privileged signs of realism overcompensate for the inability of computer graphics researchers to simulate fully such 'real scenes'.

Conclusion

In the twentieth century, new technologies of representation and simulation replace one another in rapid succession, therefore creating a perpetual lag between our experience of their effects and our understanding of this experience. A reality effect of a moving image is a case in point. As film scholars were producing increasingly detailed studies of cinematic realism, film itself was already being undermined by three-dimensional computer animation. Indeed, consider the following chronology.

Bazin's *Evolution of the Language of Cinema* is a compilation of three articles written between 1952 and 1955. In 1951 the viewers of the popular television show 'See it Now' for the first time saw a computer graphics display, generated by MIT computer Whirlwind, built in 1949. One animation was of a bouncing ball, another of a rocket's trajectory.[32]

Comolli's *Machines of the Visible* was given as a paper at the seminal conference on the cinematic apparatus in 1978. The same year saw the publication of a crucial paper for the history of computer graphics research. It presented a method to simulate bump textures, which is still one of the most powerful techniques of synthetic photo realism.[33]

Bordwell and Staiger's chapter *Technology, Style and Mode of Production* forms a part of the comprehensive *The Classical Hollywood Cinema: Film Style & Mode of Production to 1960*, published in 1985.[34] By this year, most of the fundamental photo-realistic techniques were discovered and turnkey computer animation systems were already employed by media production companies.

As three-dimensional synthetic imagery is used more and more widely in contemporary visual culture, the problem of realism has to be studied afresh. And while many theoretical accounts that developed in relation do cinema do hold when applied to synthetic imaging, we can't assume that any concept or model can be taken for granted.

As this article has tried to demonstrate, the differences between cinematic and synthetic realism begin on the level of ontology. New realism is partial and uneven, rather than analogue and uniform. The artificial reality which can be simulated with three-dimensional computer graphics is fundamentally incomplete, full of gaps and white spots.

Who determines what will be filled and what will remain a gap in the simulated world? As I already noted, the available computer graphics techniques reflect particular military and industrial needs which paid for their developments. In addition, as these techniques migrate from specialised markets toward mass consumers, they become biased in yet another way.

The amount of labour involved in constructing reality from scratch in a computer makes it hard to resist the temptation to utilise pre-assembled, standardised objects, characters and behaviours readily provided by software manufacturers – fractal landscapes, checkerboard floors, complete characters and so on. Every program comes with libraries of ready-to-use models, effects or even complete animations. While a hundred years ago the user of a Kodak camera was asked just to push a button, she/he still had the freedom to point the camera at anything. Now, the instruction 'you push the button, we do the rest' is becoming 'you push the button, we create your world'. This is yet another way in which commercial and corporate imagination has a new potential to shape our own vision of synthetic reality.

An earlier version of this essay was presented at the 1991 SAS Conference; and also published as 'Assembling Reality: Myths of Computer Graphics'. *Afterimage* 20, no. 2 (September 1992): 12–14. It also appeared in a German translation in *Illusion und Simulation*. Begegnung mit der Reality. Stefan Iglhaut, Florian Roetzer, Elizabeth Schweeger (eds). (Cantz Verlag: Ostfildern, 1995.)

Notes

1. Frederick Hartt, *Art. A History of Painting, Sculpture, Architecture* (New Jersey: Prentice Hall), 503.
2. Ibid., 504.
3. Jonathan Crary, *Techniques of the Observer* (Cambridge, MA and London: MIT Press, 1990), 1.
4. André Bazin (transl.), *What is Cinema?* Vol. 1 (Berkeley: University of California Press, 1967), 20.
5. Ibid., 21.
6. Ibid., 20.
7. Ibid., 36–37.
8. Jean-Louis Comolli, 'Machines of the Visible', in *The Cinematic Apparatus*, eds Teresa De Lauretis and Steven Health (New York: St. Martin Press, 1980), 122.
9. Ibid., 133.
10. Ibid., 132.
11. Ibid., 131.
12. Ibid., 131.
13. Ibid., 130.
14. David Bordwell and Janet Staiger, 'Technology, Style and Mode of Production', in *The Classical Hollywood Cinema*, eds David Bordwell, Janet Staiger and Kristin Thompson (New York: Columbia University Press, 1985), 247.
15. Ibid., 250.
16. Ibid., 260.
17. Ibid., 258.
18. Ibid., 260.
19. Jean-Louis Comolli, 'Machines of the Visible', in *The Cinematic Apparatus*, eds Teresa De Lauretis and Steven Health (New York: St. Martin Press, 1980), 131.
20. David Bordwell and Janet Staiger, 'Technology, Style and Mode of Production', in *The Classical Hollywood Cinema*, eds David Bordwell, Janet Staiger and Kristin Thompson (New York: Columbia University Press, 1985), 258.
21. R. Cook, L. Carpenter and E. Catull, 'The Reys Image Rendering Architecture', *Computer Graphics*, 21.4 (1987): 91–102.
22. Cynthia Goodman, *Digital Visions* (New York: Harry N. Abrams, Inc., 1987), 102.
23. L. Carpenter, A. Fournier and D. Fussell, 'Fractal Surfaces', *Communications of the ACM* (1981).
24. Geoffrey Y. Gardner, 'Simulation of Natural Scenes Using Textured Quadric Surfaces', *Computer Graphics*, 18.3 (1984): 21–30; Geoffrey Y. Gardner, 'Visual Simulation of Clouds', *Computer Graphics*, 19.3 (1985): 297–304.
25. Geoffrey Y. Gardner, 'Simulation of Natural Scenes Using Textured Quadric Surfaces', *Computer Graphics*, 18.3 (1984): 19.
26. William T. Reeves, 'Particle Systems – A Technique for Modeling a Class of Fuzzy Objects', *ACM Transactions on Graphics*, 2.3 (1983): 91–108.
27. Nadia Magnenat-Thalman and Daniel Thalman, 'The Direction of Synthetic Actors in the Film 'Rendezvous a Montreal', *IEEE Computer Graphics and Applications*, December 1987.
28. M. Carignan, Y. Yang, N. Thalmann and D. Thalmann, 'Dressing Animated Synthetic Actors with Complex Deformable Clothes', *Computer Graphics*, 26.2 (1982): 99–104.
29. K. Anjyo, Y. Usami and T. Kurihara, 'A Simple Method for Extracting the Natural Beauty of Hair', *Computer Graphics*, 26.2 (1982): 111–120.
30. Steve Neale, *Cinema and Technology* (Bloomington: Indiana University Press, 1985), 52.
31. Ken Perlin, 'An Image Synthesizer', *Computer Graphics*, 19.3 (1985): 287–296; Nelson Max, 'Vectorised procedure models for natural terrain: waves and islands in the sunset', *Computer Graphics*, 15.3. (1981); William T. Reeves and Ricki Blau, 'Approximate and Probabilistic Algorithms for Shading and Rendering Structured Particle Systems', *Computer Graphics*, 19.3

(1985): 313–322.

32.   Cynthia Goodman, *Digital Visions* (New York: Harry N. Abrams, Inc., 1987), 18–19.

33.   J.F. Blinn, 'Simulation of Wrinkled Surfaces', *Computer Graphics* (August 1978): 286–292.

34.   David Bordwell and Janet Staiger, 'Technology, Style and Mode of Production', in *The Classical Hollywood Cinema*, eds David Bordwell, Janet Staiger and Kristin Thompson (New York: Columbia University Press, 1985), 247; Lev Manovich, '"Real" Wars: Aesthetics and Professionalism in Computer Animation', *Design Issues*, 8.1 (1991).

3

Second-order realism and post-modernist aesthetics in computer animation

Andy Darley

This paper is concerned with questions of aesthetic form. It is about the relationship between computer imaging and the emergence of a new aesthetics of self – referentiality and surface play. I want to indicate some ways in which such an aesthetic is occurring, and attempt to locate and describe some of its defining characteristics and forms.

I shall do this by examining the short film *Red's Dream* (1987) – a computer animation from the domain of popular entertainment. This film is an example of what I call *secondary* or *second-order* realism; that is to say, it involves an attempt to produce old ways of seeing or representing by *other means*. There are two main points.

The first point is that the film displays unprecedented forms of imagery, which involves something more than the simple fact that a new technique or process of image origination has been used in the production of the film. In other words, the new technique of digital imaging does not produce these new forms of image – discussed in what follows – all by itself. What is being attempted with this new means involves particular kinds of contact with already established aesthetic conventions and forms.

The second point following from this is that in *Red's Dream*, such contact comprises modalities both of hybridisation and simulation. These underlie both the formal make-up of the text as a whole and the novel forms of imagery involved. The resulting aesthetic is an illuminating example of visual post-modernism. It is a particular instantiation of a generalised shift towards the increasing use of inter-textual reference, involving forms of pastiche, eclecticism and simulation. This aesthetic is an example of new levels of preoccupation with signifiers at the expense of signification and reference.

Red's Dream opens at night on a street in a contemporary cityscape. It is raining; the occasional sound of distant, rumbling thunder tells us that an electrical storm has recently passed over. The street is deserted. We are shown a bicycle storefront and through the travelling camera eye and a dissolve we enter this store. There, along with other new bikes, we find a red unicycle for sale. It leans in a corner of the showroom designated (by a sign on the wall) the 'clearance corner', and it carries a tag marked '50 percent Off'. Through a zoom into the saddle of the unicycle, the screen turns to black and the scene shifts to what we soon realise is the dream of the film's title. In this dream-sequence the unicycle appears on a stage ridden by a clown. The clown juggles three polished balls while cycling around the stage. Judging by the scattered and unappreciative clapping of the off-screen audience the clown's act is not a success. He is eventually upstaged by the unicycle which, becoming increasingly human in its behaviour, takes over and finishes the clown's juggling act to the sound of great applause. As the applause turns into the sound of the rain, we return – through a background dissolve – to the setting of the bicycle store. Here we find the unicycle ('Red') in the middle of the showroom bowing to an 'audience' which now consists of a row of mute bicycles. 'Realising' that the previous sequence was just a dream, the unicycle returns to its original place in the showroom corner, saddle hung dejectedly, confirmed in its feelings of loneliness and rejection. The cycle falls back into its original position, losing as it does so its anthropomorphic aspect (a fascinating representation of death) as it returns to an inert, lifeless object. We find ourselves outside in the street looking up at the showroom window. It is still raining, the film ends.

The scenario's apparent simplicity tends to disguise the fact that in certain other respects this film is more complicated and sophisticated than it seems. In the first place, its fictional narrative draws upon and is constructed through the established codes of both classical narrative cinema (live action) and the animated cartoon. In this respect it is a hybrid; though by no means novel in this regard. Precedents can be found in the Disney Studio's attempts, from the late 1930s to mobilise *certain* of the existing aesthetic codes of classical narrative cinema (live action) and to integrate them in a more rigorous fashion than had hitherto been the case within drawn cartoonal forms.[1] What Disney succeeded in achieving by this was a heightened sense of both naturalism and illusionism within a form (the animated cartoon) that was usually seen as, in a certain sense, inherently non-realistic. This heightened realism was largely produced by a combination of introducing unprecedented levels of spatial and temporal verisimilitude into the fictional world via the continuity system, use of psychologically rounded characters to ground and motivate the trajectory of the narrative, and an enhanced literality in the drawn imagery itself (inspired by the 'impression of reality' of live action photography).

Red's Dream brings new levels of sophistication to this tradition of cartoonal realism. The film consists of three major segments. The first establishes the overall atmosphere, setting and motivation for the rest of the narrative. The second is a dream – or fantasy – sequence. The third has two separate motivations: a return to 'reality' and the central character's reaction to this, and an equilibrium re-established through a return to the film's opening setting and location. Together, these segments or scenes comprise a quasi-circular trajectory each displaying different registers or modalities of realism. The movement is from *naturalistic observation* in the first scene, to *realistically depicted* or *rendered fantasy* in the second, which shifts to *psychological (anthromorphic) realism* or *illusion* in the third, before, finally, there is a modulated return to the opening's *naturalistic description* or *observation*.

The sound track meticulously parallels the illusionistic modalities of the unfolding image track. In the first segment, for example, when the camera enters the store, the sound of rain and distant thunder becomes muffled and combined with another ambient sound, thereby reinforcing the spectator's impression of having actually come inside. We also hear, as the camera approaches the corner in which the unicycle is leaning and as we see a bucket on the floor beside it, the sound of drops of water from a leaking roof falling into the pail. A more sophisticated example of the illusionism at work here is the contrast between the sound of flexing saddle springs, contrived to carry off the anthropomorphism when the cycle is bowing during the dream sequence, and the subsequent sound of the unicycles' saddle bouncing to rest in the scene involving the (sophisticated) metamorphosis from humanised object to inert material thing. Where deviation from this naturalist/illusionist function does occur, is with the music track – a lone, rather mournful saxophone – which runs (off-screen) under the whole of the opening segment. This music provides atmosphere, underlining the maudlin and sentimental mood of the film as a whole.

The film is clearly an example of the continued refinement of a particular tradition of cinematic realism. At the same time, however, I suggest that it involves much more. There are significant differences at the aesthetic level between this film and related predecessors.

What are these differences? They have little or nothing to do with content of meaning: in this respect *Red's Dream* is unexceptional. Rather, it is at the level of form, that the film begins to distinguish itself. From the spectator's point of view this is discernible in the first instance at the level of the image itself. There is something unusual about the imagery, though describing exactly what it is, is not easy. In terms of plasticity, texture, look (particularly the illusion of three-dimensional space) and movement, it certainly involves a much higher degree of surface accuracy than has hitherto been the case in the animated cartoon. More than this, however, it can be characterised as involving a certain ambiguity. One is uncertain of its status in terms of means of origination: is it animation, live action, a combination of these . . . or what? The imagery fascinates precisely because of this uncertainty, induced by the novelty of its appearances: the different ways in which it recasts, amalgamates and confuses familiar techniques and forms. Such fascination comes to define the primary way in which the text is received here: this entails a displacement away from concentration on the story (such as it is) towards the allure of the image itself.

To account for the features which ultimately mark *Red's Dream* as aesthetically different with respect to previous examples within the tradition, one must attempt to understand the ways in which the new means of image origination figure in the production of the text. Then one might ask how the differences at the level of production might be related to, or affects changes at, the level of reception or reading.

Existing techniques and existing aesthetic conventions or rules are two key factors shaping any emergent form of cultural production. Ostensibly, *Red's Dream* is a film. It is reproduced and distributed for exhibition in 35 mm film format. However, the means by which it was produced are radically different from those of traditional film and cartoon. The actual process of image origination and construction did not involve the usual paraphernalia of either live action or cartoon, even though the computer-synthesised moving imagery is displayed and eventually reproduced through the established media of video (CRT) and film.[2] Rather, what takes place here is that the camera, lights, locations, sets, props, actors, cel, paint, puppets and so forth, physically disappear, to be replaced by their virtual equivalents within the computer programme.

At the level of aesthetic conventions, we appear to have here an extension or development of the preoccupation with heightened realism first displayed by Disney. The crucial difference in this instance is that the new digital techniques are employed in an attempt to achieve this goal through complex forms of image simulation. Indeed, the historical form of 'cartoonal' realism associated with Disney itself becomes a partial model and reference for an attempted simulation by other means.

Perhaps paradoxically it is precisely through its 'simulational' or imitative impulse that *Red's Dream* not only continues the realist course of Disney, but at the same time produces altogether new forms of image. It does this through an original way of combining images. It is an exemplary text in this respect and constitutes an original form of image hybridisation made possible by digital techniques. The mode of combination involved here is somewhat indirect and removed from the kind of manipulation of final imagery usually associated with ways of combining and linking (i.e. through practices such as superimposition, collage, in-frame or between-shot juxtaposition). In this instance, the combination is not of already produced images – raw material awaiting some kind of work combination. Rather, it is a question of the synthetic combining through the computer of a number of prior image forms. These are: Disney-style animation, three-dimensional animation and live action cinema. Each of these kinds or forms of film provide a partial model for the programmers and animators to aim for in the search for heightened illusionism. The computer eventually brings them all together (fusing them) in the process of synthesising the final simulation or image.

In other words, the digital emulation in *Red's Dream* does not just involve the traditional cartoon form as a model, for one must recognise the way in which this form has been made to combine or become co-extensive with, the conditions which are obtained on and within the live action set. Of course, this set is a virtual one, itself a simulation created in the program of the computer. However, among other things, it is able to emulate three-dimensional spatial and temporal conditions, natural and non-natural lighting conditions and effects, surface texture, the full range of colours, the movement of objects and, as well, the complete range of movements of a virtual film camera within and around it. When cartoon characters and, just as importantly, cartoonal tropes such as anthropomorphism are then imaged through this simulacrum of the live action studio, and the resulting impression of a new level of analogical imagery is achieved within the cartoon, then this is a consequence of the peculiar crossing or fusing of traditionally distinct forms of film.

The peculiar mode of hybrid imagery which emerges from this process helps to account for what may be described as the most excessive character of this text with regard to its most obvious model, the Disney cartoon. I suggest that it helps us to understand what I referred to previously as the ambiguous character of the imagery in the text in question. In the case of *Red's Dream* – and this applies to other examples with the same goal in view[3] – the new techniques of image/text simulation produce, not a simulation that is wholly indistinguishable from its model, but ultimately, a relatively unprecedented king of image (and text).

Certainly, the ambiguity associated with the look of the imagery is reinforced by the subtle use of pastiche, the assimilation of different styles, the tacit adoption of the codes and conventions that underlie them, pervading the whole of the film. However, it is only partially correct to say that the image track in *Red's Dream*, synthesised entirely by digital computer, involves a completely new way of creating old ways of seeing. It certainly does involve this, the means and processes involved are wholly new, and 'institutional modes of representation' which developed earlier and in association with other media are assimilated by this new process in the film in question. In this case, the result of such simulation is synergetic: old ways of seeing, certainly; however, through the new simulation medium – computer synthesis – these become augmented through a kind of intensification so that they take on (in addition) an extra dimension: they escape or transcend their models.

It is precisely the detail of lighting, colour and texture – akin to cinematography, yet different somehow because it is just too pristine – the peculiar substantiality of the figures and objects, the novel way they appear to occupy and move within three-dimensional space even though represented on a two-dimensional screen, that might make even the most innocent of spectators suspect that this was somehow not like the cartoons he or she is used to watching. This has to do with specific qualities intrinsic to 'the look'; that is, the actual rendering of the simulated images themselves (and in this case, where the simulational mode is animation, to the way in which they move). The look of the imagery 'exceeds' that which is normally associated with its model(s). There is an intensification or exaggeration (a certain kind of foregrounding) at the level of the (moving) image of the analogical or mimetic aspect of these image models (i.e. of live action cinematography and photo-realist cartoon).

One might allow that it is, perhaps, just conceivable that innocent viewers believe they are watching a film which involves a combination of ordinary cinematography (or extremely realistic two-dimensional cartooning) and traditional puppet or three-dimensional animation. And yet, that portion of the film – stretching from the beginning of the dream sequence to the cycle's terminal return to the 'clearance corner' – which could most easily be mistaken for puppet animation, has a quality to it that marks it as somehow different. There is a fluidity of movement to the figures – the unicycling clown (particularly when he is cycling around the stage in mid-air), the juggling of the snooker balls and the anthropomorphic behaviour and actions of the unicycle – that is just too consistent and smooth to have been produced by even the most perfectionist of traditional three-dimensional animators.

Similarly, the spectator's view of the introductory and concluding scenes that include imagery of the city, the street and the store interior, oscillates between mistaking it for live action cinematography on the one hand or extremely accomplished naturalistic two-dimensional animation on the other. Does this ambiguity have to do with the way in which the scene is illuminated? Surely the lighting effects are too sophisticated and naturalistic for traditional animation and yet, nor do they quite constitute the illumination one usually associates with a photographed scene.[4]

The excess involved here is similar to that of so-called super- or hyper-realist painting that first emerged in the United States in the 1960s.[5] Such painting takes photography itself as its model or subject. Indeed, it is much more direct than image simulation by computer, involving the meticulous copying of a photograph (which the painter may or may not have taken him/herself).[6] What is important about such painting for present purposes is firstly, the excessive nature of the resulting imagery: the painting results in an intensification or exaggeration, and thereby a kind of foregrounding, of the realistic/analogical character of its model: the photographic medium. Secondly, it involves artifice – in this case simulation through copying – of a second order.

Of course, there is a difference between these two modes of image generation at the very least on the level of technical realisation. Producing a copy of a photograph via the meticulous and painstaking method of painting (usually with an air brush) a slide, projected (and thus enlarged) onto a canvas, is very different to producing a simulation of a particular kind of cartoon film by the techniques involved in digital image generation (a practice that uses extremely powerful computers and highly complex programmes). Yet, despite the very different techniques of production and rendering used in each case, purely at the level of the image a similar effect is achieved. Although the computer-generated images of *Red's Dream* have, subsequent to their synthesis, been recorded onto film, this only (at most) minimally modifies what might be described as the hyper-realist character of those images.

There are other ways in which parallels can be drawn between the two modes. Despite the obvious differences between their respective models – stills photography on the one hand and film on the other and the different aesthetic conventions variously established within each mode – the simulation, both in *Red's Dream* and in super-realist painting involves the reproduction of these conventions. In super-realist painting this follows simply from the act of copying a still photograph. Thus, cropping, focus, film stock, lighting, printing and the iconography (subject matter) itself – elements which are mobilised and differently codified depending upon the kind of photography taken as subject – are transposed as part of the meticulous reproduction. *Red's Dream* is not quite so simple because the simulation does not involve direct copying; rather, it is the production of a copy without an original, an instance of a certain kind or kinds of film realised through other means. Nevertheless, such methodology also entails a transposition of aesthetic codes into the simulation itself, no matter that this transposition is less direct, given the more abstract nature of the models and the origination involved in the simulation in this instance.

Unlike a super-realist painting, however, *Red's Dream* is a second-order simulation that is much more continuous with the illusionism contained in the aesthetic form(s) it uses for its model or subject. Factors at work in super-realist painting clearly distinguish it from its model, the still photograph: scale is perhaps the most important example, though viewing distance when confronting the painting itself is also crucial here. Thus, although both the photographic quality (image) and photographic conventionality (contained in the kind of photograph copied) are present in the super-realist work, it is nevertheless clear that no one will confuse the painting with a photograph or the simulation with its model (except, perhaps, if he or she sees that painting as a photographic reproduction in a book!). *Red's Dream* on the other hand, is ultimately reproduced precisely in the medium it is attempting to simulate, that is, film.

The nub of the difference between *Red's Room* and a super-realist painting is that, while both are clearly primarily about realism (i.e. two different techno-aesthetic modes, forms and styles of realism), unlike super-realism, *Red's Dream* tends to dissimulate this concern. In other words, it does not, as a super-realist painting does, disclose the realism and illusionism – the transparency – underlying its aesthetic model. Indeed, if anything it promotes the continuance of it. Thus the computer animator and technician working within this tradition appear to be striving for simulations that are indistinguishable from their model, whereas the hyper-realist painter does not. She or he knows that this is an impossible goal and besides, it is never the object of the exercise anyway, only a means to other ends.

This does not mean, however, as I have already intimated, that *Red's Dream* succeeds in its 'objective' of the perfect simulation of its model. Indeed, given my claim that its model is not one simple image as is the case with a super-realist work, but exists rather as several separate moving-image forms, it becomes hard to see how it could succeed in this sense. Hybridity lies at the heart of the simulation involved in *Red's Dream* and the excess and ambiguity produced by this unprecedented mode of image conjunction is precisely the film's aesthetic novelty. This is not, however, the result of any conscious strategy of aesthetic self-reflexivity, at least not in the sense that super-realism might be understood. It is rather, the outcome of a striving for photo realism by other means; an 'accident' almost, of the experimentation taking place in efforts to achieve the goal of computer simulations that are totally indistinguishable from photographs or films. Indeed, hybridity not only helps to constitute the aesthetic peculiarities of *Red's Dream*, it also describes something of the production practices involved in its making: a mixture of entertainment strategies and research and development objectives.[7]

I am claiming that what is important about *Red's Dream* is the peculiar way in which it is about realist and illusionary qualities, not character and plot. A preoccupation with the computer synthesis of realistic imagery was at the forefront of the minds of those who produced the film. This fascination with achieving the appearances of a prior mode of representation (i.e. moving photo-realist images) by other means is one of the central objectives of the film and computer graphics industries. A technical problem – the concrete possibility of achieving 'photography' by other means – begins to take over, and to determine the aesthetics of certain modes of contemporary visual culture. These attempts – as in *Red's Dream* – to imitate and simulate are far removed from traditional notions of representation because they displace and demote questions of reference and meaning (or if you prefer, signification); substituting instead a preoccupation with means and the image or signifier itself as a site or object of fascination.

No doubt *Red's Dream* is – as its producers believe – about producing realistic imagery: an illusionistic text. At the same time, it is much more than this because the film involves an attempt to perfect an entirely new way of creating old ways of seeing. It is simulation of a second order in the sense that prior or established modes of representation – in this case classical Hollywood and allied animated cartoonal forms and their medium, photography – are assumed as the models for entirely new techniques of reproduction. Of course, this methodology is not coincidental. It is tied to the non-indexical characteristic of computer-generated imagery. That the film should turn more readily to simulating already established forms and modes of representation rather than attempting a first-order representation of events and things in the world seems to be connected with its definitive difference from photographic recording techniques. The break is with direct analogue procedures; that is, with recording and the fidelities of recording. Computer-generated images do not involve recording, except in senses of indirect or secondary contact. Strictly speaking (and using Pierce's categories or elements of the sign), computer-generated imagery is iconic, never indexical, no matter how photo-realistic it looks, in the sense that photography is an index (not necessarily reliable) of there having been something in the world previously (staged or not).[8]

Like the super-realist paintings that precede it, the imagery in *Red's Dream* is highly arresting. However, it is arresting – and again in a similar fashion to the former – not so much for what it contains but for what it is: an imitation via the computer of imagery characteristic of other (earlier) means of representation. It is precisely this attempt to originate through other means texts containing types of imagery that are already of an extraordinary analogical accuracy which becomes the focus and governs the object of looking; everything begins and ends with the image and its relation to its prior model(s).

There are, to be sure, contending versions of what constitutes the defining characteristics of contemporary visual culture. One common recognition, which frequently cuts across differing positions, is that an aesthetic shift has occurred in which representation and its ties to reference and referential meaning has begun to disappear. First challenged in the aesthetic domain by modernist forms and practices, the suggestion is that this disappearance is increasingly manifest in a more generalised way within mass culture today. It is argued that what today replaces an aesthetic based on the idea of representation, (and this applies equally to realism's or representationalism's anti-aesthetic – radical modernism) is a new aesthetic centred on 'intertextual reference', 'pastiche', 'eclecticism', 'simulation' and 'spectacle'. The new electronic or digital imaging technologies now play a particularly important role in these developments. Their evolving techniques and processes enable various kinds of image simulation, similar to that under discussion and they are also greatly extending the speed and capacity for various forms of direct and indirect image combination. They work, for the moment, with and upon already existing images and image forms. Though I would want to resist attempts to connect these new imaging techniques in a strictly causal or deterministic way with the post-modernist aesthetics adumbrated here, there can be no doubt that a deepening connection is growing between the two.

One final question. Would an innocent spectator, as I have claimed, begin at least to suspect that there was something peculiar about the 'look' or appearance of the realistic imagery which makes up *Red's Dream*? It seems to me that the answer to this has to do with the notion of 'spectator innocence'. My claim about the text in question involves a certain degree of comparison: it is made in relation to knowledge of prior (existing) texts. Even the 'innocent' spectator of cartoon or (mainstream) narrative has the experience of previous films by which he or she can gauge this one. However, beyond this, the notion of 'innocence' is hard to sustain, given the widespread (and increasing) circulation of subsidiary forms of textuality that variously reflect upon the cinema and cinematic texts. Many spectators, for example, have already made a particular reading, or readings (in the form of a review or reviews) by the time they see a certain film for the first time.

The prior knowledge that *Red's Dream* is a film produced by computer will affect to some extent the way people receive it. Insofar as the computer imaging professional's preoccupation with realism forms the basis of popular discussions and reviews (and it does), then there will be a corresponding interest in this regard on the part of the spectator. Knowledge of how the images in *Red's Dream* were produced makes the film interesting, and certainly, for a particular kind of 'non-innocent' spectator it would seem that this element is increasingly becoming the central factor for his (such spectators are overwhelmingly male) appreciation of such images. In this instance, a fascination with the extent to which a particular technique can be made either to mimic external appearances and action, or in addition, create surface illusionism in fantastical or impossible scenarios, becomes the essential prequisite of appreciation: technique (means as ends) and the spectacle it produces are both fetishised.[9] The subsidiary texts (journalistic criticism, review and articles) which give insights into both the techniques themselves and the production of those primary texts which employed them thus become a central part of the spectating experience itself: star images and signs of authorship are here displaced by technical fascination.[10]

This paper was presented at the 1993 SAS Conference, Farnham, England.

Notes

1. The culmination of these efforts, of course, was *Snow White* (1937), a feature-length cartoon. However, the same drive is evident in countless other Disney animation shorts produced both before and after the latter. A classic in this regard is *The Old Mill* released the same year as *Snow White* as part of the *Silly Symphonies* series.

2. For the purposes of reproduction and distribution the digital image is downloaded into hard copy – CRT and then film – from the computers central processing unit and memory store.

3. Further examples from the Pixar Studio include: *Luxo Junior* (1986), *Tin Toy* (1988) and *Knick-Knack* (1989). Examples from other producers are *Tony De Peltrie* (1985), University of Montreal, *Stanley and Stella: Breaking the Ice* (1987), *Symbolics* and *Visitor On a Foggy Night* (1985), University of Hiroshima.

4. Another example of this revolves around the anthropomorphism of the unicycle; in particular, the sequence where the cycle loses its anthropomorphic character and turns once again into a lifeless object. This extraordinary visual metamorphosis would not have succeeded to anywhere near the same extent in its 'reality-illusion' objective had it been attempted using either traditional drawn animation or puppet animation; whereas, the computer synthesis of this overt visual transformation from lifelike, human behaviour to movement associated with inert matter is achieved with a seamlessness which raises the reality-illusion of the scene to a new level.

5. See for example, G. Battock (ed.) *Super Realism: A Critical Anthology* (New York: Dutton, 1975).

6. The photographs themselves run the gamut from portraiture, amateur snapshots, still-life and close-up photography, to postcards, advertising and publicity photographs, aerial photography and photographs of aspects of everyday (usually city and suburban) life.

7. Further examples that display this research exercise aspect include the computer-animated short are: *Stanley and Stella; Breaking the Ice* (1987) which, in addition to attempting surface accuracy in terms of texture and lighting, took as one of its main goals the visual simulation of flocks of birds and shoals of fish; the computer animation *Rendezvous à Montreal* (1987), which tackles the problems of computer synthesis and animating photo-realistic actors (in this case Marilyn Monroe and James Cagney); and the computer animation *Luxo Junior* (1986) which, among other things, is preoccupied with the computer generation of 'realistic-artificial' lighting effects in relation to moving objects.

8. C. S. Pierce, *Collected Papers, Volumes I–VIII*, eds C. Hartshorne and P. Weiss (Cambridge: Harvard University Press, 1931).

9. Two recent examples of this phenomenon are, of course, *Terminator 2: Judgement Day* (1992) and *Jurassic Park* (1993).

10. A typical example of this phenomenon is the cult special effects journal *Cinefex*.

The Quay brothers' *The Epic of Gilgamesh* and the 'metaphysics of obscenity'

Steve Weiner

The puppet animators Stephen and Timothy Quay, with producer Keith Griffiths, form the Atelier Koninck. Their first film, *Nocturna Artificialia* (1979), a single-puppet film and *Ein Brudermord*, a two-puppet film based on Kafka, were both heavily atmospheric. The Atelier then made a paper-puppet satire on Stravinsky and a film about the Flemish playwright De Ghelderode. Then followed three art documentaries, for which the Quays made puppet-animated inserts, on Punch and Judy, Janacek and Jan Svankmajer. *Songs of the Chief of the Officers of*

Brothers Stephen Quay (left) and Timothy Quay (right), puppet animators who, with producer Keith Griffiths, created their version of The Epic of Gilgamesh *(1985)*

© Atelier Koninck

Gilgamesh fuses puppetry with sexual psychopathology by featuring a moronic toddler who traps a flying man/insect with a woman table

©Atelier Koninck

Hunar Louse or *This Unnameable Little Broom* (1985) (called *Gilgamesh* for short), a film in which a moronic toddler traps a flying man/insect with a woman-table, changed the direction of their films by fusing puppetry to sexual psychopathology.

In 1985, Keith Griffiths received development money from London's Channel Four to make a pilot for a 9-episode, 52-minute film for actors, dancers and life-size rod puppets based on the Sumerian *Epic of Gilgamesh*. According to the tale, King Gilgamesh forced building projects and *droit de seigneur* on his subjects and to ease their burden, the gods created a rival, Enkidu, a wild man of the steppes. Gilgamesh sent a prostitute to meet with Enkidu and seduce him. Afterward, in the royal city, Gilgamesh beat Enkidu, who became his manservant. In an enchanted forest, after supernatural adventures together, Enkidu died. Gilgamesh went back to his palace, bitterly contemplating death.

Griffiths's treatment of the story, written by Alan Passes, a Swiss novelist, was ironic modernist theatre. A cropheaded Speaker narrates in a black studio-space decorated with ash and charred fragments of Biblical and musical manuscripts. Voices 'whisper history'. Architecture blatantly made of paper represents the royal city, Uruk. Gilgamesh's projects were 'part Piranesi, part Futurist'. There was an analogy to Mussolini. Rod puppets were scene changers, voyeurs, proletariats, or formed a Greek chorus.[1] Atelier Koninck chose to film the seduction of Enkidu. In Griffiths–Passes' treatment, a masked semi-naked girl drifted onto a set draped with nets and seduced him. A dance sequence was choreographed by Kim Baldstrup, a Danish film student, and filmed.

The Quays had already been toying with a different idea suggested in the work *Sobre des Angels* (Concerning the Angels, 1927–28), an 'angelology' of tormented love by the Spanish surrealist poet Rafael Alberti. In one poem, for example, the poet stumbles around his house when the violent angel of love flies in. In the Quays' sketches and notes for the idea, an angel/insect flew down towards low, mysterious lighting, tricked by perspectives to the point of suffocation by mirror-traps, and was drawn to a table –

a *machine deleriante* or *theatricum metaphysique* – that wore yellow and red stockings, sugar cubes and tea cups for breasts and played *musique automatique*. A napkin unfolded. A drawer slid open 'like a genital'. The angel put its hands on the table as on a pinball machine. Catapulted into high-tension wires, it was electrocuted. Then a devil/spider came out of a trap door, and a yellow curtain and club of thorns arrived. The angel/insect came back to life. The devil/spider beat it in the curtain, gave it a comb and invited it to the table.[2]

The Quays adapted Griffiths–Passes' treatment to their idea. At first, sketches and notations for the set bore traces of their previous film, animated inserts of benign magic for the Svankmajer documentary: a 'metaphysical room', an 'anatomical table' (graphic-art torso top), and 'neon' wires.[3] The revolving or exposed set in darkness, with pathological electrical devices, came from *Punch* and *Ein Brudermord*. They then added elements from Griffiths–Passes' treatment: 'textured bark' of the enchanted forest, created out of dandelions and stalks, and the 'pressure of a strong wind in an imaginary tunnel'. The angel, glued with feathers, mandibles, bird cartilage and conch shell from *Janacek*, became Enkidu. Sumeria, however, disappeared. The forest, in the shooting log, was *la foret*. A word on the wall, *Tabak*, a Belgian cigarette, became the calligraphed *Tepek* on a wall. Hooks that shot out of the wall resembled eighteenth-century medical prongs.

The set was lit with four front lights, two back lights, a right-side light and two angled

Above *An early sketch for the woman-table. It was based on a pin-ball machine and was part of the angel–devil premise*

©Atelier Koninck

Left *The man/insect is lured to the woman-table*

©Atelier Koninck

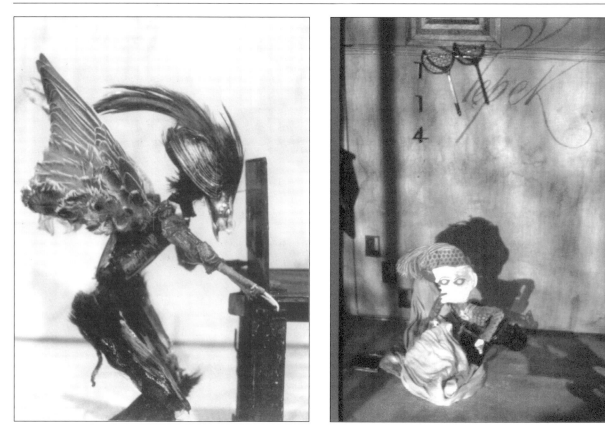

lights, with scrims and animated kooks for dappled shadows. Small mirrors provided eye lights. Low lighting created night by the film convention of shadowed upper walls. Black velvet created a pure midnight at both ends of a three-sided set made to appear, in the film, as a tunnel-box. The set, about three-feet long, three-feet high, two-feet deep, was constructed to shoot close-ups from different angles. The film became, in the words of the Quays, 'an entirely hermetic universe literally suspended out of time in a black void . . . a cruel fairy tale feel'.[4]

For the puppets the Quays reverted to the grotesque, elemental puppets they had used in *Punch and Judy*, *Ein Brudermord* and the Markopoulis woman in *Janacek*. They studied the Czech puppet film director Pojar to have their puppets acknowledge the marionette tradition by pauses or revelations of the puppeteer's control. Svankmajer's *Punch and Judy* (a.k.a. *The Coffin Factory*) (1981) had done the same with glove puppets. About six-inches tall, articulated by calliper-style joints with a ball and screw to regulate tension, the Quays' puppets moved in opposed styles: Gilgamesh pedalled, Enkidu flew. It dramatised a fundamental conflict between Enkidu of the exterior and Gilgamesh of the interior.

Influences

Traditional and modernist influences were blended into the angel/spider premise and its concessions to the *Epic*. One traditional influence was European folklore, which, except for place names and dialect, can be disconnected from social reality. Terror and dread inflect its images. Regional devils – as the Quays' spider/devil began – ruled small territories with medieval technology. They could be vindictive or have their vanity signified by feathered hats, like Gilgamesh.

The original *Epic of Gilgamesh*, written down but lost with the fall of Assyria in the seventh century BC, re-entered folklore as oral fragments. The work's 'planes of reality clothed in the appearance of primitive geography', as an expert wrote of the *Epic*, its 'vivid and sophisticated indirections', 'narrative compulsions', and 'subtle notions of time', became part-tales that 'alternated between grotesque and banal'. It was these elements of the folklore to which the Quays gravitated.

A second traditional influence was European puppet theatre. Itinerant puppeteers had for centuries carried debased versions of theatre into the countryside and poor parts of cities. They unwittingly preserved the oral, archaic powers of expression. Plays were reduced to essentials and sometimes ended without dramatic resolution.[7] Puppets, especially those representing the poor, were grotesque. Appearing as types, not personalities, their feet filled with lead, they moved stiffly without resistance.[8] Their style of motion could be, at times, metaphysical metaphors.[9]

Miniaturisation was made obvious to accentuate the object fetishism in the old puppet theatre. Nineteenth- and early twentieth-century writers on the puppet theatre had perceived it. When a child first apprehends existence, it oscillates in uncertainty about its own reality and experiences in intervals of consciousness. Objects, by their superior durability, mock the fragile self and seem to belong to a superior order.[5] Willed objects of the puppet theatre dredged up old alternations of fears of annihilation and fantasies of narcissistic power. In the Quays' words, objects and decor were:

> foregrounded as much as the puppets themselves . . . the machines and objects to act as much if not more than the puppets . . . to defy [objects'] artificiality . . . [to] perpetuate other narratives, other secret liberties.[10]

In the late nineteenth and early twentieth centuries fine artists took up puppets. By then the puppet plays were anachronistic. Cosmopolitan audiences found a 'homesickness for childhood' and strangely ungraspable emotions.[11] When the old repertoire was united to modernist sophistication, the result was often an excited unease:

> The faces [of Lotte Pritzel's dolls] are visionary, morbid . . . Fascinating, bewildering, tormenting, if you like, is the sexlessness of these dolls; in their expression and in their indeterminate dress they possess something excitedly ambiguous . . . All the perversions of a soulless, hopeless species drowning in sensuousness are here carried to extremes . . . an experience not necessarily . . . one of pleasure.[12]

The cruder European glove puppets, Punch, Kasparek, Laslo Vitez or Vasilache, with his peaked hat bent forward, frying pans to bash opponents or Jan Klaasen, Judy or Katrintje, could be violent or amoral. Kasparek, naive and brave humourist, might have expressed liberty,[13] but Punch, with his bared teeth and red-tipped nose, was a monstrous egoist, infamous for clubbing his wife. Punch's vainly red plush suit, gold trimmed, in the Quays' murderous *Punch and Judy*, reappeared as Gilgamesh's red velvet suit, hat and white feather.

Gilgamesh's development was complicated. His spider origins secretly remained. His trapdoor stayed. He was to have ridden into space so that strings from his fingers attached to an object. In the film this became a net. In suggested reshoots, Gilgamesh saw an insect along the wires and shot it down; dead Enkidu was spun in a web.

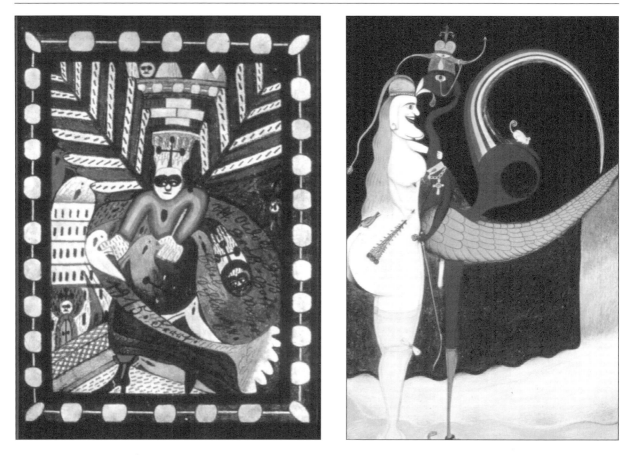

Gilgamesh turned human, but only via the 'unbearable singleminded arrogance',[14] as the Quays wrote, of three schizophrenic painters.

Adolf Wöllfli, an illiterate Swiss labourer, incarcerated near Bern, was violent, a child rapist kept in an isolated cell. Visions and punishment fantasies poured out in a prodigious quantity of drawings, paintings and musical compositions. Labyrinths of masked men, birds, icons of childhood, portrayed a cosmic order over which he ruled as the 'child divinity Saint Adolf II'.

Friedrich Schröder-Sonnenstern, the son of a Lithuanian coachman, was conscripted in the second world war but jailed as a lunatic. He was a confirmed anti-authoritarian, disgusted by the 'gangrene of civilisation'.[15] His scandalous caricatures, crimson, yellow and citrus green, revealed a 'ferocious innocence', inflamed organs and big-breasted women like 'baboons in heat', as the Quays said.

Heinrich Anton Muller, a French-speaking Swiss, invented a machine to trim grapevines. He lost the rights, withdrew from reality and suffered hallucinations. It was Muller's drawing of *Le Pere Darou* leading his pig 'Rafi' to the fair that gave Gilgamesh his bicycle and flat, white face, with eyes on the same side of his head.

Muller's *Le Pere Darou* was not psychopathological. However, *Psychopathia Sexualis*, a study of sexual perversions by Richard von Krafft-Ebing, stimulated the Quays during the period of *Gilgamesh*. Cases of hermaphrodites, idiots, cretins and fetishists documented amoral sexual cruelty. Perversion could result, according to Krafft-Ebing, in

sadism directed to 'strangling, stabbing, flagellating, or under circumstances, ridiculously silly and mean acts of violence on the other person or on any living and feeling object'. The 'tainted' could be hydrocephalic or microcephalic. Krafft-Ebing's *Case 173*, for example, had narrow, deformed facial bones, the halves of the face and ears asymmetrical, its head with a low and retreating brow, dolichomicrocephalic.[16] Gilgamesh became a 'grotesque fascist hydrocephalic child-despot wearing a red velvet suit with a feathered cap, who patrols ruthlessly his sand-box playground'.[17]

Hooks, buzz-saws, decapitating wickets and scissors immediately establish Gilgamesh's *raison d'etre*: castration. A pair of scissors is lodged overhead in wires. Gilgamesh passes a mirror-window and a buzz-saw whirls into action. They are his instruments, operated by magic, but also his reflection. The sound of the buzz-saw, to the Quays, was 'bizarre . . . perverse, the quality of the steely tinge of a vagina with metal lips'. Gilgamesh's own impotence is ridiculed as he prepares a slicing wicket with two eggs where his testes should be. The Quays regretted not having inserted glaucous, cataract eyeballs. But the autonomy of the puppet is a stubborn obstacle. As the Quays acknowledged, 'there are all the vague impulses and tuggings in which you hope to snag some tiny fragment of some deeper, elusive form'.[18] Reduced and essentialised, the puppet evolves inside a special universe of which it is the fixed point. The puppeteers obey the puppet's will.[19] Gilgamesh kept his blank, white face, his unfocused eyes off-centre and soulless, and the *insaisable regard* that had unsettled cosmopolitan devotees like the Goncourts.[20]

The Quays had grasped the puppet theatre's secret malaise. As cosmopolitan afficionados had observed, puppets move in a 'rough draft' of human representations.[21] By 'gestures of suggestion, fixation, hypnosis', a 'smirking parody of reality', they 'lead to a contempt of man' from which 'only metamorphosis' permits escape.[22] The parody becomes ominous. 'These people of wood are a bit disquieting, an empty look or interior look in their opacity of eye . . . pose, by their silence, the question of pleasure itself.'[23]

Among modernist sources, surrealism was important. The woman-table came from *La Machine Celibataire*, a surrealist catalogue of masturbatory sex machines, which included a drawing of Kafka's masochistic harrow in *The Penal Colony*. The inked torso was by M.A.E. Gautier d'Agoty, an anatomist's illustrator. The sex organ was first a porpoise mouth. Then, to suggest 'prostitute', it became pixilated red meat. Before and after Enkidu's arousal it was a squirming cricket.

That combination of erotic compulsion, castration and disgust had been developed by surrealists:

Above left
Drawing by Heinrich Anton Muller that inspired Gilgamesh's bicycle, his flat white face and eyes on the same side of his head
©Kunstmuseum, Bern/Collection: Adolf Wöllfli Foundation

Above right
The 'grotesque, fascist, hydrocephalic child-despot' Gilgamesh in his red velvet suit
©Atelier Koninck

The anatomist's illustrator M.A.E. Gautier d'Agoty's drawing, the basis for the woman-table

©Atelier Koninck

What did I admire more: the spider crawling on the mound of kisses, the phantom of scissors devouring each other or the carnivore awakening associations as uninnocent as those evoked by being fixed in solitude at the moment of orgasm?[24]

Dehumanised, headless and rigid, the woman-table and her interiors – 'intervaginal lobotomies'[25] – are available to all. She/ it was reduced in order to isolate and dramatise the disfiguring power of erotic compulsion itself. Enkidu's arousal, the pun of the waist-high drawer that slides out and his yearning leitmotif, coincides with the debasement of woman. Enkidu's catapult to electrocution upon mounting her/it, interrupts, mocks, but completes, orgasm.

The Quays admired the fables of an Austrian writer Konrad Bayer, who committed suicide in 1960. Their copy of Bayer's *Selected Works* is marked where it states that 'armed with an arsenal of ironising techniques', Bayer 'simulate[d] a world which maintained the belief in self-assertion in the midst of its created fantasies'.[26]

Bayer's 'herostrat' (titles and names are in lower case) declaims the annihilating egotism of a Gilgamesh:

> . . . i shall kill everything and decorate the towers of this darkness with the flags of my madness . . . i shall . . . freeze your eyes, freeze your ears, freeze your private parts, i shall tear out your love by the roots . . . and in this abominable coldness i will at last be alone.

The broken tennis rackets in high-tension wires was a private icon. It was used as early as *Palais des Flammes*, an early 1970s student film at the Royal College of Art in London. Electric wires had an operatic–religious flavour in *Nocturna Artificialia*, written in an Amsterdam hotel 'where the trams cast their shadows across the ceiling as they passed below, an image that has been an inspiration ever since'.[27] Trams and electric pylons reappeared in *Janacek* in the house of death. Their passing lights re-appeared in the Quays' live action feature *Institute Benjamenta* (1995). Earlier, in Poland, spitting sparks of a huge tram pylon 'like weird crucifixes caught up in fantastic congestions of wires . . . heightened the whole idea of pathological symbolism'.[28]

European folklore, puppet theatre, surrealism and psychopathology – the Quays were far too complicated to have had as sources only those mentioned here – were sources that had redefined post-war European art animation. The Quays' style – 'orthopaedic baroque' in their words – was a combination of opposites: lyric/grotesque, crude/elegant, and banal/ethereal (a hybrid principle worked out by earlier Polish graphic artists). The erotic cruelty of Walerian Borowczyk's *Jeux des Anges*, in which camera whip-pans and sounds of shots and guillotines set in a concentration camp suspended viewers' perceptions of fragmented, tortured anatomies between sadism and masochism, helped to set the standard of what an animated film could be. Jan Svankmajer's *Punch and Judy*, with its fairground music, extreme camera angles, aggressive pace, nails that pierce the body and bloody flesh juxtaposed with old, textured toys, reappeared in *Gilgamesh* with disorienting techniques: extreme angles, 180-degree reversals, impossible camera positions, whip-pans, extreme close-ups, the camera sideways on the floor then rotated up.

The child–adult sexual axis

The peculiar impact of *Gilgamesh*, its sweet terror and formal resolution but unresolved sensations, is trickier to account for.

The Quays were clear about an anti-institutional paranoia. Decor elements were called 'Gymnasium', 'medical blanket', or 'sanatorium' in the shooting log – all institutions of control. *This Unnameable Little Broom* refers to 'the petty bureaucrat [in the London visa office, who was trying to deport them due to a lapsed visa] who feels it his duty to sweep everything clean'. *Songs of the Chief of the Officers of Hunar Louse* refers to Lunar House, the Office of Immigration and Passport Control in Croydon. The broken tennis rackets on the wires meant 'one more person made to conform, useless as a tennis racket thirty miles from Wimbledon'.[29] As the Quays observed:

> Gilgamesh's little world hums beautifully and works perfectly normal, at least to him. He eliminates intruders without the slightest moral shudder. His musical theme must capture quickly this contrast: banality of evil which is his work, as a bureaucrat/civil servant.[30]

But there was a deeper paranoia. A puppet can act out desires not easily defined. As the Quays said: 'What is more noticeable in our natures is an articulated "desire" which gets played out within certain symbolic spaces.'[31] Sex and power in *Gilgamesh* are not, however, played out along a female/male axis, but along a child/adult axis.

A mixed-size scale suspends Gilgamesh between child and adult. Dandelion, scissors, an ice-cube, tongs, cricket and a tape measure show Gilgamesh to be a miniature. But his quadricycle, red vest and feathered hat, blanket, cutlery and bowl are to scale so that, with his oversized head, he looks like a toddler. However, the woman-table, tennis rackets, wires and trap door are miniaturised, which makes him look like an adult.

Further, to make the film work 'on that side we'd hoped for', the Quays asked their composer for Gilgamesh's theme to be:

> . . . a fairground type of organ and almost primitive ensemble to suggest [a] child's world of music . . . to symbolise his still being in a child's play pen [which] must on the other hand link with a serious adult frame of reference – mostly gruesome sound effects by [Larry] Sider, which the music will nudge up against . . . this contrast of the executioner with children's music.[32]

The strongest collision of child and adult frames of reference was in a shift from Gilgamesh's chamber to the exterior. The film-puppeteers, by the intrusions, provisions of props, leitmotifs, unexplained calligraphy, caricature and extreme camera movements create, inside the film, the illusion of an active, anonymous power.

Restless Gilgamesh is photographed progressively smaller, foreshortened or squeezed by camera angles against the void. The camera then moves out of the chamber snd looks back to show Gilgamesh groping ineffectively through a hole in the wall. The active, anonymous power is now ridiculing Gilgamesh. After Gilgamesh beats Enkidu and cuts off his wings, the binding yellow blanket falls, revealing the exterior's absolute black. As the Quays said:

> The forest music and the yellow cloth falling. These are both outside his grasp – they represent as it were a kind of space outside his own consciousness, areas which can't be controlled by him, hence this eternal quality.[33]

The camera suddenly moves forward independently into the forest. A long, simulated real-time shot – the shot that triggers the film's final tableau – shows a mysterious, poetic realm with cool, natural imagery such as a puff of dandelion, dappled moonlight, crickets (vaginas), and fluttering wings (potent males). Gilgamesh reacts: he humiliates Enkidu under the woman-table to end the film. But the film's new point of view squashes him and ridicules his furious ride around the table by means of an overhead angle and also turns his leitmotif to dissonant frenzy.

A psychiatrist, Edmund Bergler, not read by the Quays, echoed the kind of imagery found in *Gilgamesh*.

A baby's grandeur transforms the nursery into a place, Bergler wrote, 'magically regulated by the child . . . an executive organ of the child's sorcerer-like magic'.[34] To prevent himself from challenging the magic, the child's conscience creates punishments; in particular, castration fantasies. This turns his mind into a torture chamber, an internal concentration camp. To relieve the tension, the child acts out punishments on anything he can catch. Later, a potent intruder, the father, enters. The toddler demotes *the threatening and fear-inspiring 'witch' of babyhood from her position of power* and *makes out of the Giantess a caricature and image of his own frightened and passive self* (Bergler's italics).

In contrast to Gilgamesh's psychotic chamber, the enchanted forest is a frame of reference of adult potency

©Atelier Koninck

The child vicariously re-imagines the debased female as dominated by the 'cruelty' of sexual intercourse. But, of course, the child doesn't understand sex. The prostitute-table, electrocution, meat and cricket are images that a frightened child – or schizophrenic – might create.

The vicarious potency comes at a high price. The male toddler is now dominated by adult male potency. Gilgamesh's sadism turns to masochism. Despite the pace and gruesome sounds of the film, masochism rules, which is shown in such leitmotifs as darkness, Gilgamesh's paraplegic-like disability (he cannot get off his quadricycle), the bondage of Enkidu, the bondage of the prostitute, her wooden rigid legs forced open. Gilgamesh is caught, as the critic Rene Girard wrote about masochism, in a farcical horror in which 'this terrible caricature . . . becomes increasingly bewildered and unbalanced by a desire which nothing can satisfy'.[35]

The violation of being is the method of experience and the film's driving momentum. The 'metaphysics of obscenity'[36] that operated in the nursery unfolds into consciousness being aware of itself.

The metaphysics of puppet theatre

The psychopathology of the images is dignified by a sober metaphysics.

Puppet theatre, European and Asian, was meant to be viewed simultaneously as microcosm and macrocosm: not the dramatic character, but its collision with what surrounds him or her was dramatised. The puppet's physical limitations appeared, dramatically, as opposition to the Absolute. The 1911 *Encyclopaedia Britannica* suggested how such a restricted drama could be seen as universal:

> Every Ego [is] a living mirror . . . representative of the universe according to its point of view [and] has its correlative Non-Ego. Ego and Non-Ego, are then not merely logically a universe, but actually *the universe*.[37]

However, there is a disturbing nihilism. The late nineteenth- and early twentieth-century cosmopolitan puppet artists discovered that the non-real space of the puppet produced an oneiric zone that projected the viewer into the metaphysical. The secret order to the metaphysical, however, could never be found.[38] The play *appears* to communicate a profound message. Actually, it transcends nothing. Behind the lyrical sensations, the yearning, was an absolute lack of meaning. The puppet offered a mirror of existence, its compulsions and emotions, but without a soul.[39]

Indeed, the Quays sent their composer tapes of Zdenek Liska, Svankmajer's composer. The final, dissonant theme, they wrote, must be 'not . . . Wagnerian, Brucknerian bombast, [but] still stupidly childlike . . . [which] mustn't escalate to another level than this eternally cretinous mechanical response'. Punch and many cartoon characters also perform excessive, unexplicated, gratuitous violence.

> We are kept in a state somewhere between 'emotional seriousness' and . . . repetition-at-work coloured in with the lurid shades of aggression, madness and violent death.[40]

But what was *This Unnameable Little Broom*? Was it a grotesque reduction of Tableau II of the *Epic of Gilgamesh*, a recapitulation of the Oedipal dynamic, an allegory of sexual entrapment, a knockabout farce with deviant imagery, or a nihilist film that sadistically creates only illusions of deeper themes that are not there?

Viewers will find echoes of their own experience in this hermetic, cryptic, seductive little film, whose conflict is between infantile and adult sexuality – mutually exclusive epistemologies.

This is an extensively revised version of a paper given at the 1990 SAS Conference.

Notes

1. The *Epic of Gilgamesh*: First Draft Treatment, A Melodrama for Man, Marionette and Music, Atelier Koninck, August 1982.
2. Initial notes, n.d. and notes, 12.V.84.
3. Ibid.
4. Interview, Gallerie Kontakt, transcript, 7.
5. Maurice Rheims, 'La vie range des objets', in R.D. Bensky, *Recherches sur les structures et la symbolique de la marionnette* (Paris: Nizet, 1971), 113.
6. N.K. Sandars (trans.), *The Epic of Gilgamesh* (Baltimore: Penguin Books, 1960), 1– 45.
7. Bensky, 39, 40.
8. Max von Bohn, *Dolls and Puppets*, trans. by Josephine Nicoll (London: George G. Harrap & Co., Ltd., 1932), 396.
9. Andre-Charles Gervais, 'Grammaire elementaire de manipulation', in Bensky, 51.
10. The Brothers Quay, *In Deciphering the Pharmacist's Prescription On Lip-Reading Puppets*. Program notes or press release for *Street of Crocodiles* (1986), Griffiths's clipping file, 1–2.
11. Gunter Böhmer, *Puppets*, trans. by Gerald Moore (London: Macdonald, 1971), 7.
12. Von Bohn, 229.
13. Von Bohn, 397.
14. Letter to author, November 1993.
15. Roger Cardinal, *Outsider Art* (New York: Praeger Publishers, 1972), 155.
16. Richard von Krafft-Ebing, *Psychopathia Sexualis*, trans. by F.J. Rebman (Brooklyn: Physicians and Surgeons Book Co., 1933), 45, 82, 84, 94, 464.
17. Interview, Galerie Kontakt, transcript, 7.
18. The Brothers Quay, *In Deciphering*, 2.
19. Gervais, in Bensky, 46, 68–69.
20. Andre Leroux and Alain Guillemin, *Marionnette Traditionelle en Flandre Francaise de Langue Picarde*, Les Editions des Beffrois (Antwerp: Westhoek Editions, 1984), 7.
21. Bensky, 68.
22. Gervais, in Bensky, 64, 121, 122.
23. Leroux and Guillemin, 7.
24. Nezval, 'Le Surrealism', *Cahiers d'art* (1935), 135. Original sighted in exhibition *Czech Surrealism Between the Wars*, Church of St Roch, Stahov Monastery, Prague, July–August 1993.
25. Ibid.
26. Ulrich Janetski, foreword, in Malcolm Green (trans.), *Selected Works of Konrad Bayer* (London: Atlas Press, 1986), 11.
27. Quoted in Chris Petit, 'Picked-Up Pieces,' *Monthly Film Bulletin*, vol. 13 (June 1987): 164–165.
28. Ibid.
29. Letter to composer.
30. Ibid.
31. Interview, Galerie Kontakt, transcript, 4.
32. Letter to composer.
33. Letter to composer.
34. This extended account of the Oedipal dynamic is from Edmund Bergler, *Counterfeit Sex* (New York: Grune & Stratton, 1982).
35. Rene Girard, *Deceit, Desire and the Novel,* trans. Yvonne Freccero (Baltimore: Johns Hopkins University Press, 1949), 93, concerning the masochistic destruction of a hero.
36. Bergler, intro., xxiii. 'Metaphysics of obscenity' was an early term of abuse for psychoanalysis's obsession with pre-verbal fantasies of power and sex.

37. James Ward, author of entry 'Psychology', *Encyclopaedia Britannica*, 1911 edition, 549.
38. Bensky, 26, 81, 30.
39. Bensky, 86, 106, 123.
40. Neil Hertz in Jonathon Culler, *On Deconstruction* (Ithaca: Cornell University Press, 1982), 264, concerning the possibility that, to Freud's horror, no pathology caused repetitive deviant behaviour.

5

Narrative strategies for resistance and protest in Eastern European animation

William Moritz

Soviet Russia's domination of Eastern European countries for over 40 years (from the fall of the 'Iron Curtain' around 1947 until the 'Glasnost' of about 1990) brought mixed blessings for animation. On the one hand, Soviet policy favoured cinema as an essential, powerful popular artform and maintained busy animation studios not only for each country but also for distinct ethnic groups; animators were often tenured civil servants with guaranteed full-time employment making not only theatrical cartoons but also public service and educational animation, children's films of folk culture and titles and special effects for features. On the other hand, Soviet policy dictated sharp guidelines for subject matter and a strict censorship of both preliminary plans and finished films in order to guarantee that all films upheld general communist ideals and current party agendas. While many animators remained content to concentrate on innocent children's films or benign 'situation comedies', some artists attempted to produce allegorical or satirical works critical of totalitarian regimes, and their careful planning to outwit censorship made them, in some cases, create masterpieces of film art. Four festival prize-winners, one from each decade, demonstrate the changing strategies that their filmmakers used to speak out against totalitarian oppression.

Before the birth in 1960 of ASIFA (the International Animated film Association) with its all-animation film festivals, a newly-made Polish film, *Dom* (Home), won the grand prize at the 1958 Brussels Experimental Film Festival – a $10 000 cash prize. The two animators who collaborated on the film, Walerian Borowczyk and Jan Lenica, used the prize money to emigrate to Paris and West Berlin respectively, where they continued their animation careers in 'freedom'. They had made *Home* during a particularly touchy year in Soviet history: in October/November 1956 Russian troops crushed the Hungarian rebellion against Soviet occupation (and the hopes of neighbouring countries to escape communist domination). A year later, the successful launch of the *Sputnik* satellite put Russia in control of the skies as well.

Home addresses the issues of people trapped in a repressed world through three strategies. It sets up a complex non-linear structure that the viewer must decipher, which (1) makes it hard for a censor to ban since no individual element is obviously against the rules and the overall meaning is uncertain, and (2) requires the viewer to question the norm, which is a subversive act in itself. They also (3) focus *Home* on the plight of women, which seems to remove it from the political arena, although the thinking viewer will recognise that the ills of the woman arise to a considerable extent from the thought-control and repression of the totalitarian government.

The opening and closing scene of *Home* are the same: above the decaying façades of century-old apartment buildings, flickering patrols lurk (emphasised by Wlodzimierz Kotonski's fine pioneer electronic/concrete musical score). Decades before the helicopters of *Blade Runner* and *Blue Thunder*, these abstractions read as the omnipresent surveillance of the totalitarian state. Seven times we see the occupant of one apartment, a woman (played by Ligia Branice, Borowczyk's wife) waiting, hearing footsteps, looking up expectantly or glancing down contemplatively. Between each appearance of this heroine we see six episodes of radically different styles, which cumulatively probe the daily life of the wife in a repressive society.

The images of the first episode, mostly cut out of scientific texts, show a drill or welding gun assembling a human skull and turning on its perceptive abilities, which gradually comprehend circuitry, music as a mechanical action and furniture, culminating in that quintessential Victorian houseplant, an aspidistra on a pedestal. The sequence forces the viewer to ask: whose brain is this? Is it a man's head thinking of machinery or a woman coping with her home? And what is perception? Is it just a mechanical action? Is it human? Is it controlled by some outside force?

The second episode animates a man in sequential poses obviously cut from a manual of some kind and tinted a pastel yellow. Is it dancing, exercise or self-defense? The main question remains 'What is he doing?', which may be what the woman wonders.

The third episode prompts the question, 'What is she doing?', through an astonishing 'still life with wig'. On a kitchen table top with bottles, glasses, a cannister, an orange and a crumpled newspaper, a blonde wig roams, perusing the newspaper, pursuing the orange, drinking milk from the bottle, breaking a glass and finally scurrying away at the sound of the 'surveillance'. This wig, partly suggesting the empty-headed rambling

Left *Walerian Borowczyk and Jan Lenica working on the animation of the model husband in* Home *(1956)*

©Walerian Borowczyk and Jan Lenica

Right *The wife eagerly embraces the husband in* Home

©Walerian Borowczyk and Jan Lenica

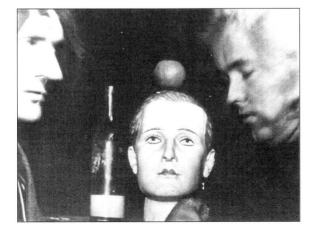

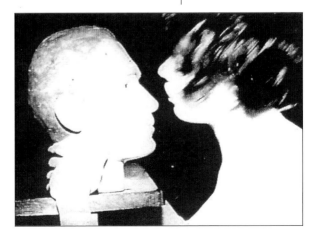

of the trapped housewife, partly the dispossessed glamour-hair of the mechanicalised head from the first episode, seems eerily subhuman, menacing, in its impossible ability to drink, break glass, and pursue.

The fourth episode, again heralded by the approaching footsteps, pictures the man as a dehumanised robot through a live action loop repeatedly showing him enter the door and hang his hat on a hook, accompanied by musical scales played on a tinny toy piano, gradually escalating in volume. The fact that the footsteps continue after this episode re-locates the mechanical husband in the mind of the wife, continually waiting (a theme in feminist literature from Natalie Barney's 1910 poem 'Waiting' to Faith Wilding's 1970s performance-piece 'Waiting').

The fifth episode delves deeper into the soul of the woman, following her reveries and longings: lying nude, she remembers 'the olden days', photographs of her grandparents, children's books, romantic church weddings, trips abroad (honeymoons?), and beautiful flowers. For a moment the footsteps intrude upon her sensuous nostalgia and her nude body quickly turns into the waiting woman again. Then in a sixth episode the live action woman approaches the handsome head of a man, which appears to be a hat-model dummy. She fondles, caresses, kisses 'him', her passionate gestures turning into flowers, one of which is tinted scarlet. But the mass-produced, uniform head collapses beneath the heat of her passion, his eye, his nose, his forehead crumbling until only a hollow shell is left. Empty reality fails to satisfy desire. The surveillance sound hovers again; the woman looks up and scurries, even as the wig had earlier. The footsteps relentlessly continue over the end credits: no answer, no solution appears for the woman's paralysed life. While evoking the tragic plight of the confined, dependent woman, *Home* also convicts as guilty the repressive society that dehumanises her and the men on which she is forced to be dependent.

Jiri Trnka's *Ruka* (The Hand), made in 1964–65 just as the Czech New Wave began to blossom, represents the more traditional mode of expressing protest through allegory. *The Hand* was also the last of Trkna's 25 films, as it threw him into official disfavour. In a 1966 interview in *Newsweek* magazine, Trnka complained, 'Too many officials think their opinion is the only one that counts . . . Official taste is bad taste'. 'Luckily', he added, 'unlike Disney, I do not have a child's soul. I do not suffer from any illusions' – a comment repeated in his obituary when he died of cancer some four years later, after the Soviet invasion of Czechoslovakia.

Trnka uses a simple, linear story: a large Hand invades the home of a potter fond of making flower-pots, demanding that he, in the future, make only images of hands. The potter refuses and tries to get rid of the Hand in several ways (hiding, nailing the doors and windows shut, refusing gifts, ripping out the phone) but the Hand foils all the potter's protests and eventually manipulates the potter with strings, like a traditional marionette, to make a monumental sculpture of a Hand. Though celebrated with state laurels for this achievement, the potter languishes and dies. Trnka managed to get the scenario and the finished film past censors by cleverly identifying the Hand with specific nationalities (the Nazi salute, the raised hand of the Statue of Liberty) considered enemies of socialism, so that the parable could be read as a protest against foreign domination – but the film nonetheless garnered international recognition (not only the Jury Prize at the 1965 Annecy, but also prizes at non-animation festivals in Oberhausen, Melbourne and Bergamo) as a denunciation of Soviet control over the arts and media. The brilliance of Trnka's masterpiece arises not only from its clever plot twists (the broken flower-pot, telephone and television as destructive tools, the seductive Hand dancing in mesh hose) but also in subtle conceptual depths: the Hand is also the animator's hand and the protagonist's unchanging wooden face is ingeniously designed and miraculously managed so that it registers dozens of different emotions, from joy to despair, simply through subtle lighting and movement.

Yuri Norstein claimed in an interview that Trnka's *The Hand* was his favourite animated film, which reminds us that these films were produced in a conscious tradition. By the late 1970s, when Yuri and his wife Francesca shot *Skazka Skazok* (Tale of Tales), several successful changes of leadership in post-Stalin Russia must have made it seem that the Soviet order would last indefinitely. So, rather than a specific protest against government policies, the message of *Tale of Tales* urges artists to accept the burden of keeping better times alive through art. Norstein still constructs his film in a complex, non-linear story that conceals the implications of his images from the blunt eye of the censor. Like *Home* and *The Hand*, *Tale of Tales* is filtered through a particular consciousness: that of a little wolf, a protagonist which Norstein freely admits to be autobiographical. At the same time, this hero derives from a traditional Russian lullaby, 'A Little Wolf could carry you away, deep into the forest', which is sung repeatedly in the film. As with Trnka's potter in *The Hand*, the wolf's paper cut-out face magically seems to mirror a hundred emotions, often deriving from the situation and subtle movement – the little tilt of the head while staring at the baby or when 'swinging' on the treadle of an abandoned sewing machine. Once in an interview, Norstein pointed out that the 'anima' in animation means putting 'soul' into something, not just life.

Within the first few minutes of this half-hour film, we glimpse a sample of all the material that will appear in variations during the rest of the film: an apple, a baby nursing, seasons passing in a forest, an abandoned house with a dazzling light pouring

The face of the Norsteins' wolf magically seems to mirror a hundred emotions. According to Yuri Norstein, 'anima' means putting 'soul' into something, not just life

©Yuri and Francesca Norstein

from its door, a luminous reverie of a bygone era (half Pushkin, half Picasso) peopled by a fisherman, a poet and a girl jumping rope with a bull, a wartime picnic-dance from which men disappear to battle and death and the heavy traffic on a contemporary highway which has now cut through the forest near the abandoned house. Each image has its characteristic sound, such as the popular tango 'The tired sun says goodbye at the sea just as you say you don't love me anymore' for the wartime scenes.

Each of these images is animated freshly and differently and the subtle changes express a growing awareness of the deeper meanings or potentials of the material. The apple in the snow, for example, is seen as a ruptured fantasy when the boy dreams of feeding the birds but it is interrupted by his drunken tyrant father, whose 'Napoleon' hat he adopts; later, this bitter childhood memory is redeemed by the excision of the parents and the successful feeding of the birds. The Pushkin reverie is first seen in vivid detail,

panning across the seaside property, pulling in for closer views of the children's play, the witty cat, the poet and his lyre, the fish and the fisherman. The second appearance transpires all in a long shot following a wanderer who passes through the same scene, but keeping everything in a larger perspective – obviously the wolf's widening point of view, which leads to his decisive intervention.

The transitions between disparate elements occur as visual analogies: the fire in a baker's oven turns into autumn leaves flaring into flame at the foot of a tree, which in turn leads to the flashing lights of autos in the highway. This constitutes the associative mental process of the wolf protagonist. The luminous door through which the wolf reaches the nostalgic past is paralleled by the light-cone of the wartime lamppost and by the luminous manuscript of the poet (flickering like a projector beam), and this cumulative chain leads to the wolf's climactic gesture of stealing the manuscript from the past and nurturing it as a baby in the present, thus preserving the precious memory of the beautiful and the tragic alike.

In addition to winning the grand prize at Zagreb, during the 1984 Olympic Games an international jury chose *Tale of Tales* as the greatest animation film of all time, a distinction well deserved by the variety of superb effects and moods, from the quiet realism of the little wolf eating a hot potato to the conceptual brilliance of scratching the phonograph record so that music is missing at the point of departure of each soldier. Trnka's *The Hand* took fourth place.

Priit Pärn's *Eine Murul* (Picnic on the Grass or *Déjeuner sur l'herbe* after Manet's painting) also won a grand prize at Zagreb in 1988, though the film had been proposed as early as 1983 and was finally approved for release in 1986, after the Chernobyl nuclear accident signalled the decline of Russian prestige. Soviet Russia had occupied and plundered Pärn's native Estonia for more than 30 years by that time, so his theme logically concentrates on desperate living conditions in a country without goods, without self-rule, redress or justice.

In making *Déjeuner sur l'herbe*, Pärn already knew both *Home* and *Tale of Tales*, so his

Below *The wolf decides to steal the manuscript of the past and nurture it as a baby in the present, thus preserving precious memories*

©Yuri and Francesca Norstein

Above left
The theme of Priit Pärn's Déjeuner sur l'herbe *concentrates on desperate living conditions*

©Priit Pärn/TallinnFilm

Above right
George must find suitable clothing for the picnic

©TallinnFilm

structure consciously became even more complex. A superficial overall pattern becomes gradually clear: four Estonian people wish to have a picnic in a public park (or, more specifically, as we find out only at the end, the picnic depicted in Manet's painting *Déjeuner sur l'herbe*), as a moment of art and respite from the brutality of daily life. Each of the four has a specific task in order to make the picnic possible and we watch each of their tales separately: Anna must get the food (symbolically an apple) necessary for the meal; George must find suitable clothing for his costume instead of the grim grey uniforms officially available in stores; Bertha, formerly an artist's model but now a faceless digit in the socialist state that prizes motherhood over art, must regain her sense of an artistically viable identity if she is to model again; Edward must manage to get the bureaucratic permit to use the park. Each is successful and for a moment, they actually realise their dream of an instant of art and respite.

The faceless Bertha cowers in bed

©Priit Pärn/TallinnFilm

Across this more obvious structure, however, flow equally obvious contradictions that make the viewer puzzle and question. Anna is awakened at precisely 9.20 in the morning by the shrieking crash of an automobile accident and later, while shopping, she drops a bag of apples (just after George sneaks by) which children pursue out into the street. In George's tale, the car crash sound occurs while he is still home (and it causes Bertha's picture to fall from the wall), yet he encounters the children running after the apples

much later and manages to grab one in order to trade it for black-market goods. In Bertha's tale, we see her daughter join the children running after the apples fallen from the bag and the car swerves and crashes in order to avoid Bertha's daughter – but the camera pulls back to show Anna, just awakened, looking out her window. This inconsistency implies that disaster happens over and over again, so time no longer matters in this moribund society.

 The frequent reoccurrence of a character that looks like Picasso (the film is ironically dedicated to 'Artists who do exactly what is expected of them') also reinforces this idea. Often 'Picasso' is being arrested by two policemen, usually pursued by seagulls, but mysteriously he sometimes performs other roles: although George had seen him arrested only minutes before, he is (with cynical common sense) a civil servant in the Bureau of Eyesight, where he is arrested again. Artists are always being arrested, just as cars are always crashing.

Picasso also gets the last word. After the lucky four enjoy their moment of art, we see the hapless Picasso lying in the road, his arm, crushed by a passing tank, squashed out into the shape of a seagull's wing. No real room for artists in the totalitarian state.

As with *Home*, *The Hand* and *Tale of Tales*, *Déjeuner sur l'herbe* offers a wealth of aesthetic and conceptual thrills that make the viewer happy to continue working to puzzle out the overall structure. Pärn's clever use of a grotesque caricature for the common man – whether the taxi driver or the black-marketeer who wants sex with Anna in exchange for an apple, they look the same – is subtly twisted and enriched by George's air-brushed *Playboy* fantasies or the remarkable instant of ecstasy that the drunken workman experiences in the snivelling baker's factory. The passing reference to the Beatles' *Yellow Submarine* when George changes the 'Shoe' sign to a blue glove or the chilling moment when Bertha draws a 'Picasso' distortion of eyes, nose and mouth on her empty face with her makeup, cause the viewer to feel more intensely the plight of intelligent, feeling prisoners of this closed system. The epic imagery of Edward's quest – his shrinking stature, the mouldy walls of the minister's building, the giant squashing a little man in the elevator, the monumental secretaries, the cyclops administrator – makes the viewer feel both the absurdity and the tragedy of this battle against bureaucracy – even as does George's ridiculous transfer (as if it were a sport like football) of black-market goods: apple for bread for shoe for glasses. And if the hidden jibes at the Russians are not always clear to a Western viewer – the Russian administrator (the film censor would have been one such) is a cyclops because the Russians only see one way to do things, and since the Estonians habitually leave the spoon in their tea while the Russians take it out, Edward can blind the Russian with a teaspoon – the Odyssean imagery carries the idea through.

Home, *Tale of Tales* and *Déjeuner sur l'herbe* all posit an 'interactive' system, in which the purposefully convoluted narrative structure must be unravelled by the viewer. While these strategies might have been devised to circumvent censors, they result in a rich experience that rewards repeated viewings, since the films are composed freshly in the viewers' minds, with new connections, new perceptions and new feelings every time. And the intricate artistry of all four filmmakers does appeal as strongly to the emotions as to the reason of the viewer, which enhances our sympathy for the characters and makes the films transcend the narrower political issues that they originally protested.

This paper was presented at the 1993 SAS Conference.

Notes

1.   Giannalberto Bendazzi, *Cartoons: One Hundred Years of Cinema Animation* (London: John Libbey, 1994), 438, for the founding of ASIFA (well indexed for all references about animation). Parker Tyler, 'New Images', *Dom, Loving, L'opera mouffe, Film Quarterly*, vol. XXI, no. 3 (Spring 1959): 50–53.

2.   Natalie Clifford Barney, 'Attendre', *Actes et Entr'actes* (Paris: Sansot, 1910), 88–89. Faith Wilding's performance piece is preserved in Johanna Demetrakis's documentary film *Womanhouse* (1974).

3.   *Jiri Trnka, der Puppenfilmer aus Prag* (Frankfurt: Deutsches Filmmuseum, 1987); Borge Trolle, 'Jiri Trnka, the Master of Puppet Animation', *The Art of Animation*, vol. 1, no. 1 (Spring 1994): 28–39.

4.   'Trnkaland', *Newsweek*, vol. 67, no. 13 (March 28, 1966): 99–100; Transition: 'Jiri Trnka', *Newsweek*, vol. 75, no. 2, (January 12, 1970): 45.

5.   J.P. Jeunet, 'Yuri Norstein', *Banc-Titre*, no. 15 (December 1980), 21–23.

6.   Mikhail Yampolsky, 'Yuri Norstein', *Kino* (Riga) (April 1985). A French version of this interview appeared in *Positif* no. 297: 48–50. *Positif* no. 288 also carried Eric Derobert's study of Norstein: 61.

7.   *The Olympiad of Animation*, June 29 – July 2, 1984, presented by The Academy of Motion Picture Arts and Sciences and ASIFA Hollywood. (Twenty-five-page program booklet.)

8.   Mikhail Yampolsky, 'The Space of the Animated Film: Khrzanovsky's *I Am with You Again* and Norstein's *Tale of Tales*, *Afterimage* no. 13 (Autumn 1987): 93–117; Karen Rosenberg, 'Yuri Norstein', *Pegbar*, vol. 1, no. 7 (Summer 1991): 18–19.

9.   Sergei Assenin, 'Drawn Paradoxes: Priit Pärn', *Etüde Eesti Multifilmidest Ja Nende Loojatest* (Estonian Animated Films and Their Creators) (Tallinn: Periodika, 1986), 296–304 (for an English-language text), plus 18 pages of unnumbered color plates on Pärn. This text covers only up to *Time Out* in 1984, but it discusses Pärn's background as a graphic artist, Arnheim theories in relation to Pärn's films, etc.

6

Putting themselves in the pictures

Images of women in the work of Joanna Quinn, Candy Guard and Alison de Vere

Sandra Law

In 1975, Laura Mulvey published her seminal article, 'Visual Pleasure and Narrative Cinema', arguing that the object of the gaze in classical Hollywood cinema is female while the subject is male.[1] Since then, many theorists have developed Mulvey's theories in more detail, though others have contested her position. Nonetheless, the issue of the representation of women in film has become, without question, a central concern within media studies, including the realm of animation.

Many filmmakers working in live action and animation have been concerned to find alternative means of portraying women and women's issues. This essay explores the animation of three British filmmakers: Joanna Quinn, Candy Guard and Alison de Vere. Though each is unique in her choice of form and content, all three use animation to explore the nature of femininity and the experience of being female.

Joanna Quinn's *Girls' Night Out* and *Body Beautiful*

The politics of Quinn's films discussed here are the politics of gender. Conscious of the continuing differences in representation of female characters in the work of male and female animators, she has suggested that, while male animators rely on the 'same old hackneyed jokes' about the female form, female animators often have a fresh approach.[2]

Although Quinn's work is not strictly political, her films do reflect the personal politics of male–female relationships. She uses humour to explore female experience. While humour is traditionally a hallmark of much mainstream animation and of the comic strip tradition that initially inspired Quinn, her humour is distinct from that seen in the comic tradition of male artists, a tradition which Betterton suggests is 'based on the humiliation of women'.[3] Joanna Quinn describes humour as a 'great weapon' to be used in the exploration of ideas and her films use humour to empower rather than to degrade their female characters.[4]

Beryl, the protagonist of both films, is a middle-aged woman who begins her cinematic life as a housewife in *Girls' Night Out* and reappears as a factory worker in a Japanese electronics firm in *Body Beautiful*. The film's action takes place primarily through the person of Beryl who is acted upon and an initiator of action herself. Beryl's person, which, at certain moments, is her literal body, becomes the battleground of what constitutes appropriate femininity.

Beryl is an 'unfamiliar' female character because she evokes none of the many stereotyped representations of women in the animated world (e.g. *Who Framed Roger Rabbit*'s sex goddess Jessica Rabbit or Tex Avery's *Red Hot Riding Hood* or the virginal innocent of Disney's *Snow White*, etc.). In designing Beryl, Quinn has overcome 'the repertoire of motifs for signalling femininity' that Antonia Lant finds in traditional animation.[5]

But, by choosing not to idealise Beryl's physical form, Quinn complicates the task of making her character a sympathetic figure. Quinn creates identification, in part, by making Beryl into a character who is a very 'ordinary' person. In *Girls' Night Out*, Beryl is shown engaged in mundane activities: washing dishes, phoning female friends and attempting to communicate with an uncommunicative husband. Because her activities are so 'ordinary', it is likely that many female viewers will identify with her as a character. A further sense of realism derives in both films from the definite geographic location, South Wales, and the use of accents and vocabulary specific to the region.

Quinn's work also foregrounds the theme of female solidarity and the justification of pleasure for female viewers. In *Girls' Night Out*, Beryl's birthday present from her friends is a visit to a local pub to see a male stripper. The film's external audience experiences the performance primarily through Beryl, though there is also a general identification with other women in the film as they obviously enjoy watching the performance.

Quinn's visual representation of the male stripper's performance appeals directly to the film's female characters and to female viewers because the subjects of the gaze, as depicted in the film, are uniformly female. While the stripper's performance could

Scene from Joanna Quinn's Girls' Night Out

©Joanna Quinn (Still courtesy of BFI Film and Video Distribution)

possibly appeal to a gay male audience the constant visual references to the female audience members in the film and their pleasure in the performance would seem to mitigate somewhat the enjoyment of men.

When Beryl and her friends arrive at the pub, they are met by a goofy-looking bull's head adorning the sign 'The Bull'. The pub is fittingly named, given the macho posing of the leather-clad gum-chewing stripper in the scenes that follow. His attitude is like that of a complacent male bovine chewing his cud. When he begins his act, the stripper is fully in control of his audience – and certain of his sexual appeal– as he struts on stage, performing acrobatic feats and swivelling his hips. Eventually, he leaves the stage to approach individual audience members. At this juncture, the point of view shifts from the female characters to the stripper, who grins toothily at Beryl in an attempt to assert his pre-eminence as the subject – not the object – of the gaze.[6] Surrounded by a golden glow, he stares down at Beryl from what seems to be a tremendous height, almost as though he were a young Greek god looking down at a lowly earth-bound human. But, in the next moment, as the stripper quaffs down an offered drink, Beryl snatches away his G-string. The stripper's distress is immediately evident, as he is transformed into a ludicrous, almost pitiable figure. His ears become enlarged and his eyes bulge as he covers his crotch to hide what Beryl has caused to be revealed. The stripper's bulging eyes at this point (and Beryl's earlier eye-popping on her first view of the stripper) make visual reference to Tex Avery's character of the literal male wolf and the female object of his desire (e.g. Red in *Red Hot Riding Hood* (1943)) and a caricatured Bette Davis in *Swing Shift Cinderella* (1945). The depictions of male/female characters of the Avery films seem to be inverted in the Quinn films discussed here: the undesirable female (known as 'granny' in *Little Red Riding Hood* and *Swing Swift Cinderella*) in Avery's films is depicted here as desiring but undesired by the male character who pursues the voluptuous young woman. The eyes of the undesired female Granny pop out when she first meets the male wolf in *Swing Shift Cinderella*. This sequence is similar to the sequence in which Beryl's eyes pop out on her first glimpse of the male stripper. But in *Girls' Night Out*, Beryl's desire is validated by her fantasy sequence with a muscled Tarzan, in which her desire is reciprocated.

Clearly, the stripper no longer has the level of control he maintained through the performance sequence. He has patronised the women by allowing them glimpses of his masculinity – his muscled body and hairy chest – but he is not willing to be fully exposed to their view. By removing his G-string, Beryl exposes the perceived source of his male power. And when she is confronted by the stripper's direct stare, Beryl does not look away – an act that underscores her empowerment.[7]

Body Beautiful is also concerned with gender representation and the dynamics of male–female relationships: the latter in both films being presented as performances. The stripper in the film *Girls' Night Out* literally performs the role of a powerful, sexually assertive male person. In *Body Beautiful*, both male *and* female characters are engaged in literal performances of their gendered roles and the film explores and highlights the differential nature of these performances. The focus in *Body Beautiful*, as in *Girls' Night Out*, is on the politics of gendered body representations and how those representations determine how women are treated by others, specifically, men.

Body Beautiful opens with a drawn 'photograph' of Vince, one of Beryl's co-workers at the factory. The viewer learns, by Vince's own account, that he is the resident factory stud/lady killer:

> Every woman, like, in this factory, and I've been here now, two years, right, every woman in this factory wants me. And I'm not exaggerating. No. No. I'm not exaggerating. See, that's me. Even the old ones, right. Well, look at, look over there now. Beryl, the fat one. Look at the love handles on that, now. Go on, you couldn't, could you, you couldn't. Oh, I love it. I give her a right going over. Been to the hair dresser have you? Eh! Was it shot? (laughs)

Vince speaks first and seems to set the fictive agenda, presenting viewers with their first impression of Beryl, whom he describes as fat (although, of course, she is included in the group of women who 'want' him).[8] He objectifies Beryl by referring to her with the relatively neutral terms 'she' and 'her', and by truncating her name to 'Ber'. Vince attempts to reduce Beryl by verbally 'cutting her down to size' (or at least to a size which he finds tolerable).

Quinn explores definitions of 'femininity' throughout *Body Beautiful*. When Beryl, in a newsagents, sees depictions of an 'ideal' female on the cover of a magazine, the shop owner suggests that, to stay so thin, a woman would have to live on air. In the next sequence, Beryl sees herself literally disappearing into 'thin air' after following the cover girl's diet. This scenario also reveals Beryl's fear of 'disappearing' in her identity as a woman outside the accepted definition of the feminine, as measured by physical difference. Vince's attacks represent his attempts and perhaps in a more global sense, society's attempts, to reduce and contain her threat. His sarcasm seems motivated by a hidden rage, rooted in Beryl's physicality. Her size and hence her undeniable physical presence represent a threat to his own sense of physical dominance. By trying to make Beryl disappear (both psychically and physically) Vince works to re-establish the status quo of male and female space and body differentials – differentials in which the male is seen as dominant and physically large, while the female is seen as submissive and small. Vince tries to compel Beryl to occupy a lesser female space, appropriate to her gender. But ultimately he fails in his attempts to diminish her and re-establish the status quo of gender identities and qualities.[9]

At certain moments in the film Beryl effaces herself by giving up the right to speak on her own behalf. In one instance, her female co-workers suggest that she complain about Vince's behaviour to a Japanese supervisor at the plant. She is reluctant and passes up an opportunity to do so. In part, her reticence seems to be part of the male–female dynamic long established in Western societies.[10] Beryl's reticence could also be partially attributed to her familiarity with verbal assaults based on the topic of her weight. She might simply have ceased to react to what has become routine and expected.

Throughout most of the film, Vince seems to maintain his position as the primary spectator, through whom Beryl and other women in the film are seen. He aggressively asserts himself, verbally and through his infringements on the physical space of Beryl and other female characters, leering at them and then winking at his audience (other characters in the film as well as the viewer), all of whom he assumes are accomplices in his ill-treatment.

When the women try to stop Vince from haranguing Beryl about her weight he says that they should go along with him because he is only joking. Similarly, when he gawks at the dancing chorus line of women, telling one of them to hold in her buttocks, he greets the objections of other male audience members by telling them to 'play the game'.

Although, on one level, Vince appears to be the narrator – the seeming authority in this story – Quinn actually subverts his primacy through his characterisation and physical representation. In the final analysis, Vince is portrayed as an obnoxious, juvenile and frequently grotesque buffoon. Indeed, Vince's sexist comments and macho posturing, coupled with his visual representation as a muscle-bound goon, establish him as an object of the ridicule for the audience rather than as an authority figure.

At several points in the narrative Vince is compared visually with an animal or something sub-human. His exaggerated, lewd gestures and gigantic incisors make him appear to be nothing more than an overgrown field rodent with an inflated view of his sexual appeal and prowess. His raucous laughter at the expense of Beryl or the other women contorts his facial features into those of a braying donkey. Even his posturing recalls non-human primates who actively display their masculinity to assert their dominance. Vince's animal nature is further underscored when one of Beryl's co-workers at the factory recounts her discovery of Vince and one of his girlfriends 'in the club':

> Guess who he's takin' out now girls. That Sharon . . . The blonde one in the office. Saw them in the club last night. Checkin' her files he was. Like animals they were!

But Vince is not the only character to be depicted as an animal. At various points, Beryl is transformed into different creatures: a whale when taunted by Vince, and a pig under the pressure of other condemning figures. However, Vince's transformations into animalistic states contrast with those of Beryl: unlike him, she never seems to lose the audience's allegiance – while Beryl's transformations are expressions of her subjectivity, Vince's are clearly caricatures.

In *Body Beautiful*, Quinn provides us with a glimpse of the possibilities animated films offer in terms of the representation of women and the experience of being female. Beryl's ability to change is under her own control and the metamorphoses she experiences reflect her potential to be whatever she chooses. The act of personal deconstruction and eventual reconstruction of her own form becomes an affirmative sequence for the film's female characters who are watching the Body Beautiful contest. It is also an affirming experience for the film's female audience.

During the Body Beautiful contest, Beryl delivers a rap song in which she asserts that her body is her own, inviting women in her audience to feel comfortable regardless of their outward appearance. In the course of her rap song, she assumes control of the transformation process, literally trumpeting her right to speak on her own behalf by metamorphosing into a chorus of brass instruments. She chants:

> My body is mine so let me be. Skinny, fat, tall or muscley. And I don't care what you think 'cause I stood here in the pink. I'm proud of every pound and I don't want to shrink. So come on all you women you've got nothing to fear.

As her rap song indicates, Beryl tries on various physical forms – a skinny one, a fat one, a tall one, a muscle-bound one and finally, that of the voluptuous blonde – all of which she rejects for her own shape. The stereotype voluptuous blonde is literally discarded by Beryl when she unzips it like a suit of clothing, playing with the idea of the feminine as a kind of masquerade.[11]

During the course of the film, Beryl experiences something that Lant refers to as the 'fantasy of reversal'; that is, she discovers that there is the possibility for a change in her present circumstances.[12] For Beryl, the first indication of this possibility comes as an epiphany in a shop where the audience sees her looking through magazines that

Beryl's co-workers stare, mouths agape, as she takes possession of the stage in Quinn's Body Beautiful *contest*

©Joanna Quinn

deal with beauty and athletics/fitness. The action depicted on the athletics magazines' covers offers an alternative to what is considered by mass-media cultures to be women's preoccupation (but a preoccupation that is authorised and validated by beauty contests, advertising campaigns and photographs of semi-nude women in tabloid newspapers) with beauty.

Beryl's fear of literal disappearance is graphically depicted as the female model on the front of *Skinny* magazine disappears as a result of what the audience can only suspect is excessive dieting. However, Beryl's fears are not limited to the nullification of her physical person. She also is fearful of the eradication of her identity, which is so intrinsically connected to her body. Beryl's personal fortunes improve once she discovers the possibilities for personal empowerment through the development of physical fitness and strength. The image of an active and fit Beryl acts as a counterpoint to the physical disempowerment of the other factory women who participate in the chorus line prior to the contest. Their singular concern is whether or not their costumes for the chorus line number will fit.

Unlike the other women in the film, Beryl takes charge of her destiny, undergoing a *Rocky*-like transformation by adherence to a disciplined fitness program. During the course of her transformation she forms friendships with some of the young men at the fitness centre. Unlike Vince, they do not feel contempt for her. Instead, a kind of comradeship develops between them. Beryl's steadfastness in following the fitness program transform her into someone fitter than her younger and more svelte co-workers. The climax of the fantasy of reversal is the Body Beautiful contest. Beryl has come into her full physical powers and uses her large self to harass and manipulate the suddenly infantilised Vince, who visibly shrinks when he loses to Beryl in the contest. Throughout Beryl's rap Vince is referred to or treated as a lesser person than Beryl. Beryl holds him over her head like an infant, she calls him 'Vincey Wincey' and later insinuates that Vince cannot handle the pace set by herself, an woman of 'twice his years'.

As she delivers her rap, Beryl tosses Vince around like a rag doll and removes his primary harassing tool, his mouth. This is an interesting act, since it locates a major source of Beryl's problems: Vince's verbal attacks on her. He is the first character to speak – the first to describe the situation and the other characters (particularly females) as he sees them. Also, he speaks frequently, as opposed to Beryl's own self-imposed silence.

Beryl's representation in this sequence is in interesting contrast to that of the older and inevitably unattractive woman in Avery's *Swing Shift Cinderella*. The label that is actually affixed to her by the animators when she tries to transform herself into a desirable female is 'Miss Repulsive of 1898', a title which directly addresses her anti-beauty queen status and which ridicules her conviction that her desire will be reciprocated, is assumed by 'Granny' who actively pursues the male wolf who in turn pursues the Cinderella of the title. Granny assaults the wolf character in much the same way that Beryl assaults Vince during her rap. When Granny tackles the Wolf, spins him about her head and finally tosses him onto the couch, she is treating him with the same negligence that Beryl treats Vince on stage.

At one point in the *Body Beautiful* contest sequence, Beryl literally absorbs Vince into her own body. His absorption renders him completely insignificant: reduced to a blob of undistinguished flesh, which feeds the appetite of the insatiable 'Ber' – an event that seems to mark the realisation of his fears, which have Freudian echoes given the sequences in which he is feminised (sprouting a tutu as he does), infantilised and absorbed by a dominant female, Beryl. But ultimately Beryl's victory over Vince and the 'reversal' of roles that takes place is not a mere supplanting of the male role by the female. Although she takes on the role of aggressor, she does so to empower herself and the women in the audience, not simply to denigrate Vince.[13]

By the end of *Body Beautiful*, Quinn displaces the apparent power of the domineering male character, Vince, as she did with the stripper in *Girls' Night Out*. However, Beryl's

victory is not only of her own doing: her success is tied into the support of other women. Quinn depicts a show of female solidarity between the two female judges and Beryl's female co-workers. The Japanese women, who are in traditional dress, could be expected to defer to the third, male judge, given women's seemingly subordinate position in Japanese society. However, they violate that expectation and pressure the male judge to rate Beryl a perfect 'ten'.

Joanna Quinn uses humour to gain the attention of her audience. However, in opposition

Top *Ever the competitor, Vince poses in body builder fashion for his audience in* Body Beautiful

©Joanna Quinn
(Still courtesy of BFI Film and Video Distribution)

Bottom *In a reversal of roles between he and Beryl, Vince becomes feminised and wears a tutu during the* Body Beautiful *contest*

©Joanna Quinn

to the norm, her work validates the experience of women in general by including progressive female characters with whom the (female) audience can identify. Quinn subverts viewer expectations when she shows Beryl triumphing as a desiring female.

Candy Guard's *Wishful Thinking, What About Me?, Fantastic Person*, and *Moanologue*

Candy Guard's animation style is simple and direct, relative to that of Joanna Quinn. The choice to make the animation 'very simple, very economical'[14] is due to her desire to focus on the characters' thoughts: 'It would be distracting if there was a very full visual style. I think more in terms of cartoons . . . It's drawn, flat, two dimensional, narrative based, it's quick, humorous.'[15] The flatness of the characters serves to make them less representative of real women: until they open their mouths.

Guard's female characters, like Quinn's, are non-idealised both in physical and behavioural terms. Their concerns vary from the everyday (such as concerns with physical appearance and male–female relationships) to the profound (relating to questions of the meaning of one's life). The significance of these concerns resides in how they affect women's experience and behaviour. Her films, as do Quinn's, act as a kind of cultural critique of the ways women choose to operate in a society that frequently judges them on grounds that are completely unrelated to their personal abilities or aptitudes. Guard's female characters are not the super-attractive or cute (or alternatively, the grotesquely

The characters in Candy Guard's Alternative Fringe *are non-idealised females in both physical and behavioural terms*

©Candy Guard

ugly) females that people many classic cartoons. What distinguishes Candy Guard's female characters is their enslavement (voluntary or not) to society's cultural mores and expectations.

Not unlike Quinn, an integral part of Guard's approach to the representation of the female and the feminine is her focus on the body, which, in the films discussed here, is the site of most of the female character's insecurities. In *Wishful Thinking* (1988), two female characters play off one another's doubts about their respective appearances as they prepare to go to a party:

Woman 1: You gonna bother changing?
Woman 2: No, think I'll just go like this?
Woman 1: Hmm, me too. I might just change my shoes.
Woman 2: I might just change my skirt.

The ante is continually upped as more and more articles of clothing are removed and others put on in their place. The two main characters act as each others mirrors, though at times they do not even appear to truly notice what the other is wearing:

Woman 2: I haven't got anything to wear.
Woman 1: What about this?
Woman 2: Does my hair look good to you?
Woman 1: Does mine?
Woman 2: What about this?
Woman 1: What about this?
Woman 2: Hmm, what about this?
Woman 1: How about a hat?
Woman 2: I'm not sure about showing my upper arms.
Woman 1: Looks nice though. My dress is riding up: it's short.
Woman 2: Looks nice though.

The relationship between the two is a conspiracy of mutual affirmation rather than mutual admiration. While they appear to register approval of one another's appearances, such approval is always conditional, as seen in *What About Me?* (1990). If one of the participants in this mirroring process lets down her co-conspirator she is punished. Here, Guard's characters are again obsessed with physical appearances:

Woman 1: And I've put on loads of weight, haven't I?
Woman 2: (distracted) Hmm.
Woman 1: What do you mean, have I?
Woman 2: No. Oh no, no. Honestly you haven't.
Woman 1: You said I had.
Woman 2: No I didn't.
Woman 1: I have though, haven't I?
Woman 2: No, I think you look very slim. Anyway, what do you think about my new dress?
Woman 1: Hmm, nice.
Woman 2: You don't like it.
Woman 1: I do, I do.
Woman 2: Look, I know you don't like it, you don't have to lie to me. I'd rather you just told me the truth.
Woman 1: (doesn't answer, just scratches her nose, tries to avoid gaze of other woman)

Woman 2: Go on you hate it, don't you?
Woman 1: All right, I hate it.
Woman 2: Fatty.

While there is a great deal of rhetoric about women's mutually supportive relationships, Candy Guard's films question the reality of this claim. The shallowness of the emotional lives of Guard's characters is a running motif. Relationships with friends and lovers are not based on mutually held interests or mutual affection. Rather it appears that the 'friendships' represent transient alliances based on shared insecurities and fears.

For these characters, changing clothes is an act of self-re-creation: representing that potential for a change in the lifestyle, identity or relationships they seem to desire. But, unlike Beryl in Quinn's films, Guard's female characters do not challenge the male gaze. Rather, they are tortuously caught by their attempts to conform to societal standards of what is deemed attractive.[16]

The conversation between the two characters parallels in many ways the clothes changing scene in *Wishful Thinking*: characters are typically absorbed in their own thoughts and aspirations. Each directs the conversation towards herself; they do not truly hear one another and as a result conversational etiquette (listening to one's interlocutor) is only nominally observed. Guard's focus on dialogue in her animated films sets her work apart from that of both Quinn and de Vere. Although there is extensive dialogue in the two Quinn films discussed here, the visual elements are the focal points of her films. The conversations in Guard's films, whether they are externalised exchanges or interior monologues, provide the literal structure of her films.

In all of Guard's films, women are looking for something, though actually – as the two characters state at the end of *Wishful Thinking* – they are not quite sure what that 'something' is.

It appears that Candy Guard's characters' attempts to find satisfaction by conforming to stereotyped notions of the ideal feminine are doomed, because the goal is unrealistic, if not unattainable. Guard's stance in her films is an ironic one, highlighting as it does the folly of her character's pursuit of the unattainable – perpetual and universal social approval. The unrealistic nature of these goals is pointedly enacted in *Fantastic Person* (1991), in which the female protagonist creates a list of tasks for the following day: including simultaneous registration in Spanish, painting and ceramic classes, the initiation of a vigorous fitness program and cleaning and redecorating her apartment! When her alarm rings early next day, she simply abandons the list and goes back to sleep. While Quinn's character, Beryl, is liberated from the need to conform to unrealistic standards of physical attractiveness, Candy Guard's characters are trapped in a perpetual and unsatisfying cycle of self-absorption.

Moanologue (1990) features a female character whose insecurities also define her relationship with others. She seems to be the stereotypical nagging woman who relentlessly and without reason pesters her mate; however, as the dialogue progresses, it seems she uses her words in an attempt to solicit the male gaze and thereby confirm her existence as a person. Most of Guard's female characters seem insecure about their right to exist independently (e.g. the 'beautiful' person giving the party in *Wishful Thinking* answers a query about her significant other's whereabouts snappily: 'he's in bed. I am my own person, you know!') and the female character in *Moanologue* is no exception (for as she says to her male partner: 'If you'd just think about me occasionally everything would be all right.').

Getting home after a hard day out in the world, Guard's protagonist asks her male partner why he doesn't look pleased to see her. This comment is the starting point for a 'moanologue' on the cruelties of inattentive men. If he was pleased to see her, she asserts, he would pay attention to her, buy her a gift, throw his arms around her or stare 'longingly' at her. She perceives his demeanour as a rejection of her as a romantic object. She colludes in her construction as simply the object of the male gaze by stating that she must be the 'ugliest woman in the world' – a line that waits to ambush anyone foolhardy enough to respond to it directly (a verbal strategy also used in *What About Me?*). Like many of Guard's females, this character is entrapped by her own image in a cycle of destructive narcissism, exemplified by her sustained glance in the mirror as she relates the events of her day to her male lover. Ironically, by not looking at him, she commits the same sin she has condemns him for: inattentiveness.

Candy Guard's work exposes, in embarrassing detail, the true nature of our own folly – our narcissism and self-absorption. In that respect, it is both painful and humorous. The eventual defeat of Guard's characters is located in their unwillingness to discard the stereotypes to which they will never be able to measure up. Quinn's Beryl does not change her essential self, she does not perform some kind of cosmetic alchemy; rather, she works with what personal resources she has (which when mobilised are considerable) and utilises them to the fullest. Conversely, Candy Guard's characters attempt to be something they are not, something, in fact, that no one is. By attempting to realise the stereotypes, they are imprisoned by them. By the end of the films, her female characters are still asking themselves questions concerning what they want out of life and their apparent lack of direction. Their lives, like the images in their mental mirrors, are fixed and unlikely to change. There is no resolution of the faltering relationships between friends/lovers, nor is there resolution of the very ambiguous feelings the women characters have about their bodies. This irresolution is probably what makes Guard's films so poignantly true to the real life experiences of many women.

Alison de Vere's *The Black Dog*

Like Quinn and Guard, Alison de Vere explores the experience of being female, but in *The Black Dog*, the 'story' is much more loosely structured. De Vere's film charts everywoman's transformation from being an inexperienced innocent to a spiritually and intellectually engaged woman. She does so through stream-of-consciousness shifts in narrative focus, using the flexibility of the animated film as a medium to meld fantasy with reality.

Stylistically, de Vere's animation is quite different than that of Quinn and Guard. While her representation of human and animal characters is fairly realistic, she introduces fantastic landscapes and creatures to define the shifts between 'real' and 'fantasy' settings.

In de Vere's film, the themes are explored through visual imagery, whereas in Guard's films, similar themes of representation, identity and human relationships are explored, primarily through dialogue. There is no dialogue in de Vere's films, a very conscious choice it would seem, to allow for the dream visioning of the female character to be liberalised.

The focus and tenor of de Vere's work is also quite distinct from that of Quinn and Guard. The camera's eye in de Vere's work is internalised and focused on the evolution of the spirit and mind.

In Alison de Vere's The
Black Dog, *the female
protagonist embarks on
a journey of enlighten-
ment. The black dog is
her spiritual guide and
conscience*

©Alison de Vere

Like Quinn and Guard, de Vere locates the experience of being female within the context of a particular female character's story (although, in contrast to the other two artists, she sets that story within a relatively abstract context, as opposed to readily identifiable locations of the 'average' home, community or job). Her female character, too, undergoes a trial involving appearances. In Quinn's *Body Beautiful*, Beryl undergoes harassment from others because of her looks, and in Guard's *Wishful Thinking*, characters bring inner crisis on themselves while attempting to perfect their outer appearances.

*Death, in the form
of a street vendor,
attempts to sell to the
central character
miniature figures of the
three female fates. Once
again she is presented
with a choice about her
future path*

©Alison de Vere

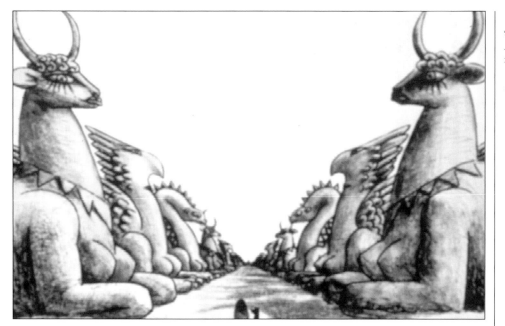

The journey takes the woman to the Complex Fata, a place of sustenance for living things

©Alison de Vere

For de Vere (even more than for Quinn), what is at issue is not simply the integrity of the female body, but also the integrity of the human spirit. The spiritual integrity of the woman is threatened by her initial focus on the appetites of the body (lust and hunger) and her surrender to the saboteurs of the spirit (avarice and vanity).

Black Dog's protagonist is an anonymous, plain-looking woman who embarks on a quest of enlightenment with the assistance of a black dog, which is at once her spiritual guide and her conscience. Her journey through spiritual death to spiritual rebirth is

The Complex Fata is an illusion; the woman is indoctrinated by fellow women into being a seductress, everywoman's fate

©Alison de Vere

The woman's appearance is reworked into a supra-female person

©Alison de Vere

realised through de Vere's use of mythical and biblical analogies. The woman is analogous to Christ as she enters the wilderness and along the way is tempted by the luxurious way of life she encounters at the Complex Fata.

This complex is a locale of fateful decision making for the female character and the vehicle through which Alison de Vere explores the distinction between destiny, which is malleable and personal, and fate, which is inevitable and global. In the film the woman discovers her personal destiny during the course of events, which are experi-

De Vere's woman enters a club accompanied by men and dances with them as part of the masquerade of femininity socially sanctioned by men

©Alison de Vere

enced in a universal sense by all women; for example, sexual initiation and the formation of their identities as women.

The Complex Fata is comprised of three buildings: a club, a restaurant and a boutique. In the rocky wilderness, it appears to be an oasis, a place of sustenance for living things. However, as the woman eventually discovers, this is far from the truth. She is transformed into a seductress after she enters the boutique at Complex Fata, her appearance reworked by the boutique proprietor through the application of 'beautifying' techniques like make-up, expensive and form-fitting clothing and hair styling. Everywoman, like multitudes of women before her, is indoctrinated by a fellow female, in this case the female fate, whose actions represent the legacy of enculturation into the necessity of signalling gender and thus signalling her femininity.[17]

The female protagonist masquerades, temporarily, as a supra-female person. What distinguishes Beryl's character (but not the other females in Quinn's films) from the female characters in de Vere's films and those of Guard is her resoluteness in rejecting the high-fashion model of femaleness. From the beginning, Beryl is who and what she is without apologies to the sensibilities of the audiences accustomed to the physically idealised representations of women that are prevalent in classical animation.

The female character in de Vere's film ultimately disavows her role as solely an object of male desire. However, prior to rejecting that role, she, like many women before her, is transformed by the female fate into a culturally defined object of beauty.[18] The woman in *The Black Dog* assumes the masquerade of socially sanctioned femininity. In the boutique, she is transformed from an ordinary woman into an object of male desire, evidenced in the scenes depicting her surrounded by male companions, at the club where she is escorted by two men to the gaming table, and in the discotheque where she dances with several men.

At this point, de Vere seems to be commenting upon women's complicity in their representation as objects to be displayed for the pleasure of other people, specifically men. The film asks us to consider how women are represented and how they seek fulfilment in life. Though these issues are explored in Guard's films, de Vere's resolution of them is quite different. Whereas Guard's characters seem caught by the images they see reflected in the mirror, de Vere's protagonist is abruptly forced from the position of narcissism into one of self-contemplation. She is compelled to turn away from her reflected image when she is expelled from Complex Fata.

Once she has indulged her various appetites, she is asked by the proprietors of the Complex Fata to pay for her pleasures. The price – her brain, hands and heart – items constituting her uniqueness as a person and her capacity to reason and feel (both physically and emotionally). As the woman discovers, the inhabitants of Complex Fata are sustained by the death of other living things. For example, the boutique proprietor kills a dove for a hat and several ermines for a fur stole. Food preparation in the restaurant occasions even more death. The restaurateur, a monstrous serpent/cat, uses her teeth to catch the fish she will later cook. The animal nature of the woman and other diners at the restaurant is revealed when they bare their teeth, as the monstrous proprietor did before them, to consume the food before them. At the club, one man kills another after a loss at the gaming tables, while death (in the form of a skeletal dowager) sits patiently nearby. The woman brings on her own spiritual death by indulging her 'base' appetites. By feeding the appetites of her body at the expense of her mind and soul, she has participated in the unthinking killing of other living things.

After her debt becomes due, the woman is forced to plunge head-long into the desolate body of water in the valley floor. As the black dog 'retrieves' her from the water and takes her to a place of relative safety, she becomes a visual analogue to the baby Moses, arriving through the rushes. She is conveyed by the black dog in a boat that has a single eye painted on either side of the prow (the eye likely signifying the Egyptian god Osiris who represents the possibility of rebirth). The black dog protects her during the night from the attacks of various evil spirits.

Two significant figures assist the woman throughout the film. One is the black dog, which has a pivotal role as guide, protector, conscience, judge and teacher. He is the one who initially wakens her from her sleep and initiates a series of events that lead her on a journey of self-discovery. He also tries to warn her away from Complex Fata, though his warnings go unheeded. Later in the story, he leads the woman to the place where she undergoes her spiritual and intellectual rebirth. He guides her and in his role as the god Anubis, wraps her body, mummifying it, in preparation for her journey through the underworld. Her time in the pyramid is the prelude to her rebirth as a spiritually and intellectually enlightened being.

The second significant male figure who appears after the woman emerges into intellectual and spiritual rebirth and enlightenment within the pyramid is a male child. This fruit of the woman's enlightenment metamorphoses from the bundle of scrolls she wraps in her shawl/head-dress and cradles as she sits, alongside the black dog, at the edge of an opening in the pyramid.

The male child is both generated by the woman and is her genitor, given that he changes places with her (in one of the final sequences of the film) in a temporal sense, when he ages, becoming a father figure and she regresses, becoming a child. As the woman and the black dog sit at the edge of the precipitous opening in the pyramid, the male child, clothed all in white, steps out onto an ephemeral bridge that magically appears beneath his feet.

The child moves easily and without fear along the bridge as he makes his way across the void between the pyramid and the other side of the valley. He provides the means for the woman to leave the desert and continue on her journey. But for the woman, the bridge proves insubstantial, crumbling beneath her feet as she anxiously pursues the child, whom she perceives to be in danger. De Vere's imagery in this sequence locates the child as a guide/saviour of the woman, given his symbolic purity (the white garments and his extreme youth, as he is little more than a infant) and his part in leading her out of the desert, the place of her spiritual downfall. The child's miraculous walk through apparent midair suggests an analogue to Christ on the water at Galilee, suggesting the child's identity as the woman's literal saviour.

The child's innocence and the woman's loss of innocence (occasioned by her sexual initiation at Complex Fata and more importantly, by her self-betrayal, when she accepts the false identity that the fate in the boutique creates for her) or perhaps, more pointedly, her experience of the world, as represented by her time in the microcosm of Complex Fata, explains why the child crosses the valley with ease, while the woman fearfully walks on the rapidly crumbling bridge. The woman's self-corruption (her denial of her true being) and her lack of belief in her own destiny appear to be the causes of the bridges' dissolution. She is reticent on the bridge, as she was reluctant at the beginning of the film, to follow the black dog into the wasteland, to face the risks entailed in the pursuit of her destiny.

It is interesting that the female protagonist's primary spiritual guide and protector is male, while the fates who lead the women into acts of personal folly are female. As in Candy Guard's films, female characters seem to be the agents of other female characters' downfalls, although the results in Guard's films are not as devastating as they are in *The Black Dog*. When Guard's characters participate in the game of mutual affirmation, the greatest penalty for failure is the censure of a female friend. But when de Vere's female protagonist submits to the ministrations of the female fates at Complex Fata and fails to pay for their services, she faces spiritual and intellectual death. Guard's main female characters in *Wishful Thinking* and *Fantastic Person* indicate that they are dissatisfied with their present lives and are searching for something that will fulfil their desires, but apparently they are searching in all the wrong places, with all the wrong motives and with the wrong people. As the woman must choose her own way, the fates simply provide the means for her self-destruction, they do not control her destiny, for only she does that. The male child and the black dog of the title, while they act as the woman's spiritual guides, are not her eventual saviours.

In the penultimate sequence we see the woman, now in a child's form, playing with a doll's house into which she places a bed and then a human figure. The figure is the woman herself as she was at the start of the film, waking to a new day: an image of the possibilities for re-birth.

Artistic creation and self-recreation are integral themes in *The Black Dog*. Although the woman in the film does not transform into different personages, as Beryl does in *Body Beautiful*, de Vere's character is depicted in her potential to occupy different roles as one individual during her lifetime. Her first transformation is marked by her change from a relatively plain person to a seductress. The woman's many other roles are visualised later, when she appears in a doctor's waiting room (after having grasped too soon for knowledge when she enters the pyramid). As the woman sits in the physician's office waiting to be treated, she is depicted simultaneously in the various identities that she has or will assume during her life, all linked by their wearing of a multi-coloured shawl. All of the woman's identities exist in the present moment that is embodied in the waiting room scene: she is at once the witch, the clown (a comic masquerade of a male with a bulbous red nose and black moustache), the business woman, the elderly person, the mother and child, the pregnant woman, the woman with the shopping bag full of groceries and the contrite woman with the shawl draped over her head and shoulders. The transience of the occupation of these identities is emphasised by the rapid pace at which various identities or personas disappear into the doctor's office for treatment. As with the changes in physical form that Beryl undergoes during the course of the Body Beautiful contest, these personae are occupied, in many cases, through personal choice and thus they are self-affirming.

While the characters of de Vere and Quinn both undergo identity changes, these transformations are much more dramatic in Quinn's films. Beryl metamorphoses rapidly into different body types and different creatures. In de Vere's film, shifts in identity are most often portrayed by the different roles assumed by women in their lifetimes and by the literal putting on of a different identity with a change of clothes. While the attempts of Guard's characters to transform themselves are mostly unsuccessful, the transformation of de Vere's character is successful, at least for a while. The most dramatic change of identity depicted in *Black Dog* is the woman's reversion to a younger stage of life. Guard's characters believe that, by putting on a different dress, they can become different people – generally people who live what are considered to be more fulfilling or exciting lives. But the superficial transformation of the female character's form in *Wishful Thinking*, for example, is ultimately destructive. The same can be said of de Vere's character's initial transformation in the boutique. This woman's exclusive focus on the embellishment of her surface (at the expense of intellect and spirit) leads to her ruin. Unlike Guard, de Vere suggests positive alternatives through the possibility of daily rebirths (as one wakes from the temporary 'death' that is sleep) and the relative immortality that can be achieved through artistic creation.

The notion of immortal artistic creation is introduced during the scene in the pyramid (prior to the woman's achievement of an enlightened state) in which various famous artists and writers (Leonardo da Vinci, Shakespeare) are depicted in the act of creation. Women are depicted as having the potential to create in a variety of ways: through the practice of their art and through their reproductive capacities. Both artistic production and procreation are portrayed as more lasting satisfactions than the shallow gratification achieved by feeding venal appetites and making superficial changes in appearance.

Conclusion

Joanna Quinn, Candy Guard and Alison de Vere, although quite different stylistically, are three artists whose work concerns female experiences and the representation of the feminine. The humour of Quinn and Guard is located in the everyday experiences of women, and in Quinn, facilitated by the use of visual and verbal exaggeration. De Vere, on the other hand, explores women's experiences through images that seem to flow one to another like events in a dream.

All three filmmakers explore the notion of the female form as something that is malleable and whose femaleness can be enhanced or reduced. In Quinn's films, Beryl rejects societal dictates of what it is to be female and instead chooses a form that is comfortable for her. Guard's characters are trapped in a continual dialogue with their mirrors as they put on the masquerade of the feminine. The literal putting on of clothes in the film *Wishful Thinking* symbolises the artificial nature of the act of putting on a feminine mask. Similarly, the female character in *The Black Dog* also chooses to put on a masquerade of the feminine before she achieves self-knowledge.

In all the films, women are depicted as complicit in their own enslavement by mirrors or by society's expectations of what femaleness represents. In *Body Beautiful* Beryl is pestered by the other women to stay on her diet so that she can fit into a costume for the dance number prior to the contest. The other female characters in *Body Beautiful* are trapped by societal beliefs about what is acceptable in the female form. In a similar way, Candy Guard's characters are dependent on their own mirrored images or the mirrors provided them in the form of their female friends. Both of these types of mirrors reflect a female image that is deemed acceptable only if it conforms to the standards set by the society in which they live.

The standard of feminine beauty in de Vere's film *The Black Dog* is set by the female fate in the boutique in Complex Fata. It represents a kind of hyper-femininity that, while it might be temporarily attainable via 'beautifying' techniques, is not realistically sustainable over extended periods of time. Further, the outcomes of techniques which seem to falsify the feminine rather than enhance it prove to be nearly fatal for de Vere's female protagonist.

The metamorphic/transformative possibilities of animation provide Quinn and de Vere with a diversity of ways to represent the female. In Quinn's work, the character of Beryl is literally transformed during the course of the film. She becomes other types of bodies (and other creatures and objects), which she tries on and then discards like pieces of clothing. Rather than try on different bodies, the characters in Guard's *Wishful Thinking* try on different articles of clothing, attempting to re-make themselves into some ideal type of femininity (represented by the other female characters at the party). The woman in *The Black Dog* changes into a range of identities.

The work of each animator discussed here deals in its own unique way with the themes of self-creation, self-determination and self-representation. Until recent decades, the animated female images that were available to female audiences were those that existed in the mind's eye of their predominantly male creators. With the entrance of more women into the field of animation as independent filmmakers, who have creative control over their subject matter, there has been a burgeoning of the types of female images available to audiences. The potential of animation to represent female experience was recognised early by the Leeds Animation Workshop.[19]

Outside of the United Kingdom there have been and continue to be female animators who are engaged in the creation of animated images of women that are expressive of their concerns and experience. Monique Renault, originally a native of France and who now lives and works in Holland, was one of the pioneers (along with Gillian Lacey and Vera Neubauer in Britain and Mary Beams in the United States) of animated films that had a distinctly feminist perspective. She uses the animated film medium to explore a number of social and political issues as they overlap with feminism.[20]

The work of female animators is characterised by its variety. The sensuality of the work of Suzan Pitt contrasts with the whimsy of Kathy Rose. However, many female animators seem to be concerned with issues of identity and this is expressed in their work, as is evident in the films of Guard, Quinn and de Vere. Lucy Lippard explains the variety seen in women's films in the following way:

> Women ... care more about variety than men and variety connects to fragmentation and to the autobiographical aspect [of their work], too – as a sort of defiance.[21]

Joanna Quinn has also expressed the belief that the films of female animators can be differentiated from men's, but in terms of the non-conventional (in terms of classical animated film) ways in which they represent the female form. She suggests that female animators do not rely on stereotyped representations that tend to mock the female form.[22] Her films like those of Guard and de Vere that were discussed here had definite feminist undertones.

Sharon Couzin provides the following definition of feminist art:

> Feminist art is art which acknowledges that difference of being a woman – i.e. what it is to be a woman – and then integrates that consciousness into the art.[23]

According to this definition, the films of the female animators discussed here all represent feminist art because they explore women's experience.

While discussions of representations of women were an early focus for discussion by feminist theorists, they generally focused on male representations of the female and to a great extent the discussion is still limited to an examination of this kind of representation (and its limitations).

With the continuing and growing participation of female animators in the field of animation, one would expect scholarship on the topic of representation to shift to the ways in which women represent themselves and other women. The effect (if any) that theoretical discussions of meaning will have on the actual work of female animators is difficult to predict. Additionally, as female animators gain greater exposure and acceptance in their field it will be interesting to see if concerns with representation (of the female) will continue to be central aspects of their work. However, as art is an intensely personal form of expression, one would expect to continue to see female animators exploring issues relating to their own experiences, impressions and concerns, as they relate to their existence as gendered persons living in societies preoccupied with issues of gender and sexuality.

This is an extensively revised version of a paper was given at the 1994 SAS Conference that was first published, in a rather different version, in the *Animation Journal* (Fall Issue, 1995).

Notes

1. Linda Mulvey first introduced the idea of the dominance of the masculine gaze in cinema in her article 'Visual Pleasure and Narrative Cinema' (*Screen* 16:3 (Autumn 1975): 6–18). Mary Ann Doane, 'The "Women's Film": Possession and Address', in *Re-Vision: Essays in Feminist Film Criticism*, eds Mary Ann Doane, Patricia Mellencamp and Linda Williams (Los Angeles: The American Film Institute, 1984), 67–82, is in basic agreement with the Mulvey thesis that classical cinema has excluded the female point of view in film but she feels that women viewers can assume one of two positions: narcissistic and female identified; or, conversely, they can act the part of 'transvestites' if they identify with the male characters. Judith Mayne, *The Woman at the Keyhole: Feminism and Women's Cinema* (Bloomington: Indiana University Press, 1990), 17, and Jill Dolan, *The Feminist Spectator as Critic*, ed. Ann Arbor (Michigan: UMI Research Press, 1988), 2, both discuss the representation in mainstream cinema of women as passive objects and men as active subjects.
2. Interview with Joanna Quinn by Linda Pariser in *Women and Animation: a compendium*, ed. Jayne Pilling (London, England: British Film Institute, 1992), 35.
3. R. Betterton: 'What's Wrong with Images of Women?', in *Looking on Images of Femininity in the Visual Arts and Media*, ed. Griselda Pollock (London: Pandora, 1987), 11.
4. Pilling, 87.
5. Antonia Lant, 'Women's Independent Cinema: The Case of Leeds Animation Workshop', in *Fires Were Started: British Cinema and Thatcherism* (Minneapolis: University of Minnesota Press, 1993), 161–187.
6. 'Whether it is a man looking at a woman on the street, the male artist's gaze at the model or the male audience for a blue movie, women do not share in the culture of looking in the same way . . . Even when roles are reversed, as for example with the male pin-up, the relativity of power and control are not so easily reversible.' It has been suggested that male spectatorship is not solely erotic but has to do with power and control over the image. In R. Betterton, 11.
7. Suzanne Moore's article 'Here's Looking at You Kid!', in *The Female Gaze: Women as Viewers of Popular Culture*, eds I.L. Gamman and M. Marshment (Seattle: The Red Comet, 1989), 44–59, suggests that in face-to-face interactions with women, men tend to stare to assert their dominance and women respond by looking away. Beryl undermines the male prerogative of the male to be the sole possessor of the gaze by returning the stripper's stare.
8. Vince uses various images of largeness to denigrate Beryl. He says that there is so much of her that 'you could hardly miss it'. During the exercise scene in which Vince puts the women through their paces, like a sexist drill sergeant, Vince asks Beryl: 'When was the last time you saw your toes love?' And, as Beryl falls over during the exercise session, we hear Vince say to the other women: 'The sinking of the Titanic.' When they react negatively to his comment he responds: 'Ah, come on. You gotta laugh!' At lunch, in the company cafeteria while the women factory workers discuss the costumes they are to wear in the chorus line routine prior to the Body Beautiful contest, Vince comes up behind Beryl and asks her what costume she could fit into: 'A whale costume?'
9. The Leeds Animation Workshop film *Out to Lunch* (1989) also examines the kinds of access and

the ways in which men and women use space. In a scene from that film, two men are seated at a table with two women. The men sprawl comfortably in their chairs, an aerial view revealing that their legs use two-thirds to three-quarters of the space under the table. The women's space has been compressed to such an extent that they occupy only a small corner of the table's area (Lant, 179).

10. Robin T. Lakoff, in *Taking Power: The Politics of Language* (New York: Basic Books, 1990), 205, argues that: 'Men's language is the language of the powerful. It is meant to be direct, clear, succinct, as would be expected of those who need not fear giving offence . . . It is the language of people who are in charge of making observable changes in the real world. Women's language developed as a way of surviving and even flourishing without control over economic, physical or social reality. Then it is necessary to listen more than speak, agree more than confront, be delicate, be indirect, say dangerous things in such a way that their impact will be felt after the speaker is out of range of the hearer's retaliation.'

11. The deliberate use of female imagery in the work of performers like Madonna, is ironic, a kind of hyper-femininity. Susan Morrison ('Girls on Film: Fantasy, Desire and Desperation', *CineAction!* (Fall, 1985): 2–6) suggests that Madonna's 'look' in the movie *Desperately Seeking Susan* – 'a man's undershirt, boxer shorts, garter belts *over* the shorts, lacy stockings and worn on top of this a man's shirt unbuttoned' – is a masquerade that 'foregrounds her femininity to excess masking the fact that she is taking the active masculine role'.

12. Quinn uses a fantasy sequence in the film *Girls' Night Out* in which Beryl imagines herself transported from the concerns of her everyday life to a desert island by a handsome, young Tarzan-like character. In the sequence, Beryl is presented as a desiring female who is not at all reticent to act on her impulses. The potential for women to return the gaze and to be an active spectator is commented upon by Jennifer Bloomer ('Big Jugs', in *The Hysterical Male. New Feminist Theory*, eds A. Kroker and M. Kroker (Montreal: New World Perspectives, 1991), 13–27. She suggests that women do return the male gaze:

> The eye of the woman bears with it, after all, the potential to return the gaze; to return not merely in a sense of the conventional female acquiescence in sexual discourse, but also to return, to deflect the power of the male gaze through a return to the repressed, through the exorbitance of the female gaze.

Ann Friedberg, in *Window Shopping. Cinema and the Post-Modern* (Berkeley: University of California Press, 1993), 184, also suggests that spectatorship is not represented by a simple 'one-to-one' correspondence between the spectator position and gender, race or sexual identity. That view of the position of the spectator acts 'as if identity were a constant, consistent continuum, unchallenged by the borrowed subjectivity of spectatorship'.

13. Ann J. Macklem, in The Popular Pleasures of Film: Feminist Perspectives (MA Thesis, Simon Fraser University, 1992), 11, suggests that a simple inversion of gender roles does not challenge male authority. However, as indicated in the text, Beryl's assumption of the role of aggressor empowers the women in the audience to be as they are and not as others feel they should be.

14. Pilling, 88.

15. Pilling, 88.

16. G. Koch ('Why Women Go to the Movies', *Jump Cut* 27 (1982): 51) suggests that narcissistic females do not challenge the male gaze. The characters of Candy Guard do not challenge the male gaze and are tortuously caught by their attempts to solicit that gaze. Linda Mulvey (1975) hypothesises that men are the primary spectators addressed by mainstream cinema. Their fantasies of the feminine are seen by Mulvey to be projected onto women. She describes the traditional role of women as that of exhibitionists. They are to be looked at and are on display. Other authors who describe the role of women in film as that of passive objects to be viewed by the active male spectator include Jill Dolan in *The Feminist Spectator as Critic*, ed. Ann Arbor (Michigan: UMI Research Press, 1988), 2 and 13; H. Sander, 'Feminism and Film', *Jump Cut* 27 (1982): 49–50; and Tania Modleski in *Feminism without Women: Culture and Criticism in a 'Post-Feminist' Age* (New York: Routledge, 1991), 108.

Jane Gaines, in 'Women and Representation: Can We Enjoy Alternative Pleasure?', *American Media and Mass Culture: Left Perspective*, ed. D. Lazare (Berkeley: University of California, 1987), 362 and 365, describes the strategy in women's films as one designed to destroy male pleasure;

that is, as being destructive of the man's view of the female object. This would seem to be the project of Joanna Quinn and Candy Guard in their films; particularly in the case of *Body Beautiful*, in which the right of the male to be the sole possessor of the gaze is directly challenged by Beryl's aggressive assertion that she has the right to determine how she is female.

17.   Betterton (1987), 7, suggests that: 'Femininity, as defined in western culture, is bound up very closely with the way in which the female body is perceived and represented . . . Women are commonly defined in terms of their appearance and relation to men . . . The visual is particularly important in the definition of femininity, both because of the significance attached to images in modern culture and because a woman's character and status are frequently judged by her appearance . . . Current ideas reinforce a view that to be feminine is to possess certain bodily attributes.' Thus, it makes it difficult to visualise a femininity outside of the existing attitudes to and representations of the female body.

18.   Annette Kuhn, in *The Power of the image: Essays on representation and sexuality* (London: Routledge & Kegan Paul, 1985), 14, suggests that glamour photography is something that promotes the ideal woman as someone 'who is put together, composed of surfaces and defined by appearances'.

19.   Lant, ibid.

20.   Pilling, 76.

21.   Sharon Couzin quoting Lucy Lippard in Pilling, 71.

22.   Pilling, 87.

23.   Couzin in Pilling, 71.

An analysis of Susan Pitt's *Asparagus* and Joanna Priestley's *All My Relations*

Sharon Couzin

To describe the woman's voice in contemporary animation requires a brief historical note on the representation of women in animation as well as their lack of participation in the planning and execution of these works. In addition, we must look to the role the feminist movement has played in both understanding and articulating the place of women in art in general – how at this point we can say the movement has re-politicised art; in this case, film.

To address these issues I wish to refer to two animations: *Asparagus* by Suzan Pitt and *All My Relations* by Joanna Priestley. While we can debate the definitions of feminist theory and female imagery, I do not think we will deny the issues, concerns, nor subject matter of these two films. I have chosen these two films, one which uses language, one which does not, because I am particularly interested in the iconographic qualities of animation in a field where the ruling ideologies of language have, in many cases, reduced or limited critical discourse by narrowly inscribing meaning.

I do not quarrel with the ideologies of feminism – the close linguistic reading was a necessary imperative to construct a field of inquiry. Laura Mulvey's seminal essay as well as the work of Julia Kristeva and Gayatri Spivak (among many, many others) advance our understanding of art, as well as of ourselves. However, they address the visual arts mainly as a subset of language.

I am interested here in exploring visual language and suggest that by examining the iconography of these films we might give a re-reading which renders both of these films powerful feminist works hinging not on text but on image alone in the case of *Asparagus*, and on the collaborative process between text and image in *All My Relations*. In the latter film there are two sets of images going on at all times: one functioning as a frame while the referential quality of the inner and outer narratives in the image create their own dialectic. In so doing, they respond to the political agenda of feminism in this case, rather than being part and parcel of the illusionism assigned to the Hollywood studio style, which is the primary focus of feminist film theory.

Historically, a woman had no voice at all in animation. The field was occupied by men in the conception, rendering and distribution. The very early individual artists who animated – for example, Winsor McCay – revealed an obsession to identify themselves as having magical creative powers. Self-figuration was as popular with the filmmakers as with the audiences. No woman figured in those early films. Studio productions depicted female characters as either unimportant, caricatured and objectified, or as lazy, stupid and aggressive, or as idealised, fantasised sex objects. *Red Hot Riding Hood* or Coal Black (from Robert Clampett's *Coal Black and De Sebben Dwarfs*) and of course Betty Boop are obvious examples of the sexual stereotypes.

But, as early as Farmer Alfalfa, the wife was depicted as a nagging, nasty one-dimensional figures. Other characters developed somewhat more rounded natures; Olive Oyl, for example or Little Lulu. Both had some sparks of independent thoughts, but quite clearly the social mores of the time dictated that the mythological position of heroic lead was male.

Ideas of the representation of self feature not only in the two animated films considered here but were absolutely central to the avant-garde film movement in America which came to prominence during the 1960s. Working in ma ny cases against conventional narrative, animators like Mary Ellen Bute (mid 1930s) and Marie Menken (late 1950s) set the stage for work done in the last twenty years.

The avant-garde filmmakers worked poetically, graphically and metaphorically, often bridging the areas between animation and live cinematography. Men as well as women worked abstractly, establishing territory which, in many instances, was only much later explored by women and then in a radically different way. Key animators like Viking Eggeling, Oskar Fischinger, Fernand Léger and Man Ray focused on the graphic, iconic order of things – allowing composition, colour and other formal elements to outweigh a secular narrative, ever popular in the studio animation film.

How did this secular narrative affect women artists? Nineteenth-century writing provides us with insights. As an art form it allowed the development of the woman's voice for self-acknowledgement. The stories written by women and about women were ones that valued domestic power, necessary for the rise of a middle class. However, that same power existed in a separate realm from the important decisions of society. Women's relations to objects, especially domestic objects, served as a surrogate region of legitimate focus, objectifying people as well as things. Without real power, women became marginalised, objectified. Their creative voices were expressed in many cases through 'women's work' such as making quilts, weaving, and doing embroidery and other handicrafts. In the twentieth century we can trace great interest in the soap opera and various forms of confessional fiction.

'But', points out Lucy Lippard, 'women also care more about variety than men and variety connects to fragmentation and to the autobiographical aspect, too – as a sort of defiance'.[1] The women's movement made questions of female imagery and feminine aesthetics central to any discussion of art made by women. What is female imagery? Is there such a thing as feminine aesthetics? Like women working in other media, by 1970 women animators began to question the common modes of representation. The idea of 'female imagery' was first used to mean 'sexual imagery'. In the world of art, body art, happenings, performances, dance and painting all used sexual imagery. Judy Chicago's work, Carolee Schneeman's films and performances, Eva Hesse's organic sculptures were all central to the iconographic background of filmmakers like Pitt and Priestley. On female imagery, Lippard states:

> I prefer [the term] female sensuality because it's vaguer and broader. There's lots of sexual imagery in woman's art – circles, domes, eggs, spheres, boxes, bimorphic shapes, maybe certain striation or layering. But it's more interesting to think about fragments, which imply a certain antilogical, antilinear approach common to many women's work.[2]

Early feminist theory thus concentrated on the representation of women and on the gender of authorship. Feminist intellectuals have engaged in increasingly sophisticated forms of theoretical argumentation and textual analysis. However, the feminist movement is also and perhaps more importantly a movement linked to a political ideology and a social movement involving a process of change. How the theoretical concepts come to be used in cultural practice cannot happen through language alone (as many literary and philosophical voices have seemed to assume).

Films like *Asparagus* and *All My Relations* are solid examples of avant-garde feminist films which are embedded with numerous political issues. Feminist art is art which acknowledges the difference of being a woman – that is, what it is to be a woman – and then integrates that consciousness into the art. It could involve a set of imagery or it might function metaphorically or poetically. Many women deal more openly with feelings, with their own and with others', and as a movement, feminist art tends to be more humanistic than formal. Making people aware through your art is a political act even if the work of art itself is not directly political.

Asparagus by Suzan Pitt is a film of social critique and is a deeply personal visual narrative on identity. The theme of identity spirals around gender, fetish, sexuality and nature. In many ways the film fulfils the requirements of nineteenth-century confessional literature. It is 'about' domesticity, power and sexual politics. Pitt's major themes of identity and gender are explored through three major motifs: the asparagus/phallus, (which she equates to nature and wholeness), the faceless woman, who is both a magician and mother figure, and the relation of objects to self (which conjoins narcissism and fetishism).

Let us examine these three motifs more carefully.

The asparagus/phallus (which Pitt equates to nature and wholeness) is a contradictory image, problematic for feminists because it clearly carries possible readings of penis envy and acceptance of the patriarchal order. The artist herself would not agree to this and reads the asparagus as an almost primeval plant with both a male and female stage in its development. After planting asparagus seeds Pitt watched the minuscule phallic shoots grow into delicate fernlike fronds – definite female images. The phallic 'other' would be claimed by many as not referring to the phallus icon but to the desire or longing to have or possess that other (which in any psychoanalytic reading would of course refer to the original 'other' – the mother). Logically then, a simple psychoanalytic reading could position the asparagus, as Pitt does, as faeces, as the castrated penis and as the powerful desiring impetus which embodies the inability of both male and female to ever completely replicate that infantile empathy at the mother's breast.

The second motif, the faceless woman, also holds the possibility of a variety of interpretations – the necessary polysemic quality – consistent with Pitt's requirement of herself in the making of the film. Pitt desired each frame to contain 'everything',

every colour, every shape, for all of the space to be compositionally occupied; for each twenty-fourth of a second to be trembling with movement. The artist here positions herself in the all-powerful role of magician/creator. But it is also the role of the all-providing mother and to the extent we accept her argument that the phallus

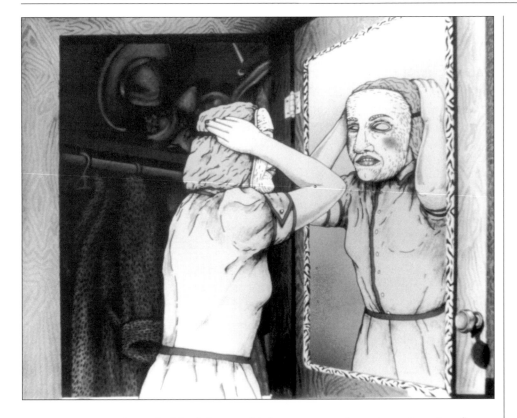

represents nature, here the blank face could also represent the universal mother figure. This countenances the linguistic notions of 'mother nature' or 'earth mother'. The blank face can be described as representing a loss of identity, but equally as abstract neutral terrain onto which the voyeuristic viewer must place an interpretation. By this account there are many possibilities, all of which force us to become an active participant in the viewing process.

This film is not presented as entertainment. It is a process, not a set of pre-existing conditions. For example, the blank face could be said to represent a lack of detail. And in the reading of Shor's book *Reading in Detail* the claim is made that, historically, details in art have been gender-attached to women. They have been equivalent to deformities and aberrations while the larger, abstract universal ideas in art have always been ascribed to men.[3] Is the artist refusing such an interpretation by reducing the face to an abstract representation of idea of face? Is it then like the asparagus, both male and female? Or does it simply make a political statement validating the worth of the female by pointing to the contradictions in the art historical system (since that same system embraces realism which is completely dependent on the veracity of the detail . . .)?

We could go farther with our inquiry into interpretation. Is the loss of identity accomplished by the destructive effects some women feel because of their desire to merge totally with a partner? We do not see a partner in Pitt's film, but then the entire film seems to represent some interior space, some stream of consciousness and to reflect mainly the protagonist's feelings. For many women the overwhelming desire for fusion with a partner, followed by rejection, is indicative of the problem of 'feeling too much'.[4]

Or does an artist experience a narcissistic dependency, reliant upon others as a means of self-validation through their art? Or, even more directly, is the lack of detail in the face a request by the artist for us to give back to her, to 'fill in the detail' as it were, with as much richness, colour and charged emotions as she has given us in the rest of the scenes? I would suggest that it is as important to recognise the array of possible interpretations as to choose a 'correct' interpretation.

The third motif, the relation of objects to self, shifts curiously from a self-absorbed narcissism to an almost fetishistic involvement with personal and domestic objects (a qualified 'domestic', however, because the site of the film is clearly an interior space; the space of dreams and fantasies). The objects in the space are all stylised, kitsch deco, often in pairs, usually decoratively detailed. The constraints of cause and effect are minimal, a feature of animation used in a manner that again directs our attention to the artist – ironic, since the artist both denies or conceals her identity within the film but clearly has created a film of spectacle and power. In this case, through unusual objects and bizarre relationships, we are consistently asked to see the protagonist as the filmmaker or creator of the film. The protagonist's relationship to the space is highly charged: the soft organic shapes of the furniture, draperies, wallpapers, lighting fixtures, etc., are all shaped and coloured in a similar manner. All seem to be a homogeneous extension of the main character.

The garden is of central importance and repeats the basic binary structure Pitt uses throughout: inner/outer. As the deep red curtains are pulled back they reveal a garden of fantastic exotic plants which begin to slowly revolve. We see two very large feet step into the garden and we watch from inside with the faceless woman as a large hand reaches down and caresses/masturbates the asparagus stalk.

This dreamlike observing of the self is echoed in the doll's house scene. The protagonist

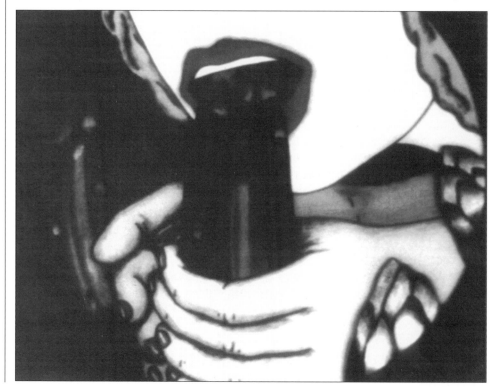

This and facing page
The dreamlike observations of the self of the faceless woman includes the masturbation of an asparagus stalk and a doll's house scene

©(Both) Susan Pitt

walks up to a table on which sits a doll's house with rooms open in front. As she reaches over to turn a knob, a close-up balloon shows her hand in detail twisting the knob. As the knob turns, the camera zooms up to one of the rooms in the doll's house that is furnished exactly like the one the protagonist has been standing in just before the camera zoomed up. Pitt creates an infinite regress, an ultimate *déjà vu* experience through a looping of the scene. The doll's house regress displaces memories of the childhood doll's house with the role of the mother and suggests two or three possible interpretations. Is it merely a comment on family rituals – the middle-class doll and the attendant doll's house accessories? Does it overtly connect to the lack of other people in this internal space? Or does it speak of the alienation and isolation of the artist's work? Or to the solitary nature of subjective work, as opposed to Hollywood-studio narrative production where hundreds of people might be involved? Certainly there are no children here. Is it a suggestion that infantile desires or anxieties continue to be played out in adulthood? Is it a formal device, a plaything of the adult which uses time rather than objects? Is the doll's house a fetish object?

As a social critique, *Asparagus* is a highly personal narrative: melancholy, evocative and enigmatic. It clearly questions the relationship of inner life with outer world and presents the dilemma of the female artist at one with herself in search of a voice. The film is not only a stunningly beautiful work of animation, but also an important document of the struggle to articulate through the image the role of the woman.

Joanna Priestley and *All My Relations*

All My Relations by Joanna Priestley was completed in 1990, a good twelve years after *Asparagus*. The film reflects many changes in American society and the woman's

movement. While *All My Relations* is filled with social critique, it is more importantly a film made by a collaborative process in which Priestley allowed the meaning of the film, in a large part, to be determined by the voices on the soundtrack.

The two narrators, Scott and Victoria Parker, were shown the film approximately 50 times and asked to improvise with no directions from Priestley. The resulting dialogue is their interpretation of Priestley's animation. Initially the narrative describes the mental and emotional states of the two main characters, represented by two abstract shapes, one a man, one a woman. The dialogue between the two begins as they walk toward and then past one another and follows a fairly typical girl finds (saves) boy narrative and humorously depicts the rapid and excited thrills of early romance which lead in the film to love, marriage, a child, a house, job, money, etc. At some point the path twists and each of the characters begins to blame the other and an extended argument/row begins with rapidly cut images to reinforce visually the emotional trauma. There is none of the personal mystery, as in *Asparagus*. Instead, a fairly public collective unconscious seems to shape much of the chronology and morality of the film, which is where the gender roles assume larger significance.

The animation formally has a particularly interesting structure – a central image composed of drawn figures which are symbolic shapes – and a surrounding frame which actually constitutes an outer film. The outer film consists of various collections of objects and artefacts, animated by eight different people. The dialectic between the two parts of the film, the inner drawn one with the more conventional narrative text, the outer 'frame' silent, but reacting to or commenting on or creating an alternative to the central story, provides an oddly satisfying narrative of its own. It is as though we hear what we are supposed to in the central narrative but are also free to construct our own interpretation of what is going on in the border. In a manner parallel to the way Priestley worked with Scott and Victoria Parker and with the collaborators of the frame section, she is also permitting, perhaps even requiring, that the audience also engage directly with the content of the film.

As in Pitt's film, colour, texture and composition give notice that a sensuous, tactile story, filled with emotion – the outer a subjective response, the inner a painful, angry and also humorous set of emotions – are both 'confessions' of an intimate personal space. Both parts of Priestley's film construct their own worlds and set up in the image a language of representation which we must accept in order to engage with this film.

Piaget in his basic research with children explored at great length how systems of representation develop. Initially, representation can occur only after imitation.[5] Sounds and phonations are his primary examples, but interestingly, image symbols develop before language symbols. Piaget describes an example of how the 'mental image', which must occur before representation takes place, is first interiorised.

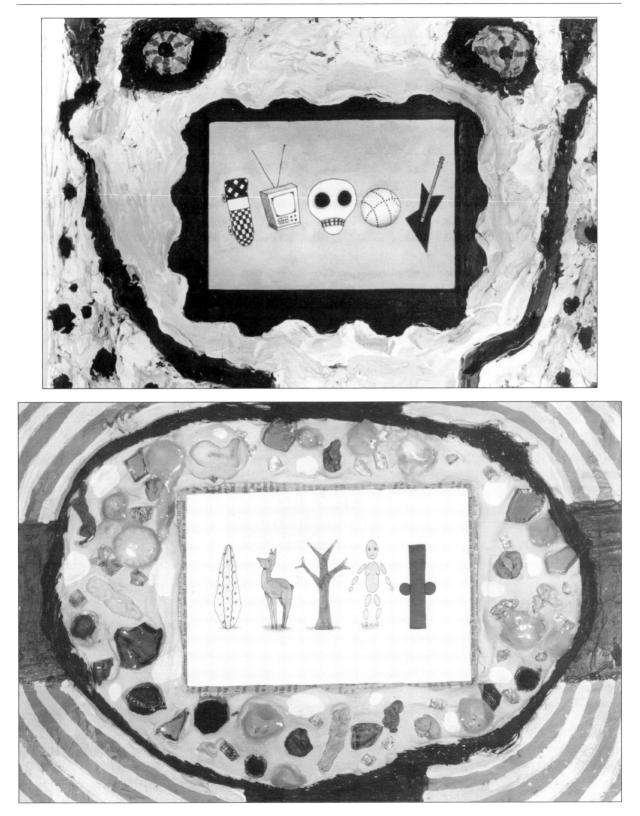

> When L. wanted to open the box which was almost closed and tried to anticipate, through representation, the future development of the situation, she resorted to opening and closing her mouth. [6]

This mental image was clearly not an imitation of external events because the event had not yet happened, it was in process. This image-forming process develops much like the processes of intelligence development. The transformation of imitation into images involves a much larger degree of interiorising than language. Even in daydreams and dreams themselves, the imitation of experienced situations and of people and things are strikingly exact to the smallest detail, is translated into images. Visual representations which spring from quite primitive (but quite basic and powerful) understandings form the basis of the central story in *All My Relations*. The story is full of detail and nuance but the drawings are really quite simple and I would suggest it is in their simplicity that they have their strength.

Piaget further claims that because images remain privately interiorised, while language becomes public, we can never share images to the extent and with subtlety that we can language. These considerations help to explain, I think, why the imagery in this film is given meaning by the language and felt as strongly as it is. I would suggest that Priestley has chosen images and scenes that are very basic and symbolically common – we can all respond to them in addition to, and even despite, the emotional chaos of the narrative.

Which brings us to the narrative. The film clearly asks for both social and personal change. It shows us the process of its making. At the moment when the camera first pulls back to reveal the frame around the picture (the drawn cels), any sense of illusion we might have imagined is gone. While this cannot be explored here, I would suggest that many successful animations create characters and situations which attain a state similar to the mimetic qualities of film without actually being so. In any case, in *All My Relations* the frame is important (the frame changes, dissolving from one to another) because it/they retain a kind of Romantic individualism; subjective, personal and separate yet part of the collaborative process in this film – much like a community quilt. The various frames include: candy, buttons, crayons, rubber dolls, fish lures, primitive paintings, flowers, cloth, crushed metal, and wadded up newspapers.

The narrative places the voice in the same place as the face in *Asparagus* but fills in the details; that is, we see the female character change from being nurturing and supportive, to being helpless and overwhelmed, to being aggressive, angry, hurt and disappointed, to being paranoid and determined, etc. A quite naturalistic scenario is played out by the central characters, mainly through the sound. In the image, Priestley uses abstraction and playfulness, a combination which is rarely seen among feminist art and is extremely successful here.

Simple drawn shapes combined with a deceptively sophisticated soundtrack are especially effective largely because the soundtrack is a fragmented and somewhat hysterical piece of realist narrative which touches on most of the topics relegated to 'women's films' of the 1940s and 1950s: sacrifice, affliction and competition. The hysteria of the woman provides a critique of emotion, of the shifting patterns of middle-class marriages – who is responsible for what – and presents a reworking of melodrama.

In this version, the man at some point says 'I'll just leave' and does, taking the child with him – probably the most obvious marker of real change in the nuclear family. The dog functions as the 'enabler' in these dysfunctional interactions and while we may or may not wish to interpret the dog symbolically, we must notice that he is always male and by biting the female provokes a sense of helplessness, anger, withdrawal and feelings of victimisation.

The female character is, however, in the process of self-transformation. She is struggling toward autonomy rather than identity and as such reviews the array of problems which face women in just the personal, domestic arena (never mind the workplace, etc.). The self-transformation evident in this film echoes the emphasis in the women's movement on the:

> …necessity of changing consciousness through personal recognition of the all-pervasive nature of female subordination. In so far as narrative constitutes one of the most important ways in which ideologies are concretised in relation to life experience, the emergence of new plots for women which emphasise autonomy rather than dependence should be welcomed as an indication of the influence of feminism upon the cultural and ideological domain.[7]

Priestley's images are simple, absract and playful. Here is the dog from All My Relations *(1990)*

©Joanna Priestley

What is important at this point in animation is to recognise the significance of women artists who take risks in creating work which radically intrudes on conventional forms, traditional 'plots', especially for women, and conventional expectations from cinema.

I would hope for a more direct investigation of the role of representation through the image and for more involvement by women at every stage of production and reception of animation. Films like *Asparagus* and *All My Relations* reinforce, enrich and privilege the opening up of representation, a process which affects all of us by building bridges between theory and embodiment.

Presented as a paper for the 1991 SAS Conference.

Notes

1.   Lucy Lippard, *From the Center*, Reprinted from *MS* 3, No. 11 (May 1975): 88.
2.   Ibid., 81.
3.   Naomi Schor, *Reading In Detail, Aesthetics and the Feminine* (New York and London: Routledge, 1987), 11–22.
4.   Rita Felski, *Beyond Feminist Aesthetics, 'On Confession'* (Methuen, 1987), 109.
5.   Jean Piaget, *Play, Dreams and Imitation in Childhood* (WW Norton and Co, Inc., 1962), 6–86.
6.   Ibid., 71.
7.   Felski, 152.

Clay animation comes out of the inkwell

The Fleischer brothers and clay animation

Michael Frierson

Clay animated films were produced in the United States as early as 1908 when Edison Manufacturing released a trick film entitled *The Sculptor's Welsh Rarebit Dream.* In 1916, clay animation became something of a fad, as an East Coast artist named Helena Smith Dayton and a West Coast animator named Willie Hopkins produced clay animated films on a wide range of subjects. Hopkins in particular was quite prolific, producing over 50 clay animated segments for the weekly *Universal Screen Magazine.* But by the 1920s, cartoon animation using either cels or the slash system was firmly established as the dominant mode of animation production. Increasingly, three-dimensional forms such as clay were driven into relative obscurity as the cel method became preferred for studio cartoon production.

Nevertheless, in 1921, clay animation appeared in a film called *Modeling*, an *Out of the Inkwell* film from the newly formed Fleischer Brothers studio. *Modeling* is one of the few known shorts using clay that was released during the 1920s. *Modeling* included animated clay in eight shots, a novel integration of the technique into an existing cartoon series and one of the rare uses of clay animation in a theatrical short from the 1920s. A closer examination of this Fleischer film is thus significant for two reasons. First, it illustrates how the clay technique 'fits' in the Fleischers' *Inkwell* series. Second, it reveals a number of traits of the *Inkwell* format itself. In particular, *Modeling* shows how the studio maintained an element of novelty in the series by integrating different animation techniques to visualise Ko-Ko the Clown's fight for corporeal existence, the unvarying central conflict of the series. This broader look at the *Inkwell* format will show that it embraced a duality of conformity and surprise, of static format and novel technique, of conventional cartoon action set in cartoon space and unconventional animation set in live action studio space. Indeed, even the central star of the series created humour by incorporating within his established 'star' persona the regular comic routines of a clown and an antagonistic tendency to leave his cartoon world, disrupting the conventions of film narrative and film space. These dualities became central to the audience's enjoyment. On the one hand, viewers are comfortable with familiar characters in a familiar format, while on the other, they came to expect from the Fleischer studio the innovative use of animation techniques to visualise Ko-Ko's on-going subversion of filmic conventions.[1] Before turning to a specific examination of Fleischers' films, an overview of the changes occurring in the emerging animation industry will show what broader impact the slash and cel techniques was having on three-dimensional forms of animation like clay.

Historical context: The emergence of division of labour in East Coast animation houses

The slash system was developed around 1914 by Raoul Barre and Bill Nolan, one of many contemporaneous developments aimed at reducing the amount of labour involved in producing drawn animation. The system involved cutting a hole in a paper background drawing so that, through careful composition, character drawings could be animated underneath. Later, the more common incarnation of the slash system was similar to cel animation: it involved cutting around the foreground character so that, through careful composition, the paper drawing could be laid over a single background drawing without obscuring the majority of it, thereby reducing the amount of the background that had to be retraced. Much of the Fleischer studio's early animation uses this form of the slash system, a method that was widely used in the early animation shops but never patented. Since slash animation required cutting each foreground drawing but did not require the payment of a licensing fee to use it, it was cheaper but more time consuming than cel animation.

By contrast, cel animation was a more expensive but faster method that also aimed to eliminate the need to redrawing backgrounds. The rise and consolidation of the cel technique – one well suited to division of labour and assembly-line production methods – to fill the demand for theatrical shorts is well documented by Crafton and others.[2] The cel system, formed by consolidating the patents of John Randolph Bray and Earl Hurd in the Bray-Hurd Process Company in 1914, is the traditional method of cartoon animation in which foreground characters are animated using a series of drawings on clear cels which overlay a single background drawing. But because the cel method eliminates the need to cut out the foreground action, it had an immediate impact on the emerging animation industry, and over the long term it became the dominant mode of production in Hollywood.

From the producer's point of view, the slash system and cel technique were manageable, industrial processes that could be 'Taylorised' through division of labour by applying the system of management that Frederick Taylor outlined in his *Principles of Scientific Management* (1911). Breaking down the substantial amount of labour involved in the production of an animated short into many specialised tasks performed by animators, inkers and cel painters, etc., presented a viable solution to the producer's problem: delivering enough product on a regular schedule to a marketplace hungry for films.[3]

By contrast, clay was and continues to be a medium that resists division of labour, since the character movements are created through manipulation in front of the camera, usually by a single animator. And as a practical matter, setting up a studio to produce clay animation circa 1914 would have been a difficult business proposition, for despite the rising popularity of sculpture in the early 1900s, the existing pool of sculptors and the existing audience for sculpture was relatively small, compared with the pool of artists and the audience for comic strips in the penny press. 'Animating sculpture' meant bringing an artform usually confined to museums, expositions and fine homes to the screen. Drawn animation could easily build on the cultural production that penny press comic strips had brought to the masses.

From the audience's point of view, early drawn animation was very accessible and familiar. Its content was an extension of famous comic strip characters and gags into a new, moving medium that retained many familiar conventions: text for dialogue in comic strip 'bubbles', 'sightlines' to indicate what a character was looking at, shot selection and staging that was similar to the strips. Grounded in the visual humour of penny press cartoons, the mass audience found familiar visual cues and many of the same characters in the weekly cartoon at the movie house. This connection to the penny press probably derives from what Conrad Smith calls 'a heritage of newsprint',[4] since many early animators, including J.S. Blackton, Winsor McCay, Paul Terry, John R. Bray and Max Fleischer were newspaper cartoonists, while others like Sidney Smith, Wallace Carlson and Raoul Barre were employed as illustrators or staff artists at newspapers.

Format: The patterning of content in the *Inkwell* series

Because it moved beyond the conventions established in early cartoons and produced cartoon 'stars' not derived from the strips, *Out of The Inkwell*, a series produced by the Fleischer Brothers from 1915 through to the 1920s,[5] is crucial to understanding the progression of American animation before the advent of sound. Much attention has been paid to the rise of the Disney studio beginning with *Steamboat Willie*, yet there is little discussion of how the *Inkwell* series explored the humorous integration of animation with live action film throughout the 1920s. During these years, the *Inkwell* series' adaptation of slash and later cel techniques shows a patterning of 'content' – what we would today call 'format' – that was very successful with audiences. In many early episodes, the basic *Inkwell* plot follows a 'visitor format' that runs like this:

1. The animator's hand brings Ko-Ko out of the inkwell by drawing him in an innovative way (i.e. the hand draws a group of ink drops that metamorphose into Ko-Ko).

2. Max is established in the studio, often working with animator Roland Crandall.

3. The action crosscuts between studio and animated scenes.

4. Gags are created that involve the movement of three-dimensional objects from the live action space into the animated space or vice versa.

5. A visitor enters the studio with an easily identifiable motive.

6. Ko-Ko enters the world of the studio to 'dissolve' the situation, creating a string of physical comedy gags that astonish all present.

7. Ko-Ko is ultimately forced to return to the inkwell.

This pattern is repeated in early shorts like *The Ouija Board* (between 1915 and 1920) and *Perpetual Motion* (between 1915 and 1920). *Modeling* also follows the 'visitor format'

Max's hand brings the clown out of the inkwell as a series of ink droplets that metamorphose into Ko-Ko. Next, Max is established at the drawing board, trying to give Ko-Ko some pep while animator Roland Crandall works at another easel. An ugly gentleman with a large nose, dressed in top hat and tails enters to examine a clay likeness that Crandall is sculpting of him in clay. After some disagreement between them – the gent thinks the bust resembles him too closely – Crandall calls for Max's help. To busy the clown, Max draws ice skates on Ko-Ko and a frozen lake for him to skate on. As Max and Crandall try to resculpt the bust, Ko-Ko skates through a series of pratfalls and gags: he chases a bear who has stolen his hat, wrestles in an ice house, rolls the bear up in a huge snowball and finally sculpts that ball into a bust of the gent. Angry at Ko-Ko's antics, Max turns to throw a wad of clay at him. As clay begins to fly back and forth, Ko-Ko escapes into the studio, hides in the nostril of the bust, is chased wiggling across the floor by Max, Crandall and the Gent, only to return to the safety of the inkwell.

As the *Inkwell* cast became established cartoon characters, later shorts relied less on the live action context and the introduction of visitors to the studio, leaving more time for interaction between live action and cartoon space and ultimately for longer bits of pure animation. In short, later *Inkwell* films have more Ko-Ko and less Max. But in the early *Inkwell* films, establishing a live action context for Ko-Ko to exercise his struggle for corporeal existence was a format that was easy to produce, since only a small percentage of the short was truly animated.

The *Inkwell* series probably adopted this format initially because of the economic realities of cartoon production in the 1920s. It became a successful format because it fulfilled the narrative needs of a five- to seven-minute short and because the Fleischers endeavoured to maintain the novelty of the series by exploring a number of animation techniques, mixing live action and stop motion footage with the central drawn character Ko-Ko. In this regard, Michael Wassenaar's description of the Fleischers' later *Popeye* series fits the *Inkwell* series equally well:

> [E]conomy is inscribed in the production process itself through a repetition of plot structures for the utmost effect . . .What is characteristic of these cartoons is a minimal amount of invention going into plot development and a maximal amount of effort going into the construction of gags within a

Below and overleaf
Patterning of content in the Inkwell *series*

©Republic Pictures (Stills courtesy US Library of Congress)

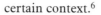

certain context.[6]

Over time, the *Inkwell* format became a comfortable, repetitive vehicle for audiences.

Technique in Fleischer films

Working within the *Inkwell* format, the Fleischers could redirect their energies from narrative construction towards the development of new techniques – rotoscoping, sound, composite imagery, the bouncing ball, setbacks – and towards tinkering with the gadgets that litter their cartoons as props. For the Fleischers, animation was the intersection of their interests in drawing and mechanics. Max's self-described 'keen and instinctive sense of mechanics'[7] is evident not only in their methods, but in their subject matter in futuristic cartoons like *Perpetual Motion* (between 1915 and 1920) *The First Man to the Moon* (1921) *Ko-Ko in 1999* (1924) and *Ko-Ko's Earth Control* (1928). Within the constraints of the *Inkwell's* repetitive plots, the Fleischers found freedom to experiment with the mechanics of animation. In the *Inkwell* series, the 'construction of gags' revolved around film techniques for visualising the interaction of the live action world and the cartoon world. As the *Inkwell* series unveiled its new technical tricks week after week, the results were successful enough to help to maintain the elevated status of cinema-as-novelty for audiences of the 1920s, audiences that were no longer fascinated by animated movement alone.

Unlike later character animation done at the Fleischer studios, the *Inkwell* films tend to rely more heavily on tricks and effects *as effects* for their entertainment. For example, although sophisticated technical tricks like setbacks were developed for later *Popeye* cartoons, they support stronger characters and narratives. In contrast, the central premise of the *Inkwell* format – Ko-Ko interacts with the live action world – coupled with the format's scant plots and limited characters forced the Fleischer studio to develop new ways to integrate live action and cartoon footage. These novel techniques sustain Ko-Ko's 'exciting habit of leaving his own world', providing a more complex filmic space and richer layers of visual imagery to decode.

Some of the animated tricks for combining live action and cartoon footage are quite simple, others are more elaborate. In *Bubbles* (1922), a simple still photograph of Max is overlaid with cels of an animated soap bubble, creating the half-hearted suggestion that Max is blowing tremendous bubbles in his living room, even though he is frozen in a still. *The Ouija Board* (between 1915 and 1920) shows Max's surprise by freezing a frame of him with mouth agape and adding an animated overlay of his hair standing on end. More elaborate interaction between Ko-Ko and the live action world is achieved in *The Clown's Little Brother* (between 1915 and 1922) where Ko-Ko rides and wrestles with a live action cat. This frame-by-frame composite of cel and live action background footage – called rotographing – grew naturally out of the Fleischer's development of the rotoscoping process in 1917 and was used to combine live action with cel in shorts as late as the 1940s.[8] The use of this kind of 'special effects' technique facilitated the integration of live action elements into *Inkwell* films and underlines their fascination with technique over story.

With live action space shown in virtually every episode, pixillation of objects is a logical method for suggesting the presence of Ko-Ko in that space. Typically, the Fleischers suggest through continuity editing that Ko-Ko climbs under a three-dimensional object in the studio space and then they pixillate that object. For example, *The Clown's Little Brother* and *Ouija Board* imply that Ko-Ko is inside a pixillated inkwell and a pixillated hat respectively. These tidy, arresting bits make Ko-Ko's presence in the live action space more concrete. In *Modeling*, the same pattern is followed, except the object Ko-Ko climbs under happens to be the nose of a clay bust. The clay is animated first on the bust, then moves to the floor of the studio. In this context, the use of clay at the Fleischer studios appears to be just another kind of raw material to pixillate, a different technique used to maintain novelty in the series and in a larger sense, to maintain cinema as a perpetual novelty.

The clay animation in *Modeling* is primitive in conception, but fairly sophisticated in execution. First, the notion that a clay bust must be used to set a context for clay animation is a quaint holdover from earlier works such as *The Sculptor's Nightmare* (1908) and *Swat the Fly* (1916), but the popular domestic sculpture seems more at home here. In the *Inkwell* series, the Fleischers cultivated an image of their studio as a homey *atelier*, bustling with all manner of artists and tinkerers, often in dressed in lab coats. Using a literal motivation like a bust to introduce a new technique into the series might be plodding, but, given the minimal amount of effort they applied to narrative development, it is pure Fleischer Brothers. Second, the primary clay form used here is a common coil – the 'snake' – often the first object rolled out by a child who plays with clay. Though simple, the form is handled well by the animator(s) (unknown), who show the clay-covered Ko-Ko inching down a real cane and along the floor. Here, the movement is well paced and suggests the frantic futility of Ko-Ko's flight. Later, the clay inchworm 'stands up and looks around' before it is captured, an expressive touch. Throughout, the accumulated expertise of the Fleischer studio with line animation shines through the simplicity of the inchworm and its movements. *Modeling* demonstrates that, in 1921, clay animation remained a simple, accessible, expressive technique, particularly for experienced animators with a knack for experimentation.

At the same time, the appearance of clay animation in only one out of six Fleischer films released that year clearly indicates that it had not established much of a foothold in the East Coast animation shops. Comparing *Modeling* to the great number of slash and cel films produced in 1921 it is clear that (a) these flat methods were becoming the central mode of production to meet the demand for theatrical shorts and (b) clay and other methods that resisted division of labour were becoming marginal production techniques. But the fact that clay was used once in the *Inkwell* series says more about a format that invited technical innovation than the perceived advantages or disadvantages of clay in a demand-driven system of production. At the Fleischer studio, clay animation was another technique that could be plugged into their format, in the same way as they used cutout animation and pixillation, to maintain an offbeat element of surprise and novelty for the audience.

The role of Ko-Ko in the *Inkwell* series: Narrative function and spatial explorations

The *Inkwell* format was characterised by a recurrent style and theme. The signature style of the *Inkwell* format revolved around whatever novel techniques could be brought to bear to visualise the filmic space where Ko-Ko's struggle for corporeal existence occurs. Thematically, this struggle was central to the *Inkwell* format: Ko-Ko's departs from his natural domain of the drawing board and explores the cartoon studio, a journey that inevitably ends when his creators return him to the inkwell.

The *Inkwell*'s central theme was also one of animation's greatest themes. As Crafton notes:

> Drawings that 'come to life' may be said to be the great theme of all animation . . . the narrative content of many animated films, especially in the silent period, may be seen as a heroic struggle by the drawings to retain their unexpected corporeal existence. This is usually expressed pictorially by having the drawings deny their obvious two-dimensionality and enter the world of real objects, with whimsical and spatially confusing results. Usually the artist succeeds in restoring order to the world; Koko must always be recapped in the Inkwell.[9]

As early as 22 February 1920, a *New York Times* review touched on this theme as a source of the *Inkwell* series' popularity:

> This little Inkwell clown has attracted much favourable attention because of a number of distinguishing characteristics . . . he has an exciting habit of leaving his own world, that of the rectangular sheet on which he is drawn and climbing all over the surrounding furniture.[10]

Here, the reviewer identifies Ko-Ko's 'habit of leaving his own world' as a primary source of audience pleasure. This weekly habit offered audiences a behind-the-scenes glimpse of the workings of an animation studio and provided a rich source of new gags for the cartoons, while locating Ko-ko's surprising transmigration within the reassurance of a fixed format. Ko-Ko provided the vehicle for moving Fleischer cartoons beyond conventional action set in cartoon space. Using 'unconventional' animation techniques like clay, pixillation and cut-outs, the early *Inkwell* films explored the clown's disruptive forays into live action studio space.

This repetitive journey, Ko-Ko's recurrent struggle within the Inkwell format fits the historical role that the archetypal clown has played in Western drama. Summarising this role, Enid Welsford states in *The Fool: His Social and Literary History*, that:

> . . . the Fool or Clown . . . as a dramatic character . . . usually stands apart from the main action of the play, having a tendency not to focus but to dissolve events and also to act as an intermediary between the stage and the audience . . . The Fool, in fact, is an amphibian, equally at home in the world of reality and the world of imagination. The serious hero focuses events, forces issues and causes catastrophes; but the Fool by his mere presence dissolves events, evades issues, throws doubt on the finality of fact.[11]

As an intermediate character between the stage and audience, the clown can comment on the action taking place, giving voice to the audience's thoughts. Though part of the story, the clown is free to defy its conventions.

Welsford's notion of the 'fool-as-amphibian' resonates throughout Fleischer cartoons, as Ko-Ko fulfills many archetypical functions: not only does he 'dissolve events,' but he also moves between the world of reality and the world of imagination. As an 'amphibian', Ko-Ko exploits the tension between narrative chaos and spatial unity in the *Inkwell* format. As an antagonist in the *Inkwell's* narratives, Ko-Ko works in many shorts to destroy the filmic space through a kind of malicious playfulness that exhibits many of the primary jokes of the clown: falls, blows, surprise, knavery, mimicry and stupidity.[12] In *Modeling*, for example, we see a rotoscoped Ko-Ko in a traditional knockabout routine attempting to ice skate, hitting the Gent with a wad of clay, surprising the Gent right off his stool by hiding in the nostril of the clay bust, mimicking the sculpting of Crandall to the exasperation of Max and stupidly lying upside down on the drawing board with a wad of clay on his head. As Ko-Ko foments a confrontation between the Gent, Crandall and Max, the momentum builds in a series of pratfalls and crude slapstick. Here, as in many of the *Inkwell* films, Ko-Ko tests the live action characters. And as the film degenerates into a kind of 'pie-fight-in-clay', the narrative premise of the short – however slight – dissolves.

As Ko-Ko dissolves the narrative unity of the film, he also disrupts the viewer's understanding of filmic space. In *Modeling* and throughout the *Inkwell* series, Ko-Ko frequently ventures forth from his drawing board into the 'real' space of the Fleischer studio. This act is, at once, the central assertion of his corporeal existence, a defiance of standard cartoon conventions and a visual confirmation of Ko-Ko's amphibian status between the worlds of imagination and reality.

The conventions of filmic space in the *Inkwell* series are firmly established at the beginning of virtually every episode, a foundation that Ko-Ko will later play against. At the beginning of most *Inkwell* shorts, we see the artist's hand (or a cutout photograph of a hand) drawing Ko-Ko, a simple act that immediately offers a wealth of cues for decoding spatial relationships in the film. Firstly, it visually differentiates cartoon space – depicted with only black and white lines – from live action space – depicted with a gray scale and realistic photographic detail. Secondly, it shows them to be 'adjacent': Max at the drawing board occupies a space relative to the cartoon space that Noel Burch in his *Theory of Film Practice* calls the fifth segment of offscreen space: 'behind the camera'.[13] Finally, the artist's hand shows the relative scale of the drawn space. These cues, taken together, establish the larger context of the live action studio space in which a smaller, drawn cartoon space exists. Given the temporal order of their presentation – the artist's hand usually draws Ko-Ko's world, the cartoon world is rarely established first – it seems clear that the Fleischers' carefully crafted this reading and not the inverse, in which Ko-Ko's cartoon space is shattered by a kind of Brechtian intrusion of the artist's hand.

This reading of the filmic space in the *Inkwell* series is consistent with the aesthetic theories articulated by Herbert Zettl in his groundbreaking text *Sight, Sound and Motion*. Zettl argues that whenever 'graphicated second order space' (e.g. a keyed-in box over the shoulder of a newscaster) is presented with 'first order space' (e.g. the newsroom set), the audience tends 'to perceive the people operating in first-order space as more "real" than the people appearing in graphicated second-order space'.[14] Throughout the *Inkwell* series, Ko-Ko's two dimensional drawing board functions like a video key, as a 'graphicated' second-order space. The black-and-white line-cartoon world of Ko-Ko is repeatedly articulated as smaller, less 'real' and adjacent to the photographic, live action world of the Fleischer studio.

Having established these spatial parameters, the early part of *Modeling* shows us either Max and Crandall in their discrete, live action space, Ko-Ko in his discrete, 'cartoon space', or the area where the two spaces adjoin; namely, Max's hand interacting with Ko-Ko on the drawing board. Longer animated segments in the middle of the film lull the viewer into accepting Ko-Ko's world, the conventional cartoon space with its drawn linear perspective and 'distant' horizon line. Each of these shots is a freestanding bit of animation having no direct interaction with the live action space, save crosscutting. During these freestanding segments, no 'live action' elements intrude in the camera's framing. Visual elements that would maintain the viewer's awareness of the 'adjacent' studio space' – such as registration pegs, the edge of the drawing board or Max's hand – are beyond the camera's frame. In these longer shots, Ko-Ko inhabits traditional cartoon space and the audience's focus shifts from curiosity about the studio and the production process to enjoyment of the clown's antics. There is one shot of almost a minute of pure animation, of sufficient duration to draw the viewer into the cartoon space without referencing the larger studio context. Although intercut with live action shots of the studio, these longer animated shots establish a conventional cartoon space the viewer is accustomed to.

Having established this cartoon space over the past few minutes, Ko-Ko's mischievous escape into the live action space becomes a more daring transmigration. In *Modeling*, the escape takes place when the background of a cartoon scene presents a hole in an ice covered lake. This drawn element in a sense 'punctures' the plane of the drawing board and as Max fishes in the drawn hole for Ko-Ko, the clown moves through it and skates into real space from behind the drawing board.[15]

Throughout, the illusion of movement into 'real space' is maintained primarily through editing. Match cutting in the *Inkwell* films suggest the temporal continuity and spatial proximity of the animated space and the 'real' studio space. Typically, Ko-Ko leaps forward 'from his drawn space', and the camera cuts to Ko-Ko 'landing' on a desk top or a carpeted floor. The cel overlays of the jump are drawn to suggest seamless and continuous action, while the background changes dramatically at the cut, from the predominantly white field of the animated space to a photographic background of the desk top or carpet. The use of photographic backgrounds that match the live action studio space and the maintenance of screen direction complete the illusion. Relying on codes of editing that were firmly entrenched by the 1920s – in particular the maintenance of motion vectors from shot to shot – the Fleischers were able to convincingly suggest Ko-Ko's movement from the drawing board into the live action filmic space. For viewers who are technically naive, this suggestion is complete enough to be transparent and the narrative flows. For viewers who are technically sophisticated, part of the 'entertainment', as it has always been in animation and special effects films, is to decode how the illusion is being created.

Eisenstein described *Merbabies,* a Disney cartoon from 1938 as a 'comical liberation from the timelock mechanism of American life. A five minute "break" for the psyche'.[16] In a sense, the *Inkwell* series served a similar function for 1920s audiences. The very format of the series – an animation studio whose work routines are constantly being thwarted by a cartoon character – embodies in it a comical liberation from the dull drudgery of work, the focus of American life. With its abundance of technical innovations, with its gags based on the magical interaction of live action and cartoon world, with its central character a knavish amphibian who moves between these two worlds, the *Inkwell* series gave audiences a comfortable format with just the right touch of chaos. As an example of clay animation from the early 1920s, the appeal of *Modeling* lies in the tension between stable format and novel technique, in the balance between traditional clown routines and the destruction of spatial conventions and ultimately, in a created character who thrives on confounding his creators, traits that support the entire series as well.

This is a revised version of a paper given at the 1990 SAS Conference and was first published, in a slightly shorter version, in the *Animation Journal,* vol. 2 issue 1 (Fall 1993). It forms part of a book by Frierson, *Clay Animation: American Highlights 1908 to the Present* (New York: Twayne Publishers, 1994), reprinted by kind permission.

Notes

1. I am indebted to Maureen Furniss for broadening my thinking on the use of static and novel elements throughout the *Inkwell* series.
2. See Donald Crafton's chapter 'The Henry Ford of Animation: John Randolph Bray', in *Before Mickey: The Animated Film 1891–28*, 137–168, and Kristin Thompson, 'Implications of the Cel Technique', *The Cinematic Apparatus* (London: The Macmillan Press Ltd., 1980), 106–120.
3. Kristin Thompson argues that as cel became the dominant production method, the net effect of this demand-driven system was a severe limitation of cel's boundaries, a trivialisation of the technique into the narrow confines of the Hollywood cartoon. Thompson writes in her essay, 'Implications of the Cel Technique', *The Cinematic Apparatus* (London: The Macmillan Press Ltd., 1980), 111, that the ideology of the cel technique – 'cartoons are secondary to live action, virtually always comic and/or fanciful, for children and trivial' – was imposed primarily by the exhibition marketplace it supplied. Cartoons were not only trivalised in the exhibition arena, but many animators past and present have found that cel technique – as it came to be used in American studio animation – trivialised and restricted their creativity. Shamus Culhane calls cel 'mind shackling' in an article entitled 'Frustration', in *Storytelling in Animation: The Art of the Animated Image Volume 2*, edited by John Canemaker (Los Angeles: The American Film Institute, 1988), 40. After viewing a program of films by National Film Board of Canada artists one night, Culhane was compelled to write: 'How totally restrictive, constrictive and dulling to freedom of expression the cel system has been. What a shock it was to realize that I have never enjoyed the excitement of making an entire film myself.'
4. Conrad Smith, 'The Early History of Animation: Saturday Morning TV Discovers 1915', *Journal of the University Film Association*, XXIX (Summer 1977): 23.

5. Leonard Maltin identifies fourteen Fleischer *Out of the Inkwell* shorts from 1915 to 1920 that were produced by John Bray and released in *Paramount Screen Magazines*. After 1927, the series was called *Inkwell Imps*. See Leonard Maltin, *Of Mice and Magic* (New York: The New American Library, 1980), 358–359.

6. Michael Wassenaar, 'Strong to the Finich: Machines, Metaphor and Popeye the Sailor', *The Velvet Light Trap*, no. 24 (Fall 1989): 28.

7. Max Fleischer writing in a studio autobiography, cited in Leslie Cabarga, *The Fleischer Story*, (New York: Nostalgia Press, 1976), chapters 2 and 6.

8. For a discussion of the Fleischer's rotoscope, see Mark Langer's introduction to a facsimile reproduction of 'The Fleischer Rotoscope Patent' in *Animation Journal*, vol. 1 issue 2 (Spring 1993).

9. Donald Crafton, 'Animation Iconography: The 'Hand of the Artist', *Quarterly Review of Film Studies*, IV (Fall 1979): 414.

10. *The New York Times* (22 February 1920), x, 9.

11. Enid Welsford, *The Fool: His Social and Literary History* (London: Faber and Faber, 1935), 320.

12. Maurice Willson Disher, *Clowns and Pantomimes* (1925; reprint New York: Benjamin Bloom, 1968), 3–23.

13. Noel Burch, *Theory of Film Practice*, translated by H.R. Lane, (Princeton: Princeton University Press, 1981), 17. Burch argues that off-screen space is divided into six segments. The four borders of the frame define four of those segments and the fifth is a distinct space located behind the camera. The sixth segment includes the space existing behind the set.

14. Herbert Zettl, *Sight, Sound and Motion: Applied Media Aesthetics*, Second Edition (Belmont, CA: Wadsworth Publishing, 1990), 206.

15. The idea of a 'punctured' background plane is found with variations throughout the series. In *Tantalising the Fly* (between 1915 and 1920), Ko-Ko goes through the puncture and ends up on the back of the sheet of paper, and in *Ko-Ko the Kop* (1927), Ko-Ko moves through the puncture to a new cartoon space.

16. Sergei Eisenstein, *Eisenstein on Disney*, edited by Jay Leyda (London: Methuen, 1988), 23.

Bartosch's *The Idea*

William Moritz

Berthold Bartosch deserves to be discussed among the important filmmakers – not just important animators – both for the intrinsic artistry of his 1932 film *The Idea* and for its seminal position as the first animation film created as an artwork with serious, even tragic, social and philosophical themes (as opposed to 'documentary', educational animations of McCay and the Fleischers or abstract animations of Ruttmann and Fischinger). That Bartosch does not always occupy a position of honour in film history stems partly from the fact that the 25-minute *Idea* has not always been easily available to viewers and partly because *The Idea* could be his only surviving film from a 45-year career that included some dozen film works.

Born in 1893 in Bohemia, Bartosch studied art in Vienna and under the influence of his socialist professor Hanslik, began (during World War I) making animated educational films on such topics as communism, humanism and the socialist theories of the Czech patriot Thomas Masaryk. After the war, he moved to the Berlin branch of the leftist Institute for Cultural Research, where he continued his film-making – and met Lotte Reiniger. He began working for her on her silhouette animations, primarily animating backgrounds and special effects, such as ocean waves, snow storms, clouds and the moving starscapes behind Prince Ahmed's flight on the magic horse in the feature-length animated film *The Adventures of Prince Ahmed*, which they shot between 1923 and 1926. In 1930 he married and moved with Maria to Paris, since the atmosphere in Germany was deteriorating for pacifists and socialists.

The publisher Kurt Wolff, who had printed about fifteen highly successful books of woodcuts – stories

Animator Berthold Bartosch working in his cramped attic studio
(Still courtesy William Moritz)

without words – by the Belgian leftist artist Frans Masereel, proposed that Bartosch collaborate with Masereel to make an animated film based on one of his wordless novels. When Masereel realised what tedious and confining work animation really was, he dropped out of the project, but Bartosch continued working alone and finished *The Idea* in the summer of 1932, working in a tiny studio on the attic floor above the Vieux Colombier Theatre in Paris. Arthur Honneger composed a brilliant score for *The Idea*, using the new electronic instrument the 'Ondes Martinot', and the sound version of the film was released in 1934, creating a sensation across Europe, except in Germany, where the Nazis banned the film, despite some brave appeals in the press.[1]

Between 1933 and 1938, with the financial aid of British filmmaker Thorold Dickinson, Bartosch created a colour animated film, about 25-minutes long, entitled *Saint Francis: Dreams and Nightmares*. This pacifist film was destroyed by the Nazis when they occupied Paris – as were the original negatives for *The Idea* and a short anti-Hitler film Bartosch had been working on. Nothing survives from the Hitler parody, but from *Saint Francis* a few still images (in black and white) show how intricate and diverse its imagery was. A still in Stefan Themerson's *The Urge to Create Visions*, attributed to *The Idea*, is also probably from *Saint Francis*, since no coal-mining sequence appears in surviving prints of *The Idea*.[2] Marie Seton makes a similar error in her 1936 article 'Medieval Tradition in Movies', as she describes Bartosch's intricate animation technique for a multiplane (no pun intended) aeroplane raid scene which she attributes to *The Idea*, although we know from one of the surviving stills that it occurred in *Saint Francis*.[3]

Bartosch also made a famous advertising film for shoes in 1939 and after the war made two other commercials which seem to have disappeared. For the last twenty years of his life, he worked on a long animation film about light and the cosmos. In 1960, a journalist from Britain named Derrick Knight rhapsodised about comets, crescent moons, prisms and crumpled paper, layers of gelatine and smeared soap – this suggests he might have seen some filmed images as well as the filmmaking process – but after Bartosch's death in 1968, no significant fragment of *Cosmos* was found.[4] For hints of what it might have been like, we can turn not only to the spectacular handling of light in *The Idea*, but also to the lovely, soft, tactile oil paintings that Bartosch executed in the 1960s.[5]

Evaluating Bartosch's *Idea* requires a parallel investigation of Frans

Below and top facing page
Stills from Berthold Bartosch's Saint Francis *(1933–38)*

Facing page bottom
Bartosch's film Cosmos *did not survive; however, some ideas of what it might have been like can be found in his tactile, soft, oil paintings such as* Nocturne *(1959)*

(Stills courtesy William Moritz)

Masereel and his book of woodcuts, *The Idea*, which Bartosch adapted. The question of authorship of the film arose in the earliest reviews. A July 1933 article in the Belgian newspaper *Vooruit* boldly proclaims 'Frans Masereel's Animation Film *The Idea*' in its headline.[6] Though the article admits briefly that 'a Czech artist Berthold Bartosch' spent more than two years working on it, they still treat the film as Masereel's. By contrast, Thorold Dickinson, in his program notes for the British premiere at the Film Society, 16 December 1934 (it had been delayed by censorship, which required the opening titles to be changed to suggest 'Idea' was a muse of inspiration) carefully states that while Masereel began to collaborate with Bartosch in Autumn 1930, he quit

after a few weeks and Bartosch continued alone. Dickinson explicitly says that Bartosch 're-shaped the scenario' and 'added to the theme a meaning beyond that in Masereel's *Idea*'.[7] Dickinson concludes that Bartosch's film constitutes 'an entirely new artistic realisation. A comparison of the book and the film provides the evidence of the extent of the divergence between the two conceptions'.

Here Dickinson was quite right: even a brief glance at Masereel's book shows that Bartosch made significant deletions and additions to make up his film scenario. But a broader look at the works of Masereel reveals many surprises.[8]

Frans Masereel, born in Ghent in 1889 (therefore just a few years older than Bartosch) came, like Bartosch, from a strict Catholic family and turned to socialism and pacifism during his years at art school. Frans Masereel fled to neutral Switzerland during World War I and worked making anti-war propaganda flyers, for which he used the woodcut technique because of its ease and low cost. He fell

in love with the technique and in 1917 began publishing book-length collections of woodcuts with thematic unity or in many cases a genuine narrative thread that qualifies them as 'Novels without words'. In addition to some hundreds of single prints and newspaper caricatures, Masereel had published sixteen of these novels before his 1930 collaboration with Bartosch. Masereel's inspiration seems not only the German Expressionists but also the classic Medieval and Renaissance woodcuts – and though the subject-matter of Masereel's books is always socialist and political in nature, definitely anti-clerical, he uses religious imagery for satirical purposes.[9]

The aesthetics of Masereel's books derives heavily from two sources: the intricate beauty of the rugged images and the sequential juxtapositions of the images in what E.M. Forster has called 'Pattern and Rhythmn'; that is, Pattern as a sense of overall direction or an arc to the action and Rhythm as the recurrence of certain motifs at irregular intervals which trigger a memory of how that motif was before and causes us to re-evaluate how it has changed or developed now.

Masereel's 1925 book *The City* demonstrates this clearly. By the way, Walter Ruttmann's 1926 film *Berlin: Symphony of the City* (note that the German word 'Großtadt' means merely 'city', not 'Great City' as so often translated) is obviously based on Masereel's best-selling book and the title claim 'From an Idea by Carl Mayer' might be a copyright cover-up – I'll wager that Mayer's 'idea' was: 'Let's make a film like Masereel's book!' From the opening shots entering the train station to the closing nightclub shots, we find an astonishing 75 per cent coincidence between Ruttmann's and Masereel's images. Many of these – say lust at the lingerie in shop windows or factory machinery – might be argued as coincidental documentary facts of city life; we know, however, that Ruttmann staged certain episodes, such as the horse fallen in traffic or the suicidal woman on the bridge and these also appear in Masereel.[10] In fact, the woman jumping from the bridge appears not only in *The City*, but at least a dozen times in Masereel's work, from separate woodcuts to book illustrations.

The City has an overall Pattern – moving from morning to night in the city, but the Rhythmic sequencing of the images also create intricate subtexts. Pictures on adjacent pages force ironic comments on the disparity between social classes and economic groups. In one sample sequence, a lawyer speaks in a courtroom with religious decor of the Last Judgement, steel workers sweat in the brilliant light of molten metal, a nebbish businessman nibbles at the nipple of a bored prostitute, a lecturer (college? legislature?) enjoys the standing ovation of his audience. Certain images that occur every five or ten pages echo one another and create another chain of irony: the bored prostitute sitting on her bed was preceded by a family mourning at a dead relative's bedside; an anatomy lesson with the cadaver obscenely displayed on a bed and a bedridden woman with only a cat to keep her company is followed by the birth of a baby at home in bed; and a bedroom murder and a despairing artist comforted in bed by his muse. Each of these 'bed' images also correlates to other motifs; for example, the delicate gesture of the cat to reach the sick woman is paralleled by one of the most beautiful possible woodcut images: a cat, alone at night, sinuously stalks down a curving staircase that parallels the shape of its tail.

Bartosch borrows some images from *The City* to use in his film *The Idea*, but he also borrows from several other Masereel books. The 1919 book *The Sun* traces the infatuation of a writer with the light of the sun, which leads him crazily to climb skyscrapers and trees and mountains until he finally reaches his goal and, like Icarus, is burnt and falls back to Earth – where he cynically recognises 'aspiration' as an idiotic human folly – a sarcastic mood very different from Bartosch, though the luminous presence of mystic light in Bartosch's *Idea* might have been partially suggested by Masereel's *Sun*. Masereel's 1918 *The Passion of a Human* provides a much more explicit sequence for Bartosch: the trial and execution of a man arrested for organising workers.

The reason Bartosch would need to annex images from other books lies in Masereel's penchant for the picaresque. Masereel's 1924 *The Idea* is truly a novel in the Victorian sense of Dickens' *David Copperfield* or *Great Expectations*, following multiple adventures of the protagonist over considerable time. The protagonist is 'The Idea' herself – and please note that no disrespect or sexist exploitation is meant by depicting the Idea as a naked woman; abstract concepts almost all have feminine gender in European languages and her nudity, the naked truth, was then an important resistance symbol, when censorship banned many works of art (e.g. James Joyce and D.H. Lawrence) for supposed pornography. Masereel's Idea is not the only or absolute Idea; however, she is one specific idea born from the head of a fallow man (with cobwebs growing from his head) in the opening pages; he mails her off into the world and then he isn't heard from again for 70 pages. She meanwhile undergoes terrifying trials and tribulations: she is forced to wear dresses and when she disobeys, she is arrested and forcibly dressed again. She has a love affair with a young man who is arrested for consorting with her; she nurses him in prison, comforts him in court, stands before him as he is shot by a firing squad and mourns him at his gravesite. She returns to city life again and again

is mocked and decried, so she flees to the countryside, where the earthy peasants piss on her. She returns to the city where a scholar slips her in a book, so she is reborn repeatedly from the printing press, manifesting on billboards, on leaflets dropped from planes. Her book is burned, but she arises from the flames and races along the telephone wires, into news cameras, along railroad trains, into parcel post, into cinemas (where people gladly watch murders but are shocked by 'the naked truth'), into band concerts, street corner orators, racing cars, underwater, flying overhead – until she arrives back

at the home of her originator. He, meanwhile, has had a new blonde Idea and disposes of the old Idea by slipping her into a crucifixion hanging on the wall, while he sadly mails the blonde Idea away, ironically beginning the cycle all over again.

These multiple adventures of the Idea – some of which occur two at a time in the same image, with the timeless juxtaposition of medieval hagiography – would have required a feature-length film of monumental intricacy to depict in time-based animation, which would have to follow through something that is suggested in only one of Masereel's woodcuts. Indeed, Bartosch does play out some of Masereel's complex images in cinematic terms: where Masereel ironically juxtaposes revellers in a nightclub in the same picture as the funeral of the hero, Bartosch intercuts the funeral procession with images of a judge sleeping soundly and the businessman dining at a luxury restaurant.

In paring down Masereel's novel, Bartosch also significantly changed the focus of the plot. The protagonist is not so much the Idea herself as the manifestation of her meaning (Liberty, Equality, Fraternity) in social terms. Bartosch creates a Pattern in which the same struggle occurs in the first and second half of the film, carefully underlined by Honneger's musical score, which repeats the same themes for 'Idea', 'struggle', 'death' and 'mourning' in both parts. In the first half, the Idea occurs to a single hero, who puts it into action by addressing the workers (borrowed from *Passion of a Human*), but he is arrested and executed; the second half moves this same struggle to a mass level, resulting in war between the money-makers and the workers – in which the common people (soldiers and their wives) suffer on both sides. The Idea, having failed on a personal and national level, returns to the absolute beauty and reason of the cosmic starscape (an apotheosis that occurs in some Masereel books, including the 1919 *My*

Illustrations from the pages of Frans Masereel's book The Idea *(1924), showing some adventures of the female protagonist*
©Redstone Press

Top *In Bartosch's work, the protagonist is not so much the Idea herself as the manifestation of her meaning (Liberty, Equality, Fraternity). Also, there is no disrespect or sexist exploitation meant by depicting the Idea as a naked woman; rather, she represents the naked truth, then an important resistance symbol when censorship banned many works of art*

Right *The hero addresses the workers, with the Idea standing behind him*

(Stills courtesy William Moritz)

Bartosch's Idea appears from a starscape. Her body remains luminous and transparent as a reminder that enlightenment is a divine phenomenon

(Stills courtesy William Moritz)

Book of Hours). The luminous presence of the cosmos becomes a Rhythm element for Bartosch, reoccurring at regular intervals. The Idea appears from a starscape at the beginning of the film – and her body remains luminous and transparent throughout

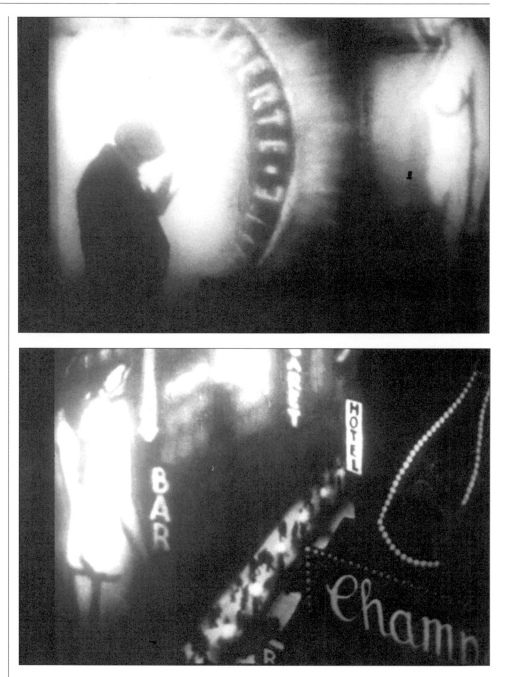

Top   *The Idea
argues with the
businessman in the light
of a luminous appari-
tion of the French franc*

Below   *When she
enters modern city life,
the light phenomena
around the Idea become
dazzling neon signs*

(Stills courtesy
William Moritz)

the film, reminding us that 'enlightenment' is a divine phenomenon. The streets through which the mailman walks to deliver the Idea's letter are haunted by spectral figures, reminders of other struggles, other aspirations. When the humiliated Idea is cast into the street clothed – with her naked truth hidden, altered, limited – she is surrounded by elegiac light phenomena, including the light-cone of a solitary street lamp (reminiscent of Magritte's painting *The Kingdom of Light*) and the serene starscape hovering over the human-scale bridge. The starscape appears again at the funeral of the political activist, placing his struggle in a cosmic perspective without cheapening it. When Idea makes her move into modern city life, the light phenomena surrounding her become dazzling neon signs. She argues with the businessman in terms of a luminous apparition of the French franc: shall it represent the 'Liberty, Equality, Fraternity' of its inscription or the gold that makes the world go round (like the cosmic starscape . . .)? And when the devastating war is over, Idea returns to the starscape from which she came.

Bartosch's tragic film exudes a grandeur and emotional power lacking in Masereel's sardonic political satire. Much of Bartosch's power arises from the subtle nuances of his animation, on multiple layers of glass, smeared with soap for soft-light haloes. Bartosch's dying words are supposed to have been: 'You can do anything with soap.' Indeed he did something very grand with it, something that only makes us sadder at the loss of *Cosmos* and his other films.

Notes

1. For example, Dr Martin Hürlimann, 'Von Micky Maus zur "Idee"', *Berliner Tageblatt*, no. 34, 1, part 4 (Sunday 20 January 1935).

2. Stefan Themerson, *The Urge to Create Visions* (Amsterdam: Gabberbochus + De Harmonie, 1983), 36.

3. Marie Seton, 'Mediaeval Tradition in Movie: The Work of Berthold Bartosch, Mystic and Philosopher', *World Film News*, vol. 1, no. 7 (October 1936): 33.

4. Derrick Knight, 'Berthold Bartosch', *Film*, no. 23 (Jan/Feb 1960): 26.

5. Exhibition catalogues published: *Bartosch: Peintures*, Musée de l'Hôtel Sandelin, Saint-Omer (12 May to 18 June 1973); and *Bartosch: Peintures*, Théatre Municipal, Annecy (June 1975).

6. G.V.H., 'Frans Masereel's Teekenfilm *Idee*', *Vooruit* (7 July 1933): 6.

7. 'The Idea', Film Society Program No. 75, 12 December 1935. *The Film Society Programmes 1925–39*, (New York: Arno Press, 1972), 307.

8. Among some dozen monographs on Masereel, the most important is Roger Avermaete, *Frans Masereel* (London: Thames and Hudson, 1977). Josef Herman's *The Radical Imagination*: *Frans Masereel 1889–1972* (London: Journeyman Press, 1980) contains a good essay on Masereel's style and ideation. London's Redstone Press reprinted in 1987 Masereel's *The Idea* and *The Passionate Journey* (My Book of Hours) including English translations of Hermann Hesse's and Thomas Mann's laudatory essays on Masereel.

9. Jan-Albert Goris's *Modern Belgian Wood-Engravers* (New York: Belgian Government Information Center, 1949) places Masereel not only in the context of other Belgian woodcut artists, but shows that others are also influenced by medieval/renaissance Belgian woodcuts.

10. Jeanpaul Goergen, *Walter Ruttmann, eine Dokumentation* (Berlin: Freunde der Deutschen Kinemathek, 1989), 25–29 and 114–121.

10

Norman McLaren and Jules Engel: Post-modernists

William Moritz

Of all the great names in animation, Norman McLaren has, paradoxically, suffered most from a kind of critical neglect. Everyone acknowledges his genius, but few discuss it. Numerous books and articles chronicle his life and describe his works, usually stressing the inventiveness of his filmic techniques, but rarely do they analyse his aesthetic qualities and achievements.[1]

Most texts oriented toward animation as a Fine Art – such as the catalogue for the massive *Film as Film* exhibition that toured Germany and England from 1977 until 1979 – ignore McLaren entirely while including Len Lye, Oskar Fischinger, Harry Smith, James Whitney and other animators who are McLaren's peers.[2] Aside from Terence Dobson's splendid paper delivered at the 1989 Society for Animation Studies conference in Los Angeles, which gave a close textual reading of McLaren's film *Synchromy* in comparison with Oskar Fischinger's *Radio Dynamics*, the only other serious critical analysis of McLaren's aesthetics comparatively is David Curtis's article 'Locating Norman McLaren'.[3] Curtis might have written the article in response to the *Film As Film* exhibition, which excluded McLaren and of which Curtis was the British co-ordinator. Curtis dares to speak the doubts that perhaps plague other serious critics, which they feel awkward about articulating.

According to Curtis, McLaren's 'work is too orthodox, too compromised or evades too many questions'. McLaren 'rejects the concern for the integrity of process and material that one associates with Modernism in Art'. In reference to McLaren's worry whether or not *Blinkety Blank* could hold an audience's attention, Curtis declares:

> This orthodoxy undermines McLaren's recognition of the legibility and iconographic strength of the single frame. His unwillingness to allow the 'blink' to free itself from narrative association denies it the reflexive relationship with the viewer associated with the avant-garde and Modernism.

Curtis concludes:

> McLaren's progress towards a Modernist position suggests that in other circumstances he might have made a substantial contribution to the dialogue of film

language pursued by the avant-garde . . . What does disqualify [McLaren's] work from participation in the avant-garde debate is his conscious adaptation and dilution of ideas to make them accessible to some notional average audience . . . No Modernist film-maker could operate under such constraint: the risk of incomprehensibility is an essential ingredient of all avant-garde work.

Curtis applies the modernist standard somewhat inconsistently. He faults McLaren for making his non-objective films 'anthropomorphic rather than abstract or concrete', yet claims that Len Lye in *Colour Box* 'emphatically draws one's attention to the origins of his marks in the interaction of paint, stencil and film celluloid' and excuses Lye's potentially compromising connections with the British Government's film unit by the lame phrase: 'The GPO slogans could be equated with the stencilled lettering in Cubist Braque or Picasso!' While Curtis avers that Lye's advertising film 'admits no other meaning' except the process and material of filmmaking, he claims that 'for McLaren it is the correspondence of drawn line with the linear fiddle tune which matters – not the nature of the brush that made it'. Lye's *Colour Box*, which Curtis judges as 'perhaps the most radical avant-garde film of the 1930s', is 'entirely abstract' because 'all its elements confirm the flatness of the "picture plane"'. Yet Curtis insists that 'McLaren's drawings imply "real" space', although he also claims that 'McLaren's oeuvre as a whole shows remarkably little interest in spatial exploration', which, given films like *Spheres*, *C'est l'aviron* and *Around is Around*, seems false.

Curtis also falls into the trap of assuming that the importance of techniques lies in priority of invention and usage. He goes to some lengths to point out that Len Lye may have had priority in drawing directly on film, though he allows that McLaren and Lye 'independently invented the idea'. Similarly, Curtis carefully notes that in the mid-

McLaren combines surrealism with an uncharacteristic lush romanticism (rendered in pastels) in the balletic A Phantasy *(1948)*

©National Film Board of Canada (Still courtesy of BFI Film and Video Distribution)

1930s, before his own experiments with drawing sound, McLaren had seen Rudolf Pfenninger's and Laszlo Moholy-Nagy's sound experiments at the Film Society (Curtis fails to note that Oskar Fischinger's ornament sound was also screened at Film Society on the same series of programs). Certainly the question should be how interestingly an artist does something, rather than whether he did it first – and both Lye and McLaren are interesting. In fact, in 1911 and 1912 the Italian painter Arnaldo Ginna made at least nine films – some abstract some representational – painted directly on blank film surface, and about that same time, the German psychologist Hans Stoltenberg also made some 'direct' film experiments, concerning which he modestly notes in his book *Pure Light Art and Its Relationship to Music* that no one who grew up with the marvellously hand-tinted films of Méliès and Zecca could resist trying to paint on film at least once.[4]

The chief flaw in Curtis's scheme is his assumption that McLaren is or ought to be or wanted to be a 'modernist' artist. Curtis judges McLaren 'extremely eclectic', 'equivocal and whimsical' and notes that 'McLaren connects with the "shared language" of animation' when, like early Disney and Fleischer studio films, he manipulates 'the dynamics of movement . . . for no other purpose than to generate pleasure through a visual sensation'. These characteristics are not those of a modernist artist but rather what we have come to think of as a 'post-modernist' artist – someone who does not reject modernism but instead recognises it as one style among many while rejecting the ideas of progress and uniqueness of the new that informed modernism; someone who loves irony and double coding, rejects the privileged status of high art as opposed to popular art, and feels free to mix elements of past and present, abstract and representational, appropriated and invented, all redefined and revealed to a new audience.

Critics weave considerable controversy and diverse specifics around post-modernism by now – as E. Ann Kaplan, for example, details in her anthology *Post-Modernism and*

Its Discontents – often under the false assumption that everything that happened after 1980 is automatically post-modern.[5] I refer rather to the simpler, clearer description of Charles Jencks in his delightful booklet *What is Post-Modernism?* – veritably a post-modernist styled text.[6] And, like Jencks, I refer you to the parable of Umberto Eco, whose test case for post-modernism is the person who feels like saying 'I love you madly' but knows that this is already a cliché, regardless of how true it might be, and so, as a post-modern person, wisely qualifies the remark with the perspective, 'As Barbara Cartland would say, I love you madly!' and thus, in an unspeakable world, is able to speak honestly.

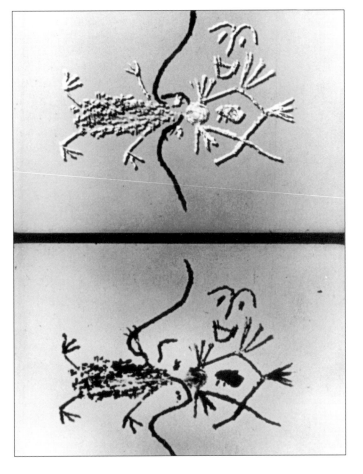

Recognising McLaren as a post-modernist opens the way to an adequate appraisal of his work. There is no reason to fault him for working in a variety of styles, both in live action and animation; he was conscious of art history and used it in fresh ways. *Fiddle-de-Dee* and *Begone Dull Care* are not failed modernist abstractions, but are rather non-objective art and visual-music, recontextualised. *Phantasy* and *Spheres* are not failed surrealism, but rather post-modernist variations and recollection and deconstructions of surrealism. There need be no embarrassment – as Curtis evinces when he refers to the opening of *Mosaic* as 'jokey' – in recognising McLaren's wit, for the reflexive beginning of *Mosaic* wherein the filmmaker sets the action in motion is no less filmic, no less meaningful and far more honest than the more aggressive and condescending modernism of, say, Peter Kubelka, Paul Sharits and Malcolm LeGrice. McLaren's association of the abstract dot patterns with a ball that the filmmaker can pull from his pocket and set in ricochet/rebound motion, actually enriches the response of the viewer in that it suggests a type of common experience that involves the sort of mathematical trajectories celebrated in this animation. Long after modernists have risked incomprehensibility and lost, McLaren can still say 'I love you madly' with his witty perspective on abstraction.

Whimsical suggestions of faces and animals cavort through abstractions in Short & Suite, *scratched directly onto film stock by Norman McLaren and Evelyn Lambart in 1959*

©National Film Board of Canada (Still courtesy of BFI Film and Video Distribution)

Or *Neighbors* (which Curtis judges to have 'no challenging aesthetic ideas of its own') has indeed a very challenging post-modern aesthetic idea: to harness the specific energy of animation, the crazy energy of pixillation (which references the silent comedy/cartoon), in order to render yet another anti-war parable suddenly visible, because the cartoon energy satirises (and forces a re-evaluation of) the gravity of politics (as Picasso did with *Guernica*) while at the same time pressing the human tragedy into fresh relief, suddenly touching in its absurdity, because of a post-modern perspective using Eco's sense.

That Norman McLaren might be a post-modernist in 1940, twenty years before Jencks dates the first flourishing of post-modernism, should not be surprising. The forces of disillusionment with the capitalist idea of progress and cumulative superiority which caused architects and artists to abandon the academic/museum money/power forces behind modernism in the 1960s had been available to McLaren two decades earlier. He had travelled to a wretched Russia and to Spain under bombardment by Nazi technology, so he had seen more of the world than many other by 1939, when he found himself literally a starving artist in New York, where the eccentric modernist whims of the Baroness Hilla Rebay von Ehrenwiesen, curator of the Museum of Non-Objective Painting and the Guggenheim Foundation must have further opened his eyes.[7] And in the short history and small world of animation, it must also have been clear to McLaren that the refined modernist experiments of Walter Ruttmann, Viking Eggeling and Hans Richter – and even Oskar Fischinger – reached far fewer people than any other animation and hence lost a great deal of their potential energy: already, less than two decades after their beginnings, all four of these artists were listed as having 'lost' films in the inventory of abstract animation which Hilla Rebay tried to assemble for her museum.

As further corroboration of the idea that McLaren might be a conscious post-modernist (even before that label was devised to describe it), I wish to cite the parallel examples of two other artists: Grant Wood and Jules Engel.

Grant Wood is usually dismissed as a 'regionalist' – which he certainly was in his devotion to Mid-West Americana – a label that excludes him from the modernist march of the 'isms' towards a more perfect future.[8] Wood suffered greatly from being stigmatised and marginalised by art critics and museums and thus, like McLaren, had good reason to doubt the validity of the academic/museum/gallery system. A careful look at his paintings shows that his reaction to modernist hegemony in the art world manifested itself by ironic stylistic tropes that closely approximate what would later be labelled 'post-modernism'. Among his serene, abstracted Iowa landscapes, Wood also painted canvases with undeniable 'post-modernist' sensibility: the 1939 *Parson Weems' Fable*, for example, directly references Charles Wilson Peale's 1822 *The Artist in His Museum* by depicting Parson Weems lifting a curtain (ironically fringed with cherries) to reveal a painting depicting the boy George Washington confessing his guilt in having cut down his father's cherry tree. Wood further deconstructs the fable by depicting George with a boy's body but the classic adult Washington head portrait rendered by Gilbert Stuart (now known from the US dollar bill) and by setting the incident not in an eighteenth-century Virginia, but in contemporary Iowa, before Wood's own home with an abstracted orchard behind it. A similar multi-layered irony pervades Wood's most famous painting, the 1930 *American Gothic*, which shows the farmer and his daughter (the butt of dirty jokes at least since Chaucer) as a formidable, sinister pair: the daughter prematurely aged in her severe plainness, with her body devoid of sensuous curves, the pattern on her dress lying flat as wallpaper; the father brandishing a lethal pitchfork to repel all travelling salesmen, the grim tightness of his stare and pursed lips forbidding, daring. Wood's 1931 *Victorian Survival*, reproducing with 'photographic realism' a woman's portrait from a mid-nineteenth-century tintype, but inserting a modern telephone beside her, offers another example of conceptual wit linked to bravura technical virtuosity – as we have come to appreciate from post-modern painters of the 1980s and 1990s.

Among the Californian colour–music artists (including Oskar Fischinger, James Whitney, Jordan Belson and Harry Smith) one artist, Jules Engel, makes work that functions very differently from the others, albeit no less brilliantly. While the others share a mystical bent coupled with a modernist faith that the very forms and processes of abstract art bear a heroic power of timeless, universal expression, Engel espouses a thoroughly post-modern sensibility: witty, eclectic, versatile, literate but accessible, classical but popular.

It could indeed have been Engel's friendship with Oskar Fischinger that freed him to an urbane contemporary perspective. Engel met Fischinger in the late 1930s when they were both working at the Disney Studios on the feature *Fantasia* and they exhibited their abstract oil paintings together during the 1940s and 1950s. Fischinger, almost tragically, embodied the archetype of the modernist: he was a very witty man and even made delightfully funny animations – but he refused to consider them as part of his genuine artistic product. Today we can see Fischinger's cigarette commercials or the rollicking adventures of two drunk men in his *Spiritual Constructions*, but he himself never showed those films together with his pure non-objective films and even threw away some of his representational work! Fischinger also failed to comprehend what he might have contributed to studio films; for *Fantasia*, he would only design and animate pure non-objective shapes – and he quit in despair when these were modified to semi-representational phenomena by the Disney staff. Years later, when the elderly Fischinger sat painting abstract oils in his front yard, a neighbour, Norman Gollin (a prominent designer) stopped by and said, 'Oskar, I saw a great movie you really should see'.

'Is it abstract?' Oskar asked.
'No,' Norman answered, 'but . . .'
'If it's not abstract, it couldn't be great,' Oskar insisted.

The lessons implicit in Fischinger's fatal confrontations with the practical everyday world were not lost on Engel. Jules had already begun creating abstract graphics in high school and at the same time discovered George Balanchine's choreography for the Ballets Russes de Monte Carlo (which used sets and costumes by many modernist artists). Jules's ardent involvement with the world of dance led him into animation, since Disney hired him to supervise the design of choreography for the dance numbers in *Fantasia*. Engel applied all his knowledge and talent to devising witty, dynamic sequences that were used in the final film: the brightly-coloured, stylised 'Russian' flowers seen from a low angle against a black background or the striking perspective shots in the 'Dance of the Hours' which show distant alignments of ostriches between the close-up ankles of the prima ballerina. Engel's subsequent work with United Productions of America (UPA), defining colour and styling on classic films like *Gerald McBoing Boing* and *Madeline* (both nominated for an Academy Award) further demonstrated how he could blend the refined 'high' plastic sensibility of modernist art with the 'low' cartoon, producing a fresh, engaging experience.

In Engel's own personal animation films, elements of dance choreography (not only ballet, but also modern dance and Broadway jazz dancing) intertwine with a variety of graphic styles that often reference modernist art only to recontextualise it. Above all, Engel builds conceptual wit into many pieces that challenges their status as 'high' art even as the formal elements threaten to function as pure modernism. Engel's *Landscape*, consisting of pure colour flickers, he designates as 'Color Field Painting in Time', a certain contradiction that challenges the purity of the gallery/museum system validation of the long meditative stare, the rigorous study of the canvas. *Villa Rospigliosi* and *Gallery*

3 similarly posit imaginary museums that show moving images, some from Engel's own oil paintings or Cy Twombly's ascetic calligraphy – and others referencing the thaumatrope and such 'archaeology of cinema' philosophical toys – forcing us to think of how we see 'high' and 'low'. Another kind of conceptual puzzle emerges in *Accident*, a film constructed after an actual dream Engel had: we see a greyhound from one of Muybridge's motion studies, which is gradually erased, seemingly by accident, but actually by painfully careful repeated animation drawings. Engel comments: 'My aim is to discover problems, not to solve them. I want to find things that you didn't know existed.'

Wet Paint provides a parallel instance of conceptual reflexiveness in a wholly non-objective film: the graceful liquidity of drawn animated choreography seems to be interrupted by the insinuation of accidentally spilled ink that seems to run across the paper in random, aleatory oozes – all, of course planned and executed in repeated paintings. The title is a 'ready-made', an object Engel found on a park bench. A parallel in Engel's gallery art might be his small wooden sculptures of chairs, almost like toy furniture, painted in Mondrian's neo-plastic primary colours, but each slightly eccentric in its balance or angles, weight and perspective.

Like McLaren, Engel has worked in live action and documentary film as well as a range of animation techniques, including computer graphics. His masterwork, *Coaraze*, combines several techniques to render visible elusive universal aspects of everyday life. In a small village perched among remote French mountains, Engel's cameras follow the dizzy pitch of cobbled walkways and the regimented tiles of sagging roofs, exposing the miracle of light and shade, positive and negative, with astonishing freshness recalling the luminous intensity of Vermeer and Weston. He contrasts the flowing camera with stationary viewpoints (are these still photos? or still lives?), a silent choreography that questions the nature of movement and of accomplishment. He ruthlessly pursues the savage play of school children in the street, kicking and jeering one another in an uncomfortably familiar fashion – the violence of their 'choreography' redefining the serenity of passive architecture, of innocence and maturity – for this medieval environment co-exists today to be exploited by high-tech cameras, which reveal that these 'primitive', quaint people are painfully like us.

These elements of what would later be called post-modernism arose in the work of McLaren, Wood and Engel by a spontaneous process that linked their natural sense of humour, their conceptual wit and insight, to their disillusionment in the absolute, sacred power of art and the perfectibility of modern art. Their work was not a doctrinaire post-modernism, not part of a movement, but it must be honoured nonetheless, perhaps more so, precisely because it was personal and original for these artists.

Notes

1.   This would include such volumes as: Maynard Collins, *Norman McLaren* (Ottawa: Canadian Film Institute, 1976), Valliere Richard's *Norman McLaren, Manipulator of Movement* (London: Associated University Presses, 1982), or the special issue of the journal *Sequences*, no. 82 (October 1975), devoted entirely to McLaren, in which, for example, the four-page article of Gilles Blain 'The Place of Norman McLaren in the History of Animation', 122–125, speaks only of McLaren as an absolute experimenter. The best critical text about McLaren (this is written before the publication of presumably major works by Terence Dobson and Donald McWilliams) is Alfio Bastiancich's *L'Opera di Norman McLaren* (Turin: Giappichelli, 1981), which contains, in addition to thorough biographical and filmographic information, 65 pages of texts by McLaren,

and 25 pages of critical analysis by Bastiancich wherein he refers to McLaren as a 'retro-garde experimentor' and relates his work to theories of Rudolf Arnheim and Noel Burch – all in Italian.

2. Wulf Herzogenrath and Birgit Hein, eds, *Film als Film* (Kölnischer Kunstverein, 1977). A very different English version is: *Film as Film: Formal Experiment in Film 1910–75* (London: Hayward Gallery, 1979).

3. David Curtis, 'Where Does One Put Norman McLaren?', *Norman McLaren Exhibition and Films* (Scottish Arts Council, 1977), 47–53. David Curtis, 'Locating McLaren', *Undercut*, no. 13 (Winter 1984–85), 1–7.

4. Hans Lorenz Stoltenberg, *Reine Farbkunst in Raum und Zeit, und ihr Verhältnis zur Tonkunst* (Leipzig: Unesma, 1920). Reprinted in 1937, in an enlarged edition, despite the Nazi ban on abstract art.

5. E. Ann Kaplan, *Post-Modernism and Its Discontents* (London: Verso, 1988).

6. Charles Jencks, *What is Post-Modernism?* (New York; St. Martin's, 1987). The Umberto Eco parable appears on 16.

7. William Moritz, 'You Can't Get Then from Now', *Los Angeles Institute of Contemporary Arts Journal* 29 (Summer 1981): 26–40 and 70–72. Joan Lukach's *Hilla Rebay: In Search of the Spirit in Art* (New York: Braziller, 1983), produced under the auspices of the Guggenheim Museum and the Hilla Rebay Founation, minimises the eccentricities of Rebay by careful excerpting from documents.

8. Wanda M. Corn, *Grant Wood, The Regionalist Vision* (New Haven: Yale University Press, 1983).

11

Disney, Warner Bros. and Japanese animation

Three world views

Luca Raffaelli

This paper essays an analysis of the philosophy behind two of the most prolific cartoon producers, Disney cartoons and the Japanese cartoon industry, while also examining that of contemporaneous non-Disney American cartoon studios. All were involved in serial production; that is, studios organised for the continuous production of animated films whether they were shorts or feature films for the cinema, television or the video-cassette market or television episodes or specials.

I concentrate on the birth and refinement of Disney's philosophy during those years when Walt was working his hardest to promote the growth of his studios; that is, the period from 1928 (the creation of Mickey Mouse) to 1941 (the strike). Hence the emphasis on production for cinema, which was at that time Disney's main concern. The development of the philosphy behind Japanese cartoons, on the other hand, happened in the 1960s; that is, in the television era, although cinema still played an important role (as did videos in later years).

These were the two animated cartoon worlds which influenced cinema audiences more than any other, yet they are very different.

The section on Disney is entitled 'One for all'. In a nation which extols freedom and openness and exalts the individual and his potential, one can see how Disney's philosophy manages to unite, in the same story, the success of the individual and the apotheosis of the group. All celebrate the winner's (often the two winners') good fortune together: the important thing is for everybody to be united and to celebrate together.

The section on the Japanese cartoon is entitled 'All for one', as here, in a sense, the tables are turned. In a nation where loyalty to the group is paramount, animated cartoons have sought to exalt the actions of the individual, such actions always directed, however, towards collective success if not the salvation of that greatest group of all: the whole of humanity.

Our brief look at Warner Bros., Fleischer and MGM is entitled 'All against all'. Their anti-Disneyan characters live in a society with little structure where most of the characters are in conflict with one another. They fight, too, with their own conflicting personalities, their wild nature vying with their social personae.

Three very different ways, therefore, of looking at life (and animated cartoons). Different, too, in their stylistic modes and methods of production. And just as an ugly antique vase is always considered worthy of interest, while a product designed for the younger generation is nearly always considered junk, so, between those who love Disney (and united in the name of gag/cartoon humour, also love what I will describe as anti-Disneyan productions) and those enamoured of Japanese cartoons, a war began almost immediately; a war in which those who suffered most were, as might be expected, the younger generation, enthusiasts for the Japanese cartoon.

An aside on television

Television is given too great a responsibility in its role as baby-sitter or parking ground for adolescents. Unfortunately, this has not, generally, generated an increased interest in productions intended for younger audiences, but rather an irrational fear of the possible consequences of the latter watching them; feelings that have arisen, surely, out of a sense of guilt for having dumped the kids in front of the small screen, or for not having created more opportunities for a dialogue that would have drawn them away from their silent TV viewing.

In this essay, frequent references are made to childhood, as the world of animated cartoons is closely linked with that of the child. I believe that many events and modes of behaviour occurring in our adult world can be explained by comparing them to the drives, needs and games of our childhood.

Cartoon animation, with its enormous range of techniques and its ability to adapt to all forms of language, has generated an enormous range of products, suited to all ages and all possible uses. At the same time the animated cartoon has succeeded, more fully than any other language form in the world, in endearing itself to audiences of different ages, united, through the years and in all corners of the globe, in watching one film. It might be that we can comprehend more from one simple drawing than from the most sophisticated reconstruction or reinterpretation of the real world.

Japanese cartoons are often criticised for their violence and in some cases, violent sex scenes (in which it is often the heroine herself who is the victim). This essay concentrates on the birth of Japanese cartoons in relation to the American models and does not address these later developments. One could, on some other occasion, examine how, starting from *Heidi* and *manga*, the Japanese cartoons moved on to deal, at times in somewhat dubious ways, with more disconcerting sexual themes, but it would be a grave error in judgement to take as most significant those facts which are merely most surprising or shocking.

Disney: The soundtrack and the philosophy are born

It was the innovation of the soundtrack which led to the blossoming of Disney philosophy (although historically, *Steamboat Willie* (1928), the third *Mickey Mouse* film made by Walt Disney with Ub Iwerks was not, as is usually thought, the first talking movie cartoon.[1] *Steamboat Willie* was in fact initially designed as a silent movie but, after completing the scene in which the steamboat slides into the water and Mickey climbs aboard, Disney stopped work on the production to carry out an experiment. He wished to verify whether or not sound, synchronised with cartoon images, could be made credible. It was a great step forward. Cartoons could not only make people laugh and marvel: they could make people believe in them.

At the time of *Steamboat Willie*, characters in animated series were an assemblage of drawings of rubber-like tubes: two for the legs, two for the arms and a bigger one for the trunk (what has come to be called the rubber-hose style). The head was a resilient ball and thus one of the many circles (e.g. also the palms of the hands, the belly and the ears) which facilitated the task of the cartoonist.

Even the circles, however, had this rubber-hose quality. The animated characters could thus roll themselves up or bounce around, be flattened in one scene and come back, safe and round, in the next. We imagine rubber tubes to be black, like the inner tubes of a bicycle. The tubes of these cartoon characters were also black and so the American characters of the first cartoon serials had black 'skin'. On black-and-white film this facilitated the contrast with the lighter background.

What is the plot of *Steamboat Willie?* It's the 'story' of a little mouse, playing like a child. With eyes narrowed to mere slits, he communicates his sheer satisfaction in playing. A child who, through his game, controls the entire Universe, changing its views, widening its vocabulary, turning logic upside down. A cow's teeth are not musical instruments yet they become so, thanks to him. Mickey is creator of his world.

One of the reasons why Disney might initially have felt that soundtracks might not work was that *Steamboat Willie*, like many other cartoons, recreates a child's fantasy world, which does not naturally translate into adult language. George Groddeck, in his book *The Language of Es*, writes:

> To us adults a chair is a chair, but to the child it is also many other things: a carriage, a house a dog or a child [...]. The adult forces himself to remove and hide symbolism whereas the child immediately sees symbols, he cannot act other than in a clearly symbolic way.[2]

In the film, adulthood is represented by the big, vulgar and evil cat who never plays around, who never plays at all. His job is to pilot the steamboat; he must make it work. The adult plays the role which fits him best: that of 'producer'. He can treat Mickey badly, forcing him to be useful and productive, such as peeling potatoes, as happens at the end of the film. But, of the two, the only one to express any feelings of happiness in the course of the film, is the mouse. A parrot makes fun of the sulking Mickey as he peels potatoes – perhaps he is the mouse's guilty conscience, awakened by the envy of the adult. But the film ends with Mickey managing to hit the bird with a tuber: a not entirely happy ending but an open one. The game has not been entirely quashed.

Felix the cat, Bimbo the dog, Oswald the rabbit and Bosko – all live in poor, rural America where it is necessary to work hard each day to earn a living, thinking up, where possible, an idea which will allow an amusing adventure. Rubber-hose characters have a very limited repertory of action and expression, drawing upon conventions of silent film comedy.

Mickey was born one of many such characters in this genre and created as a mouse, without any pretensions to originality. Mice like him had been seen in their hundreds and not only in the cartoons of Walt Disney. But none of them had ever reached stardom in the way that Mickey did. Having verified the possibility of achieving credibility through sound, Walt Disney realised that by investing a lot of money, artists, time and effort he could revolutionise cartoons. He asked: We can convince audiences that Mickey is playing music on a cow? Fine, then we'll convince them that animated characters are real. Audiences will no longer merely laugh at their gags but, through them, will be moved, suffer, feel sympathy. In other words, they will identify with these characters and believe in their world. And to achieve this goal, away with the rubber-hose style and everything else that has already become tradition! The game, started in *Steamboat Willie*, becomes ever more serious and even death will makes its appearance. Disney needed to do away with the merely playful. He wanted to be taken seriously, to transform his playworld into real life, into productive activity: to find a compromise between Mickey and the steamboat cat. He had to show the world the importance of his work while still remaining in his chosen arena of game-playing. In any case, many jobs are none other than the games and emotions of childhood transposed in productive terms. Businessmen, entrepreneurs, politicians? They all seem like big children.

So Disney started to play in earnest. In the course of seven years, he put together a staff of 750 artists capable of following him in his revolutionary research, reaching his goal with *Snow White and the Seven Dwarfs* (1937). Ollie Johnston and Frank Thomas, two of Disney's cartoonists described the twelve rules which changed animation in their first book, *Disneyan Animation: The Illusion of Life*.[3] These represented the basis of Disney's so called plausible–impossible philosophy: following these rules, the cartoonist learns how to transform a rubber-hose creature into an expressive and credible character and to create a world which is extravagant but not entirely removed from the real one.

Through the application of these rules, Disney sought to bring animation to its maturity, to widen its vocabulary, its expressive potential. Only thus could one create characters that are fully formed psychological personalities; only thus could an interchange of emotions be brought into play. Only thus could a film hold an audience's attention for over an hour. Only with these rules could he, the creator Walt, be taken seriously and jump from the second division of short films to the first division of feature films. While remaining in the playworld of cartoons, to become, finally, an adult figure to whom attention and credit is paid. With these twelve rules, Walt raised his childhood needs and desires to the highest levels of business (and who was joking now with so much money involved?) and to the level of cinematographic art: to the level of Art with a capital A.

Disney was the first to make a colour cartoon (*Flowers and Trees*, 1932); the first to build the 'multiplane' camera,[4] the first to study and perfect the technique of lip synchronisation. Nothing was left unexplored in the quest for maximum credibility.

Here it should perhaps be emphasised that Disney had never been interested in realism *per se*. He did not intend to interpret reality so much as to invent a parallel reality. For this reason, Disneyan exaggeration refers only to the personalities of his characters and only in a limited manner to the contraposition of his laws of animation to those of the natural laws of physics. In the real world, a car driving away does not bend back on itself for extra push. With Disney this can happen because communication, even more than spectacularisation, requires it. A fat man walking along, in Disney's cartoons, bounces his belly on the ground: this serves to re-invent reality in a caricatural key, but not to go beyond it (as happens in Warner and MGM cartoons).

One of the marvels of Disney lies precisely in the creation of an animated satire on behaviour. The example of the fat-bellied man is perhaps too obvious: there are much subtler nuances in the cartoon's ability to make the characters display not only the obvious emotions but also those taken for granted or hidden, as if there were a rule of Secondary Emotion in addition to that of Secondary Action.

Disney's animation reveals those modes of expression, of feeling, that we do not get to know since we cannot live our lives in front of a mirror. We have, however, glimpsed them in others and felt their existence in ourselves when we try to maintain self-control, not showing our true feelings. Through their characters, Disney's cartoonists were able to show the whole range of feelings, bringing them out, superimposing one on another but, above all, exaggerating their manifestation. Emotions are never unambiguous, the last is allowed to linger on as we catch a glimpse of those to come. And that is not all: the most manifest hide those we don't even know we have, those we do not even confess to having. It is this system of signals, this mix of emotions that Disney, with his revolutionary techniques in animation was able to reveal. 'Real', that is, live action, cinema cannot do so much.

There is a sequence in *Bambi*, relevant here, where the young rabbit Thumper, having watched young Bambi's awkward attempts at walking, says: 'He doesn't walk very good, does he?' His mother promptly intervenes: 'Thumper!' 'Yes, Mama', answers the little rabbit (sadly shrugging his shoulders, as Disney's note underlines[5]). 'What did your father tell you this morning?' Thumper sighs and then recites, as by rote: 'If you can't say something nice . . . don't say anything at all.' As he pronounces this last phrase, the face of the young rabbit fills the screen: the scene is all his. In sixteen seconds of footage as many as eleven different expressions pass over his face. They are difficult to categorise, one merging into another, resurfacing, becoming hidden then re-emerging once again. The instructions for the young actor Peter Behn, voicing Thumper's character, were as follows: 'Thumper starts to speak almost mechanically, then he stops stiff to think.' In Milt Kahl's animation, the little rabbit takes a breath before starting to answer, in obvious frustration. He starts to rotate his big left foot on the ground, as is his habit in moments of agitation. Then he closes his eyes and pushes his little muzzle forward to let out the lesson which his father has dictated to him. Here there is a pause, in which, it seems, Thumper can no longer remember anything. He raises his eyes to the sky as if searching for the rest of the phrase, then starts to speak again. He leans to the ground with his ears down glancing timidly at his mother, seeking her approval. As he is about to finish he looks directly at her, his chest swelling with pride. A moment later it hits him that he is in fact being well and truly humiliated. Thumper's chest deflates and his whole body assumes a position which is sulky and at the same time, submissive. He rises and starts to sniff the air (and therefore to act like a normal little rabbit) when our attention is transferred to Bambi. And all this, as we have said, in an amazing sixteen seconds. Particular note should be taken, incidentally, of Thumper's ears: all through the scene described here they move in such a way as to emphasise his facial expressions, acting as a counter-balance, giving the character the stability and solidity needed for the credibility Disney so expressly demanded. Who could ask for more?

But what had Thumper done to deserve such a lesson? He had merely expressed an opinion, not even a daring one and certainly not offensive. In fact, the character of Thumper fulfills the role of the little tyke, the enterprising youngster who still doesn't know the rules of polite society and has yet to deny his spontaneous reactions and emotions. This reference to paternal authority is an exception in Disneyan filmography, in which fathers hardly ever play a determining role. In *Pinocchio* we have a failed father figure, in *Cinderella*, the King, father of the heroine's future bridegroom, is a foolish, dizzy and silly character, dominated by his role as buffoon, unable to express any serious feelings. Cinderella has no mother, instead she has a step-mother, no sisters but step-sisters. And the step-mother is not only the mother but the father of the family.

The father figure, when it exists, provides no moral example. In *Bambi* he is a legend, in *Cinderella* a clown, in *The 101 Dalmatians* another timid eccentric. In short, the father figure is notable for its absence: it as though paternal authority can only be found among the evil characters (and here we come back to Walt's personal history).[6] Disney's films lack a precise moral directive, an effective, positive figure of authority. Disney always points out where evil is: good consists in its absence. The evil characters are the ones who intend to control the world, to determine how it is to be ordered. They impose their own desires and make life miserable for the defenceless. It is with them that the only true Disneyan father figure resides. In the absence of a wicked authority lies Good, says Disney, and here lies his universal effectiveness: he proposes no recipe other than the future to come, in which evil will have been vanquished.

At the beginning of the film there must always be a problem: Snow White, Cinderella and Dumbo all have different problems, but all have a certain faith in the future. They know happiness can be achieved by maintaining their sense of self and letting the present take care of the future. And if there is someone who wishes them harm, sooner or later that someone will be defeated. After pain there is joy; pain is a transition, joy is the present which unfailingly arrives, more or less an hour into the film.

Disney tends towards paradise, to the final picture which blocks reality in an infinite, immutable time: a legendary time. To achieve this, Walt reads to his universal audience universal fairy tales, recreating, through cinema, the ideal of family life he had sought in his childhood.[7]

It is truly remarkable how Disneyan discourse manages to merge with the American model. It seems to be both its inspiration and its consequence, allowing the exaltation of the individual in the apotheosis of the community. Cinderella wins thanks to team spirit, thanks to the little mice and birds who sew her dress and to the good Fairy Godmother who protects her. Cinderella's dream is an ambitious one: but everything is allowed, everything is possible in America so long as you hold onto your dreams, as long as you don't throw away the opportunity when it comes (see, for example, the ballroom scene). Cinderella lifts her eyes to heaven and silently plans her future.

Cinderella triumphs because 'that's how it's meant to be', relying on a series of coincidences foreseeable only in the laws of probability. From a certain point of view, her story is anything but optimistic because she alone, out of many, manages to triumph. The others remain as slaves, as step-mothers or step-sisters. Anyway, in our everyday world, fairies don't exist. So what can people who don't live in films do? Be prepared: that is Cinderella's advice and that of Walt Disney – because in America, a lucky strike happens to us all, sooner or later.

The positive characters in Disney's cartoons never question their own behaviour. In any case, they never have serious problems or dramatic contradictions: there is no need to reflect deeply on life, on the world or on destiny. What's more, this formula of Disneyan simplicity rules that the good characters are often shy and awkward. Nor is it accidental that this is particularly the case with nearly all the male characters confronted with female desire. It is the females who take the first steps and the males who look down, bashful, when this happens. Their legs tremble while the female, who knows everything and rules all, has already taken the situation in hand. Disney exalts the poverty of spirit of the good characters, simplifying them as much as possible, in social terms, though not, as we have seen in Thumper's case, in psychological terms. Nor do the evil characters live through personal dramas: they are evil, by their very nature, and that's it.

After the great techno-expressive revolution of the plausible–impossible, it was the feature films which became important to Disney. Short films became of secondary importance and Disney gave them more superficial attention. With the passage of time and film, his Mickey moved from the world of poor farmers to that of the big city. He is no longer a child in search of adventure but a middle-class citizen occupied in day-to-day dealings with various incidents and characters. Mickey, like his creator, becomes enamoured of convenience and comfort, of his armchair and of Pluto who fetches his newspaper. During the 1930s, Walt had also become a rich man who felt novelty as a threat. Mickey became truly the portrait of his co-author[8] and producer. Disney favoured Mickey for he was the only character born in short films.[9]

In the feature films the wicked characters are killed, because life must go on. But they live on in legend. It is the same process which Disney had experienced personally, keeping the memory of his father as a legend while removing his person as soon as possible – that is, on reaching adulthood – in order to enjoy the conquest of his autonomy. Passing through these contradictions, Disneyan communication finds its route through childish emotions, as seen through the eyes of a child but placed in the position of an adult.

In order that such a representation be popular, in order, in other words, that the child Disney be definitely and globally accepted, Disney the producer had to approach 'real cinema' (not only by making feature films, but by making them a force to be reckoned with in the film industry) with adult logic and make yet another step towards great Art. In this way, he would continue his success in mixing the child with the adult (for what can be less concretely productive than art for Art's sake?), low culture with high culture (animated cartoons with great illustration, great painting, great music), and feelings with reason (the necessity of self-expression with that of not risking too many debts).

It is well known that Disney started his career as a cartoonist and draughtsman but, with the industrialisation of the cartoon business, he gradually moved away from the drawing table to take on the role of conductor of his orchestra. He knew how to pick people and assign them their tasks, how to get what he wanted out of the people most suited to following him. He knew, as few others did, how to discuss and create the stories to be told and find the best way to do it.

'I am like a little bee. I go from place to place collecting pollen to offer to all', is a remark of Disney's which renders very effectively the idea of Disney the author-producer, creator of a great family whose goals were dictated, not to be questioned, challenged or appealed against.

And even here, in the everyday working of his studios, the paternal model returns: *talis pater, talis filius*. Walt Disney was a personality revered by those who remained enchanted by his fascination and his ideas, by anyone who did not question his concepts of life, of show business and of animated pictures, by people who were not put off by his manias. Those who need a boss to fear and to whom they can offer their best, those who need a paternal figure who, though stingy with compliments, knows how to reward faithfulness to a common ideal; anyone with talent as a cartoonist or draughtsman, story writer or director, able to mediate with a supervisor who is expected to know at any time what choices are to be made: such would have found themselves at home with Walt Disney. Anyone with ideas of his or her own or a different view on life from that of Walt, anyone who could see more of his defects than his good points, would not last long in the company.

For Disney, art was, above all, the art of communication: to communicate in the sense of being able to make oneself understood; to tell a story and express the feelings in a story clearly; and to find, without renouncing artistic potential, the way and the form through which the images, the music and the text can come to touch the most sensitive emotional chords.

But, as set out in the Disneyan rules, everything must be manifest, expressed, resolved: there is no room for the unexplored, the obscure, the unknowable. The games and rules must be clear. Again it is here that Disneyan ambiguity lies. This desire, this Disneyan necessity to render everything clear, visible and accessible, it would seem, is an antidote to treachery. For this reason, the characters are stable in their roles and characters, the wicked die wicked, the virtuous survive to live virtuously. There is no treachery, no change, no risk. Everything has already been determined.

Something, however, that Disney did not perhaps realise was that within such careful organisation of characters and of their movements lies hidden the complexity of life. It is in the animations realised by his collaborators, in the subtleties of Thumper's movements that mystery, the possibility of disorder and the struggle of opposing feelings are to be found. If the Disneyan structure were not so ironcast, a momentary feeling might emerge which was not foreseen by Disney: Thumper might react to his mother's humiliation without submitting. But the script is stronger than the individual scene and a subversive picture (in the sense of a single image) cannot undermine the plot or its structure.

Walt's dream was to tell the world wonderful stories just as his mother had told him in the happiest days of his childhood, but to tell them to a crowd, a crowd which would become united thanks to those stories and to his films. Who would thank him as one thanks a father who has allowed so great a feeling of unity, so much shared joy, such unquestionable understanding, concord and solidarity? It is easy to unite against evil when evil is so unquestionable. To make such a union plausible, to truly cement the feelings of his public, the Disneyan world had to be entirely credible to elicit emotions through the characters with whom one can identify.

The limits of 'Disneyanity'

Like the houses in animated cartoons, the Disneyan structure can stand serious quakes and rock dangerously, yet stay on its feet. Extreme situations can be found in the short films, above all in those with typically Disneyan characters. Here the pace must be the trigger, there is more space for over the top invention, for the 'straight ahead'.[10]

Disney had built a convincing world which must remain so right up to the last frame. When the lights go up we return to real world but not, Disney hopes, without a certain nostalgia for the world we have just left behind.

Cinema, a group ritual

Mickey Mouse and company were born into the world of cinema. In a darkened auditorium, the audience laughs, becomes emotional and is afraid together. Disney's cartoons are directed at this group of people who, through their laughter and their emotions, stimulate one another. It is a cinema designed for the group. Disney's cinema always deals with a band of characters – for example, Mickey Mouse, Donald Duck and Goofy, Snow White and the Seven Dwarfs, and the 101 Dalmatians – who act in the name of Goodness. Good characters predominate, overwhelmingly.[11]

It is a naive world crammed with childish dreams:

> To the animistic wish of the child the stone is alive because it can move so it rolls down a hill. Even a twelve year old is convinced that a river is alive and has a will because its waters flow. He believes that the sun, the stone and the water are inhabited by spirits rather similar to people, who therefore feel and act like people . . .

So writes Bruno Bettelheim in *The Uses of Enchantment: The Meaning and Importance of Fairy Tales*. He continues:

> If we do not understand what the rocks, trees and animals have to tell us, it is because we are not truly in harmony with them. For the child who is trying to understand the world, it seems reasonable to expect an answer from those objects which excite our interest. And, given that children are egocentric, they expect that animals will talk about the things which are truly important to them, as do animals in fairy tales and as the child himself does with his pets or toy animals. The child is convinced that the animal understands and feels with him even if it does not show it openly.[12]

Disneyan cinema is like this; animistic and egocentric, like a child. It concentrates, in fact, entirely on the main characters for whom all the world is ready to cheer at the end of their misadventures and in the unequivocally happy ending. For this, it is important to Disney that America be behind him as well as the many people in the movie theatres who show his films. For the ritual to work in fact there must be plenty of spectators to experience the final catharthis as a collective one.

Headover heedlessly

It is worth exploring an example of a non-Disneyan scene: a rabbit is falling, together with a dog, from a dizzying height. The two scream out their desperation as they look down on the ground, miles below them. The images show us a city seen from a height of 8000 or 9000 metres. The streets spin sickeningly. The pair cover their eyes as the rabbit continues to nibble his carrot, between one scream and the next. The sequence continues for several seconds, amid the howls, terror and weeping which anticipate their imminent crash. The tension mounts: something has to happen. And something does. Just before they touch the ground the pair pull on imaginary brakes and land gently on the ground. The rabbit – it is, of course, Bugs Bunny – turns to the audience and says: 'Fooled ya, didn't we!'

Another example: an aeroplane nose-dives, hurtling towards the audience. Bugs Bunny is terrified. The violence of the inexorable descent is such that the contact with the air rips the wings from the craft as the typical birds-eye view of the city, seen from high above, spins like a top. Bugs is as white as a sheet (the little gremlin plays with a yo-yo and when a Warner Brother character plays with the yo-yo, it demonstrates a lack of concern in a very dangerous situation). The speedometer spins ever more rapidly until it can no longer be read, then it stops abruptly; but instead of numbers, a message appears: 'Isn't this incredible?'

Bugs is now green, he starts screaming in rhythmic spasms and rightly so, for the impact is imminent (the scene has been going on now for over a minute), when the aeroplane stops just a few inches from the ground. 'Sorry folks, we've run out of petrol', says the gremlin, eating a banana. 'It happens with this kind of bombers', Bugs Bunny explains, ironically a moment before the film ends. Then comes the final motto of the Warner Bros. cartoons: 'That's all, folks!'

The non-Disneyan character of the Warner cartoons is synthesised in these two sequences:

(1) Disney's cinema would never contain so much terror, unless it was caused by the evil character, not even if the terror was dissolved into some kind of gag. Even when Mickey Mouse, Donald Duck and Goofy battle with ghosts, their fear is always in fun, just touched upon, like a game of peek-a-boo. It is never like the solid fear of death, which only appears, in the feature films, due to the presence of the evil character.

(2) There is the question of the characters' physicality. In comic strips and in cartoons it is normal for a character to fall from the roof of a house and to get up with only his cloths torn or at most, slightly stunned, and that is as far as Mickey or Dopey can go. They would never be allowed to break in mid-air, moments before crashing to the ground. This would destroy their credibility.

(3) The reason the characters are falling precipitously is because of the dynamics of their antagonistic relationship, not because of the existence or the wicked design of some evil character. It is simply because, as in the first case, one is a dog the other a rabbit or, as in the second, that one is a rabbit, the other a saboteur gremlin. Nobody is good or bad: more likely one is wily, the other dumb, one is a winner the other a loser, but all without any drama, in what is clearly only a game of roles.

(4) The director addresses himself directly to the audience with that comment: 'Isn't this incredible?' One already knows that everything will end with a laugh, but with this intervention, the element of play becomes even more obvious.

(5) Bugs Bunny, the dog and the gremlin also speak directly to the audience. Obviously, even the characters are in the conspiracy, accomplices of the staff who have devised the big joke. Disney would never have allowed such a gag because it reveals what is make-believe (the cartoon) as opposed to the reality of an audience watching a film.

Above all, it is the decision to address the audience directly which is so absolutely anti-Disneyan. Mickey and company allow themselves to do so only during the presentation of one of their shows or in other very exceptional cases. But when fiction begins, the characters of Disney are part of one world and the audience is part of another. Only in this way can the viewer believe in that world and participate emotionally in the stories which unfold there.

The philosophy behind the Warner Bros. cartoons was developing in the late 1930s, just as the Disneyan one was approaching its apotheosis with the production of *Snow White*. Stylistically and technically, Disney was already a reference point for all the other American cartoon studios and his films were carefully scrutinised to grasp their secrets.

The work of Warner's writers was a direct reaction to the language and basic themes of Disney. The message they are constantly trying to send to the audience is: 'It's only a film, we're behind it all, don't believe what you see.'

It is not a very reassuring message: by laying bare role-playing and pretence, the Warner directors disrobed the king and ripped the book of fairy tales from the grandmother's knee, so that finally she might tell her own, saucy tales. They eliminate any religious (and eschatological) elements from their stories. Paradise, they say, is an invention, just like these films of ours. In the total anarchy of Bugs Bunny and company, both the fear of authority (typically Disneyan) and the doubts about the credibility of our own world, are simply irrelevant.

If the world of Disney is a paradise which we must fight to attain (with a god to respect, whether it be Walt, Education, America or God himself), Warner's cartoons proceed instead to conquer the truth which lies hidden behind social order: there are no rules to respect and nothing to expect from one's own destiny. One must enjoy oneself, ignoring or torturing any authority which one decides to corner. There is no world to build but there is our own world to lay bare.

Character conflict as story vehicle

It's worth considering the role of character conflict as story vehicle, which is common to all the other cartoon studios competing with Disney: Popeye versus Pluto, Bugs Bunny versus Daffy Duck or Elmer Fudd, Wile Coyote versus the Roadrunner and so on.

This fact could give rise to two hypotheses, both of which contain an element of truth:

(1) Only Disney with his well-developed philosophy could have created such a family of enthralling good characters, the other studios would not have been able to do so.

(2) The non-Disneyan studios were anti-Disneyan (the truth was that the team of script writers, cartoonists, directors and musicians at Warner's, MGM, Paramount and Colombia were ruled more by production costs than by any philosophy).

While Disney changed the course of his work with the advent of sound, the other studios continued the tradition of cinematic comedy that go back to silent live action comedy and which was still evident in the clash between Mickey and the steamboat cat. It is the traditional theme of conflict: the policeman against the tramp; the pair of comedians against the world; the bashful lovers contending with difficult parents; cats, poor and dreamers, against the police dogs. And it was from this great stock of conflicts that the new era of non-Disneyan talking cartoons took their impetus. They agreed with Walt on one point, however: rubber tubes were by now old hat – cartoon characters could no longer be mere caricatures. They had to grow and become rounded psychological personalities.

To have is to be

There is, however, another difference between Disney and Warner. Disney's characters, after a period as poor farmers, acquire houses and belongings and through these possessions determine their relationship with the world and even with their own personality. The Warner characters, on the other hand, are penniless vagabonds. Bugs Bunny lives in a burrow whose interior we never see, with an entrance hole that can move or transform itself into an elevator to aid the rabbit's escape.[13]

The violence in these cartoons is the violence of great emotions. It is fiction – the cheerful allegory of physical and psychological conflict. It is in all cases a response to the initial violence which gives rise to confrontation. As these are cartoons made up of movement, sound and noise, the conflict must occur: it cannot be avoided. But it is the duel of emotions, of nerves and muscles, which is portrayed through the most complete, liberating and devastating physicality. It is a kind of animated expressionism of feelings: as Disney suggested, everything must be made evident, but here it is overwhelmingly exaggerated.

These reactions are so unreal and yet so true, they express perfectly the sense of what is happening inside us, which we usually try at all costs not to show: an idea similar to that put forward for Thumper, only here the hidden behaviour is no longer to be found between the lines; it is manifest, overwhelming everything, for here it is clear that it's all in fun.

It is this eulogy to feeling, this demand of the characters to be completely themselves, even to the detriment of social order, that renders the Warner cartoon so un-Disneyan. Here Thumper's mother would be slapped on the face, ridiculed amidst a chorus of boos, while Thumper would be finally enabled to express himself as he wished.

Thumper's mother ridiculed? What a suggestion to impute to these anti-Disneyans! The answer is very simple: it is because the Warner group had the luxury of having no real authority within their own studios. A string of highly amusing anecdotes about the Warner producers Schlesinger and Selzer, highlights the uselessness of their roles and their absolute incompetence in the field of cartoons, together with their total inability to make themselves respected or instil fear in others.

Chuck Jones writes: 'For Schlesinger the only method of determining the quality of a cartoon was by ensuring that it was made on a shoestring.'[14] A short-length film made by Warner cost six to ten times less than one made by Disney. And while Walt and his collaborators checked and rechecked every scene before the final editing, at Warner's each scene made just had to be okay.

From where, then, does this attitude of complete derision towards authority derive? Clearly it dates a long way back to that comic quality based on conflict, those eternal jokes making fun of policemen, guards, businessmen and big politicians. But there is something else, something personal, which goes beyond tradition and even beyond the evident incompetence of their producers and managers. Here, too, we have stories of fathers, parents and offspring.[15] They differ, however, from Disney's, either because the conflict is much less intense or because it manifests itself with more awareness.

Jones said that the best loved actors and those who make us laugh the most 'are those who know how to portray our own errors, our shortcomings and our misfortunes. Maybe, subliminally, they reassure us by showing us through laughter that we are not alone'.[16] In these words lies all the melancholy typical of the pure comedian, which is

also anti-Disneyan. For, whereas Disney uses gags to develop and make understood his vision of the world (or how it should be), Warner's use of gags is determined by their vision of the world: they pour everything they have into being funny, on this they base all their characters, situations and conflict, both desperate and comic at the same time.

All for one: the Japanese *anime*

The little orphan Heidi who had found affection and serenity with her grandfather in the mountains is brought to Frankfurt by her aunt by trickery – she is told that she will be able to go back to her grandfather that same evening. Naturally this does not happen: Heidi is brought to the city to live with the Sesemanns as a companion to their invalid daughter who is a few years older than Heidi. Being a guest, Heidi must obey the household rules and submit to the iron discipline of Fraulein Rottenmeier, the governess, who regards total submission and the renunciation of any expression of feeling whatsoever to be the highest achievement of a correct education.

Heidi's face is distorted with grief at the idea of having been betrayed by her aunt, and during the first lesson with Fraulein Rottenmeier, Heidi, stricken with homesickness, sees a carriage through the window. She is sure it is her grandfather, come to find her and take her back to the mountains. Overjoyed, she jumps up from her desk, knocking over a bottle of ink. But, alas, there is no one waiting for her at the front door.

What I am describing are a few of the scenes from *Heidi of the Alps* (Alps no shojo Heidi), one of the most famous series of the Japanese animated cartoons (or *anime* as they are known in cinema jargon) produced in 52 episodes by Zuiyo in 1974. One of the first Japanese cartoons to be broadcast in Italy by state television channel RAI, it was so successful it was endlessly repeated.

Heidi is therefore both a prototype and a classic. An analysis reveals a number of constants in Japanese cartoon serials. Its heroine is an orphan and characters without a family are a typical feature of the *anime*. Secondly it follows, more or less faithfully, the story taken from a novel by a famous European author, another common feature of many *anime* (and one of the reasons behind the international success of Japanese cartoons). Heidi itself was inspired by the work of the Swiss author Johanna Spyri. Up to where we broke off our story the Swiss novel and the animated cartoon coincide perfectly.

The serial's producers found it necessary to make two essential modifications to the original novel: firstly, they had to lengthen the plot (the serial was 25 hours long). To do so, they extended the part dedicated to the battle between Heidi and Fraulein

Rottenmeier, fierce even in the book but shorter. Secondly, they eliminated all reference (and there are many) to the Catholic religion with its call to bear suffering. Spyri's book, in fact, portrays Heidi as the model for a young saint: the little girl puts up with all the vexations of the adult world because she entrusts her fate to God. In Chapter 10 Clara's grandmother says to her:

> 'Then, dear child, let me tell you what to do: you know that when we are in great trouble and cannot speak about it to anybody, we must turn to God and pray Him to help, for He can deliver us from every care that oppresses us. You understand that, do you not? You say your prayers every evening to the dear God in Heaven and thank Him for all He has done for you and pray him to keep you from all evil, do you not?'

> 'No, I never say any prayers', answered Heidi.

> 'Have you never been taught to pray, Heidi? Do you not know even what it means?'

> 'I used to say prayers with the first grandmother, but that is a long time ago and I have forgotten them.'

> 'That is the reason, Heidi, that you are so unhappy, because you know no one who can help you. Think what a comfort it is when the heart is heavy with grief to be able at any moment to go and tell everything to God and pray Him for the help that no one else can give us. And He can help us and give us everything that will make us happy again.'

> A sudden gleam of joy came into Heidi's eyes. 'May I tell Him everything?'

> 'Yes, everything, Heidi, everything.'[17]

This last sentence, taken from Spyri's book, highlights the point of contact between European children's literature and Japanese animation. It is often precisely this inability to find anyone to whom they can recount their feelings that causes the children in Japanese serials to suffer (and not only the children in cartoons). Let me quote just a few more lines from Chapter 11 of the novel:

> As Heidi continued her weeping, the lady, who was evidently getting impatient with her, went up to Heidi and said with decision, 'Now, Adelaide, that is enough of all this causeless lamentation. I will tell you once for all, if there are any more scenes like this while you are reading, I shall take the book away from you and shall not let you have it again'.

> Her words had immediate effect on Heidi, who turned pale with fear. The book was her one great treasure. She quickly dried her tears and swallowed her sobs as best she could, so that no further sound of them should be heard. The threat did its work, for Heidi never cried aloud again whatever she might be reading, but she had often to struggle hard to keep back her tears, so that Clara would look at her and say, 'What faces you are making, Heidi, I never saw anything like it!'

This then is what a child must do to respect the rules of the adult world and learn how to behave in society – hide their real feelings and never again give way to tears. This, basically, is what is the only positive suggestion in the novel published in 1880. The moral of the book is: pray, trust in God, have faith even in the most painful situations and you will be rewarded.[18]

Eliminating the religious theme, as the Japanese did (to make the story comprehensible to audiences in their own country), the moral becomes rather different: fight your battles on equal terms, child, and if you are brave and lucky, if you do not let yourself be overcome by depression but keep your hopes high and believe in yourself, then you will be able to make yourself respected, to change your situation in life and even that of others. And, in fact, without believing in any divine providence, Heidi manages to return to her grandfather and bring to her beloved mountains all the adults she has met and loved or hated in the course of her adventures. She manages to convince them that it is healthier to live a life where feelings can be expressed (among the mountains, in the open air) than to live a life (in the city, shut up in a house) where good manners lead to one's own annihilation.

But we still have not arrived at the true final event: in the mountains Clara regains the use of her legs, both in the book and in the cartoon series. In the cartoon, however, Divine Providence is lacking, thus the miracle seems to be performed by the little heroine herself. It is Heidi who is able to show the adults the possibility of seeing the world from a different point of view, to get up and observe the city from on high while breathing the clean air deep into their lungs. She is the one who believes in Clara's recovery, who understands that hers is a psychosomatic illness. The adults, limited by their own preconceptions, had, naturally, never considered such a possibility. Many people feel the cartoon version of Heidi to be affected and sickly sweet but that is a very superficial view. If anything its apparent affectedness originates in the somewhat dated European version, which has nevertheless sold many copies in the Western world, even in our century. A cartoon series is something to be marketed: it is therefore an intelligent choice to pick a traditional European novel, to remove those elements which limit its universal appeal while keeping its air of gentility and tender packaging. Only a very attentive observer, however, will be able to see Heidi the liberator, the standard-bearer of adolescent revenge. Whether this message was conscious, either as commercial consideration or personal feelings of its creators, is hard to determine. What is certain is that this theme was repeated, as we shall see, too frequently in the history of Japanese animation for it to be considered accidental.

In January 1963, animated television cartoons as an industry were born in Japan with a black-and-white series called *Tetsuwan Atom*, produced by Mushi, one of the first production studios in the history of Japanese animated cartoons. By the end of 1966, the series had reached 193 episodes. The story played out by American silent cartoons repeated itself here: Atom was the child of a highly successful comic strip – a *manga* as they are called in Japan – published for ten years by Osamu Tezuka. Before that date, animated productions in Japan had been limited, made soley on the initiative of artists working in a completely artisan way.

Tezuka's commic book *Goast Man & Onward to Victory*

Long before Astro Boy *in America,* Tetsuwan Atom *produced by the Mushi studios in 1963 was one of the Japanese cartoon industry's first animated series and its most successful strip*

©1963 Tezuka Productions/Mushi Productions

Animated Television Series

ASTRO BOY

©1963 Tezuka Productions/ Mushi Productions

1963

was published in Japan when he was just sixteen. In this story, all the characters' eyes are rounded ovals, sometimes circles filled with black, sometimes empty circles with a little black dot. However, the eyes are prominent in relation to the characters' other facial features. This is how Tezuka conceived his characters, several years before the Japanese comic strip and animated cartoons became an industry. Furthermore, in two of the last frames of the story, Tezuka brings on characters from *Bringing Up Father* (in Italy known as Arciboldo and Petronilla), the famous American comic strip created in 1913 by George McManus.

The Japanese animated cartoon industry was born nearly 50 years after the American one and was born under its influence. But the *anime* were born with sound and for television. American cartoons originated from comic strips and therefore, from situations with very simple, humorous developments. The *anime* were inspired by the printed magazines or comic books, *manga*. It is true that, in many cases, the Japanese style did not respect the rules dictated by that master of animation, Norman McLaren (according to whom one must not move the drawing but draw the movement). Japanese cartoons were created to a much more static formula than those of America in the 1920s. However, it is worth remembering that, in the years in which Japanese cartoons were being developed, the world's animated cartoon industry was going through a serious economic crisis. Television productions budgets did not allow levels of quality high enough to maintain even Disney's image, who was also struggling to survive in the feature film market). The only ones able to adapt to the situation were Hanna & Barbera with their limited animation films. What, then, could the Japanese do? Having eliminated the possibility of drawing twelve frames a second and also eliminating, finally, the idea of imitating Disney (animated film studios the world over had tried to do this, usually with embarrassing results), the Japanese invented another path to follow: that of the subjective. The cartoons of the group or the family became, in Japan, that of the individual.

So, technically we no longer have two or three frames per drawing but 5 or 6, sometimes even more. This means that any movement becomes a series of more or less perceptible jerks, abandoning a fundamental element of the American style: fluidity. Furthermore, there are long walk or run sequences in which the characters are no longer flat against the background, as in the chases of Tom and Jerry and company: in Japanese cartoons the character often runs or walks along a line leading in or out of the horizon, as if he was the centre of the world, the only living being there. Obviously the animators save on intermediate movements, leaving the extreme ones (which in Disney last for only one or two frames) fixed through several poses. Thus, a character gazing at some terrible situation with a terrified look on his face will have (typically) a drop of sweat fixed on his forehead and his mouth wide open for a long time. The character's thoughts or the narrators comments are heard as a voice over describing the emotions clearly evident on screen, a form of stream-of-consciousness interior monologue. But one might also hear only the sound of the wind or the panting of a runner. Approaching characters are often seen coming closer without any intermediate drawings, but with cross-fadings. The reason, obviously, is to save time and work, but the effect on the story is often positive. There is something fascinating in such continuous appearing and disappearing combined with gripping music and epic commentary.

The angles of the shots are chosen in a functional manner within the limits of the animation and are constantly changing. Then there are the camera movements, optional, at no cost. A fixed close-up can be drawn in with a zoom lens and made more interesting

Top row and bottom left   *Comic strips such as* Goast Man *&* Onward to Victory *published by Osamu Tezuka were precursors to Japanese anime, just as American animated cartoons originated from their comic strips.*

©*Osamu Tezuka*

Bottom right   *With limited costs available, the focus of the Japanese anime changed from being on the group to being on the individual*

©*1986 Toei Animation Co. Ltd*

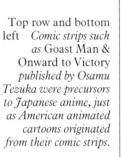

by rotating the camera or changing the intensity of the light. Such camera moves do not require the work nor the cost of an animator.

In short, anime could be considered, broadly speaking, as a kind of animated comic strip, just as the *manga* cut out the action between one cartoon and the next, the *anime* leave to the imagination of the viewer any movement which is not strictly necessary to show.

In Japanese cartoons, each emotion exists in time. Time is often, in fact, slowed down, offering us the chance to follow the thought that comments on, transforms and experiences that particular moment of emotional perturbation. This slowing down, however, is also an indication of the extreme concentration of the central character with regards to the situation being experienced. It shows, therefore, the perception of daily life in a timeless dimension, in certain respects as meditative. Japanese culture is particularly sensitive to time and to the steadiness of waiting. In Japanese cartoons, the characters are often waiting for something for a clash with the enemy, for a match, for a love encounter. These moments are savoured, lived in and are full, moment by moment. It is like a sumo wrestling match where the careful reciprocal sizing up by the two contestants offers to Japanese audiences an emotion as intense as the final, brief, decisive match.

In Japanese films, characters' thoughts or narrators' comments are heards as voice overs, which describe the emotions clearly evident on the characters' faces

©Daimaru

It might be pertinent here to quote a passage from the book *Myths To Live By* by Joseph Campbell, in the chapter dedicated to inspiration in oriental art:

> The sin of inadvertence, not being alert, not quite awake, is the sin of missing the moment of life; whereas the whole of the art of the nonaction that is action (wu-wei) is unremitting alertness. One is then fully conscious all the time and since life is an expression of consciousness, life is then lived, as it were, of itself. There is no need to instruct it or direct it. Of itself it moves. Of itself it lives. Of itself it speak and acts.[19]

This frequent stretching of time does not interfere with narrative continuity. The scene may be slowed down or move forward jerkily but the soundtrack binds it together, unfolds it, gives it depth. Japanese animation renounces only the fluidity of motion but, at the same time, with its technique it develops new narrative potential. If we were to compare them with the moving mouths and blinking eyes of the early American television cartoons (Hanna & Barbera in particular) we would find that these jerky Japanese characters have a different fascination. But such a comparison would be out of place. It would be like comparing the style and contents of the Japanese cinema of Ozu with that of the American director, Altman, or that of Disney with McLaren.

In short, the skill of the Japanese was precisely in finding a style of animation that had nothing to do with the expensive fluidity of Disney. Thus, despite the fact that, on occasion and thanks to bigger budgets, some *anime* achieve fluidity, we can conclude that fluidity is not necessary to the narrative, Japanese cartoon uses a different language.

If Western prejudice and preconceptions about what constitutes 'good' animation can be laid aside, one will discover that Japanese-style cartoons can enthral their audiences, bringing them into a close relationship to the characters, fascinating them with spectacular visuals, often repeated but not deprived of an intriguing range of variations on the theme.

The Japanese cartoon as we know it was created for television. And television quickly ceased to be a meeting point, uniting different families under one roof.[20] It soon became an indispensable object in every household. More and more frequently, it became a source of home entertainment for solitary viewers. The Japanese cartoon industry realised this and chose to aim its films, in particular, at the child who watches television alone, the single child, the child of separated couples or of divorcees, the child of working parents, in Japan as in the rest of the world.

Japanese cartoon series often tell stories of orphans and robots to these lonely children, but that is not all: they also often take sport as subject – netball, tennis, football, gymnastics and baseball – the Japanese national sport. Historically, the first series about sport was *Mach Go Go Go* (1967), about car-racing. The first to be dedicated to a female audience was *Attack Number 1* (1969), which was about netball. One would assume that in sport cartoons it would be obvious to focus on a team and therefore, a group. But they do not. Representing, as it were, the problems of an individual within a nation-team, they focus their attention on a single player, a member of the team undergoing a crisis. Maybe he or she was once the best player but can no longer live up to his/her reputation, yet must do their best, because needed by the team. The narrative themes of the various sports *anime* are very similar to one another and naturally, they often end up with the triumph of the player in difficulty. But sometimes, also to avoid the obvious, it is enough, after being defeated, for the player to have the courage to go on and rediscover hope in the future. Sometimes the crisis is a physical one; at other times it is psychological or simply the result of inexplicable malevolent forces. Nearly always the suffering is hard to communicate to others; in any case, the relationship with the other team members is tainted by feelings of guilt at personal failure. As opposed to Hanna & Barbera, who invented continuous dialogue between characters to make up for the lack of action (too expensive to animate), the *anime* created interior monologue. Nor was this a make-shift solution, for the sequences are extraordinarily effective. Hanna & Barbera's television characters have very few expressions, never exaggerated, created, above all, by movements of the eyes and eyebrows. The heroes of the Japanese television cartoons, on the other hand, have opted to display their great emotions. Thus, in the customary moments of breathless suspense, they open their enormous mouths, dilate their shining eyes and come close up to show more clearly their most intimate emotions, in complete contrast to the model of Japanese behaviour. Their reactions appear exaggerated (remember Disney?) also due to the lack of intermediate drawings. A Disneyan character uses many drawings to constantly change its behaviour, whereas the Japanese are often petrified with fear or joy. They cannot feign indifference or act nonchalantly, partly because it is not affordable (drawings are expensive), partly by choice.

It is interesting to note how in both America and Japan comics and cartoons concentrated in their early stages on children, terrible children, in such comic strips as the Yellow Kid, The Katzenjammer Kids, Buster Brown and Little Jimmy. All are, to some extent, orphans, children of poverty or riches, and they rebel, with the weapons of games and practical jokes, against the rules dictated to them by adults; rigid, hypocritical rules which they cannot negotiate but at least have fun sabotaging. In doing so they lay bare the littleness of the adult world, causing them to fall about laughing with great, bitter guffaws.

Japanese cartoon orphans do not have the courage to play tricks; if they do, like Heidi, they find it is far better to show no emotion. These Japanese orphans internalise the tragedy of childhood, the struggle against an adult world which no longer remembers, which never wants to remember, how hard, how exhausting and how dramatic it is to grow up.

It would be easy, at this point, to embark on speculation about the problems of children in Japan, on the social pressures exerted on its youth, from a very early age, on the relentless emphasis on competition, on the many hours each day rigidly devoted to various duties, on the few hours of sleep allowed each night, on the killing regime imposed at school and in universities.

It would certainly be an interesting subject and one from which it is easy to draw one conclusion: no wonder they recognise themselves in those cartoon characters, deprived of affection, misunderstood and without a family! However, I think it is far more interesting to try to understand why these characters met with such success in Western cultures and why it is that European children found it so easy to identify with these situations as to render some Japanese cartoons series classics, their memories indelible even in adulthood.

Many Japanese characters use violent methods because the world in which they live their adventures is so filled with violence that is seems to be the only language through which they can communicate. Just like children. This being the premise, Japanese cartoon heroes/heroines always place themselves on the side of what is right and good. They always come to the aid of some defenceless character in need of help. They are

champions of Right, the heroes of survival in a world, like that of Ken the warrior, 'dominated by barbarians'. And there is no doubt that, watching certain Japanese cartoons, for example, Katsuhiro Otomo's famous *Akira* (highly successful in the United States and which contains some truly memorable sequences), one has the feeling that

Japanese *anime* filmmakers are searching for ever stronger emotions to offer to their audiences, skyscrapers crumbling to the ground, roads opening up to swallow screaming crowds, buildings and whole neighbourhoods, characters swelling to the size of mountains and becoming hideously deformed – scenes of destructive power in the face of which their characters can only try, desperately, to flee.

Man has always loved the sensation of fear when he knows there is no real danger, but in certain *anime* this sensation would seem to have become a genuine need. Maybe this is a consequence of the national trauma suffered after the tragedy of Hiroshima; in the movies or in television the experience is relived, cleansed of any real consequence and therefore rendered innocuous. But perhaps we should also attribute it to the Japanese culture and education, which expects any expression of feeling or emotion to be severely repressed. Can it be that this society, in some way, comes back to life with these scenes of cathartic demolition?

What is more, these destructive powers, as in *Akira*, often belong to men, concealed in supernaturally powerful psychic forces. This would seem to say, yet again, that education suppresses vital forces, which could one day explode.

Europeans feel themselves to be light years away from the Japanese universe, from its culture and its life style. And yet, quite apart from the undoubted narrative quality of certain productions, Japanese cartoons have portrayed situations in which children from other cultures have recognised and continue to recognise themselves. This does not happen simply because the Japanese know how to sell their products, but because, with regard to its youth, Western culture, our culture, is much more repressive than we would wish to believe. Instead of trying to understand what it is that makes them so attractive to our youth, the adult world has chosen to condemn that which presented itself as new or different or incomprehensible. It is a story that repeats itself and which, if we stay within the realm of cartoons, took place a generation ago, when children with a passion for Flash Gordon, Mandrake and American comic strips besieged the newsstands in search of their magazines.

Many adults fail to understand this new Japanese phenomenon and greet the passion of their children with sufferance, if not with downright disgust. The Japanese protagonists rebel against prohibitions and injustice. Faced with the prohibition against watching these cartoons and the injustice of forbidding what is not known, merely on principle, the reaction of children could not be other than great sorrow. The cartoon characters, not the adults, were the ones to understand children's feelings. But their parents, assuming they noticed this frustration, did not accept it. Thus they wrote letters to the press and the teleision stations, generated the anti-robot mania and caused certain programmes to be suppressed. The child who sought consolation in these cartoons found only emptiness and anger.[21]

It is fortunate that older fans of Japanese animation have meanwhile grown up and have continued to follow (at times with maniacal devotion, but such is the fruit of opposition) the Japanese characters and their inventors. And they, as those before them, the devotees of Flash Gordon and Mandrake, were able (and continue to be able) to publish magazines and organise festivals and conventions to celebrate such work. In the space of a few years we will see a re-discovery and a re-evaluation of the Japanese cartoon and all this will become past history. There will merely be some added resistance, with respect to American comic strips, since Japanese culture is more remote and might make us suspicious.

Hope goes beyond this: when the children of these fanatics of Japanese *anime* will fall for some new, fantastic heroes (undoubtedly extremely dangerous and violent) coming from some other part of the world, maybe their parents will be able to refrain from shouting at the scandal and instead will watch, come to know and understand them.

This is a revised version of a paper given at the 1995 SAS Conference at Greenboro. The paper explores some of the issues explored in his book *Le Anime Disegnate*, published in 1994, which won a special mention.

Notes

1. Another cartoon with a synchronised soundtrack had been made a few weeks earlier: *Dinner Time* was directed by Paul Terry and produced by Van Beuren for the Aesop's *Fables* series. Disney saw it at a private showing and his comment, (written in capitals) in a letter to his brother, ran 'MY GOSH – TERRIBLE!'. The soundtrack had seemed to him a mere jangle of noise.

2. G. Groddeck, Psychoanalytische Schriften zur Psychosomatik, published in a collection entitled *Il linguaggio dell'es*, translated by Maria Gregorio (Milan: Bompiani, 1987).

3. Ollie Johnson and Frank Thames, *Disney Animation: The Illusion of Life* (New York: Abbeville, 1983).

4. Footnote on Thumper in *The Encyclopaedia of Walt Disney's Animated Characters* (Twickenham: Hamlyn, 1987).

   (On reflection, Thumper's mother behaves like a bitch. In order to demonstrate to everybody that she knows exactly how one behaves in polite company she doesn't spare her charming young offspring a public humiliation. The youngster is forced to recite aloud a lesson he has learnt by heart but entirely failed to assimilate. A lesson which is anyway completely out of proportion in this context.

   Had the mother been as well brought up as she would have us to believe she would have spoken to Thumper later, calmly and gently, in private. For one demonstrates what good manners are, one doesn't teach them. (As discussed, this needs explicating in terms of what is considered 'normal'.)

5. Although recent research has cast doubts on this oft-repeated claim; for example, Maltin in *Of Mice and Magic* said 'Ub Iwerks had developed something similar in the mid-1930s, but he never carried it to this degree of intimacy'; also, Max Fleischer in the same period created experimental forms of multiplane.

6. If the evil one is not there, if there is no father figure, as in that week spent with his mother and younger siblings, one can listen to stories and time thus becomes perfect, joyful and infinite. We need to block that time, destroy the wicked one, after which there will be no need to build anything, for happiness is now.

7. The relationship between Disney and his neurotic and violent father is described in every Disney biography; for example, Bob Thomas, *Walt Disney: An American Original* (New York, Pocket Books, 1976); Leonard Mosely, *Disney's World* (Chelsea: Scarborough House, 1990); Marc Eliot, *Walt Disney: Hollywood's Dark Prince* (New York: Birch Lane Press, 1993).

8. Ub Iwerks.

9. He was also the one meant to disobey the wizard. The apprentice Mickey repeats, in *Fantasia*, what he has already done in *Steamboat Willie*, rendering spectacular and unproductive the magic of his gloomy master in the dream scene. A sequence not to be found in either *Goethe* or in the original fairytale.

10. Thus in *The Brave Little Tailor*, a short film made in 1938, we see a giant rolling a cigarette from a haystack with Mickey inside. By strange coincidence it is he who has been chosen to eliminate the mighty man, so Mickey during his mission finds himself, after many vicissitudes, inside the huge cigarette which the giant is smoking. Here we are at the limits of Disneyanity.

    In *The Art of Self Defense* made in 1941, a boxing Goofy must undergo a lengthy breathing exercise. At the end of the sequence he is blown up like a balloon and just like a balloon, rapidly deflates, floating around the gymnasium. There is a similar gag in *Beach and Picnic* made two years earlier: here it is Pluto who must struggle with a big blown up duck which exhales all its air onto him, with similar consequences.

11. In Disney, Nature itself is good, even in the documentaries, where it is manipulated at will. Disney expects the world to be transformed in accordance with his own thoughts, his own ideas, his personal needs. The animals that Snow White meets in the woods are timid, frightened, as nearly everybody is good in the world of Disney. They hesitate to trust her and, once they feel safe to do it, they all unite in a true big family which then protects the whole story. The small animals, the little birds and rabbits, even the little tortoise who arrives always just a bit too late,

protect Snow White and the seven dwarfs. They weep with them at the heroine's presumed demise and join in the celebrations when the Prince brings her back to life and carries her away.

12. Bruno Bettelheim, *The Uses of Enchantment: The Meaning And Importance Of Fairy Tales* (New York: Alfred A. Knopf Inc., 1976). From an Italian translation by Andrea D'Anna (Milan: Giangiacomo Feltrinelli Editore, 1977), 47.

13. In some of his films, Bugs Bunny appears carrying the typical bundle of the child who has run away from home. He presents himself thus, for example, in *Racketeer Rabbit* (1946) directed by Freleng and written by Maltese. Here he sets about drilling a hole in the floor of an abandoned house where he can burrow into sleep, before getting involved in a bloody battle between gangsters.

   Sylvester the cat is the guest of a human household and might get kicked out at any moment. Of Daffy Duck's address we know nothing. Only in one of the full-length Bugs Bunny feature films (made by building original sequences out of several short-length films) – *The Bugs Bunny/Road Runner Movie* (1979) directed by Chuck Jones – does the rabbit own a large mansion with a swimming pool, adorned with the images of his creators. But it was just a way of parodying Hollywood stars, who receive their guests, as he does, in their dressing gowns. This indifference towards possessions is a clear symptom of the of the internal freedom of Bugs and company characters.

14. Chuck Jones recounts many examples of Warner Bros.' animation artists difficult relationships with their fathers in *Chuck Amuck: The Life and Times of Animated Cartoons* (London: Simon & Schuster, 1989).

15. Jones, ibid.

16. Jones, ibid.

17. Johanna Spyri, *Heidi* (New York: Children's Classix, a division of Dilithium Press, 1986), 154.

18. Spyri, ibid., 162.

19. Joseph Campbell, *Myths to Live By* (London: Bantam, 1981), 123.

20. In Italy, this campaign led to the cessation of many Japanese cartoon series being shown on television.

21. In the early days of television it was often the case in tenement style buildings in Italy that one television would be shared by several families.

The thief of Buena Vista

Disney's *Aladdin* and Orientalism

Leslie Felperin

We begin with a true story, but one so dense with stories within its stories, so layered with conflicting versions of the truth, that it seems to have garnered the narrational generative capacities of myth. It would take a modern Sheherezade far more than a thousand-and-one nights to unravel the complex skein of fact and fiction that surrounds the ur-narrative of the Gulf War of 1990. But that is not the purpose of this essay: here we are concerned with tracing how that vast story-cycle of fact is entangled with another story, the fictional film *Aladdin*, which is itself enmeshed in a dense mesh of true stories and tall tales, a whole discourse of ideas about the Middle East and about 'Otherness'.

Once upon a time, not too long ago, relations between Islamic states in the Middle East were fraught with political tensions. Meanwhile, in a land called Buena Vista, far to the West, some artists constructed a film set in a Middle East that looked very different from the one people saw on the news. The land they painted was filled with magic and fantasy, while the other was filled with strife and anger. This paper concerns what enabled two such contradictory visions of the Middle East to manifest themselves.

Representations of the 'Orient' no matter how seemingly innocent, are charged with meanings about cultural relations. In 1991, the West was bombarded with infrared images of the Gulf War and a wrecked Baghdad. A year later, Walt Disney's *Aladdin* was released. Set in a mythical city called Agrabah, a near acronym of Baghdad, the film presents a different picture of the Middle East. Although these two portraits are very dissimilar, they share more than just a common cultural origin. Both texts are informed by the discourse of Orientalism, which can be broadly defined as set of readings and writings that Western institutions impose on the what used to be called the Orient, especially its most proximate part, the Middle East. The film *Aladdin* is as rooted in the complex discourse of Orientalism as the news coverage of the Gulf War. By looking at this film and some texts surrounding it, this paper will discuss some ways in which Orientalism, as it is represented through the story of Aladdin in several forms, operates in popular culture. I will suggest that recent visual interpretations of the story are used for three purposes: to allay fears about the Oriental 'Other', to display technical innovations, and finally to buttress a discourse of Western technological superiority *through* the textual appropriation of a story of the Oriental Other.

Edward Said, whose influential book *Orientalism*[1] had a radical impact on post-colonial criticism, defines his the Orientalism broadly as, among other things, 'a certain will or intention to understand, in some cases to control, manipulate, even to incorporate, what is a manifestly different (or alternative or novel) world'.[2] He writes of the 'sheer knitted-togetherness' of Orientalist texts, their propensity to cross-reference one another to a such an extreme degree that at times they seem to describe not a 'real' Orient, but a virtual, wholly textually defined one.

Aladdin has been controversial ever since its release. Spokespeople for Arab–American groups and devout Muslims have been especially vocal in denouncing the film's use of stereotypes.[3] In contrast, some viewers the author spoke to informally applauded the film's attempt to reflect Arab culture and physiognomy within the limitations of a caricatured form. I do not wish to endorse simplistically either position. Instead, I believe this debate is symptomatic of the unstable infrastructure of the larger cultural discourse of ethnicity, whose parameters are constantly being redrawn by the intervention of hitherto silenced ethnic and religious groups. In other words, the fact that *Aladdin* is contentious at all demonstrates that there are now new groups of interlocutors who will not accept unproblematically Western representations of themselves.

I would like to touch briefly on how these perspectives might by contextualised with reference to past representations of the Orient and the Aladdin story in particular, in animation, live action film and other media.

In order to understand the cultural work of *Aladdin*, it is vital we understand the matrix from whence it sprang. Said suggests that 'European culture gained in strength and identity by setting itself off against the Orient as a sort of surrogate and even underground self'.[4] Hence, one of the covert projects of Orientalism is to define the West as the Orient's Other through a series of binary definitions. The 'Occident' is light and enlightened while the Orient is dark and benighted. The former is rational and just, the latter sensual and despotic. One is scientific and rigorous, the other magical and imaginative and so forth. Post-colonial critics like Said, Reza Hammami and Rana Kabbani describe how the circulation of these definitions was and is one of the projects of a large collection of orientalist texts that encompass a range of topics including philology, history, travel, anthropology, and of course, fiction.

Like many fictional Orientalist texts, *Aladdin* is quite literally a projection, in the psychoanalytic and cinematic senses of the word, of Western fears of and desires for the Orient. Many of the dualisms outlined above are replayed in the surface of its narrative. The Oriental world it depicts is one of despotism and irrationality, an image congruent with traditional figuring of the Orient. The laws, like the one that decrees Jasmine must marry, are arbitrarily enforced and revoked. Evil despots like Jafar seize power through the misappropriation of magical technology. These elements are certainly present in earlier versions of the story, but the film chooses to underline their current political relevance by dropping allusions like Jafar's ominous threat, 'There's a new order now', which echoes George Bush's famous phrase. Complimentarily, the film recasts Western fantasies of the Orient as a place of sensuality and pleasure. Journalists and reviewers at the time of the film's release remarked on the sexiness of its heroine, Jasmine, practically the only woman in the film, who was described by one animator as a 'super-babe'.[5] The figuration of Jasmine parallels representations of Middle Eastern women that is discussed in the work of Malek Alloula.[6]

The filmmakers have described how the film was visually inspired by a mixture of 'original' Middle Eastern material and Western depictions of the East. The studio sponsored book on the making of the film asserts that the production designers developed the style of *Aladdin* from the study of the following:

(1) Persian miniature paintings from approximately AD 1000 to 1500;

(2) various Victorian paintings of Eastern cultures;

(3) numerous photo-essay and coffee-table books on the Middle East;

(4) Disney animated films from the mid-1940s to the mid-1950s;

(5) Alexander Korda's 1940 film, *The Thief of Baghdad*.[7]

Apart from the mention of the Persian Miniatures, all the sources just cited are Western in provenance. Better than anything I could have drawn from a viewing of the film, this list illustrates the 'knitted-togetherness' of Orientalist discourse in practice. Like many other Orientalist texts, *Aladdin* is far less concerned with a representation of any real Middle East than it is with re-presenting older Western representations of the Orient and the story. This self-referential tradition can be traced back to the beginning of the story's circulation in the West.

The corpus of tales known as the *Arabian Nights* or *The Thousand and One Nights*, translated into Western languages at the beginning of the eighteenth century was one of the first Islamic fictional works to circulate in the West and gain widespread popularity. Consequently, not only were the *Nights* crucial to the formation of popular Western conceptions about the Orient, but their subsequent forms were also filtered by those very conceptions they helped to foster.

Antoine Galland, for example, one of the *Nights'* earliest 'translators', was also one of the first to incorporate the story of Aladdin into the tales where most scholars now agree it should never have been. He was also one of the first Westerners to excise some of the more salacious passages he had heard from Arab storytellers from the story and the cycle as a whole. Robert Irwin, the eminent scholar of the *Arabian Nights*, even suggests that 'it is conceivable that Galland himself wrote the story, drawing as much on European sources as oriental ones'.[8] Thus, the intermingling of Oriental fancy dress and European fantasy that marks the story of *Aladdin* throughout its history might be traceable back to its very conception.

It is interesting to note that as far back as the first wave of interest in the *Nights*, they were seen not only as light entertainment for adults, but as especially suitable reading for the young. Gibbon, for example, wrote that:

> Before I left Kingston school I was well acquainted with Pope's *Homer* and the *Arabian Nights* entertainments, two books which will always please by the moving picture of human manners and specious miracles.[9]

The pleasure of 'specious miracles' that the *Nights* offer is often central to their reception and one that comes to gloss ideas of the Orient as a land of both miracle and chicanery. Furthermore, their association with childhood pleasure is gradually elided with the Western notion that Orientals themselves are essentially childish. In the 'Translator's

Foreward' to his *Plain and Literal Translation* of the *Nights*, Sir Richard F. Burton berates his predecessors for what he sees as their misappropriation of the book, decrying that, 'one and all degrade a *chef d'oeuvre* of the highest anthropological and ethnographical interest and importance to a mere fairy-book, a nice present for little boys'.[10] Burton's translation restores material excised from Galland's version in an attempt to recapture the original's 'authenticity' and thereby drag the book out of the nursery. At the same time, he figures Arabs in the Foreword as childlike in their credulity, noting, as *they* listen to *his* telling of the stories at a fireside encampment that, 'the most fantastic flights of fancy, most impossible of impossibilities, appear to them utterly natural, mere matters of everyday occurrence'.[11]

Despite Burton's efforts to give the *Nights* and the anthropological context, the stories continued to be published mainly under the aegis of children's fiction throughout the nineteenth century. The *Aladdin* story, along with *Sindbad the Sailor* and *Ali Baba and the Forty Thieves*, soon emerged as particular favourites and were often published on their own, retold by new authors and vividly illustrated by well-known artists like Aubrey Beardsley, Heath Robinson and Tenniel.

Soon pantomimes were being made of these stories. Accounts of these early pantos stress their use of clever theatrical devices in order to help carpets fly and genies seem to appear magically. Many British theatre-goers will attest that little has changed technologically in the Christmas pantos of today. These early performances of *Aladdin* are noteworthy for their use of spectacle. One of the earliest cinematic adaptations of the story, by Pathé Frères from 1906, seems to be either closely inspired or even based upon a stage version. The theatricality of the staging of the final scene is apparent.

Timothy Mitchell, in his book *Colonising Egypt*,[12] reports on how Egyptian students, like Ibrahim Pasha in Paris during the nineteenth century, wrote of how curious they found the West's obsession with *le spéctacle*, a word for which they could find no equivalent in Arabic. Pasha was particularly puzzled by the Western spectacles of the East, the masques and operas, the panoramas of Cairo and the Great Exhibition of 1873, which reproduced the city in miniature, with chaotic streets and dirtied paintwork. Mitchell observes that:

> Spectacles like the world exhibition and the Orientalist congress set up the world as a picture. They ordered it up before an audience as an object on display, to be viewed, experienced and investigated.

The continuity between these nineteenth-century technologies and early cinema has been well discussed elsewhere. For the present, my point is that this specular activity, the machinery of the power of the gaze, offered another way to frame and contain the Orient, just as scholarly Orientalism described it through the power-knowledge of the written text.

The Aladdin story was subsumed into this specular world view through the new visual machinery of the cinema. The 1906 Pathé Frère version used a combination stage effects and trick film effects in order to create genies with rudimentary animation techniques. Many prints of this film were hand-tinted. None of this technology was original at the time, but it is interesting that the story should have invited the use of relatively new techniques. In fact, the Aladdin story and cognates of it like the two *Thief of Bagdad* movies of 1924 and 1940, repeatedly serve as showcases for new cinematic special effects techniques. It is as if an attempt is made to literalise the story, with its all-powerful genie, creating an impossible world through cinematic 'magic' of animation. In other words, in many ways the Aladdin story serves as a trope for the animation process itself.

The logic of this trope is that Western technology is the genie which Aladdin/the animator commands and the world that they manipulate together is a fictive one that represents the Orient. Since fictional representations of the Orient are so scarce, this delightful land of fantasy might become the only way the West can imagine the Orient, as a hybrid place, using a Western language and in Arab fancy dress, somewhere between Tehran and Veronica Lake, as a Warner Bros. movie *Ali Baba Bunny* puts it. Films like *1001 Arabian Nights* (1959) by the United Productions of America (UPA) studio and *Aladdin* are deeply marked by this hybridity. On the one hand they try to emulate the look of Orient in various ways, while maintaining an emphatically Western world view in the narrative frame of reference.

The UPA version of the film, for example, emphasises the studio's distinctively 'flat' graphic style in order to enhance the Oriental look of the film, suggested by the non-representational quality of Middle Eastern art. Yet Aladdin is tellingly displaced as central character by the studio star, Mr. Magoo.

A similar displacement is at work in *Aladdin*. The publicity surrounding the film continually stresses the pains the artists took to incorporate the look of the Middle East. However, this look is literally part of the background of the film, an element in the art direction, supplementary to the foreground's characters who look like Tom Cruise. Oriental imagery becomes one of many special effects, something that superior Western technology, like the weaponry in the Gulf War, can create and control. For example, in *Disney's Aladdin*, a book on the making of the film, special effects supervisor Don Paul explains how the smoke and fire was based on Arabic calligraphy and stylised 'to make them more arabesque in design'. Paul cheerfully states that though they made an effort to use arabesque images, 'we try not to hold their shapes too long. Otherwise, we may be saying words we don't know we're saying'.[13]

For some viewers of the film these good intentions to 'authenticate' the film's look seemed superficial in practice. Khalil Barhoum, a professor of linguistics at Stanford University in California, was reported as saying of the film's storefront signs were 'scribblings' and that his 'children recognise Arabic writing and were puzzled by the animators failure to draw simple letters'.[14]

What Barhoum's children have failed to recognise is that *Aladdin* is not really addressed to them. *Aladdin* is a fictional orientalist text, engaged with a dialogue with other fictional orientalist texts. The scrawls it depicts are a unique language, one without a referent except to the animated world in which they are embedded. Furthermore, as Said and others have suggested, the 'Orient' itself is a discursive construct, one which only makes sense in opposition to a complementary 'Occident'. It is therefore fitting that one of the most financially successful cinematic visualisations of this construct should be animated.

After all, animation is a discursive construct in its own way, one marginalised, like the East, that signifies only through its opposition to the dominant that is live action cinema.

Notes

1. Edward W. Said, *Orientalism: Western Conceptions of the Orient* (London: Penguin, 1991).
2. Ibid., 12.
3. See, for example, 'Disney's *Aladdin* rubs Arabs up the wrong way' by Christopher Walker, the

Times (22 May 1993) and 'Arabian Slights' by Richard Scheinin, *San Jose Mercury News* (2 Jan. 1993), to site but two.

4. Ibid., 3.

5. *Aladdin Sane* by Mimi Avins in *Premiere* (December 1993).

6. See Malek Alloula, *The Colonial Harem* (Minneapolis and Manchester: University of Minnesota Press and Manchester University Press, 1986).

7. John Culhane, *Disney's Aladdin: The Making of an Animated Film* (New York: Hyperion, 1992), 89.

8. 'There's the rub . . . and there too' by Robert Irwin, *Times Literary Supplement* (24 December 1993).

9. Edward Gibbon, *Memoirs of My Life*, ed. Georges A. Bonnard (London: Thomas Nelson, 1966), 36. Quoted from Peter L. Caracciolo, 'Introduction: "Such a store house of ingenious fiction and of splendid imagery" ', in *The Arabian Nights in English Literature*, ed. Caracciolo (London: Macmillan Press, 1988), 2.

10. Richard F. Burton, *A Plain and Literal translation of the Arabian Nights* (Benares: Kamashastra Society, 1885).

11. Ibid., viii.

12. Timothy Mitchell, *Colonising Eygpt* (Cambridge: Cambridge University Press, 1988).

13. Culhane, 113.

14. Quoted in Scheinin, 'Arabian Slights', *San Jose Mercury News* (2 January 1993).

13

Animatophilia, cultural production and corporate interests

The case of *Ren & Stimpy*

Mark Langer

One of the best-publicised events related to animation and video during 1992 was the conflict between Nickelodeon and filmmaker John Kricfalusi over the cablecast animation series *The Ren & Stimpy Show*. Critics have hailed Kricfalusi as 'a man of genius' and the series as 'the best animated cartoon to come along since the glory days of the 1940s'.[1] Nickelodeon owned the rights to the programme and characters devised by Kricfalusi. Despite the acclaim for the filmmaker and the series, Nickelodeon transferred production from Kricfalusi's Spumco studio to a new Games Productions studio, which used many former Spumco staff. Nickelodeon maintained that they were forced into this position because of Kricfalusi's erratic performance. The filmmaker allegedly missed production deadlines and exceeded budgets on a regular basis. Kricfalusi claimed that Nickelodeon did not understand the series. Confronted with something that was too innovative and creative for pedestrian minds, averred the filmmaker, the company chose to remove Kricfalusi in order to produce a more conventional and low-budget series.

Much of the debate over this issue has centred around time-honoured myths of the artist in conflict with a corporate entity, and has been documented largely through interviewees' accusations of corporate phillistinism or individual irresponsibility. A paradigmatic comment on the situation was offered by Richard Gehr of *The Village Voice*, who maintained: 'Wrenching *Ren & Stimpy* away from Kricfalusi is like taking *Twin Peaks* away from David Lynch and Mark Frost and handing it over to Quinn-Martin...' Or, as John Kricfalusi says with utter seriousness: 'They didn't really deserve *The Ren & Stimpy Show*.' *The Simpsons* creator Matt Groening has said: 'It's like taking Dr Frankenstein away from his monster.'[2] This study will not examine the Nickelodeon/Kricfalusi conflict from the point of view of artistic martyrdom or of individuality versus corporatism. Instead, it will discuss the issue in terms of questions relating to the creation and marketing of products for specific taste groups within a North American context, and in terms of the shifting position of animation within the cultural landscape.

Film historians tend to regard their domain as the study of artists, art or the corporate figures and institutions of the film industry. Alison Butler observes that among the basic strategies informing contemporary film histories is the treatment of cinema as an autonomous artistic-industrial practice separate from its socio-cultural context.[3] Although the cinema is overwhelmingly a popular culture phenomenon, the influence of popular culture on the filmmaking process frequently is disregarded in historical considerations. Herbert Gans has described this problem with the questions:

> Is popular culture something that is created in New York and Hollywood by skilled profit-seeking enterprises which have enough of a monopoly over the supply of entertainment and information that they can impose almost anything they think will sell on the American public, particularly on the television public – a captive audience to a handful of channels? Or are these enterprises themselves often unwitting agents of a culture in the anthropological sense, of a shared set of values or norms that they must try to express if they are to attract an audience and make their profits?[4]

This article will examine *The Ren & Stimpy Show* with the assumption that both individuals and creators are agents of culture. Culture itself is not a monolithic institution, but is made up of many subcultures, which participate to varying degrees

The Ren & Stimpy
Show *logo*

©1991 Nickelodeon

in the total culture. Individuals and creators can be agents of specific subcultures. It will be argued that much of the difficulty arising between Nickelodeon and Kricfalusi was due to the fact that they were agents of different cultural entities, and consequently did not share a congruent set of values or norms.

Animation – which for the purposes of this paper will mean commercial, studio animation – was for a long time a marginalised form of expression with little cultural capital. Pierre Bordieu has pointed out that capital is not solely a matter of economics. He defined capital as 'the set of actually useable resources and powers'. Capital can be either economic, cultural or social. The total combined volume of these different kinds of capital varies according to social class. The dominant class, which includes members of the professions with high incomes and qualifications, has greater access to material and cultural goods. Unskilled workers and labourers have the lowest access to such resources. People who stem from these different classes will have access to different amounts of capital, based on the amount of economic, cultural or social capital with which they begin life. Within different realms of society, the proportion of one's capital can vary. Thus, artists and industrialists can both be seen as belonging to an upper class, but will differ in the kinds of capital that they have acquired. An artist will have much cultural capital but less economic capital. The proportion might be quite the opposite for an industrialist. Each group often will give cultural legitimacy to different forms of cultural goods. For example, while theatre might be patronised by artists and industrialists, more avant-garde works would be consumed by the former than by the latter, since the former depends on its specialised knowledge in this area as part of its cultural capital. Both of these theatrical forms are legitimated by their association with this class.[5] Forms of theatrical practice patronised by the lower classes, such as wrestling, have little cultural capital.

During the 1960s, when film became institutionalised as a form of intellectual discourse with academic journals and university programmes, expressions of interest in mainstream 'Hollywood' animation at best were ignored. At worst, these expressions were dismissed on intellectual and aesthetic grounds. Affected by widespread misogelastic tendencies among arbiters of film culture, animation was relegated to reaches of a cultural limbo even beyond those occupied by other film forms with a touch of levity, such as the musical or comedy. Popular cultural discourse joined with intellectual discourse in its rejection of animation as coherent with high or even middlebrow thought. Within mainstream culture and its organs of legitimation, animation was devoid of cultural capital. This characterisation applies only to commercial animation, not to experimental or independent animation. While books such as Ralph Stevenson's *Animation in the Cinema* (London: Zwemmer/Barnes, 1967) castigated most commercial animation, the work of independents was praised. However, independent animation tended to be marginalised as a minor subclassification of experimental filmmaking.

This view began to change around the mid-1970s following such events as the New York Lincoln Center Disney retrospective in 1973, the Jay Cocks's 1973 article on Chuck Jones in *Time*, the animation issue of *Film Comment* edited by Greg Ford in 1975 and the Whitney Museum Disney show in 1981.[6] In this period, institutions of higher learning began to introduce animation as part of general scholarly film curricula, rather than as ghettoised craft courses or programmes in the Fine Arts. For example, in New York, the New School for Social Research introduced a course on the history of animation in 1973. By 1975, a similar course was offered in the Film Division of the Graduate School of Arts at Columbia University.[7]

Consecutive editions of a standard introductory text demonstrate this increased emphasis on animation within the discipline of Film Studies. In 1979, Kristin Thompson and David Bordwell's *Film Art: An Introduction* mentioned animation in a scant three pages. By the second edition, this increased to five. In the third edition, fourteen pages dealt, at least in part, with the subject. By 1993, the fourth edition contained thirty-six pages with references to animation, and included a section devoted to analyses of animated films.[8] Concurrent with this movement in academe, *Cinema Journal*, *Screen*, *The Velvet Light Trap* and *Film History* now routinely publish articles on topics previously covered only in such underground animation periodicals or fan magazines as *Funnyworld*, *Film Fan Monthly*, *Starlog* or *Mindrot*. Emulating the institutions of traditional art forms, the study of animation has created its own agents of cultural respectability. The discipline has been served by its own scholarly society since 1986 (the Society of Animation Studies) and by its own refereed academic publications since 1992 (*Animation Journal*).

The growing acceptance of animation by the institutions of high culture coincided with its acceptance by more broadly-based social institutions. Certain areas of animation have been validated by mainstream culture as something other than simple-minded entertainment directed toward a juvenile audience. For example, Christopher Finch's *The Art of Walt Disney*, Thomas and Johnston's *Disney Animation: The Illusion of Life*, John Canemaker's *Treasures of Disney Animation Art* and Patrick Brion's *Tex Avery: Les Dessins* led a trend to produce expensive coffee-table art books presenting the work of the Disney, Warner Bros. and MGM studios in a manner coherent with that used to merchandise the Old Masters;[9] mainstream publishers, such as St. Martin's Press and Farrar Straus Giroux, market memoirs of Shamus Culhane and Chuck Jones;[10] and cel art galleries operate in every major city. Through this cultural imprimature, animation history is transformed into a variety of consumer goods that cater to a now-popular taste.

All of this has profoundly changed the position of animatophiles on the cultural terrain. Animatophiles are a taste group characterised by a high degree of knowledge about animation. Animatophiles consist of a tiny total culture, wherein its participants exist largely apart from the mainstream and a bigger partial culture, whose participants exist mainly within the dominant total culture, but function as animatophiles on a part-time basis. Animatophilia, as a total culture in itself, has participants who are animation company owners and employees, animation scholars, devoted fans and obsessive consumers of animation and its ancillary products. This core is composed of those animatophiles with the highest degree of specialised knowledge about the subject and whose lives revolve around animation. As participants in a partial culture, animatophiles include buyers of animation art, casual fans and other people with an interest in animation beyond that of the total culture. In other words, the culture of animatophiles has a core of people whose lives are completely devoted to animation, surrounded by a more diffuse but larger body of animation fans who more or less live predominantly within the total culture. The member group of animatophiles might also intersect with the membership of other taste groups.[11]

The specialised knowledge of core animatophiles forms a different kind of cultural capital which is defined by its opposition to, or separateness from, the tastes of mainstream culture. Taste groups, as forms of social distinction, do not depend on traditional notions of class determination through economic ranking. Within a consumer society, people are confronted with an enormous range of goods. As they select and classify goods from all of the possibilities offered, they position themselves within a particular social space which can be determined not only by economic position, but by taste.[12] Goods with a low-cultural status, like Liberace recordings, can cost as much or more than goods with high-cultural status, like Phillip Glass or Bach recordings. Consequently, taste can be more important than economics as a means of social positioning. As Pierre Bordieu has stated: 'Nothing classifies somebody more than the way he or she classifies.'[13]

Animatophiles share characteristics with other post-industrial marginalised taste groups (such as Trekkies, Transcendentalists, jazz 78 rpm recording collectors, or forms of both black and adolescent culture) in that they maintain a certain degree of 'hipness'. Don Wallace has pointed out that hipness:

> . . . differentiates through the discovery of the exotic, through the legitimation of the illegitimate, and therefore its power is not in knowledge *per se* but in the ability to confer on the otherwise forbidden the status of rarity and desirability.

Wallace goes on to observe 'hip is a category that is always in motion: by increasing the desirability of a practice, there is the risk that it will be popularised and therefore devalued'.[14] Hipness becomes a game of displaced authenticity that often derives its meaning and value from the exclusive nature of the code used by a particular taste group. Once the code is decipherable by the total culture, it ceases to be exclusive and loses its value to members of the group.[15] In other words, the cultural capital of this code depends on its ownership by a particular taste group.[16]

The fans and creators of comics form another taste group similar to animatophiles. Like animatophiles, they grew in strength during the post-war baby boom period, and like their animation counterparts, were considered to be an outlaw or fringe taste group. In response to a general condemnation of comics as trash, the late 1940s and early 1950s saw the emergence of artists such as Basil Wolverton and the team of Will Elder and Harvey Kurtzman of *Mad* magazine. These artists exemplify certain trends in this sort of cultural sub-grouping. First of all, Wolverton, through the exaggerated grotesquery of his style, deliberately violated the aesthetic norms of graphic arts.[17] Will Elder and Harvey Kurtzman's satires of popular mainstream comics (including *Women Wonder!*, *Starchie*, *Mickey Rodent!*, *Outer Sanctum* and the *Classic Comics* takeoff of *Robinson Crusoe* [with Jack Webb as Friday]) relied on a reader's sophisticated level of knowledge about this manifestation of popular culture.[18] Forms and conventions of comic art were recombined to create new, and often ironic, meanings. Indeed, Kurtzman has been described by Art Spiegelman as America's first post-modern humourist, laying the groundwork for such contemporary humour and satire as *Saturday Night Live*, *Monty Python*, and the *Naked Gun*. Spiegelman called Kurtzman 'the spiritual godfather of underground comics'.[19]

Mad catered to a taste group that asserted its cultural space through the legitimation of an illegitimate art form. Attacks on publications such as *Mad* for their bad taste and their inappropriateness for a juvenile audience resulted in the establishment of a Comics Code, which effectively suppressed such expression for a number of years.[20] Nevertheless, *Mad* prevailed and was finally accepted by mainstream culture.

Through its popularity, the cultural capital of *Mad* was devalued among comic fans, even as its cultural capital rose within society as a whole. The specialised knowledge inherent among such fans of comic books as *Mad* readers became diffused throughout society. Once an outlaw form of culture, comics became legitimised as part of the total culture.[21] Exhibitions of pop art based on comics became commonplace during the 1960s, when comic art visual and narrative conventions were appropriated by such artists as Roy Lichtenstein, Oyvind Fahlström or Bernard Rancillac,[22] redefining comic art hipness in terms of the total culture's notion of Fine Art. Hipness in the comic book taste group moved on to underground publications. These underground comics further pushed beyond the norms of legitimised tastes in narrative and visual aesthetics through their examination of such topics as black culture, drugs, sex and new-left politics and through their abandonment of colour images for the cheaper use of black and white.

Film history often deals with issues through analogy to other entertainment forms. For example, much scholarship on the subject of early cinema has examined the medium in relation to theatre, vaudeville, magic lanterns, magic shows and other nineteenth-century modes of performance.[23] By means of analogy, patterns similar to the *Mad* phenomenon can be observed in the social positioning of animatophiles. Mainstream culture has valorised classical American studio animation into a system of taste norms. Within scholarship, the study of animation has aped time-honoured forms of academic practice. Until recent years, there has been a tradition of analysing animated cartoons by attributing their characteristic features to the particular achievements of an individual, paralleling *auteur* methodology in the study of live action film. Scholars or enthusiasts in journals like *Funnyworld* or *Mindrot* identified unheralded artists of animation in emulation of the treatment of live action counterparts identified by such publications as *Cahiers du Cinéma*, *Movie* and *Film Comment*. True artists of animation were seen as those who ran the institution (like Disney or Lantz) or they were seen as *auteur* escape-artists who wriggled out of studio straightjackets made by producers like Schlesinger at Warners or Quimby at MGM.[24]

Academic discourse established a hagiography of great animation artists as early as 1975. In the ground-breaking *The Hollywood Cartoon* issue of *Film Comment*, Winsor McCay, Chuck Jones, Grim Natwick, Walt Disney, Tex Avery, Max and Dave Fleischer, as well as Bill Hanna and Joe Barbera (in their *Tom and Jerry* period) were singled out as artists. Television animation was dismissed in the same issue as ' . . . the Muzak of animation', 'an insistent assault of mediocrity' and as 'assembly-line shorts grudgingly executed by cartoon veterans who hate what they're doing. What's missing here is not money, but imagination'.[25] A similar distinction can be noted in the reception of animation by the general public. As knowledge of animation became commodified, it followed the 'great man/great artist' model originally adopted in the scholarly treatment of animation. Artifacts and ephemera associated with important artists such as Disney, Avery, or Hanna and Barbera have had their status revised in terms of cultural capital. For example, twenty years ago, probably no one could have imagined a time when Annette Michelson, high-brow avatar of such *auteurs* as Eisenstein and Vertov and co-founder of *October*, would translate a coffee-table art book that reproduced images for *Tom and Jerry* cartoons.[26]

One can track this revision through examination of the changing status of cels and other forms of animation artwork. Cels were once considered the detritus of the industry. Black-and-white cels were commonly washed of their images and reused. This was not possible to do with colour cels, which were most commonly thrown away after use. The current practice of collecting animation art work began in the late 1960s and early 1970s, but at first was strictly a low-budget affair restricted to animatophiles. Early ads in fanzines and other dealer offerings marketed original art work for ten to twenty dollars.[27]

With the acceptance of certain figures as 'masters of animation', the animation art market boomed. In 1989, a black-and-white cel from *Orphan's Benefit* (1934) was sold for $286 000 at an auction at Christie's. Seventy-nine Disney drawings, watercolours and cels were offered for sale at Sotheby's in New York on 27 June 1992. The firm estimated that this sale would realise $1.5 million.[28] Background art from Disney's *Beauty and the Beast* (1001), with gouache cel-overlay replicas of characters from the film, were auctioned at estimates of $1000 to $10 000 by Sotheby's in Los Angeles in October 1992. Seventeen-thousand catalogues – a record for an auction house – were printed for the sale.[29] Now animation art is sold by the same institutions that deal in high-culture art or by specialist galleries that mimic the behaviour of major art dealers. Animation art has attained the cultural respectability of an investment, albeit (in the words of one gallery), 'an investment that makes you smile'.[30] One straight-faced gallery owner likens cel art to 'the painting off the ceiling of the Sistine Chapel'.[31] What was once the pursuit of marginalised fan culture now has been redefined into conventional notions of a commodity merchandised within Fine Art commerce.

As animation was redefined to cohere to dominant cultural conceptions, notions of connoisseurship have been applied to the medium. John Halas, arguing in favour of a 'masters of animation' approach, claimed that:

> . . . animation . . . still lacks serious critical appreciation. Compared with other media such as the fine arts, cinema or music, animation is by and large, a badly neglected form. It has few critics who are able to analyse what is good or bad, or who know what values to look for in an animated film. Many make the mistake of comparing animation with live action productions, making unfair comparisons between two very different disciplines. Moreover, general audiences have only been exposed to one type of animation, that of popular, funny and usually American, cartoons, as if there were only 'pop' music and no other kind.[32]

Halas's distinction between a low-culture animation (categorised as popular entertainment and the traditional domain of animatophiles) and a high-culture animation (which would be recognised as art by the larger culture) increasingly is made untenable by the crossover of low culture into high. With the growing acceptance of popular animation as art and of commercial Hollywood figures like Disney and Avery as artists, the boundary between high and low has shifted.

This tendency toward absorption on the part of dominant culture threatens the existence of animatophiles as a taste group distinct by the nature of its specialised knowledge. Consequently, animatophiles distinguish themselves as a taste group by resorting to strategies earlier mapped out in other comic media. Core animatophiles seek out more obscure sources to locate forms of expression that have not been legitimated by popular consumer culture. Since the 1970s, as 'classical Hollywood' animation joined the mainstream, and as its codes became the new norm of taste, the cutting edge of animatophilia moved from the cult of Disney and Warner products to such sources as early television animation, children's broadcasting, commercials and other forms of expression that remain disenfranchised by both mass culture and the academic/art establishment. As the code of hipness is deciphered by total culture, animatophiles create new codes from the detritus of animation. In this sense, animatophilia becomes a trash aesthetic (or perhaps more correctly, a trash practice), which examines the detritus of mass culture and recombines it to produce cultural capital. The violation of taste norms becomes a key element of this animatophile practice.

By pushing further into the realm of cultural illegitimacy, animatophiles redefine themselves as a taste group hipper in terms of animation than the general Disney/Warner Bros.-loving public. A glance at a publication like the *Whole Toon Catalog* (whose very title conjures up the counter-culture stance of *The Whole Earth Catalog*) testifies to the recent shift of interest to past series' like *The Beany and Cecil Show*, which is marketed as being 'Created by the great Bob Clampett . . . Brilliant and inventive, much of the adult-oriented punning will go over younger children's heads'. Conventional criteria of quality such as links to cartoon *auteurs* now are applied to previously unvalued animated works like 'classic Raid commercials, Shamus Culhane's Muriel Cigar commercials, the Hamm's Bear, Ez-Pop popcorn and Westinghouse'. Other entries in *The Whole Toon Catalog* testify to the popularity of such 1950s and 1960s 'trash' as 'Colonel Bleep', 'Clutch Cargo' or vintage animated cereal commercials.[33] Within the cultural shift in animatophilia, certain graphic styles, limited animation, the use of public domain music or formulaic advertising jingles, etc. – still hallmarks of cheapness and bad taste within the total culture – now are icons of rarity and desirability among animatophiles.

Animatophilia and related tastes have had an effect on the production of Nickelodeon's *Ren & Stimpy* cartoon series. *Ren & Stimpy* originally was conceived in terms of legitimised forms of children's broadcasting. According to Karen Flischel, Vice-President of Research at Nickelodeon:

> It is made for children . . . "Ren & Stimpy" follows the "Looney Tunes" or "Bullwinkle" model, where there are two levels of appeal – the gross look for kids and the zany humour for the older crowd.[34]

In other words, the series was intended to appeal to both the tastes of children and their parents, who would watch television in a family environment. An early press release described the series as being in 'the tradition of Laurel and Hardy, Abbott and Costello and Flintstone and Rubble . . .'. *Ren & Stimpy* was announced as part of a 90-minute block of new animation, following the highly conventional series *Rugrats* and *Doug*, both of which emphasise family life, non-violence and moral values.[35]

For twelve years Nickelodeon was cable television's only channel devoted solely to children's broadcasting. However, the high cost of animation prevented the network from developing its own original programming. With the takeover of Nickelodeon's parent company Viacom by media tycoon Sumner Redstone in 1987 and the restructuring of the company's debt over the next few years, came a massive infusion of new capital. Redstone invested $40 million into the development of new animated programmes for Nickelodeon.[36] Drawing on the experience of other studios, such as Disney and Warner Bros., whose work has entered the cultural pantheon, Nickelodeon executives realised that animation offers attractive long-term financial prospects. 'We know that kids like animation, and that good quality animation lasts forever', said Nickelodeon president Geraldine Laybourne, '*Looney Tunes* are 50 years old and they still play today'.[37] Nickelodeon wanted what Todd Gitlin would call a 'recombinant' animation series, where older forms are repackaged in slightly different variations from the originals.[38] In the tradition of the Disney and Warner Bros. studios, Nickelodeon sought to find styles and characters that would create a distinctive product identity in order to differentiate its product from the product of other companies.[39] *Ren & Stimpy* was to become a mass-marketable form of cultural capital for Nickelodeon, following the model of other animated series that had attained cultural capital within society at large.

Nickelodeon's Vice President of animation, in charge of the series, was Vanessa Coffey. Coffey, who previously worked on the successful recombinant series *Muppet Babies* and *Teenage Mutant Ninja Turtles* elsewhere, was no stranger to this kind of marketing strategy.

While the owner and distributor of *Ren & Stimpy* had this agenda, it was not completely coherent with the agenda of director John Kricfalusi and his colleagues at Spumco, the manufacturers of the series. As an animatophile, Kricfalusi's work was informed by the tastes of this cultural group. Within the *Ren & Stimpy* series, as in his earlier work on the ill-fated *Mighty Mouse: The New Adventures* or *The New Beany & Cecil Show*, Kricfalusi constantly made reference to the detritus of American culture, and deliberately violated norms of good taste. The first of the *Ren & Stimpy* episodes to be aired, 'Stimpy's Big Day' (4 August 1991), serves as a useful example of this orientation.[40] The story of 'Stimpy's Big Day' is fairly rudimentary. The programme begins with Stimpson J. Cat watching television in a fabulous 1950s-decorated room. Although the viewer cannot see Stimpy's TV screen, one can hear the sound track, which consists exclusively of boings, crashes and honks. Stimpy's partner Ren Hoek,[41] a demented chihuahua, enters and berates Stimpy for watching cartoons, stating 'Cartoons aren't real . . . they're PUPPETS!'. Their conversation is interrupted by the beginning of the *Muddy Mudskipper Show*. Stimpy, a devoted fan, turns from Ren to the screen. During the commercial break, Ren and Stimpy learn of a contest organised by the show's sponsor, Gritty Kitty Litter. The winner of the best poem praising the qualities of Gritty Kitty Litter's product will become eligible for prizes of up to forty-seven million dollars, plus an appearance on the *Muddy Mudskipper Show*. Despite Ren's discouragement, Stimpy sends in his entry and wins.

In Hollywood, Stimpy meets Muddy Mudskipper and goes thorough make-up in preparation for his guest appearance on the show. The appearance is a sensation. At

'Fabulous Fifties' back-ground sketch for The Ren & Stimpy Show

©1991 Nickelodeon

"Cartoons aren't real... they're PUPPETS!"

LOG BIOGRAPHY AND SONG LYRICS .... **Characters** ....

LOG™

Log is the pet rock of the 90's. There's log for girls with beautiful hair to comb, dream date log with dress up fashions, baby-wet-myself-log, frontier log, visible log, invisible log, and anatomically correct log. Accessories include; Log helmet, log underwear, and log lunch box. Log from BLAMMO™."

The LOG theme song

"*What rolls downstairs alone or in pairs,*
  rolls over your neighbors dog?
It's great for a snack, it fits on your back.
  It's log, log. log!
It's log. It's log. It's big, it's heavy, it's wood!
It's log, it's log. It's better than bad. It's good!
Everyone loves the log. Come on and get your log!"

Top   *Storyboard sketch for 'Stimpy's Big Day'*

©1991 Nickelodeon

Bottom   *Kricfalusi's hommage to John Hubley in the 'Log' commercial*

©1991 Nickelodeon

home, Ren's gradual deterioration parallels Stimpy's climb to stardom. Stimpy becomes the star of several television series, but he finally rejects fame and fortune to return home and live with Ren. Ren and Stimpy embrace in friendship, but the narrative ends with Ren berating Stimpy ('You filthy worm!') for giving away forty-seven million dollars.

'Stimpy's Big Day' has a basic narrative that in many ways is unremarkable by children's show standards. It emphasises loyalty between two child-like characters and reinforces popular myths about success and social mores. But, the story of 'Stimpy's Big Day' can also be seen as a post-modernist ironic commentary on the seminal 1950s film *A Star is Born* (1954) through its hip restatements of the high-budget 'serious examination of show business' concerns of Cukor's film into the low-budget, cultural trash form of children's television animation. The relationship between Stimpy and Muddy Mud-skipper recalls that between Esther Blodgett and Norman Main. Stimpy's preparation in the make-up room for his first television appearance seems modelled on the overly enthusiastic styling that Esther endures in *A Star is Born*. Other filmic references include the use of the Hollywood sign and Kirk Douglas's face as icons introducing Hollywood.

Although there is a tendency to recombine elements of cinema for purposes of parody in 'Stimpy's Big Day', Kricfalusi primarily foregrounds his debt to the cultural detritus of past television forms like commercials and low-budget animation. 'Stimpy's Big Day' not only uses public-domain music, which is common given the low budgets of early television animation, it also recycles music from the television show *Truth or Consequences* (1950–58).[42] Stimpy's success on television is marked by his appearance in a string of programmes such as 'Marshall Stimpy', 'Stimpy the Jungle Boy', 'Sergeant Stimpy of the Klondike', 'Ask Dr Stupid' and 'I Love Stimpy', which are derived from past television programming. The episode ends with a sequence where Ren and Stimpy

Storyboard sketch from a John Hubley 'Marky Maypo' commercial

©Storyboard Productions

appear on stage before a curtain to bid the audience farewell, as was customary with the television comedy teams of Martin and Lewis on the *Colgate Comedy Hour* (1950–55) or Burns and Allen on *The George Burns and Gracie Allen Show* (1950–58).

But it is in the handling of narrative and other conventions that the influence of animatophilia becomes most obvious. The story of 'Stimpy's Big Day' is preceded by an advertisement for a fictitious product called 'Log'. Log is a piece of merchandise in the tradition of the Slinky, Silly Putty or the Frisbee, which were created for a juvenile market. Just as these products were fundamentally only a spring, a glob of malleable plastic and a pie plate – Log is just a log. Its fictional manufacture, Blammo, has a name reminiscent of Whammo, the manufacturer of the Frisbee. The 'Log' song combines and spoofs advertising jingles for earlier products, with its children's chorus touting Log's ability to roll down stairs (as did the 'Slinky' song), run over the neighbour's dog or serve as a great snack. The central character in the 'Log' advertisement bears and unmistakable resemblance in both design and petulance to John Hubley's 'Marky Maypo' character used in Maypo cereal advertising campaign of 1956.[43]

A scene depicting Stimpy and Muddy on the *Stimpy and Muddy Show* indicates that Kricfalusi's concern with the cultural detritus of television centres on the conventions of past animation series. Muddy and Stimpy's dialogue consists almost entirely of past clichés and catch phrases from earlier cartoons produced for or shown on, television,

The Stimpy and Muddy Show

'Get your hands out of that pic-i-nic basket!'

including 'Get your hand out of that picnic basket!' from *Yogi Bear*, 'I hate meeses to pieces!' from *Pixie and Dixie*, 'Well blow me down!' from *Popeye* and Elmer Fudd's 'I'm huntun' for a wabbit!' from the *Bugs Bunny* animated films.

While Nickelodeon press releases for *Ren & Stimpy* promised 'the anarchic physical comedy of the great Warner Brothers [sic] cartoons of the 1940s and 1950s' with 'lovable stars of animation',[44] the reception of the product – both positive and negative – emphasised its appeal to animatophiles through the recycling of animation and pop-culture conventions. Richard Gehr, writing in *The Village Voice* noted that the show was 'preceded by *Doug* and *Rugrats*, two sensitive failures in a post-*Simpsons* mode', but also commented that:

> *Ren & Stimpy* . . . is the first TV cartoon aimed at practically everyone *but* children. Underground comics' influence – especially Peter Bagge's *Hate* and Daniel Clowes's *Eightball* – is apparent in Ren's violent mood swings and the show's fabulous 1950s background. The music is nostalgic with generic library stock, bongos and guitars alternating with DNA-embedded classics like Rossini's 'Thieving Magpie', heard in 'Space Madness' as a nod to both *2001* and *A Clockwork Orange*.[45]

Early market research indicated that *Ren & Stimpy* doubled Nickelodeon's rating among children aged two to eleven, increasing the total number of viewers to 1.2 million. It also had one of the largest adult concentrations of any Nickelodeon show. About 35 per cent of *Ren & Stimpy*'s audience was aged eighteen or over. With an eye to increasing audience share, the animation department at Nickelodeon requested that Viacom, owner of Nickelodeon, run the series on Saturday nights on another Viacom network, MTV, which catered to adolescents and young adults. This was done in order to get the MTV audience and bring it to Nickelodeon for Sunday morning *Ren & Stimpy* cablecasts.[46] The result was a near-doubling of viewers to 2.2 million households with 45 per cent

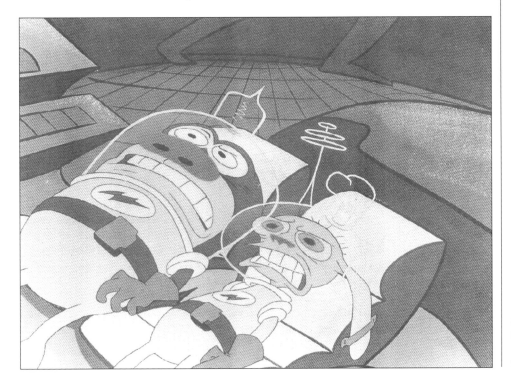

Ren and Stimpy blast off in 'Space Madness'

©1992 Nickelodeon

of the audience being aged eighteen or over.[47] Ren and Stimpy became icons of adolescent culture, with extensive coverage in such magazines as *Dirt* and *Film Threat*. The hip stance of the animatophile trash aesthetic suddenly was absorbed by the larger taste group of adolescent and young adult culture.[48]

Institutional and marketing considerations turned this demographic shift into a problem for Nickelodeon. The corporate cultures of Nickelodeon and MTV, which are highly competitive and occasionally non-cooperative, resulted in *Ren & Stimpy*'s withdrawal from the rock music network.[49] From Nickelodeon's point of view, the eight weeks of MTV cablecast had served its purpose. The series was withdrawn despite MTV's request to prolong it.

While Nickelodeon was committed to children's broadcasting, Kricfalusi and his co-workers increasingly created programming that catered to his cult following among animatophiles and allied youth taste groups addicted to the show's hip references, deliberate bad taste and trash aesthetic. Observed *Ren & Stimpy* writer Bob Camp,

'... Nickelodeon's target market is ten- to twelve-year-olds – but we're not aiming the stuff at little kids ... We want to really push the envelope – disembowelment gags and all'.[50] Nickelodeon looked towards Disney and Warner Bros. as models. Kricfalusi and his staff leaned towards the early *Mad* approach to culture. Spumco staff member Bill Wray maintained: 'If we could find some budding Harvey Kurtzmans who could draw ... they'd have a job here. That's what we're looking for.'[51]

Nickelodeon story editors continually requested script and other modifications, which were resisted by Kricfalusi. Revisions to 'Stimpy's Big Day' included the deletion of a character sniffing kitty litter and use of the word 'Ragu'. The original ending of this episode was to show Stimpy present himself for a smacking. Nickelodeon story editors deemed this to be 'Too masochistic for the younger viewers'. Other suggestions for the changes were resisted by the filmmaker. When Nickelodeon asked why the perspective on a car in 'Stimpy's Big Day' looked as if it were from a second story window, Kricfalusi retorted, 'Because we can't draw cars, let alone perspective'.[52] Kricfalusi removed his name from 'Nurse Stimpy' (1991) because of changes that Nickelodeon urged that he make to the script.[53] Although Standards and Practices at Nickelodeon withheld network approval from such items as the episode titles 'Ren and Stimpy Bugger Christmas' and 'Stimpy's First Fart', Kricfalusi strained harder and harder against these production constraints. Nickelodeon began to receive finished episodes that had to be censored in part.[54] Eventually, two episodes featuring a new character named George Liquor were deemed unsuitable for broadcast altogether. 'Man's Best Friend' featured Ren clubbing George Liquor with an oar in a black-and-white slow motion parody of *Raging Bull* (1980).[55] In 'Dog Show', George Liquor tormented Ren and Stimpy to make them competitive in a dog show. 'Powdered Toast Man' (1992) did make it to air. This was a spoof of animated superhero conventions dating back at least as far as the Fleischer *Superman* series of 1941–42. The 'Powdered Toast Man' episode featured the Pope clinging tenaciously to Powdered Toast Man's buttocks and showed the hero using the Bill of Rights and the Constitution as kindling. When viewers complained to the FCC, Nickelodeon dropped the episode from replay on future air-dates.[56] These shows presented real problems for the cable network. Each episode represented an investment of approximately $400 000. Nickelodeon could not pump money into a programme that did not conform to corporate perceptions regarding the needs of the 55 per cent of its audience that was under eighteen.

This consideration was particularly important in light of the marketing deal Nickelodeon signed with Mattel to license *Ren & Stimpy* products to children – a deal that *Variety* considered 'One of the entertainment industry's major licenses this year'.[57] The licensing of products based on animated characters has been a vital economic factor in the animation industry since the 1920s.[58] Positioning *Ren & Stimpy* outside of a juvenile taste group might have jeopardised the popularity of the series among potential Mattel toy purchasers, adversely affecting the value of the license and the profitability of *Ren & Stimpy* to Nickelodeon. One can only imagine the reaction of Nickelodeon executives when Kricfalusi's partner Bob Camp told the press about Spumco's merchandising ideas:

> We're gonna [sic] do great stuff! Enema bags, butt plugs ... we want really stupid toys, not your regular GI Joe crap. We want toys that leak on you and explode in your face – *real* fun stuff![59]

The Nickelodeon/Spumco tensions were compounded by production problems.

Spumco simply could not manage the delivery of product on time or on budget. A Nickelodeon story editor observed that 'Nickelodeon have one of the hottest shows in the country right now, and a potential merchandising bonanza if they can get new shows to the public. And John [Kricfalusi] is sitting on the shows'.[60] Nickelodeon claimed that Kricfalusi was not only responsible for missing deadlines, but also for going over budget. Kricfalusi appeared intransigent about changing either programme content or his working methods. Instead, the filmmaker blamed Nickelodeon for the missed deadlines through its delays on script approval and story comments.

In light of these problems, Nickelodeon's parent company, Viacom, decided to end the relationship with Kricfalusi. Nickelodeon arranged with Kricfalusi's more compliant partner Bob Camp to take over production of the series by a reorganised Games Production studio for the manufacture of 'Ren & Stimpy Nicktoons'. As Linda Simensky of Nickelodeon observed:

> If the problem were just one of taste and censorship, we probably could have solved it here. The decision to get John [Kricfalusi] off *Ren & Stimpy* was based in part on taste considerations, but mainly was motivated by problems with budget and schedules. We *were* constantly confronted with all sorts of in-jokes and obscure references in *Ren & Stimpy* that staff at Nickelodeon didn't feel were funny or understandable by anyone.[62]

Kricfalusi maintained that the problem was one of taste. In a statement given to *Variety* after he lost control of the series, the director disavowed the scatological humour that characterised *The Ren & Stimpy Show*. A supposedly repentant Kricfalusi said, 'Farts are behind me'.[63]

It would be too much to claim that Kricfalusi's animatophilia was solely responsible for his removal from *The Ren & Stimpy Show*. It was certainly a strong contributing factor. As the aesthetic of a group that continually redefines itself outside the taste norms of mainstream society, animatophilia is an aesthetic alternate to that of mainstream culture. Nickelodeon sought profit by mass-merchandising products to mainstream culture. Consequently, Kricfalusi's fate was probably inevitable.

A preliminary version of this paper was given at the Society for Animation Studies Conference at the California Institute of the Arts in Valencia, California on 24 October 1992. The author is indebted to Don Wallace and Dave Marshall for their insights on taste groups and popular culture and to Linda Simensky for her information about corporate strategies at Nickelodeon. This paper was written at the instigation of Tom Knott of the Canadian Film Institute, who drew the author's attention to the vitality of contemporary television animation and served as an excellent source of research material. Will Ryan's knowledge about *Mad* is rivalled only by Jerry Beck, who remains this author's guru on all things animated. Further assistance was given by Karen Flischel and Bronwyn McElroy of Nickelodeon, Harvey Deneroff of the *Animation Report*, Karl Cohen, Bill Mikulak, Susan Kelly, Hank Sartin, Myron Waldman, Sybil del Gaudio, Ron Magliozzi, Will Straw, Chris Faulkner and Janet Staiger.

Notes

1.   Wheeler Winston Dixon, 'Interview with John Kricfalusi', *Film Criticism*, vol. XVII no. 1(Fall 1992): 39.

2.   Richard Gehr, 'You Filthy Worms! Ren and Stimpy's Creator Gives Hell to Nickelodeon', *The Village Voice* (17 November 1992): 58. 'Who, Where, Ren?' *Entertainment Weekly* (20 November 1992): 8. Other comments include: 'It's like someone saying, "We like this Little Tramp character, but let's get rid of that Chaplin guy" ', from David Silverman, quoted in 'Cheers 'n' Jeers', *TV Guide* (17 October 1992): 4. Elsewhere, Kricfalusi's loss of the series has been likened to a similar experience early in Walt Disney's career, with Nickelodeon, by implication, cast in the role of

the odious producer Charles Mintz. Harvey Deneroff, 'Of Bluth and Spumco', *The Animation Report*, vol. 1, no. 7 (September 1992): 2.

3. Alison Butler, 'New Film Histories and the Politics of Location', *Screen*, vol. 33, no. 4 (Winter 1992): 414.

4. Herbert J. Gans, *Popular Culture and High Culture* (New York: Basic Books, 1974), 7–9.

5. Pierre Bordieu, *Distinction: A Social Critique of the Judgement of Taste* (Cambridge: Harvard University Press, 1984), 114–120.

6. Ford, a key figure in the legitimation of animation, curated the 1981 Whitney show and programmed the influential 1979 *Cartoonal Knowledge* series at New York's Thalia theatre. Jay Cocks, 'The World Jones Made', *Time* (17 December 1973): 17; 'The Hollywood Cartoon', special issue of *Film Comment*, vol. 11, no. 1 (January–February 1975).

7. The former was taught by Leonard Maltin, the latter by the author.

8. David Bordwell and Kristin Thompson, *Film Art: An Introduction* (Reading, Mass.: Addison-Wesley, 1979), 17, 22, 218; *Film Art: An Introduction*, 2nd edn (New York: Alfred A Knopf, 1986), 14, 19, 148, 168, 176; *Film Art: An Introduction*, 3rd edn (New York: McGraw-Hill, 1990), 21, 24, 174–175, 185, 253, 301, 347–353; *Film Art: An Introduction*, 4th edn (New York: McGraw-Hill, 1993), 10, 24–25, 29, 122, 135, 158, 163–64, 167, 181, 200–211, 221–222, 239, 304, 306, 328, 331, 345, 361, 402, 405, 417-424, 446.

9. Christopher Finch, *The Art of Walt Disney* (New York: Abrams, 1973); Frank Thomas and Ollie Johnston, *Disney Animation: The Illusion of Life* (New York: Abbeville, 1981); John Canemaker, *Treasure of Disney Animation* (New York: Abbeville, 1982); Patrick Brion, *Tex Avery: Les Dessins* (Paris: Éditions Nathan Image, 1988).

10. Shamus Culhane, *Talking Animals and Other People* (New York: St. Martin's Press, 1986); Chuck Jones, *Chuck Amuck* (New York: Farrar, Straus, Giroux, 1990).

11. Gans, 94–100. Within this article, I will not explore the more politically charged notions of resistance or subversion employed in many cultural studies examinations of subculture.

12. I am indebted to Don Wallace for this insight. Ian Angus observes, '. . . commodities are produced for "Individuals" who define themselves through their difference from other production groups'. Ian H. Angus, 'Circumscribing Post-Modern Culture', *Cultural Politics in Contemporary America*, eds Ian Angus and Sut Jhally (New York: Routledge, 1989), 101.

13. Pierre Bordieu, *In Other Words: Essays Towards a Reflexive Sociology*, trans. Matthew Adamson (Stanford: Stanford University Press, 1990), 132.

14. Don Wallace, *Consumption, Class and Taste: The Construction of the Market for Popular Literature*. Unpublished thesis (Carleton University, 1992), 57. It should be noted that one man's hipster is another man's nerd. Hipness or nerdness lie in the eye of the beholder. For example, the hippest of a youth taste group might appear as just another sulking adolescent to other taste groups. Hipness varies from one taste group to another. However, the hip are recognised as arbiters of taste norms within their particular taste group.

15. I am indebted to Dave Marshall for this insight.

16. While this article centres on the importance of 'hipness', other factors come into play in defending taste groups and similar social organisations. These will not be dealt with directly in this study. In a critique of this article, William Mikulak correctly observes:

> There are numerous specialised taste/consumption/fandom groups that overlap in today's popular culture landscape . . . They each encompass a wide range of modes of relating the shared interest beyond a mere knowledge gradient . . . There are differing degrees of sincerity toward the subject ranging from zealous religiosity toward canonical texts to high campiness. Psychic immersion varies from passive spectatorship to intensive role playing, complete with costumes. Fans may appropriate favourite characters for use in their own narratives and art objects, extending the fictive universe to suit their needs. Sometimes it seems as if rather than opposing the mainstream, they choose to ignore it while in their insular fan communities, focusing vast energies on arguing the fine points of each other's interpretation of the subject matter.
>
> Thus, while you are no doubt correct in arguing that taste groups respond to the main-streaming of the marginal tastes by seeking even more marginal subjects, more insular groups may use esoterica as a means to make distinctions among group members. Here I see a parallel between animatophile taste groups and academic researchers intent on uncovering ever more

obscure corners of filmdom on which to stake their claims as experts.

William Mikulak, letter to the author, 15 January 1993.

17. See, for example, Basil Wolverton, 'Mad Hats', *Mad* #36 and 'Mad Reader', *Mad* #11, reprinted in Maria Reidelbach, *Completely Mad: A History of the Comic Book Magazine* (Boston: Little, Brown & Co., 1991), 190, 199.

18. Harvey Kurtzman and Will Elder, 'Woman Wonder!', *Mad* #10 in Reidelbach, 34–35; 'Mickey Rodent!' *Mad* #13 in Reidelbach, 29; 'Outer Sanctum' in Williams Gaines (ed.), *The Bedside Mad* (NY: Signet, 1959), 6–29; 'Robinson Crusoe' in Gaines, 158–178; Les Daniels, *Comix: A History of Comic Books in America* (NY: Bonzanza Books, 1971), 61–70. Similar satires were done by Wally Wood ('Batboy and Rubin' and 'Flesh Garden'), Jack Davis, ('High Noon') and others.

19. Richard D. Lyons, 'Harvey Kurtzman Is Dead at 68; Cartoonist Was Creator of Mad', *The New York Times* (23 February 1993): B7.

20. *Comix*, 83–90; Frederic Wertham, *Seduction of the Innocent* (New York: Rinehart and Winston, 1954).

21. One indicator of this mass popularity can be seen by the increasing acceptance of American television series based on comics, beginning with *Dick Tracy* (1950–51), *The Adventures of Superman* (1952–57), *Flash Gordon* (1953–54) and *Steve Canyon* (1958–60). The proliferation and longevity of such shows peaked in the 1960s with *Dennis the Menace* (1959–63), *Hazel* (1961–66), *The Addams Family* (1964–66), *Batman* (1966–68), *Tarzan* (1966–69) and *My World and Welcome to It* (1969–72), before tapering off in the 1970s with *Wonder Women* (1976–79) and *Buck Rogers in the 25th Century* (1979–81). Occasionally, these programs reinforced condescending attitudes toward their comic sources by emphasising the 'camp' nature of the work. This was particularly stressed in the *Batman* series.

22. Pierre Couperie and Maurice C. Horn, *Bande Dessinée et Figuration Narrative* (Paris: Societe Civile D'Etudes et de Recherches des Littératures Dessinéesm, 1967), reprinted as *A History of the Comic Strip* (New York: Crown, 1968), 228–252.

23. See, for example, Robert C. Allen, *Vaudeville and Film 1895–1915: A Study in Media Interaction. (New York: Arno, 1980); Erik Barnouw, The Magician and the Cinema* (New York: Oxford University Press, 1981) and C.W. Ceram, *The Archaeology of the Cinema* (New York: Harcourt, Brace & World, 1965).

24. Frank Tashlin embodied an important transitional point in the study of animation, largely because his career spanned live action and animated films. His reputation spread as early as Jean-Luc Godard's appreciation in *Cahiers du cinéma*, reprinted in *Godard on Goddard*, ed. Tom Milne (New York: Viking, 1972), 35–36, 57–59; the article by Roger Tailleur in *Positif* no. 29 (1958) translated by Paul Willemen as 'Anything Goes' in *Frank Tashlin* (Edinburgh: Edinburgh Film Festival, 1973), 17–31; Ian Cameron, 'Frank Tashlin and the New World', *Movie*, no. 16 (Winter 1968–69): 38–39; Mike Barrier, 'Interview' *Frank Tashlin*, 45–53, etc. Similar consideration of other animation *auteurs* can be found in Mike Barrier, 'Screenwriter for a Duck', *Funnyworld*, no. 21: 9–14; Jeff Missine, 'Walter Lantz: Cartune-ist', *Mindrot*, no. 10 (20 April 1978): 12–21; Joe Adamson, *Tex Avery: King of Cartoons* (New York: Popular Library, 1975) and *The Walter Lantz Story with Wood Woodpecker and Friends* (New York: G. P. Putnam & Sons, 1985); and in many of the essays in *The American Animated Cartoon*, ed. Danny Peary and Gerald Peary (New York: Dutton, 1980).

25. Leonard Maltin, 'TV Animation', *Film Comment*, vol. 11, no. 1 (January–February 1975): 77. See also, Greg Ford and Richard Thompson, ' Chuck Jones'; John Canemaker, 'Winsor McCay' and 'Grim Natwick'; Mark Langer, 'Max and Dave Fleischer'; Jonathan Rosenbaum, 'Walt Disney' and 'Tex Avery' and Mark Kausler, 'Tom and Jerry' in ibid., 21–38, 44–56, 57–61, 64–75.

26. Patrick Brion, *Tom and Jerry*, trans. Annette Michelson (NY: Crescent/Nathan, 1987).

27. This interest in cels parallels that of an earlier period when Disney's work was held in high regard by both critics and the public. A critic in the 1940s unobserved, 'The original drawings and paintings of Walt Disney's "Dumbo" are already being shown in the Harlow, Keppel & Co. gallery and are interesting the usual public. This is "art for the people" very distinctly and has been so from the beginning'. With a lessening in interest by high culture critics for Disney films, came a diminishment of the market for animation art. Cel art no longer was sold in galleries. For years, animation art was relatively valueless within total culture and became almost exclusively marketed within animatophile taste group. For example, in the late 1970s, one dealer offered original animation drawings of Bugs and Elmer from *What's Opera Doc?* (1957) for $20 each,

while Gallery Lainzberg offered cels and animation drawings from $20, including customer matting. Even taking account of inflation's effect, these are bargains in terms of today's prices for such items. H. McB. 'Attractions in the Galleries', *The New York Sun* (31 October 1941): n.p.; Timothy White, 'From Disney to Warner Bros: The Critical Shift', unpublished paper, Society from Cinema Studies Conference, Washington D.C., 28 May 1990; Brian Tischler, letters to the author, 5 and 13 December, 1978; Gallery Lainzberg advertisement, *Mindrot*, no. 7 (15 June 1977): 19.

28. Rita Reif, 'Are Cartoon Stills Still a Hot Ticket'? *The New York Times* (12 April 1992): 33.

29. Rita Reif, 'Animation Auction is Questioned', *The New York Times* (17 October 1992): 17.

30. Silver Stone Gallery advertisement, *Storyboard/The Art of Laughter* (Dec./Jan. 1992–93): 38.

31. Howard Lowery, quoted in Joanne Kirschner, 'Collecting Toons for Fun & Profit', *Rapport*, vol. 17 no. 2 (December 1992–January 1993): 9.

32. John Halas, *Masters of Animation* (Topsfield Mass.: Salem House, 1987): 9.

33. *Animated Commercials #1*, *Animated Commercials #5*, *Beany and Cecil*, *Clutch Cargo*, vol. 1 and *Colonel Bleep* vol. 1, *The Whole Toon Catalog* no. 8 (November 1992): 18, 20, 29.

34. Flischel, interview with author, 6 September 1992.

35. 'Nickelodeon to Debut Original Block Sunday, August 11 Featuring: *Rugrats*, *The Ren and Stimpy Show* and *Doug*', *Anymator* (May 1991): 2–3.

36. Viacom International owns MTV, VH-1, Showtime and a number of syndicated series such as *The Cosby Show* and *Roseanne*. Nickelodeon had 55 million subscribers and earned $169 million in revenue during 1991. Mark Langler and Geoffrey Smith, 'The MTV Tycoon', *Business Week* (21 September 1992): 56–62.

37. Daniel Cerone, 'Eye on TV', *The Star-Ledger* (10 August 1991): 23.

38. Todd Gitlin, *Inside Prime Time* (NY: Pantheon Books, 1983): 77–85.

39. 'We were looking for a Nicktoons style with a Nicktoons identity.' Linda Simensky, interview with the author, 16 October 1992.

40. 'Stimpy's Big Day' and 'The Big Shot!' will be treated as one episode in this article. Both were broadcast as consecutive halves of the same series episode. 'The Big Shot!' is simply the concluding half of 'Stimpy's Big Day's narrative.

41. Terms for bodily exudates are common in Kricfalusi's series. Hoek is pronounced 'hork', which is a slang term for the expectoration of phlegm. The first four letters of Kricfalusi's company name – Spumco – suggests a slang term for semen. Early in 'Stimpy's Big Day', Ren eats the contents of Stimpy's kitty litter box in an act of coprophilia. At the end of 'The Big Shot!', Stimpy exhibits his collection of 'magic nose goblins'. 'I picked them myself', proudly says the character, displaying his nose to the viewer. Freud has observed that much humour '. . . includes what is *common* to both sexes and to which the feeling of shame extends – that is to say, what is excremental in the most comprehensive sense. This is, however, the sense covered by sexuality in childhood, an age at which there is, as it were, a cloaca within which what is sexual and what is excremental are barely or not at all distinguished', Sigmund Freud, *Jokes and Their Relation to the Unconscious*, trans. by James Strachey (NY: W.W. Norton, 1963), 97–98. While *The Ren & Stimpy Show* serves as an excellent subject for psychoanalytic analysis, such analysis will only be suggested by this study.

42. Dave Mackay, 'Sour Persimmons # 1', *Apatoons #63* (June–July 1992), n.p. Use of recycled material such as jingles or theme music from television is common in contemporary animation. Another example is the use of music from *The Price is Right* in John Lasseter's *Tin Toy* (1988).

43. Later 'Log' commercials included *Log for Girls*, *High Fashion Log for Girls*, *Action Log*, *G.I. Log*, *The Visible Log* and *Anatomically Correct Log*. These spots parodied such ads and products as *GI Joe* and *The Visible Man*. Other Kricfalusi ads included the breakfast cereal spoofs 'Powdered Toast' and 'Sugar Frosted Milk', which stays lumpy, even in cereal.
The Maypo commercials featured the characters Marky Maypo and his Uncle Ralph and concerned the attempts by Uncle Ralph to get his nephew to eat a new maple-flavoured breakfast cereal. Each commercial concluded with the line, 'I want my Maypo!' which became one of the most successful advertising slogans of the 1950s. These spots were produced by John and Faith Hubley, directed by John Hubley and animated by Emery Hawkins, for the advertising agency of Fletcher Richards, Calkins & Holdin, Inc. and their client Heublin, Inc. At least four separate Maypo advertisements were created by Hubleys' Storyboard Productions. Sybil del Gaudio, interview with the author, 1 February 1993; Alice C. Wolf, *The History of American Television*

Commercials 1947–77, *Millimeter*, vol. 5, no. 4 (April 1977): 22–24, 27, 46, 58–61.

44. Bronwyn Smith, 'Animated Duo Takes to the Road on Nickelodeon for the Premier of *The Ren & Stimpy Show*' (25 July 1991): 2; Bronwyn McElroy, 'Hey, Man, *The Ren & Stimpy Show* Premieres All-New Episodes when the Nicktoons Hit Begins Airing on "Snick" ' (Press Release, 15 August, 6 July 1992): 1.

45. Richard Gehr, 'Maim That Toon', *The Village Voice* (8 October 1991): 49.

46. Simensky, 16 October 1992.

47. Flischel interview, Stefan Kanfer, 'Loonier Toon Tales', *Time* (13 April 1992): 79; Mark Robichaux, 'For Nickelodeon, Crude Toon Is Big Hit', *The Wall Street Journal* (27 January 1992): B1.

48. Ren and Stimpy were on the cover of *Utne Readers*, (October–November) 1992; A.A. Perry, 'The Great Unwritten rules of Comedy', *Dirt*, no. 2 (1992): 12; Christine Gore, 'Celling Out', *Film Threat*, no. 7, (December 1992): 22–25, 28, 39; Alice Pinch and Stiffy Miller, *The Screechin' Ren & Stimpy Episode Log* (ibid.): 26–7. The series is used in the marketing of other adolescent culture products attempting to position themselves within changing parameters of hipness. Among the first signs of *Ren & Stimpy* losing hip status is the ad copy for Slave Labour Graphics: 'Ren & Stimpy? Bah! Milk and Cheese. Dairy Products Gone Bad! They're Drunk! They're Violent! They're Dairy products Gone Bad and They're rampaging their way across America! Get your copy of Milk & Cheese before they too become hip & trendy'! Slave Labour Graphics advertisement, *Film Threat*, no. 8 (February 1993): 12.

49. Linda Simensky, interview with the author, 3 October 1992.

50. Pam and Doug Murray, 'Ren & Stimpy's Pals', *Comics Scene*, no. 28 (August 1992): 10.

51. 'Bill Wray Interview', *Pure Images*, no. 5 (1992): n.p.

52. 'Revision made', memo from Will McRobb to John Kricfalusi, 2 April 1991 and 'Revisions in Contention', memo from Will McRobb to John Kricfalusi, with annotations by John Kricfalusi, 2 April 1991 (private collection).

53. The credits eventually read 'Directed by Raymond Spum', Cerone, *Toontown Terrors*: 90.

54. Will McRobb, memo to Libby Simon, 2 October 1991 (private collection). In 'Stimpy's Big Day', a microphone that was inserted into Stimpy's mouth was deemed to phallic: in 'Space Madness', lines emulating dialogue from *Gilda* ('You're not like the others, Johnnie, you hate the same things I hate . . . perfume-smelling things . . . lacy things, things with curly hair') were altered; in 'Stimpy's Inventions', a scene where Ren licks Stimpy's armpit was cut, etc. Pinch and Miller: 26.

55. At the time of writing this article, it is rumoured in one trade publication that an edited and re-animated version of this episode is being prepared by Games Production. Karl Cohen, 'Oh No, Not Another 'Ren and Stimpy' Update!', *Asifa-San Francisco Bulletin* (March 1993): 6.

56. Daniel Cerone, 'Ren and Stimpy and Its Creator: A Parting of Ways', *Los Angeles Times* (28 September 1992): F12; Jennifer Pendleton, 'Gearing Sides with 'Ren Artist', *Daily Variety* (25 September 1992): 22; Dan Persons, 'Ren & Stimpy', *Cinefantastique*, vol. 23 no. 5 (February 1993): 5. The abandonment of replay dates only applied to the US market. 'Powdered Toast Man' was aired over the Canadian cable network Much Music on 4 March 1993. Much Music caters to an adolescent, rather than a juvenile audience.

57. Jennifer Pendleton, 'Nick Faves Launch New Mattel Line', *Daily Variety* (12 June 1992): 3, 10.

58. Walt Disney and Pat Sullivan were particularly successful practioners of product licensing. John Canemaker, *Felix the Cat: The Twisted Tale of the World's Most Famous Cat* (New York: Pantheon, 1991), 64–65, 71, 85, 88; *Annual Report Fiscal Year Ended 28 September 1940* (Burbank: Walt Disney Productions, 1940).

59. Murray & Murray: 12.

60. 'Ren & Stimpy and Its Creator: A parting of the Ways': F12.

61. Persons, 60.

62. Linda Simensky, interview with the author, 14 October 1992.

63. Daniel Cerone, 'Ren & Stimpy Creator Fired', *Los Angeles Times* (26 September 1992): D1; Jennifer Pendleton, '*Ren & Stimpy* goes to camp; Kricfalusi sings new toon', *Variety* (5 October 1992): 26.

14

Francis Bacon and Walt Disney revisited

Simon Pummell

Francis Bacon and Walt Disney is the provocative title of an essay by John Berger.[1] The provocation is in the link between 'High Art' and 'Low Art' as seen by the bourgeois art world and Berger uses the link to question the quality of Bacon's work. However, he does so in such detail and in such a way that he reveals a potential link far more complex and suggestive than the dismissive intent of his essay. Berger is always incisive and he uncovers connections where previously cultural assumptions concealed the tracks.

The opening of the essay brings together three strands of evidence in a manner clearly designed for ironic effect. He describes Bacon's subject matter in a way which emphasises the violence and degradation he sees in them: 'A carcass with splints on it. A man on a chair smoking. One walks past his painting as if through some gigantic institution...', and he punctuates the list with evidence of Bacon's high standing in the art world: 'According to the magazine *Connaissance des Arts*, Bacon became the first of the top ten most important artists' while also ceding:

> Bacon is a painter of extraordinary skill, a master. Nobody who is familiar with the problems of figurative oil-painting can remain unimpressed with his solutions. Such mastery which is rare is the result of great dedication and extreme lucidity about the medium.

The third strand of evidence is quotation from Bacon himself, such as: 'I've always hoped to put things over as directly as I possibly can and perhaps if a thing comes across directly, they feel that it is horrific'.

After four quotations from Bacon, Berger summarises Bacon's aims as follows:

> The appearance of the body suffers the accident of involuntary marks being made upon it. Its distorted image then comes across directly onto the nervous system of the viewer (or painter), who rediscovers the appearance of the body through or beneath the marks it bears.

This summary needs some examination. The four quotations used by Berger to represent

Bacon's views are taken from *Interviews with Francis Bacon 1962–79*.[2] We hear Bacon's struggle to define his painting aims and practices, which are not reducible to any bald statement of unambiguous practice or intention. They reveal something far more productive: the process of searching and Bacons's terms and language need to be read in conjunction with the paintings. At the beginning of interview five, Bacon says:

> I think that in our previous discussions, when we've talked about the possibility of making appearances out of something which was not illustration, I've over talked about it. Because, in spite of theoretically longing for the image to be made up of irrational marks inevitably illustration has to come into it to make certain parts of the head and face which if one left them out, one would only be making an abstract design.

The last of the four quotations cited by Berger can be re-read by putting it back into the context of the sequence of interviews from which it was culled, and such a reading casts some light on Berger's approach to Bacon:

> What I want to do is to distort the thing far beyond appearance but in the distortion to bring it back to a recording of the appearance.

If read as Berger wishes, this statement is merely a statement of the artist's will to distort, to force the viewers to find their way back to some pre-existent, unitary appearance. As Berger's summary states:

> [the viewer] rediscovers the appearance of the body through or beneath the marks it bears.

It is 'through' or 'beneath' which is significant as it ignores the profound transformation of the word 'appearance' that Bacon's paintings strive for and that elsewhere he articulates more clearly as an aim. Bacon attempts to express this a number of times in his interviews:

> . . . It's the violence also of the suggestions within the image itself which can only be conveyed through paint. When I look at you across the table, I don't only see you but I see a whole emanation which has to do with personality and everything else. And to put that over in a painting, as I would like to be able to do in a portrait, means that it would appear violent in paint.

> . . . and it needs a sort of magic to coagulate colour and form so that it gets the equivalent of appearance, the appearance that you see at any moment, because so called appearance is only riveted for one moment as that appearance. In a second you may blink your eyes or turn your head slightly and you look again and the appearance has changed. I mean, appearance is like a continuously floating thing. . .

> Well, its a complicated thing. I very often think of people's bodies that I've known, I think of the contours of those bodies that have particularly affected me, but then they're grafted onto Muybridges bodies. I manipulate the Muybridge bodies into the form of the bodies I have known. But of course, in my case, with this disruption all of the time of the image – or distortion or whatever you like to call it – it's an elliptical way of coming to the appearance of the particular body . . .

In response to a *joint examination* of how often Bacon had been seeing people he painted, the interviewer David Sylvester (D.S.) says:

So, although you weren't actually painting from them, you might have seen them the night before and that would have made the memory of them vivid again. It all suggests that really, the photographs are much less important than your memory of how people are.

This all suggests that the profound transformation Bacon seeks is to introduce obsession with time and change into the single image of traditional oil painting. To Bacon, appearance is inextricable from time and change and so, memory and mortality. Before we look at how Berger erases this and his grounds for a link with Disney, I wish to examine an example of Bacon's work in the light of the issues raised here.

Triptych August 1972, Tate Gallery[3]

I have chosen the triptych in the Tate partly because it is so accessible and also well known so it is likely any reader will have experienced the painting first hand. It is also one of Bacon's finest paintings and as a focal point for discussing his methods it incorporates much that would allow it to be posed as a representative Bacon painting.

It is a particularly symmetrical triptych. The outer panels appear to be two moments in the same dramatic situation – a man sits on a chair (he appears to be George Dyer), while the central panel is of two men having sex, clearly based on a Muybridge plate.[4] So if the two outer plates are based on a mixture of memory and presence, the centre works by the mixture of grafting memory on to a found image selected for its general and formal resonance.

The Muybridge quotation and the sequential relationship between the two outer panels immediately introduce time as a formal catalyst. One of the first things that reinforces the implication of time is the calligraphic quality of Bacon's brush marks, underlined by his remark, 'Painting has nothing to do with colouring surfaces'.[5] The paint is also often laid on so thinly as to be simultaneously there and not there; a trace rather than a definite presence. So to begin to understand Bacon's painting one can make reference to Rawson's work on drawing:

> The curved stroke, the variety of which is immense, is based upon the concept of change; for a curved stroke is drawn by an instrument that is continuously changing its direction across the ground. The qualities of curves and their content of experience of change, are one of the most important sources of artistic vitality, for they extend the meaning of drawn forms via the suggestion of change into the dimension of time.[6]

If one compares the centre panel of the painting to its reference in Muybridge, it is this transformation of two distinct clear-edged forms into an interpenetrating set of calligraphic curved forms which is striking. And the power of the image derives from the way in which this dissolution of the form into a set of traces of movement still manages to imply a full range of anatomical facts. It is this which gives the impression not of another set of boring self-referential graphic marks but of the mutability of flesh itself. And additional energy is added to the image by certain almost free-floating marks clearly executed very quickly. All this is set against very cool rectilinear framing devices in black, grey and white, painted in a meticulous flat way, revealing no movement of brush or hand whatsoever.

It is this mixture of graphic implications which John Russell seems to be driving at, although succumbing to mystification, when he discusses Leiris who opposed straight and curve, dexter and sinister as mythical elements of beauty (in passages particularly prized by Bacon).

> The equivocal couplings of which Leiris speaks are figured directly in paintings like the *Two Figures* of 1953 and although the popular idea of Bacon is, one might say, all sinister and no dexter, the poignancy of his distortions comes precisely from the fact that the straight line is present, unseen as the complement of the curved line . . .[7]

This mixture of quietude and frenzy, monumental stasis and the slightness of continuous motion is at the heart of Bacon's work and the source of it is examined more thoroughly later in this paper.

The mix of free marks and control and of abstractions and anatomical information is the set of a master and the route to the solution can be traced through successive transformation of the same Muybridge frame.[8]

The route is of course not some simple progress from problem to solution. But to look at each is to understand the balance between the distortions of mutability and the beauty recaptured from it, and why the 1972 *Triptych* is a masterpiece. Each stroke sits on the canvas with no sense of its being wilful: the distortion is beautiful as well as conveying a poignancy born of the destructive inevitability of flux. While in a canvas such as *3 Studies of Figures on Beds* (1972), the distortion lacks such a luminous beauty and so is open to the criticism of reductiveness (Russell tellingly comments on the failure as 'mere sensationalism, flat and cartoonish'). And if this balance is reached in *Triptych August 1972*, it is reached at a different level of formal complexity/freedom in *Two Figures 1953*. But what Russell says of this canvas is worth considering in relation to the 1972 *Triptych*:

> Bacon has not negotiated . . . the tricky moment at which complete definition of the body is succeeded by complete definition of an individual face.

By 1972, Bacon appears to have triumphed over the problem, typically by a lateral move. The shifting bodies in erotic embrace have faces of even more ambiguity, but some of the answers are waiting in the wings.

The outer panels are clearly the same man, and so must relate to the portrait genre, the aim of which is concisely described by Gombrich as:

> . . . there is a hierarchy that extends from the permanent frame of the body to the fleeting ripple of a mobile expression. Somewhere within this hierarchic sequence we must locate what we experience as the more permanent expression or disposition that constitutes for us such an important element in the 'essence' of a personality.[9]

Bacon's point of concentration along this hierarchy clearly takes far more serious account the 'fleeting ripple' than most portrait painting. And at a psychological level, this raises the question of the construction of a stable, unified ego.

The images of Dyer are both provisional (each is read against the other) and fragmented, yet they also have some tranquillity. The forms again are articulated in beautifully interlocking curves which owe more to Michelangelo's annotation of musculature than any previous modernist fragmentation. And when the figure is incomplete, it seems not to be injury, but a lack of a trace. A concept of trace, so central to the deconstruction theories of the mid-1970s to the early 1980s and its attempts to discover movement and flux in traditional philosophical systems, is prefigured in the way Bacon is attempting to storm the citadel of 'High Art Oil Painting'.

> Fact leaves its ghost is another favourite saying of Bacon's and in these portraits the ghost and the fact are both present and in such a way that no one can tell them apart. [10]

To read the two-portrait frames one must:

(1) Accept and appreciate the significance of his line.

(2) Accept a semi-transparent film of oil paint as simultaneously 'there and not there'. It should be noted here that in Berger's summary, which was the departure point of our examination, '[the viewer] rediscovers the appearance of the body through or beneath the marks it bears' is inapplicable. Bacon's paintings constitute appearance entirely through such marks. The idea of such an originary appearance which is overlaid by the textuality of brushmarks is practically invalid when confronted by a painting such as *Triptych August 1972*. It is an approach also theoretically open to attack by any post-Derridean system of analysis.

(3) Be prepared to read the two images against each other (as in a film cut or subliminal film frames).

(4) Come to terms with the psychological implication of this decentring of a subject of a portrait.

And the sense of George Dyer that this process gives the viewer can be grafted back onto the centre frame – the figures have faces as clearly as a film actor who momentarily turns away from the camera or a lover who is walking away. The experience for the viewer is dynamic, dialectical, almost cinematic.

All this suggests that the transformation Bacon seeks is to allow the implications of movement in time in traditional oil painting. To Bacon, appearance is inextricable from time and change and so from memory and mortality. The difference between expressionistic distortion and this process is revealed clearly in Bacon's wavering between two nouns:

> Disruption all the time of the image . . . or distortion.

Although one can distort a static image, one needs a flow – in this case temporal – to disrupt it. It is this fundamental obsession which Berger erases:

> There are no alternatives offered in Bacon's world, no ways out. Consciousness of time or change does not exist. Bacon often starts working on a painting from an image taken from a photograph. A photograph records for a moment. In the process of painting, Bacon seeks the accident which will turn that moment into all moments. In life the moment which ousts all preceding and following moments is most commonly a moment of physical pain.

This statement, which is at the heart of Berger's assessment of Bacon, is reductive in a number of ways. As we have seen, it ignores the transformative effect of Bacon's formal process and here it attempts to give the action a false dramatic effect. It does so by assuming Bacon's paintings represent 'moments' and that his accidents are to create that moment. But when asked about that ambition by his interviewer Sylvester, it is significant that what Berger calls 'moment', Bacon calls 'image':

> No, I don't now. I suppose as I get older I feel I want to cover wider areas. I don't

think I have that other feeling any longer – perhaps because I hope to go on painting until I die and of course, if you did the one perfect image, you would never do anything more.

Berger's equation of image and moment is supported by his reference to the painter's use of photography. Further examination of the Sylvester interviews reveals something almost diametrically opposed to Berger's analysis. The first and clearest point is that a major source of photographs for Bacon is Muybridge's work:

> Well, of course they were an attempt to make a recording of human motion – a dictionary, in a sense. And the thing of doing series may possibly have come from looking at those books of Muybridge with the stages of movement shown in separate photographs.

Thus each photograph is part of a sequence recording movement in progress like a strip of film frames, and each frame derives its meaning in its relationship to the others. In fact, they are as far removed as possible from the nature of photography Berger refers to. So, rather than reinforcing the idea of a single moment, Bacon's painting activity always seeks not to make that moment archetypal but to re-integrate the image with a reality that 'is like a continuously floating thing'. The central influence of Muybridge's photographs informs his use of other photographs:

> But I don't only look at Muybridge's photographs of the figure. I look all the time at photographs in magazines of footballers and boxers and all that kind of thing – especially boxers. And I also look at animal photographs all the time because animal movements and human movements are continually linked in my imagery of human movement.

Again, the use of the image is dialectical: the photograph is in no way fetishised as a moment of supreme, self-identifiable significance. In fact, is explicitly seen as a trace, which is meaningless without the activity of reinvention in the memory:

> It's true to say I couldn't attempt to do a portrait from photographs of somebody I didn't know. But, if I both knew them and have photographs of them, I find it easier to work than actually having their presence in the room. I think that, if I have the presence of the image there, I am not able to drift so freely as I am able to through the photographic image.

D.S. 'Are you saying that painting is almost a way of bringing somebody back, that the process of painting is almost like the process of recalling?'

F.B. 'I am saying it. And I think the methods by which this is done are so artificial that the model before you, in my case, inhibits the artificiality by which this thing can be brought back.'

To begin to understand this we must try and see afresh the demands of traditional portrait painting on the sitter, demands which were carried over into photography, initially for technical reasons. But, later, as deference to our received notions from portrait painting continued; that is, that of a stable portrait face as a matrix on which expression is an overlay, it manifests itself in a hierarchy of likeness from studio portrait to snapshot. Imagine the effect of having a rigid 'model' would have on the recreation of a face described by Gombrich:

> In real life we are aided in this, as we are aided in the perception of space and colour, by the effect of movement in time. We see the relatively mobile ones and thus form a provisional estimate of their interaction.[11]

Having examined the interaction of the panels of the *Triptych August 1972* it allows us to re-assess Berger's assertion that they are symptomatic of the extreme alienation of all Bacon's work:

> The triptych form, in which each figure is isolated within his own canvas and yet visible to others, is symptomatic.

Underlying this comment is the assumption that the triptych is somehow a unified dramatic form. To expect dramatic interrelation between the figures in Bacon's triptychs is as misplaced as to expect a figure in a film strip to reach out to characters in adjoining frames.[12] Such an expectation simply serves to conceal the formal and temporal relationship that is discoverable between each unit of the triptych.

D.S. 'You paint a lot in series, of course.'

F.B. 'I do, partly because I see every image all the time in a shifting way and almost in shifting sequences. So that one can take it from a more or less what is called ordinary figuration to a very far point.'

D.S. 'When you're doing a series, do you paint them one after another or do you work on them concurrently?'

F.B. 'I do them one after the other. One suggests the other.'

'Cobwebs on the screen'[13]

> *There are two main approaches to animation. The first is known as straight ahead action because the animator works straight ahead from his first drawing after another, getting new ideas as he goes along, until he reaches the end of the scene . . . Both the drawings and the action have a fresh slightly zany look, as the animator keeps the whole process very creative.*[14]

The juxtaposition of the above quotation with Bacon's description of working in series forces many dissimilarities to the fore: European high art, American cartoon art; reticence, brashness. But, there remains a residue of basic similarity in technical approach. Only by looking at the reason for similar technical formal approaches can we review Berger's conclusion about Bacon and Disney:

> Both men make propositions about the alienated behaviour of our societies; and both, in a different way, persuade the viewer to accept what is . . . The surprising formal similarities of their work – the way limbs are distorted . . . The overall shapes of bodies, the relation of figures to background and to one another, the use of neat tailor's clothes, the gesture of hands, the range of colours used – are the result of both men having complementary attitudes to the same crisis.

He goes on to argue that their complementary attitude is acceptance of alienation. On the basis of our review of his description of Bacon's painting we can tentatively substitute some notion of change in time; movement as a shared concern that has crucial formal consequences.

Walt Disney's studio was undoubtedly the central studio in the American cartoon industry. His studio developed a complex rhetoric of animation and explicitly developed a figurative animation that took as its premise the necessity of complete interpenetration of form and movement. That the final films are saccharine and devoted to naturalising the moral values of Middle America through distortion of folk and fairy tales and a highly sentimental anthropomorphism is something one cannot contest. But in the process of making the films, the Disney Studio poured most creative effort into the animation stage leading to pencil tests. Animation directly drawn; rough, shimmering pencil lines defining form and movement. The viewing of the tests, known as sweat-boxing, was repeated over and over again until the animated movement satisfied Disney.

It is a truism that the animators preferred line test to the final film, that the potential of the form was seen to lie there. In interviews and writing by traditional American animators, they re-appear constantly as the focal point for the love of an involvement with the form. Chuck Jones summed up the attitude:

> Animation is itself an art form and that's the point I always think needs clarification. The animation exists without any background or any colour or any sound or anything else. You don't even have to have a camera. I don't know if you've ever taken any of the great Disney animation or even some barfly animation and held any of those big thick scenes in your hand and flicked them. God! It's so beautiful you can't believe it. That pink elephant sequence in *Dumbo* is a perfect example of what I'm talking about; there are no backgrounds, no nothing. Animation does everything.[15]

And the paradox, that more was less, also piqued the Disney Studio:

> In the late 1930s, Alexander Woolcott, author and critic, visited the studio and was greatly impressed with the appearance of the rough pencil tests he was shown. All the extra lines that helped construct the characters and search out the movement were little more than cobwebs on the screen, yet, somehow, they seemed to coalesce into a character, causing Woolcott to state that there was more creativity in this form than in any finished animation. Walt always like the vitality of the rough animation, but he never found a way to use it properly in a picture. Could it be combined with live action to suggest the inner ideas or dreams of some character? Could it represent a fantasy of wandering thoughts, of visions, of half-formed notions? Could it be a mystical character that was not earthbound and only partially formed most of the time? In one discussion, Mel Shaw commented: 'It just seems to me that there's even more of an art form in an expressionistic medium out there, somewhere. We haven't experimented.'[16]

The description of the Disney Studio's fascination with animation in this form and yet its association with the unconscious and the alien and their eventual failure to use its potential is significant.

Disney's animation is in the paradoxical situation of being a highly self-conscious art form predicated on a very naive value system (an inverse folk art of a society in which ability to articulate in technical ways outstripped any moral or philosophical framework of thought available).

So rather than interrogate the final films for the values they reveal I wish to examine the rudiments of form for a potential that is later erased.

Such an examination is based on sources such as contemporary documents published within the studio as explicit guidelines to animators: records and descriptions of the 'Action Analysis Classes' classes instituted by Walt Disney in 1932 and run by Donald Graham, a draughtsman and teacher with a background in engineering, which attempted to create a formal framework for the interrelation of movement and form in a series of drawings; and historical accounts of the development of animation written by the animators themselves. In conjunction with these documented sources, there are certain formal qualities in the films which can be seen to be isolatable and it can be argued, precede other qualities in the chronological development of the work.

As one reads this material it becomes clear an academic form of animation is being created, with the idea of necessary distortion as its axis:

Squash and Stretch

Anything composed of living flesh, no matter how bony, will show considerable movement within its shape in progressing through an action . . . The squashed position can depict the form either flattened out by great pressure or bunched up and pushed together. The stretched position always shows the same form in a very extended condition. Immediately, the animators tried to outdo each other in making drawings with more and more squash and stretch, pushing those principles to the very limits of solid draughtsmanship.[17]

Follow Through and Drag

The loose flesh on a figure, such as its cheeks, or Donald Duck's body and almost all of Goofy, will move at a slower speed than the skeletal parts . . . In effect, the animator is drawing in the fourth dimension, for he is depicting a figure the way it would be at only that precise moment. The drawings are not designed to be viewed by themselves, but only in a series projected at an established speed.[18]

To further underline the parallel with Bacon, they made full use of precisely the range of photographs that he makes use of, from Muybridge to news photos:

On the sports page of the daily newspapers we found a gold mine that had been showing the elasticity of the human body in every kind of reach and stretch and human action.[19]

This elasticity was systematically analysed in Don Graham's analysis classes where a section of film was run again and again until the relationship between weight and motion in an action was eventually clarified. Looking both at animation and live action source material, Graham also attempted to build a critical language that would allow techniques to be clarified and formalised.

He built one system around the drawing of Bill Tytler. An examination of his work provides a focal point for understanding the work in the Disney Studio. Tytler was one of the few Disney animators with an art education – after art school in New York he studied sculpture in Paris. He was also considered to be one of the best draughtsmen at the studio. Highly enthusiastic about Graham's classes, Tytler's work and attitudes reflect the mixture of the studio.

In a class given in 1937 he elaborated upon drawing movement, talking about accent – both in the flow of drawings and in individual work:

Whether you handle 1, 2, 3 or 7 characters you must phrase or force or define so the eye always follows. Very often you must do things you might call bad drawing in order to accent or force. We all realise that in animation one drawing is just part of 100 or 300 drawings. In itself it is nothing – just a continuation of a vast whole. If you always try to keep perfect form, you will not get the feeling across – it will be just something that continues without any flavour.

You can give a drawing an accent – you can twist an eyebrow or a mouth – you can force or accent if you can do something to the little character's shoulder or chest; but it is a continuous flow; and it always comes back to its original shape.[20]

Graham attempted to formalise this intuitive sense of accent and distortion in a principle he dubbed 'Forces and Forms' which isolated the leading edges of forms in movement and used them as the fulcrum of the complete drawing. A method of locating forms without baldly stating them, the theory never seems to have been widely applied in the studio perhaps because any suggestion of ambiguity was a problem. But, with this theory in mind, it is interesting to examine a short series of drawings from *Snow White* that Tytler animated.[21]

To see the drawings as two stages of finish allows one to see the two sets of diametrically opposed principles working in the Disney Studio.

The roughs clearly relate to the ideas of animatable form and the ambiguous definition of one form against another and of the dialectical relationship of one drawing to another. The flow of line can be seen to run in overlapping patterns from one drawing to another. The trajectory of lines in the first drawing already implies the position of the line in the second drawing. This allows for the concept of any line as a trace of gesture and so must foreground the *work* of the film to some extent: a quality that Disney's fantasy of realism could never make space for in the finished film. This element of calligraphic energy gives the drawings a real force and leads to an ambiguous relation between the forms in any drawing, which adds to the drawings' feeling of flux. Whereas, in the cleaned up drawings, the lines cease to function in any dynamic or ambiguous way and are unequivocal descriptions of static form, reticent, reduced to 'realistic' outlines in which the drawing gesture is subdued to invisibility.

These two opposing drives in Disney's development of animation are reflected in the studio handouts on the design and action of the characters such as Donald Duck. Donald as a cartoon character from quite early in the Disney stable is a relatively abstract figure, designed to be dynamic rather than to conform to any norms of a realism. He 'has a pear shaped body: is short, squatty, and is drawn to show weight in the body' and the instructions take into account the dynamism of line 'when drawing Donald for a line of action try to make the whole thing curl in one line to give directness'. Yet the level of detail about Donald's form from the precise thickness of his webs to the number of ribbons on his hat presages the rigidity of attitude which leads to more and more obsession with realism and to the demise of the more abstract character.

Finally, much of the formal responses to the demands of drawings movement was suppressed in favour of clarity. Disney's conventions for figurative animation are shot through with this fundamental contradiction. The desire to produce graphic art concerned with flux and movement led to a form which was modernist. But Disney's value forces him to suppress and to continue with (as much as possible) a nineteenth-century realism in the behaviour of his characters and the graphic finish to the animation. One studio circular listed as its priorities:

> …main considerations in story animation: (1) Simplicity and clarity. (2) Caricature: we should make action stronger than it would be in human life. Otherwise we are not taking advantage of our medium.

Again and again, animators are told to ensure clarity is always maintained. Disney's caricature has no ambiguous moral relationship to what it depicts, so its level of connotation was constantly minimised. A special 'Silhouette Test' was developed to erase any ambiguous poses and the use of gesture was always based on a direct emotion–gesture link. Model sheets were developed to show exact expressions for anger, happiness, or shyness, etc. The logical conclusion of this suppression of ambiguity was the cleaning up of all drawings to single lines to act as definite outlines and their subsequent tracing onto plastic cel and colouring.

A careful viewing of much of Disney's work reveals the contrast of a potentially disruptive and problematic dynamism of form then laid over with the sickly colours of a rigid sentimentality.

Disney's animation is a form unrealised, a form developed and then suppressed in which all the clues to the form it might be are in earlier stages. The form was discovered, fully developed by the 1930s, and then the studio's resources went entirely into re-aligning, normalising and personalising a form which basically expresses the plasticity and mutability of bodies and so the fluxiveness and lability of identity.

Disney's earlier films clearly show a response to this flux as violent. The *tension* of such uncontrollable plasticity is discharged in comedy charged with violence. *Steamboat Willie* is full of animals 'played' as musical instruments in a variety of ingenious and violent ways. When we laugh as an ostrich is made to sing by being grabbed around the neck by Mickey Mouse and rhythmically stretched and squeezed, the notes choked out of it, the projection of anxiety about squash and stretch and its expulsion through sadism and comedy is painfully clear. The most extreme example of this is *The Mad Doctor* (1935). This film has Mickey Mouse rescuing Pluto from the clutches of a vivisector and is distinguished in being the only Disney film to be banned by the censor. In one scene, Pluto, trembling with fear and strapped into an operating table, becomes transparent; and as the doctor approaches his ribs and heart collapse in on themselves and fall to the bottom of his quivering translucent carcass. A brilliant graphic shorthand which powerfully expresses fear, yet timed for comic effect, such a sequence is unimaginable in the cloying context of later films such as *101 Dalmations* where similar material is milked for maximum sentimentality, and emotion is strictly portrayed through the illustrational representations of dramatic expression by characters.

As Disney 'refined' his medium, his response to the threat of flux as violence was no longer released by the valve of laughter but concealed as much as possible, both in the treatment of narrative and the rationalisation of the animation. But a nucleus of films can be recognised as fitting Erwin Panofsky's description:

> Within their self-imposed limitations the earlier Disney films and certain sequences in the later ones, represent as it were, a chemically pure distillation of cinematic possibilities. They retain the most important folkloristic elements – sadism, pornography, the humour engendered by both . . . and they also retain undisguised the discovery of a new graphic form which baldly and powerfully describes the absolute flux of material objects and flesh in the world.[22]

Obviously, it is not simply a matter of celebrating this violence. But the combination of physicality in flux and a dramatic disruption of the hermetic order of the body links the films to a tradition of popular grotesque and festivity which is an area rich in possibilities, for the disruption is the disturbance of all that is normative and hierarchical:

> Far from construing this attempt at erosion as a mere embrace of barbarism or of chaos, it is possible to discern it as a desire for something excluded from cultural order – more specifically, for all that is in opposition to the capitalist and patriarchal order which has been dominant in Western society over the last two centuries.[23]

It is a path for exploration of the threat of material dissolution and the concomitant threat to identity, and a space in which the possibilities and the real fear and pain of that threat can be impacted together.

And so, to what extent does Berger's assessment of the links between Disney and Bacon hold? Berger locates the similarity around 'the alienated behaviour of our societies' and decides:

> The surprising formal similarities of their work – the way limbs are distorted, the overall shapes of bodies, the relation of figures to background and to one another, the use of neat tailors clothes, the gestures of hands, the range of colours used – are the result of both men having complementary attitudes to the same crisis . . .

It is true that both men are positioned within a crisis, but I think that a belief that their work uncritically and directly transcribes alienated social behaviour is inadequate. What we have discussed as the common formal qualities in their work is also the source of the crisis. Both men have discovered a means to render a state Panofsky describes in Disney's films: the very concept of stationary existence is completely abolished.

Yet for both men, a phallocentric obsession with flux as violence is always a factor in their work, which each seeks to deal with through formal decisions.

Disney was unable to resolve the problem and so his forms have a ruinous contradiction running through them. Potentially labile form is combined with flattening colour and stable, illusionist backgrounds; and an obsessive repetition of the concept of personality acting.

Bacon's position is more complex. Both by looking at the paintings and from his comments it is clear that he regards the flux he perceives as violent. His choice to paint oil paintings, his relation to that tradition and the idea of a single great image (reinforced by the associations of oil painting with the bourgeois fantasy of owning the original) is part of the resistance to that perception. The conflicts in his situation are best expressed by his decision to make portraits. By doing so, he intervenes at a point of real crisis in a culture where the concept of stable and unified ego is embattled. In his best paintings, he resolves the opposing forces in a form of rare beauty where tragically the solidity of anatomical fact simultaneously exists only as traces of movement. By remaining scrupulously honest about his perception of the impossibility of stationary existence and the pain of desiring flesh destined to fade, he has developed forms which any serious attempt at a graphic description of flux must take into account.

Bacon and Disney indeed share, to some degree, discoveries and fears, but whereas Bacon braves his fear to look straight at the flux, even if sometimes his own fear is what he sees, Disney had no choice but to bury the grotesquerie of squash and stretch under paint and plastic and middle American sentiment. And yet, the paradoxical relationship between the two is more complex still.

Bacon's relationship to the bourgeois culture of easel painting mixes destructiveness and epitomisation in equally burning parts. Disney, although always true to his *petit bourgeois* Middle American values, developed a form of enormous potential that was open for use by a democratic and socialist modernism, a popular form of great complexity, inspiring admiration from Eisenstein in *Film Sense* and the Mexican muralist David Siqueiros to say in 'How To Paint A Mural':

> I still have to mention something which I think will be of importance to what we might call the poly art of the future . . . Everyone knows the animated cartoon film which resulted from a combination of drawing, colour and the cinema; Walt Disney

was the most famous producer of these cartoons. The cartoon makes me wonder whether it would be possible to arrive at a relationship between formal mural painting and the cinema. Would it come to the point where a finished work of art would actually be the colour film made out of it? It has always been difficult for me to understand why modern painters, having seen these cartoons, have not looked for relationships between polychromed abstract forms. Now we can understand they failed to do so because they were not up to date in their material technique and their so called modernity was in fact archaeological . . . Painting and cinema can do wonderful things together.[24]

This is a slightly revised version of a paper given at the 1993 SAS Conference, Farnham, England. The author would like to thank Ray Durgnat who supervised the original MIA paper at the Royal College of Art in London upon which this essay is based.

Notes

1. John Berger, 'Francis Bacon and Walt Disney', in *Ways of Seeing* (London: Writers and Readers, 1972).
2. David Sylvester, *Interviews with Francis Bacon 1962–1979* (London: Thames and Hudson, 1975).
3. This essay has its origins in a slide show/lecture; however, the paintings discussed in this essay hare available in several collections of reproductions of Francis Bacon's paintings, for example, *Francis Bacon*, eds D. Ades and A. Forge (London: Thames and Hudson, 1985).
4. Frame II of Plate 68 in *Muybridge: The Human Figure in Motion* (London: Dover Photographic Library, 1955).
5. John Russell, *F. Bacon* (London: Thames and Hudson, 1971).
6. Philip Rawson, *Drawing; The Appreciation of the Arts 3* (London: OUP, 1969).
7. John Russell, op. cit.
8. All plate numbers from *Francis Bacon* by Lorenza Trucchi (Milan: Fabbri Editori, 1975), trans. by John Shepley (London: Thames & Hudson, 1976).
    Plate 35. *Two Figures 1953*.
    Plate 39. *Two Figures in the Grass 1954*.
    Plate 143. *Studies from the Human Body Triptych*.
    Plate 157. *3 Studies of Figures on Beds 1972*.
    Plate 166. *Triptych 1972*.
    Plate 176. *Two Figures with a Monkey 1973*.
9. E.H. Gombrich, 'The Mask. The Perception of Physiognomic Likeness in Life and Art'. One of three lectures, John Hopkins University, 1970.
10. John Russell, op. cit.
11. E.H. Gombrich, 'The Mask. The Perception of Physiognomic Likeness in Life and Art'. One of three lectures, John Hopkins University, 1970.
12. In an essay prefacing the catalogue to the 1985 Tate Gallery retrospective of Bacon's work, Andrew Forge writes: 'There is nothing cinematic in Bacon, at least not in the obvious sense of a discrete form being in motion in front of a fixed viewpoint.' The argument he develops of time ruptured is undoubtedly more closely related to the possibilities of film than he allows by limiting the term of 'cinematic' so narrowly. Cinema is rarely a document of 'discrete form being in motion in front of a fixed viewpoint'. Moving camera and the cut were established early in the cinema and constitute part of its basic vocabulary. Theoretical writing as early as Walter Benjamin's 'The Work of Art in the Age of Mechanical Reproduction' (in Illuminations, ed. Hannah Arendt, trans. Harry Zohn (London: New Left Books, 1973)) positioned films in explicit relation to notions of continuity and discontinuity, for example:

    . . . less a matter of time captured than time ruptured. The act of reaching for a lighter or a spoon is a familiar routine, yet we hardly know what really goes on between hand and metal, not to mention how this fluctuates with our moods. Here the camera intervenes with the resources of its lowerings and liftings, its interruptions and isolations, its extensions and accelerations, its enlargements and reductions.

Certainly, such a description fits the graphic representation of a look to one side in a painting such as *George Dyer Crouching 1966*.

13. Frank Thomas and Ollie Johnstone, *Disney Animation: The Illusion of Life* (New York: Abbeville, 1983).
14. Frank Thomas and Ollie Johnstone, op. cit.
15. Interview with Chuck Jones by Greg Ford and Richard Thompson, *Film Comment* (Jan–Feb 1975).
16. Frank Thomas and Ollie Johnstone, op. cit.
17. Frank Thomas and Ollie Johnstone, op. cit.
18. Frank Thomas and Ollie Johnstone, op. cit.
19. Frank Thomas and Ollie Johnstone, op. cit.
20. Frank Thomas and Ollie Johnstone, op. cit.
21. This essay has its origins in an illustrated slide show/lecture. The relevant drawings can be found in Frank Thomas and Ollie Johnstone, op. cit.
22. Erwin Panofsky, 'Style and Medium in the Motion Pictures', (1934, revised 1947) in *Film Theory and Criticism*, eds Gerald Mast and Marshall Cohen (New York: OUP, 1979).
23. *Fantasy, the Literature of Subversion*, Rosemary Jackson (London: Methuen, 1981).
24. David Sequieros, 'How to Paint a Mural', in *Art and Revolution* (London: Methuen, Camelot Press, 1973).

15

Body consciousness in the films of Jan Svankmajer

Paul Wells

I believe that body, figure, extension, movement and place are only fictions of my mind. What, then, shall be considered true? Perhaps only this, that there is nothing certain in the world.[1]
– Rene Descartes

We shall never completely master nature; and our bodily organism, itself a part of that nature, will always remain a transient structure with a limited capacity for adaptation and achievement. This recognition does not have a paralysing effect. On the contrary, it points the direction for our activity.[2]
– Sigmund Freud

The work of Jan Svankmajer, celebrated Czechoslovakian animator and avant-garde filmmaker, demonstrates an ongoing pre-occupation with the codes and conditions of bodily function and identity. His fictions are characterised by the recognition of transience in the body and the place of the body as a defining instrument in socio-cultural mechanisms and indeed, as a socio-cultural mechanism. Svankmajer uses the unique vocabulary of animation in expressing these principles and essentially re-defines the conditions by which the body might be represented and re-defined aesthetically and politically.

This essay examines three main areas of address in Svankmajer's work. Firstly, the body in transition; secondly, the body as mechanism; and thirdly, the body under threat. Svankmajer is largely concerned with the idea of de-rationalising the body from its assumed functions and properties. To this end, he defines the body materially, playing out its corporeality in clay, its identity through objects and its relationship to the codes and conditions of lived existence through its opposite in automata.

Svankmajer attempts to use his representations of the body to engage with discourses of power. He views the human condition as subject to increasing states of flux and disorder and the body as the site onto which humankind projects its desire, its fear and its uncertainty. Michael O'Pray suggests that this level of address is located within further discourses where surrealism conjoins with the conditions of post-modernity.[3]

Importantly, though, Svankmajer's view of his own work as in the realm of 'fantastic documentary' perhaps helps to root the works in less abstracted soil, stressing that its conditions are not merely aesthetic but are sociologically determined. Bryan Turner makes a useful distinction between being a body and having a body and implies a structural framework for viewing Svankmajer's films that recognises the very tension between biological functionalism and ideological determinism, a structure predicated on what Turner terms as 'the four "r"s – reproduction, representation, regulation and restraint'.[4] These terms can be understood in a variety of ways, but they signify particular views of the body as it has been defined within social contexts. This raises issues about how the body has been socially constructed; subjected to rules and regulations which contain its physical expression; defined by historicised codes and conventions of inhibition and repression; and rendered 'safe' by its containment.

The body in transition

Svankmajer's films make few concessions to the notion of character, but instead seek to translate quasi-human formations into ciphers for symbolic meaning. Few are given dialogue, but become narrational vehicles in themselves for specific ideas about how the body responds to change. Though Svankmajer contextualises aspects of this representation in what the viewer might understand to be a surrealistic space or dream-state, he is, most often, creating a fictionalised notion of consciousness, which, if imagined 'real', both recalls the playful and liberal apparatus of childhood and makes concrete the irony and contradiction of the adult sensibility. Svankmajer's notion of 'documentary', therefore, is at the service of making films of record that engage with psycho-somatic states as they have been historically determined.

Dimensions of Dialogue (1982) contains three separate, but related narratives, each examining different levels of human exchange. The first, 'Exhaustive Discussion', depicts a variation of the game, 'Stone, Paper, Scissors', where three heads composed out of objects in the Mannerist style of Arcimboldo take turns to devour one another, regurgitating the materials previously swallowed into newly formed, if fragmented, heads, until finally the heads are 'pulped' into a series of clay busts. In his work on Arcimboldo's paintings, Pontus Hulten has suggested three fundamental interpretations that could be applied to the images. He notes that they can be seen as an 'amusing work of fantasy and invention', an allegory related to the Hapsburg Empire and sixteenth century science' or 'a metaphorical statement [about] a new vision of man'.[5]

'Exhaustive Discussion' directly echoes Arcimboldo's paintings in both compositional structure and metaphorical implication. Svankmajer's heads are made of metal objects, fruits and vegetables and office stationary, which can be read as metaphors for, respectively, industrialism, nature and bureaucracy – embodiments of the tensions in Czechoslovakia in regard to its former status as a satellite to the authoritarian regimes of the former Soviet Union or indeed, as Nazi-occupied territory, in World War II. Svankmajer seeks to play out a greater universality in the rendering of his metaphor, using the body and particularly the face to engage in allegories of colonisation, consumption and change. A repeating choreography shows the head composed of metallic objects consuming the head made of fruit and vegetables, pulping the fruit and eventually regurgitating it to form a corrupted hybrid head made up of the decomposed materials. This is followed by the head composed of office stationary devouring the metal head and finally, the fruit and vegetable head consuming and regurgitating the paper head.

This repetition suggests a destructive continuum in the relationship between human nature, the industrial process and the governing bureaucracy. Played out as a children's game, the processes of mutually condoned power relations are executed in a spirit of ironic naivety, in which Svankmajer implicitly criticises the ways in which the body passively services the continuum, part securing its quasi-erotic pleasures in modes of orality, part rendering itself as a vehicle subservient only to autocratic ends. His irony is doubly served by the notion that the body cannot help its subversion, but will let the very appetites that inform it become subject to constraint. The industrial process consumes nature; bureaucracy overwhelms the industrial process; but is itself undermined or challenged by the force of nature as it expressed through the body. This continuum has the appearance of both a social flux and a social status quo, where conflict seems synonymous with progress and change.

Svankmajer implicitly suggests, however, that these dialectics produce a merely reductive synthesis, which ultimately collapses democratic principles and the possibility of a progressive social structure which will properly serve humankind. The film evokes the notion of reproduction as a regressive process, yet ironically, this first section of the film concludes with the final regurgitation of numerous clay heads – perhaps an intimation of immortality in the sense that 'clay', in representing the very essence of life, somehow survives the exigencies of the structures through which it finds itself regulated, restrained and represented.

Svankmajer might be suggesting that the body can survive its mis-representation and its own historically conditioned culpability. This recalls Michel Foucault's view that 'there is little question that one of the primordial forms of class consciousness is the affirmation of the body', which he suggests emerges out of a desire within an exploited proletariat to resist 'a whole technology of control' that is necessary to sustain codes of bourgeois hegemony.[6] Svankmajer demonstrates both the mechanism of continuum in the maintenance of bourgeois hegemony and the body as a mode of resistance in its inevitable undoing. His reproduction is ultimately about deregulation emerging out of restraint and re-defining aspects of representation. It is this theme that he develops in the second section of the *Dimensions of Dialogue,* entitled *Passionate Discourse.*

Passionate Discourse specifically genders its participants, only then to blur the distinctions of gender and finally, to render them indistinguishable in their self-destructive imperatives. Clay figures of a man and woman sit opposite each other at a table, exchange glances and smiles, before tentatively touching and kissing, whereupon they make love. Svankmajer shows his protagonists moving beyond the everyday functionalism of their bodies into the liberation of expressed physical desire. Their bodies literally meld, operating as the symbolic embodiment of body consciousness, as it experiences the freedoms of sensual pleasure beyond social repressions and initially, unrelated to ideas of reproduction. The body here simply negates any function it might possess within the socio-cultural framework.

The sexual act is used as a premise to liberate the body from its ideologically determined roles. Its state of impersonality, half-formed, malleable, without shape, echoes the theme of body consciousness in Svankmajer's films as it expressed as a relationship between childhood polymorphous perversity and adult determinacy. Svankmajer here resists the post-modern tendency to fragment the body, providing an example of sex and sexuality in a fluid and adherent bodily form. This more impressionistic representation

of making love includes glimpses of hands on breasts, kisses and so forth, but perhaps most strikingly, animation is used to redefine profoundly the size and scale of the body, to depict the vagina as a synecdoche for the female form, as it experiences labial pleasure.

Svankmajer's use of metamorphosis here achieves a number of potentially subversive ends. He shows the process of symbolic unison and the breakdown of a gendered order, thus destabilising the phallic emphasis of patriarchal social structures. Once more, as Foucault suggests, 'sex is the most speculative, most ideal and most internal element in a deployment of sexuality organised by power in its grip on bodies and their materiality, their forces, energies, sensations and pleasures'.[7] Thus Svankmajer's depiction of the sexual act expresses particular contradictions, most notably, how the achievement of personal liberation through the pleasure of re-determining the body is inevitably tempered by historically determined socio-cultural power relations which have colonised its very physiognomy. This is cleverly illustrated by the sequence that follows the couple's love-making: they become separate forms once again, seated in opposite chairs. Their sexual union results in a piece of clay being left on the tabletop and Svankmajer's decision not to specifically shape or gender the clay clearly asks the viewer to interpret it metaphorically.

Although the piece of clay is given appealing anthropomorphic qualities, which engage the sympathy of the viewer as it attempts to solicit the affection of its 'parents', Svankmajer refuses the idea that this piece of clay is merely 'a baby'. In not being explicit and literal, he engages with what Foucault calls 'the bio-politics of population'[8] simply; here the mechanistic and regulatory controls that are played out through the body, which inevitably affect the psychological and emotional agendas of the individual, and more importantly, the ways by which social and ideological orthodoxies, are maintained. The piece of clay could represent a fatal and unaddressed flaw in the relationship; the refusal to take responsibility for actions which have cause and effect; the essential difference between men and women; or perhaps, most fundamentally, the idea of consequence and culpability in a social structure, which suggests individual pleasure is not possible without repercussion at the social level. If the former melding of clay was concerned with an uninhibited imperative to move beyond social frameworks, the latter melding when the couple literally and brutally, tear each other apart, is allied to the view that the context in which the relationship takes place is inevitably oppressive, inescapable and leads to destructive tendencies.

Passionate Discourse, therefore, plays out power relations as they have been historically determined by gender and sexual behaviour within societal limits – a bio-politic which

seek to contain modes of liberation and specifically direct human endeavour into available social frameworks which maintain, in Svankmajer's view, a wholly self-destructive order, a concept he takes to its logical conclusion in the film's third segment, 'Factual Conversation'.

Svankmajer has suggested that 'to revive the general impoverishment of sensibility in our civilisation, the sense of touch may play a very important part'.[9] His view is clearly endorsed in *Passionate Discourse*, yet refuted by the ways in which the body has become a contradictory vehicle of expression and identity, half-positively driven to express its nature and half naturalised by the historically determined, political functions that have shaped biological imperatives. Returning to the more universal themes, *Factual Dialogue* once more uses heads, which maintain a constant distance from each other while defensively circling and occasionally spewing particular objects. At no point do the heads move close or touch and thus only communicate at a distance. Initially, the objects that are disgorged from the mouths of each of the two protagonists are related and essentially 'match' – a toothbrush with toothpaste, bread with butter, a pencil is sharpened by a sharpener emerging on one of the tongues. This signifies co-operation and the possibility of understanding, principally in regard to modes of consumption and commodity.

The second phase of the piece shows the objects mismatching, and in the style of *Exhaustive Discussion*, these objects destroy and pulp each other. This could be read as inappropriate and destructive exchange. The third and final part of the sequence shows the same objects emerging from the mouths simultaneously and clashing, once more destroying each other. The objects are merely waste materials, lost commodities in a false mode of relationship. Though this relationship might be viewed as an individual conflict, it is also metaphor for the global struggle between East and West when the ambiguous terms of the Cold War were still operational.

The consequence of the conflict is two-fold. Svankmajer clearly suggests that the conditions of capitalist exchange are corrupted and cannot maintain the credibility of the economic and social core of late industrial societies, in the light of inequalities found in other (Third World) contexts. The very ordinariness of the objects Svankmajer uses point to the taken-for-granted aspects of commodity culture and the self-evident waste that informs its level of exchange. This 'commodity culture' also defines the body not as a model of resistance but as a vehicle for exploitation in the face of a necessarily productive work ethos. As Richard Dyer has noted:

> The rhetoric of capitalism insists that it is capital that makes things happen; capital has the magic property of growing, stimulating. What this conceals is the fact that it is human labour and in the last instance the labour of the body, that makes things happen.[10]

This idea usefully underpins an interpretation of Svankmajer's texts in terms of his concern with the ways in which the body in transition is inevitably progressive and creative and indeed, sometimes irrational, but the frameworks within which it finds itself inhibit that progress and creativity by once more rationalising its purpose. Svankmajer sophisticatedly uses animation as an irrational form to express this tension, ultimately demonstrating that the body is intrinsically bound up with economic life but exists in a system that is literally 'exhausted' of its value and appropriateness. As Dyer also notes, 'how we use and organise the capacities of the body is how we produce and re-produce life itself'[11] and it is this theme that informs another of Svankmajer's films that I would like to address within the broad context of body in transition.

Darkness, Light, Darkness (1990), which echoes the bleakness and black humour of the Samuel Beckett absurdist canon,[12] attempts to delineate the oppressive frameworks that the body attempts to develop within. Reminiscent of many of the short films from the Zagreb studio, most notably Dragic's *Passing Days* (1969), and operating in the tradition exemplified by fellow Czechoslovakian Jiri Trnka in *The Hand* (1965) and up-dated by Rbycznski in *Tango* (1988), *Darkness, Light, Darkness* takes place in a small domestic room which houses an individual but which is acted upon and changed by oppressive and interventionary social forces. Svankmajer shows the gradual construction of a human torso within a room for which it finally grows too big. The first elements of the body to arrive in the room are the sensory apparatus: the eyes, the ears (arriving as a fluttering butterfly), the nose, the teeth and the tongue, the latter real dentures and flesh and finally, the hands and feet. The figure becomes self-conscious about its own creation, monitoring its own awkwardness and difficulty. Svankmajer implies that the figure might be read as a child slowly coming to terms with its sensual and physical faculties. The encroachment of puberty and adolescence is signalled by the specific gendering of the figure and the masculine imperatives which then seem to inform the process of 'growing up'. This is amusingly played out as the other parts of the body mobilise in the attempt to resist the entry of the genitals into the room. Just who or what is 'banging' on the door is unknown to the audience until the other parts of the body dowse what the viewer could assume was a previously erect penis, now entering the room in a forlorn and flaccid state. Even when it attaches itself to the torso, it is dismissively 'flicked' to get rid of the drops of water and its former phallic power is reduced to being understood as a mere body part with specific rather than metaphysical functions. With this 'gendering' of the figure comes the implied gendering of the space and this issue is particularly important in this reading of the film because Svankmajer has privileged the man and absented female figures to over-determine the space as

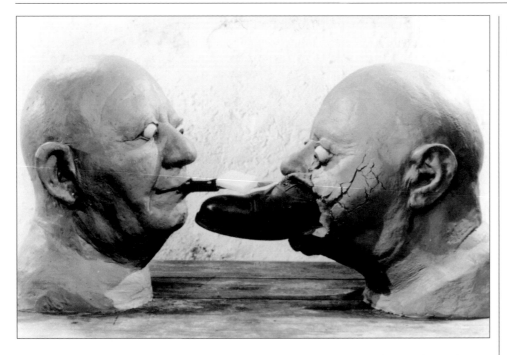

historically masculine and thus implicitly subject to patriarchal hierarchies and ideological orthodoxy.

As the rest of the body literally floods into the room and constructs the torso, it is clear that Svankmajer once again plays with the ambiguity of the transition from communist oppression to implied capitalist freedoms. The body is too big for the room, yet is foetally compressed as if in a womb. At the point of greatest entrapment, the body politic, it seems, has the possibility of rebirth. In true absurdist style, though, Svankmajer enjoys a bleak humour in letting the body emerge out of darkness into light, only to once again switch off the light at the ambiguous point of suffocation or new life. He suggests that the social order predetermines the capacity of the body and prevents it from breaking out of its limits both biologically and socially. Under these terms, then, the body seems purely a mechanism of state power.

Body as mechanism

This theme Svankmajer explores in a series of films in which he views the body as a mechanism:

> Body as Mechanism . . . its disciplining, the optimisation of its capabilities, the extortion of its forces, the parallel increase of its usefulness and its docility, its integration into systems of efficient and economic controls, all this was ensured by procedures of power that characterised the disciplines: an anatomo-politics of the human body.[13]

The figure in *Darkness, Light, Darkness* embodies the self-conscious realisation of Foucault's conception of anatomo-politics, playing out a suicidal impulse that rejects the premise of biological evolution as ideological passivity. If the figure symbolises the death of authoritarian modes of socialism, a theme more specifically explored in Svankmajer's post-perestroika agitprop film *The Death of Stalinism in Bohemia* (1990), then it is a figure that desires what Jonathan Miller has called 'the physiological constancy of the internal environment'[14] and not the modification of external conditions.

In *Food* (1992), Svankmajer looks at the tensions between the physiological imperatives to merely nourish the body and maintain its health and well-being and the social conditions which once again contain and define even these imperatives within ideological parameters. Like *Dimensions of Dialogue*, the film is divided into three sections called 'Breakfast', 'Lunch' and 'Dinner', each looking at how the body is reduced to a particular mechanism in the service of an oppressive class structure. Svankmajer uses pixillation to heighten the mechanistic effects of the film and as a Brechtian alienation technique that simultaneously draws attention to the self-conscious mode of address in the film – the black humour that informs it and the political agendas he is engaging with.

In the first sequence, two blue-collar workers try to get their breakfast and each treats the other like a dispensing machine for food. Literally, when each figure is fed some coins, its body becomes 'a dumb waiter' serving sausage, mustard, bread and beer. The figures clearly operate as metaphors for utilitarianism, producing and consuming, supplying and demanding, literally 'feeding off their fellow human beings' in what could be termed 'mechannibalism'. The body, here, is defined by the biological and labour functions of its class and has no identity or indeed, personality or purpose beyond this. One person literally replaces another as each one demands food: they are physiognomies merely conditioned to accept the premises of socio-economic status quo.

In the next sequence, 'Lunch', the working-class cafe is replaced by the aspirant middle-class restaurant and two diners fall into conflict about the nature of their consumption and greed. The two men start to compete as they wait to be served – and devour cutlery, flowers on the table, their glasses, serviettes, and their own clothing. When the figures are naked, they go on to eat their plates, the tablecloth, the table and the chairs, and just when it seems that nothing more can be consumed, the more overtly middle-class protagonist regurgitates his cutlery and eats his working-class companion.

In what might be viewed as an over-determined metaphor, Svankmajer stresses how the status quo is established and maintained by the necessity for the middle-class to satiate and sustain itself by the exploitation of the working class. Upward mobility is achieved by a mechannibalism that endorses the disposability of human needs and values in the face of a commodity culture. Everything is consumable; everything is property; nothing is outside this value system – a system which can only be maintained if the body has the ontological equivalence of a material object. Svankmajer's use of the animated form compounds this issue in the sense that the animation can redefine the status and equitability of figures, objects and environments, empower the weak, and move things that cannot move, or de-stabilise a space. His treatment of the human form enables him to re-enact the politics of the body through representations of the body in a more literal and explicit form.

'Dinner' takes this to its most surreal and satiric extreme, where dinner is the privilege of the upper class and aspirant middle class. The protagonist here attends a banquet, enjoying the platters of food with exotic sauces and pickles, but in order to do so literally nails a fork to his hand. This conjunction of man and metal is the most basic construction of body as mechanism. The figure embodies Foucault's notion of anatomo-politics because he is rendered as the most mechannibalistic in that he symbolises a dominant class, which determines social structure and necessarily lives off the other classes. The

fact that he is served breast and penis as delicacies is a recognition of the de-sexualisa-tion/castration of masculine/feminine forms in the service of the rationalised order. This is a patriarchal order that oppresses women and undermines men who aspire to

Like Dimensions in Dialogue, *Jan Svankmajer's film* Food *(1992) is divided into three sections; in this case, 'Breakfast', 'Lunch' and 'Dinner'. The characters partaking in each meal adopt social-class roles and thus the act of consuming food is extended to represent, for example, the rapacious effects of the classes upon one another*

©Channel Four Television/Heart of Europe/ Koninck International/ Krátký Film Praha

challenge other men with power whose agenda it serves to maintain the body as something which Dyer suggests has had 'its predominant use . . . as labour of the majority in the interests of the few'.[15] Svankmajer shows how the body can be de-personalised and thus distanced from the problems of its nature, operating as if it were automata in certain historically determined social codes.

The body as mechanism, when it is spectacularised in aesthetic or theatrical contexts, was an issue addressed in two of Svankmajer's earliest pieces, *The Last Trick* and *Punch and Judy*, both made in 1966. The puppet and marionette tradition in Czechoslovakia was important in sustaining the Czech cultural and aesthetic identity in the face of other influences, particularly that of the German language. Fully aware of this tradition, Svankmajer sought to develop aspects of the popular theatricality and folk literacy of the marionette show in the animated form. Michael O'Pray suggests his most successful attempt to do this was actually in *Don Juan* (1970):

> Svankmajer's *Don Juan* is a homage to the *commedia dell-arte* influenced marionette theatre and is an astonishing merger of its traditional features with cinematic animation. Svankmajer also uses the relatively innovative idea of using actors in the roles of marionettes. Equipped with large wooden heads and mock strings, Svankmajer's characters leave the theatre and fight and connive in the streets.[16]

This relationship between the 'real' body and its primitive synthetic creation in the guise of a puppet or marionette demonstrates the body's resistance to becoming automata. Svankmajer uses the overt artifice of the puppet/marionette show to demonstrate how the body as an aesthetic construct inevitably critiques the conditions of its context and construction. Playing out tensions between function and performance, Svankmajer reveals how utilitarian notions of control could be subverted by the spontaneous art of performance, using the live action 'body' to reject the rigidity and limits of its representation as automata. In many senses, Svankmajer uses the animated form to continually breach these parameters, but the early puppet films serve a political end in using established traditions of creative performance to both celebrate 'magical illusions' and the freedoms they offer and critique the political context that informs them.

In *The Last Trick*, two magicians (each with marionette heads on real bodies) compete to see who can perform the best trick. The performance is theatrically staged and literally reveals both the stage machinery and the internal machinery of the magician figures. The role of the magician is important because, as Jonathan Miller suggests, 'the reputation of the magician depends not so much on what he brings about, as on the personal aura which he projects'.[17] Svankmajer subverts this notion of personal aura by negating the personality traits of his magician figures; their lack of individual identity heightens the impersonality and distance of their achievements as magicians. The disturbing distinction thus produced emphasises the horror of their 'tricks' and determines a performance vocabulary that uses conflict to resist conformity, but with the consequence of simultaneously revealing inevitable social collapse.

This ambivalent and contradictory stance characterises much of Svankmajer's work because it recognises the need for change, but shows that the process towards change will be underpinned by a code of conduct which is inevitably violent and not necessarily progressive. Svankmajer uses the ritual of performance to suggest a model of difference only to imply that humankind will always fall prey to its own inability to properly reconcile the repeated failings and flaws of its evolutionary sensibility. The two magicians in *The Last Trick* are metaphors for Svankmajer's social vision as it is played out through the contradiction inherent in the body as it is simultaneously liberated through art but mechanised by socio-cultural practice. Svankmajer's quasi-surrealist approach represents the magician as a mechanism which possesses the inherent possibility of failing. The 'blue' magician throws a wooden fish into his head only for it to magically re-emerge as a set of fishbones; the machinery in his head having stripped the fish of its 'flesh'. The machinery sparks and burns. An insect crawls from the magician's head. Svankmajer intimates possible failure. The 'red' magician, in turn, responds by revealing that his head is a violin case. He then ties a rope to a chair and makes objects dance along the rope in the shape of a dog. The 'blue' magician plays numerous instruments and two violins emerge from his head. The 'red' magician juggles three heads and balances them on one finger, while the 'blue' magician plays tricks with chairs.

As their competitiveness escalates, so too does its physical expression and later the two figures literally tear each other apart. Only 'arms' remain, mechanically moving and shaking hands – consolidating Svankmajer's irony in depicting the very humanness informing the automata who act out the show. The insect is essentially the catalyst by which the interface between man and machine fails. An agent of disorder and a Kafkaesque harbinger of supernatural change, the insect enables Svankmajer to show the inappropriacy of a (man-made) mechanism to accommodate the limits of human expression. Once more, using Turner's terms, the body, subject to a mode of representation (i.e. as 'the magician') in the act of quasi-reproduction (i.e. of 'the trick'), fails both in relation to its regulation (i.e. the workings of the machinery) and the maintenance of restraint (i.e. the violence which emerges out of the ritual of performance).

Punch and Judy (a.k.a. *The Coffin Factory* and *The Lynchgate*) repeats these motifs by

mixing hand-puppets and a live guinea pig. Real hands are placed within the puppets in a similar fashion to the way he melded marionette heads and live bodies in *The Last Trick*. Punch strokes and feeds the guinea pig and refuses to sell it to the harlequin. A fight ensues and Punch mallets the harlequin and puts him into a coffin; the harlequin re-emerges, however, and does the same to him. As O'Pray suggests, the presence of the guinea pig as a self-evidently non-human yet living creature plays out 'both untrammelled desire, unmediated by conscience, morality or convention and almost paradoxically, its opposite, order and innocence, which can never partake in the aggression of the "constructed creatures" (marionette-humans) whose world they cannot share'.[18] If the insect in *The Last Trick* was a catalyst for chaos, a narrational provocateur by which Svankmajer could reveal the rebellion in the construction of the contemporary body, then the guinea pig plays a more basic role in providing a comparison to the mechanised body, suggesting the very organism from which it has become alienated. Thus, these two films provide ironic spectacles of physical estrangement, the body is literally and metaphorically managed and manipulated, struggling to impose its innate qualities, qualities which, even when they find recognition, are corrupted and without positive purpose.

Body under threat

Svankmajer's concern for the contemporary body focuses on its increasing instability in acts of transition and its powerlessness when subject to mechanistic intervention and control. He thus shows how the body has become alienated from itself and subject to pre-dominantly utilitarian functions. It has already been suggested that the body's more primal energies sometimes offer unconscious or misdirected resistance to these processes, or indeed, either through the impersonality of sexual or performance art rituals find temporary release or relief.

In Svankmajer's universe, these latter modes of resistance are often seen to be even more counter-productive and compound his cultural pessimism. Svankmajer's 1973 film *Leonardo's Diary* led to the filmmaker being forbidden to make films for seven years and he was subjected to constant government surveillance. His animation of Da Vinci's anatomical drawings, mixed with live action footage of sporting activities and social uprising, drew too close a link between art as the embodiment of human progress and achievement and its necessary relationship to revolutionary activity. The film's essential theme is the way that the body has been socially directed anatomo-politically and the necessity that it breaks free from these contexts to express dissent. Svankmajer uses the self-evident classicist achievement of Da Vinci's work to authenticate, yet disguise, his desire to re-figure the body as an agent of action and change. The complicity of the body as a passive, ideologically contained social vehicle is revoked in Svankmajer's fast-cut montage, implying an incitement to violent action.

Svankmajer implicitly stresses the need to revolt against those social and historical processes that have misrepresented the body and created the body in a spirit which is alien to its actual nature. The consequences of this revolt, however, are uncertain, and while Svankmajer suggests that revolt is inevitable given the way the body has been repressed, it is still likely that the desire to recall the primitive and organic in the body will only result in self-defeating ends.

Interestingly, Svankmajer ultimately makes a film that shows how the supposedly safe channelling of subversive physical energies into sporting activity might actually be a legitimate context in which violence can take place without restraint. *Virile Games* (1988) mixes live action, fast pictorial montage, cut-out figures, real objects and clay heads to show how football violence operates on and off the field, leading to multiple deaths and the over-riding conclusion that humankind can sometimes demonstrate a horrific indifference and contempt for life. This partly echoed the Heysel stadium tragedy and

other stories of 'hooliganism' which then characterised European football, but the film's main emphases lie in the degree and extent to which the body could be completely devalued and abused and further, how the body became a vehicle for its own destruction.

A man watches football on television, having ritualistically prepared himself with enough beer and biscuits for the duration of the match. This simple prelude establishes notions of consumption and an unabated appetite as the underpinning conditions for the expression of aggressive impulses. As the man watches the game, he fantasises that he is every member of both teams and the referee! Svankmajer creates a balletic lyricism to the game's execution only to counterpoint the action with excessively brutal acts of violence played out on the heads and bodies of the players. These acts constitute 'the score' in the game as each player dies. When the viewer watches 'the football' being played, Svankmajer uses cut-outs to represent the players, who are pixillated to show a dance-like fluidity and an often impossible dexterity to their skills. This is accompanied by a sentimentalised arrangement of orchestrated strings which lend a comic feel to the sequence, which is starkly interrupted by the foregrounding of a clay head which is subjected to violent acts perpetrated by off-screen hands. The oscillation between the two-dimensionality of the pixillated ballet and the three-dimensionality of the clay heads serves to heighten the corporeal vulnerability of the body. The heads are crushed by pot lids; a water tap literally drains away a face as if it was liquid; scissors cut up a face's features; a syringe is plunged into the middle of a face ultimately inflating and exploding the head; heads are minced in a grinder; trains run through facial features; and corkscrews pull away a face's eyes, nose and mouth.

In a Warner Bros. cartoon, such acts would, ironically, have less serious implications. Here, with Svankmajer stressing the very 'fleshliness' of the head and body, the actions take on a greater degree of what Svankmajer would call 'fantastic realism'. Also, this 'realism' is reinforced by the Svankmajer's subtle implication of motivation. The objects that are used in the violent acts are ordinary objects available in the domestic space and most specifically, in the male viewer's kitchen drawer – the drawer being Svankmajer's most consistent symbol for the unconscious. The spectator is clearly involved in a sadistic and masochistic fantasy, facilitated by the context of the football match.

Svankmajer continues the black humour of the piece, having every player who is stretchered off with injury being taken directly to a coffin. The coffins then play against one another, but this is merely a prelude to the excesses of the second half when the ball is kicked out of the ground and lands in the spectator's flat, when both teams leave the ground to reclaim it. The crowd riots and the football match continues in the small flat, resulting in full scale brutality until all the players are dead. The 'referee', previously at best inept, if not certainly irrelevant, concludes the game and leaves the flat. The spectator returns to his seat in front of the television only to discover that he has sat on one of the player's clay faces, which has attached itself to his bottom. This is the film's final image and the greatest signifier of Svankmajer's concern that the body is held in contempt and subjected only to the abuse of its social context and the lack of directed coherence in its response to oppression. The body, chiefly designated here through the face, is shown as both the subject and the object of excess. Primal impulses are not contained within the regulative aspects of the game, nor in the normal context of everyday existence and emerge as vicious, murderous acts. These are not premeditated politicised acts, however, but the consequence of the rejection of politicised restraint. The excessive, random brutalities accord the body no value but, ironically, release the body from anatomo-political function. The body's rebellion is thus characterised by contradiction. In order to de-historicise itself, it is prone to self-destruction, a theme played out in Svankmajer's most historically specific film, *The Death of Stalinism in Bohemia* (1990).

Jan Svankmajer's Virile Games *(1988) suggests that sporting activities are a legitimate context through which physical energies and violence (at least the fantasies thereof) can be channelled.*

©Krátký Film Praha (Still courtesy of BFI Film and Video Distribution)

Top *Svankmajer moves beyond the innocence of cartoonal violence by demonstrating the excesses of physical brutality that underpin sporting contests*

Below *A production shot of the meticulous preparation required for the image above*

©(Both) Krátký Film Praha

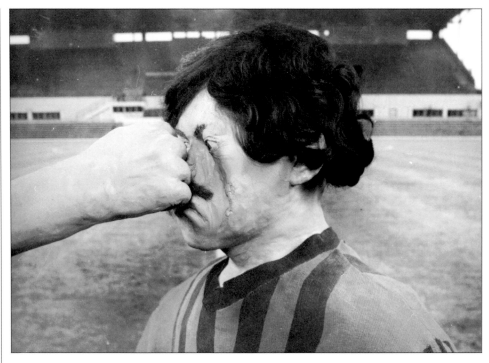

Death shows how the rejection of the 'body politic' of Stalinism in Bohemian Czechoslovakia results in an uncertainty of purpose, direction and identity. Stalin's body is represented as a concrete bust and in a mock-birth which initiates the historical narrative

Svankmajer plays out, a further bust, that of Klement Gottwald, the first communist president of Czechoslovakia, is born of a Stalinist body, its umbilical cord ceremonially cut, yet highly evocative of Gottwald's puppet-like status and the satellite status of the nation. Gottwald is dramatised through the use of his voice on a radio broadcast and some live action footage of apparently contented crowds of people. This is merely a façade, of course, as Svankmajer shows a conveyor belt process in which clay figures are created, hung and have their bodies returned to a bucket.

This reproduction of the body represents the political necessity of conformity, which is regulated by state policing. The process also reflects the show trials of leading political figures, including the first communist party secretary Rudolf Slansky who was executed as part of the supposed demonstration of state democracy, which self-evidently hid political corruption and totalitarian government. The body is once again seen as without value, subject to mechanistic processes and ultimately disposable. Portraits of Stalin, Gottwald, Brezhnev and Hasak (Czechoslovakia's president 1975–89, responsible for the 'normalisation' policy after the 1968 uprising) all hide skeletons who reveal themselves by eating through the pictures. These signify the sinister imperatives of leaders in the preservation of power through the oppression of the body and the systematic denial of individual or social mobilisation.

Czech liberation is demonstrated by the painting of the Czech flag on its material resources, but Svankmajer's scepticism about the future of the nation in the face of the history it has endured is reflected in the film's final images in which a bust of Stalin, painted in Czech colours, is used to bare 'the baby' that is the future of Czechoslovakia. Significantly, no 'baby' is actually shown. Svankmajer refuses to embody the future, when its 'father' is a denial of the organic and the maintenance of the socio-symbolic. Svankmajer suggests that there is no new body, merely the legacy of skeletons and statues.

Svankmajer clearly feels that even though it is the case that the body can and should be instrumental in the progressive recovery of the culture and is the fundamental essence of organic life at its most pure; the context in which it exists has only undergone cosmetic transformation and still cannot accommodate or constructively situate the body's potency. Though Svankmajer could be seen as a cultural pessimist in this respect, his work remains progressive in playing out the submerged social and political discourses of the body in a highly controversial form that both defines his own view of his films as 'fantastic documentaries', predicated on the surrealistic re-evaluation of the taken-for-granted naturalised conditions of contemporary society, and as animations which continually push back the frontiers of the art form itself.

Notes

1. R. Descartes, 'Second Meditation', *Discourse on Method and the Meditations* (London: Penguin, 1971), 102.
2. S. Freud, 'Civilization and Its Discontents', *Civilisation, Society and Religion*, Penguin Freud Library, vol. 12 (London: Penguin, 1985), 274.
3. M. O'Pray, 'Jan Svankmajer: A Mannerist Surrealist', P. Hames (ed.), *Dark Alchemy: The Films of Jan Svankmajer* (Trowbridge: Flicks Books, 1995), 48–78.
4. See B. Turner, *The Body and Society* (Oxford: Blackwell, 1984).
5. P. Hulten, 'Three Different Kinds of Interpretation', from F. Benvutti (ed.), *The Arcimboldo Effect* (London: Thames and Hudson, 1987), 18.
6. M. Foucault, *The History of Sexuality* (London: Penguin, 1976), 176. Foucault contextualises this

view by suggesting:

> The living conditions that were dealt to the proletariat, particularly, in the first half of the nineteenth century, show that that there was anything but concern for its body and sex: it was of little importance whether those people lived or died, since their reproduction was something that took care of itself in any case. Conflicts were necessary (in particular, conflicts over urban space: cohabitation, proximity, contamination, epidemics such as the cholera outbreak of 1832 or again, prostitution and venereal diseases). In order for the proletariat to be granted a body and a sexuality, economic emergencies had to arise (the development of heavy industry with the need for a steady and competent labour force, the obligation to regulate population flow and apply demographic controls); lastly, there had to be established a whole technology of control which made it possible to keep that body and sexuality finally conceded to them under surveillance (schooling, the politics of housing, public hygiene, institutions of relief and insurance, the general medicalisation of the population), in short, an entire administrative and technical machinery made it possible to safely import the deployment of sexuality into the exploited class.

7.   M. Foucault, ibid., 155.
8.   M. Foucault, ibid., 139.
9.   P. Hames (ed.), *Dark Alchemy: The Films of Jan Svankmajer* (Trowbridge: Flicks Books, 1995), 110.
10. R. Dyer, *Heavenly Bodies* (Basingstoke: Macmillam, 1987), 138.
11. R. Dyer, ibid., 138.
12. Samuel Beckett's Absurdist Theatre is characterised by an address of the ways in which humankind is intrinsically bound up in inescapable patterns of existence, subject to repeating the conditions of its own downfall in the pursuit of purpose and meaning. The fact that humankind endures this apparently bleak scenario informs the idea of 'the absurd' – simply, the degree and extent of such hopelessness becomes the subject for black humour.
13. M. Foucault, op. cit., 139.
14. J. Miller, *The Body in Question* (Basingstoke: Macmillan, 1978), 288.
15. R. Dyer, op. cit., 138.
16. M. O'Pray, 'Svankmajer: An Inventory', *Afterimage*, vol. 13 (Autumn 1987): 15.
17. J. Miller, op. cit., 93.
18. M. O'Pray, 1987, op. cit., 18.

Eisenstein and Stokes on Disney

Film animation and omnipotence

Michael O'Pray

Sergei Eisenstein loved the cartoon figure Mickey Mouse. The Soviet film director not only admired Walt Disney's films but also made them part of the subject matter of his theoretical studies. With his characteristic ambition, these theoretical explorations of Disney's animation were intended to serve as the bases for understanding animation and developing questions alluding to the nature of art itself.[1] Most of these writings are from the early 1940s, some years after his return from Hollywood where he had met Disney in 1937.[2] He was also reconsidering or at least reformulating his theoretical ideas, especially that of montage. That Disney should play a part in Eisenstein's fresh thoughts on cinema is characteristic of the latter's eclectic approach to ideas, borrowing from all the arts, especially painting and literature.

By no means does this essay attempt to unravel fully Eisenstein's insights into Disney and the issues of film animation; rather, it settles more modestly on a particular aspect relating to a question of aesthetics that is articulated by Eisenstein in primarily psychological terms. It was prompted largely by the intriguing fact that Adrian Stokes, the English aesthete in the same period, also refers briefly but fascinatingly to Disney's *Silly Symphonies* and Mickey Mouse in his book *Tonight the Ballet*,[3] published in 1935. Although Stokes's references are less sustained than Eisenstein's, they betray similarities in their associations with an idea of omnipotence, one that I wish to discuss here. As we shall see, Disney haunts the discourse on classical ballet in Britain during the 1930s and 1940s.

Adrian Stokes[4] began his studies of the visual arts, initially in early Renaissance architecture and sculpture, under the influence of the nineteenth-century English aesthetic tradition of late romanticism, especially that of John Ruskin and Walter Pater and then, through his own analysis with Melanie Klein in the 1930s, of Kleinian psychoanalysis. In the same decade, he published two astonishing books on architecture and sculpture – *The Quattro Cento*[5] and *Stones of Rimini*[6] – in which Kleinian ideas (although never overt) helped to shape his thoughts on these two areas of the visual arts. More radically, in his post-World War I writings, Stokes set out quite explicitly to ground aesthetic experience and artistic practice in the early and fundamental infantile structures formulated by Klein; namely, the depressive and paranoid–schizoid phases or positions. Originally, he connected these two positions with what at first was a technical (albeit ancient) distinction in sculpture between carving and modelling. The paranoid–schizoid position was aligned with a strong overwhelming and manipulation of the spectator by the art object – what broadly speaking we might understand as intense identifications. This was aligned with modelling. The depressive position was related to a conception of the art object whereby it had an independence and autonomy[7] and was strongly associated with carving. During the same period – the 1930s – Stokes was a ballet critic for the *Spectator* and wrote two popular books on the subject, *Russian Ballets*[8] (in honour of the Ballet Russes) and *Tonight the Ballet*. This was also a time in which classical ballet in Britain under the impact of Diaghilev enjoyed a unequalled reputation.[9] Powell and Pressburger's *The Red Shoes*, made in 1947, lends this phenomenon its crowning filmic and highly romantic moment.[10] Interestingly, Powell had the dancer and choreographer Leonide Massine play a role in the film and it is to Massine that Stokes's *Tonight the Ballet* is dedicated.

One explanation for this mutual interest in a Hollywood cartoon director, of course, is the almost universal popularity of Disney's films in that period, when cinema attendance, even among aesthetes like Stokes, was regular.[11] Perhaps it is no accident that Stokes especially, and to some extent Eisenstein, found themselves writing about Mickey Mouse. In England, Stokes was not alone in in making comparisons with Disney's work and the classical ballet of the period. For example, the film director Anthony Asquith, in an essay on filming the ballet that was published in 1936, cites Disney's *Silly Symphonies* as an example of 'ballet constructed in film terms' and not 'merely a film treatment of a theatrical ballet'.[12] There seemed to be a general fascination with ballet among filmmakers at the the time. The animator Len Lye was reported in 1935 as planning a ballet film using real dance for an advert for Savings Bank,[13] the classic *Rainbow Dance*. In 1934, the author of *Balletomania* Arnold Haskell discusses film with the ballet choreographer Balanchine and again Disney is cited by Haskell:

> Micky Mouse seems to provide the ballet need on film; a strong personality artificially created out of a pattern. Musically, too, it would be difficult to imagine a more perfect screen ballet.[14]

Ten years later, George Borodin in his book *This Thing Called Ballet*, published in 1945, was still referring to Disney but noting that the 'beauty and unity of those first *Silly Symphonies*' was superior to Mickey Mouse and especially Donald Duck. Of the *Silly Symphonies* especially, Borodin states:

> . . . there has never been a purer expression of the union of music and movement in any public performance, a union all the more complete, because the story in the *Silly Symphonies* was quite immaterial. One may with every justification, liken them to *Les Sylphides*.[15]

In ruminating on these ideas thrown up by Eisenstein and Stokes, it seemed that there were similarities in what they said about Disney's films even if their approaches and conceptual frameworks are quite different. Importantly, they both shared some idea of the role of omnipotence, of an all-powerfulness which they associated with the notions of control and virtuosity. What follows is largely addressed to this issue as it relates to film animation.

For Stokes, classical ballet was the supreme form of the combination of dance or bodily movement with music. Music placed alongside movement transforms it. As Stokes puts it:

> Music that breaks in upon the scenes of movement gives rebirth not only of feeling but of perception.[16]

An example of this power he suggests is in a commonplace scene of the 1930s in Europe:

> Think how the streets spring to life when the bolder kind of barrel-organ grinds its tune! At once the streets become a *mise-en-scène*, the movement of passers-by and of traffic becomes a ballet of sorts.[17]

In such a situation, for Stokes, life takes on an outwardness as of a spectacle. And in a more psychoanalytical, and specifically Kleinian, vein, he remarks:

> So many things that lay in pieces in the mind and which were projected into the external world as piecemeal, rhythmless, living death, are gathered together, organised and drilled by the music.[18]

What was accidental and arbitrary is given shape and form by the music. At this point in *Tonight the Ballet*, Stokes turns to film: 'Was not the old silent film and its accompanying music a kind of ballet?', he asks.[19] What separates out music like the barrel-organ in relation to passers-by in the streets from ballet itself is the synchronisation achieved between the music and the movements in ballet. Stokes connects this synchronisation with omnipotence:

> Any action is pointed by the synchronisation of a precise sound. Just think of the noises employed by the music-hall to stress the *tours de force* of acrobats. It is as if instead of thumping the earth they struck a real musical note by the brilliancy of their leaps: every time they hit the bell. An almost omnipotent neatness of movement is thus expressed; and since we wish that all our aims were executed with this intense organisation, this slick clock-work precision, we derive pleasure from the synchronisation of any noise that seems to denote the power of human movement.[20]

The context for 'omnipotence' in this passage relates to that which is achieved by the juncture of music and movement so that the latter in its 'neatness' gives pleasure to the spectator who desires such a movement for him or herself. Here the fantasy of a desire is given expression through art albeit the musical hall, circus, classical ballet or Disney cartoon.

According to Stokes, such characteristics, found in the Ballets Russes during the 1920s and 1930s, are fascinatingly passed on to Disney when Stokes, lamenting the death of Diaghilev,[21] remarks:

> Mickey Mouse and Silly Symphonies were the only things that helped to fill the gap for the London ballet lover.[22]

Other ballet companies only filled Stokes and others with nostalgia for the Ballets Russes company. Mickey Mouse, on the other hand, 'does not fill one with nostalgia'. In what Stokes calls:

> Disney's miniature theatre of grotesqueries ... we recognise immediately the quality of expressive but infinitely precise movements which make the synchronised sounds so lovable.[23]

Stokes goes on to describe the qualities of Mickey:

> There is a patness in everything that occurs, the vital wit that belongs to situations

expressed in terms of agility or graceful movement.[24]

In his first piece of writing on Disney in 1941, Eisenstein makes a similar observation to Stokes's. Describing Walt Disney himself, Eisenstein remarks that 'Mickey has the same grace, ease of gesture and elegance'.[25] At a later point, Eisenstein says something quite remarkable:

> I'm sometimes frightened when I watch his films. Frightened because of some absolute perfection in what he does.[26]

I shall return to this 'frightening' business. Eisenstein goes on to make parallels with other forms and creators of art. He compares Disney's films with Francis of Assissi's sermons, Fra Angelico's paintings, butterflies flying, flowers growing, brooks meandering, Hans Christian Andersen, Lewis Carroll and Hoffmann. This list suggests that Eisenstein is struggling to make the point that there is both a simplicity, a child-like primitiveness about the films – like a stream, a flower or a butterfly – and something displaying an 'absolute freedom from all categories, all conventions'.[27] Stokes too uses a list. It is an equally fascinating one. He remarks:

> To my mind a *Punch and Judy* show is far better entertainment than Noel Coward's *Cavalcade*. Mickey Mouse, like Charlie Chaplin, like the Harlequin, like the ballet dancer, like marionettes, like the pre-Wagnerian opera singers, like the Clown, is a mask, a figure, an emblem. Nothing escapes.[28]

If Eisenstein's list seems to be making a point about the feeling that Disney's animation produces in the viewer, then Stokes is comparing Disney's work with other kinds of cultural objects, ones that all share a certain mode of representation in which outwardness is a central and important quality. All these objects or forms share an immediacy of sorts – 'nothing escapes'. Stokes compares Lotte Reineger's shadow animation *Prince Achmed* unfavourably with Walt Disney's films, for the former does not reveal its 'inner processes'.[29] Disney's films, he believes, like the classical ballet, fully project themselves in an externalisation so that 'Mickey Mouse . . . cannot fail to express the world'. In his use of the notions of 'mask' and 'emblem' Stokes is interpreting Mickey Mouse quite differently to Eisenstein whose list does not have the implication of something standing for something else as implied by the notions of mask and emblem. Stokes's commitment to the emblematic was founded in his allegiance to the art of the *quattrocento*, which he redescribed conceptually as the Quattro Cento in which art as 'the turning of subject into object' is somehow 'transparent to the eye',[30] having an immediacy that Stokes felt at the time was only to be found in *quattrocento* art. Ezra Pound's own allegiance to the *quattrocento* involved an understanding of the emblematic. Pound makes a distinction between art that is 'clean' and that which is 'muzzy'.[31]

There are so many routes one could take from these fairly casual remarks by Stokes and Eisenstein. But what I want to identify and develop is what both men are characterising here in relation to animation and to do that we have to take a step back to consider Freud's concept of the omnipotence of thoughts.[32] This latter notion is one that Freud used quite substantially in his case study of the Rat Man. The omnipotence of thoughts is an early, we might say primitive, defence mechanism against anxiety used by the infant in order to experience an all-powerfulness and hence control, which in fact is quite illusory. By necessity, this mechanism is a conception of the mind itself, for in the case of the unfortunate Rat Man, he believed that by *thinking* that an event had occurred, it had done so in reality. Put another way, his desire for *x* was enough to make it seem to have been satisfied; hence the phrase, 'the omnipotence of thought'.

This is the model that Freud offered for the structure and the function of the omnipotence of thoughts, which he used extensively in *Totem and Taboo*. For example, in *Totem and Taboo*, it explains animism and notions of magic found in primitive tribes.[33]

Stokes's remarks on Mickey Mouse involve the idea that in watching the animated character's utter control of his movement we see fulfilled our own desire to have such an organisation of our own 'aims'. It is this idea of omnipotence that is central to Stokes's view of Mickey Mouse. This control is partly achieved through Disney's presentation of his cartoon character in an emblematic form. Part of what Stokes understood by the emblematic was its relationship to the artistic process or creation itself. In renaissance art 'the act of artistic creation was itself the specific symbol of release that men were feeling or desiring'.[34]

For Eisenstein, Mickey Mouse and Disney's cartoons of the period in question were related to two notions of omnipotence. The first is the most obscure and complex and it must be remembered that Eisenstein never gathered these notes and drafts together into a worked-over piece. We must expect difficulties working with such material. At various points, Eisenstein speaks of the plasmatic characteristic of Disney's films and other art works (mainly drawings). According to Naum Kleiman, Eisenstein's view of Disney's kind of animation led the Soviet director to:

> . . . the theme of 'protoplasmaticness', which lowered the 'level of attractiveness' to the verge of 'the physiology of the sense organs'. In Eisenstein's view, the very mechanism of a flowing 'omnipotent' contour was an echo of the most concealed depths of pre-memory.[35]

This plasma is connected to the prenatal and is a primitive force that he associates with his concept of ecstasy. These prenatal elements are 'expressed not as a process, but as an object'.[36] Eisenstein believes that Disney 'appeals to this realm . . . through elements of form'.[37] This 'plasma appeal' can be seen in varying contours – necks and legs expanding, and the variation of species – octopuses becoming elephants and so forth. He calls this the 'omnipotence of plasma which contains in "liquid" form all possibilities of future species and forms'.[38] He remarks in an earlier passage that:

> . . . ecstasy is a sensing and experiencing of the primal omnipotence – the element of coming into being – the plasmaticness of existence, from which everything can arise. And it is beyond any image, without an image, beyond tangibility – like a pure sensation.[39]

Further explication of these ideas are given in Eisenstein when he talks about the outline of a drawing taking 'on an independent life, independent of the figures themselves'.[40] Based on the view that any representation comprises both the lines themselves and 'the image that arises from them',[41] then plasmaticness is concerned with form. Eisenstein understands that this primitive all-powerfulness of the line in drawing takes an image that comes to express that omnipotence. So, form is aligned with omnipotence of the plasmatic which in turn for Eisenstein causes us to respond as spectators in a certain way. This merging of an organicist metaphysics with a reflexive psychology comprises the theoretical framework in much of his discussion of Disney.

The other notion of omnipotence that Eisenstein uses when speaking of Disney is a more straightforward one in that relates it to the idea of fantasy:

> As an unforgettable symbol of [Disney's] whole creative work, there stands before me family of octopuses on four legs, with a fifth serving as a tail and a sixth – a

trunk. How much (imaginary!) divine omnipotence there is in this! What magic of reconstructing the world according to one's fantasy and will.[42]

This view is only another confirmation of Freud's remark in *Totem and Taboo* that '[I]n only a single field of our civilisation has the omnipotence of thoughts been retained and that is in the field of art'.[43] So much needs to be explored and unpacked in all of this, but for our present purposes I would like to offer the following thoughts that might link Eisenstein with Freud and to some extent with Stokes.

The central concern here seems to be the idea of a certain pleasure achieved by animation (not all of course) wherein we identify with its virtuosity. Stokes and Eisenstein speak respectively of a 'patness' and an 'absolute perfection' (one, we should remember, that frightened Eisenstein). They stress the force of this virtuosity. It is not simply a characteristic of the animation but somehow is an integral part of how its affects us. In this virtuosity where form and content reach a perfection, there is the deepest pleasure because we are confronted with a control and importantly, the very fantasy of that control in the animated figures.[44] In other words, in the plasmatic element – the sheer virtuosity of of the lines, say, in Disney, or for that matter, in the animation films of Robert Breer or Len Lye – we have an objectification of our own desire for omnipotence. Our desire to will something without in fact acting upon it is acted out in the animation itself through the virtuoso use of forms.

In this way, it could be suggested that Eisenstein's terror at Disney's perfection is not only of the representation of the omnipotence of thought but also of the ensuing idealised nature of the images. Our fear (Eisenstein's fright) is of the image's fragility; that is to say, the danger it evokes in terms of the potential failure of its ambitions (like watching a tightrope walker). The fear could also be attributed to our anxiety for a fantasy pushed to its ideal limits – the bounds of the imagination – but always precisely and finely controlled through formal and imaginative virtuosity.

In one of Eisenstein's extensive footnotes on the animism of drawing, he touches on this issue in terms of 'magic':

> Here, magic is not just an empty phrase of speech. For art (true art) artificially returns the viewer to the stage of sensuous thought – which is also the stage of a magical relationship with nature. When you achieve, for example, a synthetic blending of sound and image – you have subjected the viewer's perception to the conditions of sensuous thought, where synthetic perception is the only kind possible – there is not yet any differentiation of perceptions. and our viewer is 'rebuilt' in accord with norms not of the present, but those of primordially sensuous perception – he is 'returned' to the conditions of the magical stage of experiencing the world. and an Idea, carried by means of *such a system* of influence, given form *through such means* – irresistibly controls emotion. For the senses and consciousness in such a condition – are subjugated and controlled almost as if in *a trance*. And because of the passively-magical state of the perceiver, art is simultaneously – actively-magical in terms of influence and control over the viewer by the artist-magician.[45]

If art is the 'influence and control over the viewer by the artist magician' as Eisenstein suggests, we take some of the sting out of that artist-centred remark by considering that such influence and control only seems possible if it finds some response in similar terms in the spectator. For it seems part of the omnipotence of thoughts that influence and control is projected onto some other object whereby it can satisfy a desire that must remain necessarily unfulfilled in the actual world. In Mickey Mouse, such a state is achieved in Eisensteinian terms through his idea of omnipotence. But it is important to stress that this is not simply a matter of fantasy, otherwise much of film would satisfy us in the same way. On the contrary, in animation especially, the satisfaction depends not simply on the ability to represent other impossible worlds, but rather to remind us that the skill and virtuosity involved in form is supreme and fundamental in achieving this world. In this way, it is true that animation is often at its best when we marvel not only at the subject matter, so to speak, but at its means of achievement. We are conscious of technique here in the way that we are often not in mainstream narrative film.

So, if in animation we witness the omnipotence of thought, we also witness necessarily the means of achieving that omnipotence and to that extent animation separates itself from other kinds of cinema. In animation, at its best, we thrill to the means of representation and not only the representation.

This is a revised version of a paper presented at the 1993 SAS conference, Farnham, England and was first published as a Working Paper by the School of Art and Design University of East London, 1995.

I would like to thank Ray Durgnat for his comments on an earlier draft of this article.

Notes

1. See Edoardo G. Grossi, 'Eisenstein as theoretician: a preliminary consideration', *Eisenstein Rediscovered*, eds Ian Christie and Richard Taylor (London: Routledge, 1993).
2. These writings are collected in *Eisenstein on Disney*, ed. Jay Leyda (London: Methuen, 1988).
3. *Tonight the Ballet*, Adrian Stokes (London: Faber & Faber, 1942).
4. For an excellent introduction to Stokes, see R. Wollheim, 'Adrian Stokes' in *On Art and the Mind*, Richard Wollheim (London: Allen Lane, 1973).
5. In *The Critical Writings of Adrian Stokes*, vol. 1, ed. Lawrence Gowing (London: Thames and Hudson, 1978), 29–180.
6. Ibid., 181–302.
7. For a fuller account of the relationship between Stokes and the ideas of Melanie Klein, see 'Adrian Stokes', Wollheim, op. cit.
8. *Russian Ballets*, Adrian Stokes (London: Faber & Faber, 1935).
9. Of course, Diaghilev's impact had been felt for many years. See Richard Buckle, *Diaghilev* (London: Weidenfeld, 1993).
10. See Michael Powell, *A Life in the Movies* (London: Heinemann, 1986), 97. Arnold Haskell's response to the film is to be found in *In His True Centre: An Interim Biography*, Arnold L. Haskell, (London: A&C Black, 1951), 164–166.
11. For an example of the debate about film in literary circles during the inter-war years, see Francis Mulhern, *The Moment of 'Scrutiny'* (London: Verso, 1981), esp. 51–52.
12. See Anthony Asquith, 'Ballet and the Film', in *Footnotes to the Ballet*, ed. Caryl Brahms (London: Peter Davies Ltd, 1944), 249.
13. 'Avant-garde to the Rescue: Revolution in Advertising', *World Film News* (April 1936), in *Traditions of Independence: British Cinema in the Thirties*, ed. Don Macpherson (London: British Film Institute, 1980), 183–184.
14. *Balletomania: The Story of an Obsession*, Arnold L. Haskell (London: Gollancz, 1934), 154.
15. *This Thing Called Ballet*, George Borodin (London: Macdonald, 1945), 206.
16. *Tonight the Ballet*, op. cit., 13.
17. Ibid., 13.
18. Ibid., 13.
19. Stokes also discusses, among other films, John Grierson's classic documentary *Drifters*, which fascinatingly also receives attention from William Empson in his *Some Versions of Pastoral*, published in 1935. Of course, Empson was a contemporary of the GPO filmmaker Humphrey Jennings at Cambridge University.
20. *Tonight the Ballet*, op. cit., 20.
21. Diaghilev died in 1929 and the company was taken over by de Basil.

22. Tonight the Ballet, op. cit., 20.

23. Ibid., 21.

24. Ibid., 21.

25. *Eisenstein on Disney*, op. cit., 1.

26. Ibid., 2.

27. Ibid., 2.

28. *Tonight the Ballet*, op. cit., 23–24.

29. Ibid., 64–65.

30. Richard Wollheim, 'Introduction', in *The Image in Form: Selected Writings of Adrian Stokes*, ed. Richard Wollheim (Harmondsworth: Penguin, 1972), 15.

31. On Pound and Stokes and the emblematic, see Peter Robinson, 'Ezra Pound and Italian Art', in *Pound's Artists: Ezra Pound and the Visual Arts in London, Paris and Italy* (London: Tate Gallery, 1985).

32. On the omnipotence of thought, see Wollheim on what he calls the Master Thought in 'Imagination and Identification' in *On Art and the Mind* (London: Allen Lane, 1973).

33. I have examined the link between the omnipotence of thought and magic elsewhere in relation to the Czech animator Jan Svankmajer. See, 'Animisme, magie en de almacht van Ideen in de films van Jan Svankmajer', in *Het Ludicatief Principe: Jan Svankmajer* (Antwerp: Antwerpe Film Stichtung, 1990), 58–62.

34. In Wollheim, *The Image in Form*, 43.

35. Naum Kleiman, 'Introduction', in *Eisenstein on Disney*, op. cit., xi.

36. *Eisenstein on Disney*, 64.

37. Ibid., 64.

38. Ibid., 64.

39. Ibid., 46.

40. Ibid., 59.

41. Ibid., 57.

42. Ibid., 3.

43. Sigmund Freud, *Totem and Taboo* (London: Routledge & Kegan Paul, 1960), 90.

44. 'Figures' is to be understood in its widest sense here, incorporating the more abstract shapes of, say, Len Lye's or Stan Brakhage's 'animated' films.

45. *Eisenstein on Disney*, op. cit., 94–95, footnote number 46.

17

Towards a post-modern animated discourse

Bakhtin, intertextuality and the cartoon carnival

Terrance R. Lindvall and J. Matthew Melton

Mikhail Bakhtin complained that the wit of Voltaire and the Enlightenment era lacked the full-bodied comedy of the Medieval marketplace. In *Rabelais and His World*, Bakhtin celebrated the universal, ambivalent and grotesque 'carnival comedy' of the sixteenth century.[1] Enlightenment laughter is primarily mocking and satiric, subverting the folly of the hierarchy in its feasts of fools, asses and administrators. Medieval comedy, however, affirmed, renewed and revitalised the old, bringing forth new birth, life, hope and laughter. It simultaneously took apart and put together the Body of Humanity and the Christian Church. By means of deconstruction and then reconstruction, carnival laughter simultaneously derided and delighted in the social and cultural apparatus of its era.

Medieval laughter reduced the mysteries of social and religious existence by *playing* with their forms without *denying* them. The highest form stood with the lowest; the vulgar gave the pre-eminent meaning; the clown sat on the throne. Nonsense ruled sense's domain; and humour was intertwined with the humility and humanity of all those who came from the dust (or *humus*, the root of humanity, humility and humour) and would return unto it.

A frequently overlooked contemporary (or post-modern) form sharing the playful dynamism of the carnival spirit is the self-reflexive animated cartoon, particularly that of the comic genre. (*Animation* as a genre extends beyond the realm of the *cartoon*, which is defined in this paper as *comic animation*.) Like medieval comedy, the cartoon mocks itself, romping with its audience. It re-creates (makes again) and recreates (enjoys) its own being. In ways that will be shown, Bakhtin's notion of carnival provides an inspired model for analysis of comic genres like the animated film, genres often overshadowed by more 'significant' cinemas. Where the clown once ruled or misruled, in medieval comedy, it is now the turn of the animator to show his motley.

Theoretical heritage

The casual way in which animation and the cartoon are treated by film theorists is due in part to the self-deprecating humour of the cartoon itself. Like the post-modernism of Jean-Francois Lyotard, the cartoon is a playful art. Without pretensions, it teases both those who neglect it and those who take it too seriously. Vladimir Propp's discovery of a basic morphology in the Russian fairytale should encourage us not to despise the little, common, vulgar things of this world.[2] But, when modernist Siegfried Kracauer separated animated cartoons from true photographic film, he essentially banished them from his theory, warning that in certain cartoons of Disney, a 'false devotion to the cinematic approach inexorably stifles the draftsman's imagination'.[3]

Jean Mitry treated animation with little more attention, though he did praise the assimilation of image and sound in Alexander Alexeieff and Claire Parker's non-comic pinscreen animation, *A Night on Bald Mountain* (1934). It offered, he claimed, 'a succession of imprecise, ghostly, hallucinatory forms, that Moussorgsky's work seems to call up from the underworld, animating with a glorious, life-giving breath'.[4] This 'inspired' view of animation was echoed by Erwin Panofsky, who said the 'very virtue of the animated cartoon is to animate; that is to say, endow lifeless things with life or living things with a different kind of life. It effects a metamorphosis'.[5]

One of the most significant treatments of animated film is Dana Polan's 'A Brechtian Cinema? Towards a Politics of Self-Reflexive Film'. Polan suggests that a Hollywood cartoon like *Duck Amuck* (1953) embodies a consciously apolitical self-reflexivity. It is a playfully disengaged art form wholly concerned with 'the nature of animation technique itself'.[6] Post-modern sensibilities are stylistically realised in this art form with the fusion of high and low art, the tinkering with hybrid forms, the tones of irony and parody, the incredulity toward meta-narratives and the principle of double coding, all of which frolic merrily in the realm of the intertextual. The self-reflexive cartoon is a cultural practice operating as one of Lyotard's language games where rules and players are in constant flux. It comically renders transparent the workings of the text, providing a Brechtian distance from the work and upending the dominant classical narrative style to revitalise traditional pleasure in the act of viewing.

The animated film mediates between two competing epistemological methods, between what Paul Ricoeur designates in hermeneutics as *synthetic* and *analytic*.[7] C.S. Lewis expresses it as the difference between 'looking along' and 'looking at', corresponding respectively to the French verbs *connaître* and *savoir*.[8] The first is a knowledge by acquaintance; the latter a knowledge by description. One might define them as a hermeneutics of faith and a hermeneutics of suspicion – both being necessary for a full knowledge of the object.

As the cartoon reflects upon its own construction and its relationship to the context out of which it has been created, it deconstructs the imposed reality of cinematic discourse. The cartoon, in Polan's terms, 'explicitly signals its cartoon-ness' and an awareness of its means and motives of production.[9]

Self-reflexive cartoons

Animated films demonstrate self-reflexivity in three general and overlapping ways. First, by commenting on filmmaking and the film industry and by unveiling the raw materials and methods of the filmmaking process, cartoons reveal their own textuality.

Second, animated films possess the ability to function as discourse, speaking directly to their audiences. Third, animated films reflect their relationships to their creators. The animators themselves enter their cartoons and become deconstructive agents of their own artifice. Animated film is a genre in which the *auteur* is not only dominant, but able to speak directly to her or his audience. As Steve Schneider notes, 'animation is probably the ultimate auteurist cinema'.[10]

The irony of filmmaking as the subject of film draws attention to the craft, the business and the visions behind such enterprises. The writer/director is able to explore his or her work and question it, its techniques and its values. These films are not mere exercises in vain speculation, but serve as excursions into the fundamental nature and purposes of film.

Many cartoons have demonstrated this ability to reflect upon their own nature as drawn, celluloid products.

Reflexivity in animation

Cartoons about the art of filmmaking appeared early in film history. Cartoonist Winsor McCay bet comedian John Bunny and company that he could make his lightning sketches move and proceeded to show his merry comrades the wonders of how he brought *Little Nemo* and his cartoon characters to life. The secrets of the enchanted drawings were revealed within the text itself, demythologising the mysteries of the esoteric art.

Two animated films from the silent era unveil the art of filmmaking (with subtextual commentary on the act of adultery within the industry) in narratives about filmmakers. In *Revenge of the Kinematograph Cameraman* (1912), entomologist Wladislaw Starewicz produced a satirical puppet film with waxed insects. A businessbug from the country, Mr Zhukov (a beetle), leaves his bugwife and goes to the city where he succumbs to the lusty temptation of a Dragon-fly cabaret dancer. A jilted suitor, the grasshopper, who happens to be a cameraman, bicycles around and films the bad beetle and his paramour from behind bushes and through the keyhole of a hotel bedroom door.

The completed film is then shown at an outdoor cinema that Mr Zhukov and his wife are unsuspectingly attending. Mrs Zhukov sees the sin of her husband on the big screen and enraged, demolishes both her husband and the screen. The film within the film exposes the hypocritical behaviours of the bugs and insinuates a parallel within the real film community. All the insects attending the premiere become neighbourhood voyeurs, sharing in the spy work of the grasshopper cameraman. The consciousness of the spectator in recognising or projecting one's life onto the screen is played out in all its irony as the beetle's lovemaking scene has been recorded, even as one of Kracauer's 'found stories', wherein the spectator catches 'nature in the act'.

Starewicz portrays the insect's drudgery of filmmaking, of loading and transporting equipment, of setting up and shooting and finally, of the exhilaration of exhibiting one's work. The function of film is shown to be the confrontation of the spectator with hidden and expressed desire.

Catching 'nature in THE act' is also an implicit theme of Otto Mesmer's *Flim Flam Films* (1927). After Felix the Cat buys a movie camera, he turns it over to his mischievous kids. They use the camera to capture their dad's dalliance with a bathing beauty, getting Felix in loads of trouble with his infuriated spouse. Felix's cartoon shows problems inherent in the filmmaking process, such as improper framing, disjointed camera angles and inverted images. The power of the camera in this jazz age cartoon is its ability to reconstruct such events as feline infidelity.

Porky Pig also produced his own cartoon in Tex Avery's *Porky's Preview* (1941). Holding a special screening for animal friends, Porky revels in his crude, stick-figure scrawls, which Leonard Maltin points out bear a remarkable resemblance to the later UPA animation. Porky brags that it wasn't hard because, 'shucks, I'm an artist'. Avery's text is a gentle piece of self-mockery and irony on the low 'art' of animated cartoons.

Another film in which animated characters both make and watch cartoons is Tony Sarg's impressive silhouette animation of 1922, *The Original Movie*. Sarg explores the entire process of filmmaking from the perspective of a stone-age filmmaker. A screenwriter hires Stonehenge Film Co. to produce his film. They cast the parts and shoot his script of 'Who's the Goat?' using a monkey camera-operator hanging from a dinosaur's neck for a primitive crane shot. Censors arrive to cut up Mr A. Flintpebble's film. The final product is a very short film that its writer cannot recognise. The intertitles announce Sarg's cynical moral: 'It's a wise scenario that knows its own author after it gets in the movies.'

From the Van Beuren studio in 1931 came the clever, frenetic *Making 'Em Move* (a.k.a *In a Cartoon Studio*). This unusually delightful exception to the run-of-the-mill Aesop Fables series sneaks a cartoon character and us into the secret recesses of a cartoon studio. Ominous signs along the corridor leading to the inner sanctum demand 'SILENCE'. Dozens of cartoon artists are diligently drawing in what appears to be a Taylorised, capitalistic animation factory. A typical menagerie of cartoon animals form a busy musical band to keep the peon animators from rebelling or forming a union. The enslaved but happy animators create flipbooks of a hootchy-kootchy dancer, which are then shot by a camera on a tripod. The little band is placed on the film to produce the sound track. Finally, the film premieres with the titles announcing: 'A Movie Cartoon Today – Fables Animals Presents "LITTLE NELL"'. The sawmill melodrama is acted out by stick figures (twice or thrice removed from the real). The actors bow and when the villain appears the crowd hisses and boos. The villain responds with Bronx cheers for which the audience punches in the screen. The cartoon points up the madcap lunacy of the animators and the creative anarchy that reigns in the cartoon studio.

From Moscow, Fedor Khitruk's stylised *Film, Film, Film* (1969) offered a playful satire on filmmaking. The Halas and Batchelor *History of the Cinema* (1958) deconstructed the story of film, from the inverted image of the Magic Lantern to the wide-screen cinemascope images. Michel Valma spoofs both film and psychoanalysis in his witty and succinct *Freud S'Explique Sur le Cinema*. Bruno Bozzetto's *Sigmund* (1984) showed the famous psychoanalyst as an impressionable boy spectator sitting in front of a television and projecting himself into an oneiric state of Olympic athletic fantasies. The voyeur finds his pleasure by becoming, in Kenneth Burke's terms, consubstantial with the heroic images, all without leaving the cushions of a giant armchair. Andrew Stantan's *A Story* (1987) portrays a clown character, a macabre Ronald McDonald, who breaks the barrier of the television screen by reaching out and trying to pull a mesmerised kid into Tedland. The attempted kidnapping only results in a hole in the screen and the clown wondering why it is that when he tries to pull a kid into his television program, 'the kid gets a concussion'.

Carl Sturges produced *At The Movies* (1979), a festive piece of clay animation celebrating some of the unique frustrations of going to a movie theatre. Zlatko Grgic and Ivo Vrbanic parodied various national movie treatments of romance, from American Westerns to Swedish nudity to Soviet propaganda, in their *Love and Film* (1961). All these cartoons are affectionate footnotes to the magic of film and television, simultaneously debunking that magic by dismantling the cinematic apparatus.

Cartoons commonly quote and refer to other cartoons and cinematic texts. *Who Framed Roger Rabbit?* (1988) cascades with animated allusions, inside references and jokes, such as the ubiquitous ACME or Daffy Duck complaining in his customarily irascible fashion that he can't understand the squawking of Donald Duck. The practice of inter-textual footnoting originated much earlier. Even Walt Disney in his sketchy *Puss 'N Boots* (1922) advertised not only the Newman Kingville Theater, as it was supposed to do, but a Rudolph Valentino character as well, who would, it was promised, 'throw the bull in six parts'. Through association with recognisable Hollywood personalities or places, the cartoon character can leave Toontown and enter the studio system. For example, in *You Ought To Be In Pictures* (1940), Porky Pig meets with Leon Schleschinger to discuss his contract.

Some cartoons are endowed with a sense of consciousness that humorously connects them to points of art and culture outside themselves. Stanley Cavell points out that the 'lows of culture' generally do burlesque 'the conditions of high art, [as] the highs often need decanting and the lows are often deeper and more joyful'. The lowly cartoon is a most apt vehicle for cracking the pretensions of the dominant cinema. Silent cartoons often followed the same formulas of second-rate filmmaking. When a character or genre succeeded, it was immediately imitated. Both minor comics and cartoons copied Charlie Chaplin endlessly. Dozens of cartoons have paid tribute to Hollywood, its stars and its films. Caricatures of famous film luminaries are spotlighted in 1933's *Mickey's Gala Premiere* (Greta Garbo embraces a giggling Mickey Mouse) and Tex Avery's 1944 *Hollywood Steps Out* (Clark Gable is recognised by his oversized elephantine ears). Such cartoons were peppered with playfully coded references to the cultural texts of Hollywood. The same pattern pops up with Flip the Frog in *Movie Mad* (1931) from Ub Iwerks and in T.E. Hee's caricatures in *Coo-Coo Nut Grove* (1936). Donald Crafton notes the irony of the Pat Sullivan/Otto Mesmer production of Felix in Hollywood that ends 'with Cecil B. DeMille handing Felix one of those long-term contracts just when Sullivan and Winkler were haggling over renewal'.

Caricature has functioned as a point of contrast with the real world, parodying the Hollywood Star System. Scores of back-handed tributes are played with the dominant characteristics and circulating gossip of key actors and actresses. Mae West rumbled her way into the 1935 parody, *Who Killed Cock Robin?* Katharine Hepburn made cartoon cameos as frequently as Laurel and Hardy. In Disney's *Mother Goose in Hollywood* (1938), she is a forlorn Little Bo Peep, while her distinctive voice pervades the silly *Hamateur Night* (1939). Humphrey Bogart and sizzling Lauren Bacall ('BeCool'), whistling like a construction worker, are the focus of *Bacall to Arms* (1946). Gregory Peck cuts his steak with a *Spellbound*-like knife in *Slick Hair* (1947). These parodies stretched the idiosyncratic characteristics of the stars (like making Jimmy Stewart's drawl interminably long.) Inside jokes on Bing Crosby and his obsession with horse racing decorate many cartoons like *Hollywood Daffy* (1946) in which Daffy also disguises himself as duck versions of Chaplin, Durante and even the Oscar statuette.

The list of quotation films is almost inexhaustible: *Gabby Goose* (1937), *Film Fan* (1939), *A Star is Hatched* (1938), *Porky's 5 & 10* (1938), *Porky's Movie Mystery* (1939), *Bosko's Picture Show* (1933), *What's Cookin' Doc?* (1944), *Hollywood Capers* (1935) and *Bunny and Claude* (1968). *Daffy Duck in Hollywood* (1938) mocked the studio world of Wonder Pictures where the motto was, 'If We Make It, It's a Wonder!'. In *Stage Door* (1944), Bugs Bunny and Yosemite Sam watch a black and white cartoon, 'One 'o them thar B.B. cartoonies!'. A film clip of Errol Flynn as Robin Hood punctuates the finale of *Rabbit Hood* (1949). After cutting away to Flynn, a sceptical Bugs Bunny looks into the camera and mutters: 'Naw, that's silly. It couldn't be him.' The episode cleverly inverts the concepts of reality and illusion by allowing the cartoon to pass judgement on the live action film, even denying its plausibility. A parodic apotheosis occurs in *Hollywood Canine Canteen* (1946), in which all the actors and actresses are dogs. In the Academy Award-winning Pete Burness cartoon *When Magoo Flew* (1955), old Mr Magoo boards a plane that he mistakes for the Rialto Theater. He watches real life policemen chase a crook on the plane and thinks he is watching a 'realistic 3-D' movie. His only complaint when he leaves the plane is that there was no cartoon played onboard: 'You don't happen to show cartoons of that funny little near-sighted man, do you?'

Of all genres, cartoons seem particularly suited to deconstructing the ontological nature of the film medium itself. Films like Robert Swarthe's *Kick Me* (1975) and Wolfgang Urchs' *Contraste* (1964) dabble with the limits of the frame. Swarthe's camera-less animation begins by announcing: 'Ladies and Gentlemen, this animated film is made of tiny little pictures drawn on Motion Picture film.' The protagonist, a stick figure, falls outside the frames on a strip of celluloid. Trying to get back, he is chased by a large black spider from frame to frame. Just as he is to be caught, he is rescued *deus ex machina*, by what appears to be the burning of the film. However, the burning becomes a new pursuer. (A brief segment in *Allegro Non Troppo* (1976), Bruno Bozzetto's grand parody of Disney's *Fantasia* features a little fellow who discovers the transitory, flammable nature of film. As the paper on which he was drawn burns him into oblivion, he bravely waves farewell.)

In *Contraste*, a rumpled housewife decides to modernise her home. She trades in traditional furniture for abstract, fashionable objects: a classic piano for a new technological music machine, Renaissance paintings for contemporary art works. Finally, she exchanges her pipe-smoking, traditional husband for a Picasso-like lover, who immediately seeks to find himself a more-up-to-date mate. Realising she has discarded what was truly valuable to her, she stops the cartoon by stepping out of the frame to the sprocket holes and begins to reverse the flow of time. By speeding the frames in reverse, the *hausfrau* is able to restore her life to the beginning of the film, bringing back all her drab furniture and retrieving her original dull, but faithful, husband.

The 1985 Grand Prize-winner at the Hiroshima Animation Festival was Osamu Tezuka's hilarious *Broken Down Film*, a delightful homage to American Westerns, with gags borrowed from Keaton and other silent comedians. The cartoon is a projectionist's nightmare with two countdown leaders, inverted title cards, shifting frame lines, scratches drawn on the film and animated hairs apparently stuck in the gate. In Tezuka's film, humour arises out of the breaking of spectator expectations. The frame-play breaks the illusion of watching a film. *Broken Down Film* disrupts the set of shared codes for even an animated film, deconstructing the conventional grammar and reworking the codes into a fresh perspective on the nature of film itself. By highlighting the artifice deployed in its own invention, the film reaffirms the presence and validity of normative codes. It confirms an unconscious awareness of the tacit rules of conventional and classic film production by breaking our expectations in the act of watching film.

This self-consciousness about textuality exhibits itself in several ways: (1) exposing and dismantling the filmmaking process; (2) alluding to other texts and contexts beyond itself, thus grounding itself in reality; or (3) addressing the plastic nature and raw material of celluloid and the frame itself.

The dynamic cartoon text extends into other texts, the filmmaking processes, the Hollywood industry (e.g. the interdependence of cartoon to the studio system is evidenced by the Fleischer cartoons utilising and dismantling Paramount's musical scores) and the raw material of film itself. The cartoon also unveils the classical cinematic disguise of being a self-contained, closed structure by becoming open to the experience of the reader as well. By acknowledging familiar topics, issues and personalities, these cartoons begin to establish a common ground for communication with their readers.

Discursive cartoons: the text and reader

How does a text invite a relation with its reader? What kind of reading(s) does a discursive cartoon demand? Can cartoons call to the reader, as Ricoeur argues, as a person calls to another? Or in Bakhtian fashion, can we find dialogism, the 'necessary relation of any utterance to other utterance' in a cartoonic complex of signs?

Many cartoons, particularly those of Disney, are narratives constructed in the classical cinema mode, the *histoire*. But some cartoons have a playfully perverse tendency to disrupt the normal codes of a hermetic narrative. Other cartoons, placed under the rubric of comedy, follow the disruptive strand and fit very neatly into Steve Seidman's generic category of comedian comedy.[11]

Comedian comedy comes from vaudeville and burlesque where the on-stage or on-screen character addresses the audience directly. We see this when Bugs Bunny speaks directly into the camera at the conclusion of *Duck Amuck*: 'Quite a little stinker, ain't I?' This is discourse, an animated dialogue between the polyphonic text and the reader.

Even as Barthes called for a playful science of signs and imaginative pleasure to replace 'theological' science, a proper reading of the cartoon text should evoke anarchic pleasure. This translates as a reception of the text itself, a surrender to the posture a film demands of the reader. C.S. Lewis distinguished 'receiving' a work of art from 'using' it, as in forcing psychoanalytical or Marxist paradigms on a textual structure that recommends its own hermeneutic. Lewis's crucial objection to 'using' an aesthetic text was that, as readers, we 'are so busy doing things with the work that we give it too little chance to work on us. Thus increasingly *we meet only ourselves*'.[12] We contemplate, but do not enjoy; or as Ricoeur would put it, we place priority on structure over interpretation.

A film text offers a network of discourses. This calls for responsibility on the part of the reader, who is always tempted to force the text onto his or her Procrustean bed of analysis. By interacting with the voice of the author, the reader may discover the *sensus plenoir* of the text. This 'fuller meaning' emerges only after proper exegesis in which the reader listens to the text in light of its historical, linguistic and ideological/theological contexts.

Cartoons, however, do not need the consistency or internal logic of a realist film. New codes can emerge when a reader encounters the unpredictable articulations of the cartoon. The super-textual can break into the text at any moment. It might even be planted as an integral part of the text, derailing it from the inside to transform the narrative into discourse, into dialogue with the reader.

Tex Avery's slow but supernaturally speedy dog, Droopy, engages in regular dialogues with his audience. In the beginning of *Dumb Hounded* (1943), Droopy introduces the cartoon by announcing: 'Hello all you happy people. You know what? I'm the hero.' Later, when he breaks 'character' by barking back to another dog, he explains to us humans, looking directly and plainly into the camera: 'Dog talk.' Manipulating cinematic time and space, Droopy is invariably located beside the dog desperately fleeing from him. At one point, the escaping dog races through several sets (à la *Blazing Saddles*) so quickly that he skids beyond the sprocket holes. Scampering back to the safe confines of the cartoon world, he hides in a darkened room. Droopy stands right behind him, of course, and drawls: 'Here we go again.' This Tex Avery trademark also appears in a similar scene in *Northwest Hounded Police* (1946) where Droopy deadpans: 'Monotonous, isn't it?' Droopy's ironic detachment, what Mast calls *katastasis*, addresses the spectator with wry commentary, as though confiding to us the contrived nature of the cartoon. 'I surprise him like this all through the picture', Droopy explains in his funereal voice.

The Brechtian style of address subverts the self-contained universe of the conventional narrative, bringing the enunciator down from the screen, as in Woody Allen's *Purple Rose of Cairo*. The character becomes a more objective cultural identity. This might not hold for Bob Hope or Woody Allen, who have actual personalities beyond the dramatic persona. But there is no possibility of bumping into Porky Pig no matter how many bars or sties we frequent.

When the text acknowledges the presence of a generalised reader, it procures from the audience the plausibility of existence. It is imbued with life – animated – much as Tinker Bell came alive when Peter Pan persuaded the children to clap. Daffy Duck speaks to his spectators, appealing to their good sense. Bugs is like the dapper French comedian Max Linder, who, as Andre Bazin noted, plays 'directly to the audience, winks at them and calls on them to witness his embarrassment and does not shrink from asides'.[13] Bugs Bunny's discursive behaviour enables the spectator to attribute more actuality to him than to either Popeye or even Donald Duck.

Woody Allen talking to us is unremarkable. But for Bugs and his ilk, the word and image become the miracle of new creation. He who has no being, whose presence in film is a veritable absence, now exists in a phenomenological encounter. We listen to him as he weaves his witty spells. He gets us to laugh, to join in his conspiracy. He gets us to believe in him and surrender to his magic or at least to appreciate his magical creators.

Chuck Jones's unparalleled classic *Duck Amuck* (1953) involves the reader in one of the most discursive and hilarious self-reflexive texts. Leonard Maltin cites Louis Black on the levels of interpretation offered the spectator in *Duck Amuck*:

> The cartoon stands as an almost clinical study of deconstruction of a text, in the way it presents a whole at the beginning and then dismembers every facet of the cartoon, only to put them together at the end.[14]

Daffy Duck not only performs for us, but begs, cajoles and berates his spectators and more significantly, his spectating Creator. The film draws attention to the art of making cartoons, to the mysteries of production and to the dependent nature of the cartoon character. Maltin observed that when 'Daffy yells for a close-up, the camera moves in so far that the screen is filled with Daffy's bloodshot eyes'.[15] Daffy, as a cartoon Job, is stuck in a seemingly arbitrary and nonsensical universe. After the setting changes arbitrarily from old MacDonald's farm to an Arctic setting with igloo, Daffy asks: 'Would it be too much to ask if we could make up our minds? Hmmm?' When all the backgrounds are erased, Daffy grits his beak and declares: 'Buster, it may come as a complete surprise to you to find that this is an animated cartoon and in animated cartoons they have scenery.' He appeals to the normal grammar of cartoon syntax to recover some regularity for this world gone askew.

At the mercy of an unseen and whimsical power, Daffy seeks to adapt to the chaotic changes in his environment and the bizarre metamorphoses of his own image. 'Who is responsible for this?', he screams. 'I demand that you show yourself! Who are you?' A mysterious and sovereign creator whose malevolent whimsy makes sport with him frustrates him at every turn. Finally, the camera pulls back to show the unseen artist as Bugs Bunny. 'He is his own auteur', wrote Richard Corliss, 'the cartoon director's alter-ego. He knows what's going to happen, in the next frame or three scenes away and he knows how to control it.'[16]

Daffy's appeals for us to help him uncover the source of his troubles go unheeded as the spectator himself or herself is at the mercy of the dynamic comedy. The final unveiling of Bugs Bunny as the tormenting 'stinker' behind the whole mess elicits one last laugh, but also leads the audience to an awareness of the supernatural or supercelluloid Artist, who does exist and seems to 'play' with the creatures. The joke expands and culminates as one realises that the impish and sadistic rabbit exists only as the impish imaginative expression of another – albeit genuine – cartoonist. In the chaotic world of the simulacra one finds not a referent, but an author.

Transcendent 'toons: the text and author

If the cartoon is discourse, who is the discourse-maker? For Barthes, 'the birth of the reader must be at the cost of the death of the Author'.[17] In the discursive cartoon, this is not so. To have discourse, one must have communicating subjects, one of whom is the author (or *auteur*). This revived and reformed 'auteurist' approach must distinguish between the independent animator and the studio-driven, mass-produced cartoon. Yet, even in the latter, the voices of many authors whisper through the Studio Babel. The consciousness of the reader (his/her birth) occurs in encountering the author(s) in the words and images of the created text. The reader is neither a passive consumer of unyielding ideologies nor an independent constructor of brave new worlds, but one who seeks a meeting of minds in the text.

Cartoon authorship could involve a screwy coterie of animators on Termite Terrace or just one *auteur* like the incomparable Norman McLaren, but the cartoon is a genre, like the avant-garde film, that highlights the name below the title. The authors leave their signatures or thumbprints on their work. G.K. Chesterton observed that 'as God made a pigmy-image of Himself and called it Man, so man made a pigmy-image of creation and called it art'.[18] Men and women, as *imago Dei*, imitate their Creator, becoming what J.R.R. Tolkien called 'sub-creators'.[19] Their cartoons carry what Peter Berger has called 'signals of transcendence', clues and hints to a reality beyond their two-dimensional existence.

Signals of transcendence occur most clearly when the author personally enters the text, like Woody Allen's Mr Kugelmass, a bored character who lusts after the ideal women of literature and goes to live and love in books like *Madame Bovary*. (Students reading this work would ask their teachers: 'Who is this character on page 100? A bald Jew is kissing Madame Bovary?')[20] The entrance of the other-worldly creator into the world of his or her creation is a sort of incarnation or 'incartoonation' and occurs in both live action alloys and in full animation. The intrusion of an outer reality, even as small as the cartoonist's hand or drawing tools, transforms the cartoon world. The presence of the maker endows the inanimate with a magical ontological concreteness; that is, it somehow makes the imaginary cartoon character, Felix or Dinky or Bugs, more real.

Crafton makes this point in relation to the silent animated film, arguing that self-figuration, the 'tendency of the filmmaker to interject himself into his film . . . can take several forms; it can be direct or indirect and more or less camouflaged'. Early on, animators interjected themselves audaciously into their work; but later, the practice took on a subtler, cleverer, almost heirophanous quality. The animator, Crafton notes, not only bestowed a mythological status on his or her role, but imaged the artist as 'a demigod, a purveyor of life itself'.[21]

The grand incarnation of animator into animation can be found in Otto Messner's *Felix the Cat*. Felix, Crafton avers, is 'an index of a real personality . . .

> One realises that the personality is that of the creator. With Felix, the quest for self-figuration reaches its end. Messmer no longer feels obliged to physically enter the image (although in *Comicalities* he did briefly toy with the 'hand of the artist' convention). Instead, he enters the film through total identification with the character.[22]

Felix follows the generic signs of self-figuration associated with animator-artist Emile Cohl's clown, the character being an 'incoherent' theophany of the incoherent artist.[23]

Animators inside animation

Cartoons and their creators have made joint appearances since Winsor McCay interacted on stage with Gertie. In a stage act, McCay would time commands and conversations with his paper dinosaur. At one point, McCay disappears behind the screen and appears, still wearing a tuxedo and top hat, on the screen as an animated figure on Gertie's back. Other cartoonists, like Fontaine Fox and Rube Goldberg, appeared with their respective characters, Boob McNutt and the Skipper of Toonerville Trolley, in cartoon live-action alloys.

More engaging than these straightforward interviews was the work being done under the auspices of the John R. Bray studio. Walter Lantz worked as a straight-man in the Dinky Doodles cartoons, a harbinger of his later television program with his irascible Woody Woodpecker. The charm of Lantz, Earl Hurd or Max Fleischer interacting with Pete the Pup, Bobby Bumps or Koko the Clown stemmed partly from the magical mixture of cartoon characters and live backgrounds. Characters left the magic worlds of cartoonland, now known as Toon Town, and joined their human creators. The artistic gods sat, talked and toyed with the creatures made in their images, creatures that disobeyed the laws of their creators as rebelliously as Adam and Eve.

This relationship between author and text can be traced back to McCay, John Stuart Blackton and Emile Cohl, all paternity claimants to the animated film. These artists would invade the illusory worlds they had made with their own presence. They were more akin to lightning-sketch performers than magicians; in fact, rather than jealously guarding the secrets of their magic, these cartoonists seemed to revel in exposing them. In *The Enchanted Drawing* (1900), Blackton used this stage tradition not only to showcase his lightning talents, but to present himself. The artist interacts with his sketch of a man, snatching a bottle of liquor from his powerless subject. Having interrupted the pleasure of his creature, Blackton bows and takes his leave.

As an adherent of Andre Gill, Cohl belonged to an anti-rationalist, Bohemian group called the Incoherents. Cohl's aesthetic approach combined wild and crazy metamorphoses with a gamesome surrealism. In 1908, he invented a lively stick figure named Fantoche (the puppet), who was at the whim of his deterministic, anarchical animator and would suffer a series of phantasmogorical transformations. At one point, the little clown Fantoche falls from an upper story window and is decapitated. The illusion of this fictional world is broken as Cohl's hand enters and like a Michelangelean hand of God toward Adam, patches the little fellow's broken neck with a paste pot. In an Einsteinian universe, where time and space are relative and a Creator can stand outside this time–space continuum watching his or her world and its chronology unfold, the Author/Creator can be omnipotent, omniscient and eternal and thus enter it for such miraculous interruptions of natural cartoon laws.

Wallace Carlson and Harry Dunkinson established a smoother double-exposure technique for the combination of animation and live action in 1916, but the experimenters at the Bray studio were the ones who exploited it. Bobby Bumps would sit on Earl Hurd's hand (and be ordered by his Master through written intertitles: 'Get off my hand!') and Pete the Pup or Dinky Doodle would hide from a dapper, young Lantz. In a 1927 Hot Dog cartoon, *The Lunch Hound*, Lantz enticed Pete out from behind a rock by drawing a roast turkey (much like McCay cajoling Gertie out into public with flattering words). Later, in a 1957–58 series on ABC, an obnoxious, staccato Woodpecker would introduce Lantz as 'my boss'. The two would then offer quick peeks or revelations at what went on behind the scenes in a cartoonist's *atelier*. This television series followed the first prime-time series in 1955, the CBS Cartoon Theater. Wooley noted that 'in his living room, host Dick Van Dyke would chit chat with Terry Toon characters who responded on film clips'. The actor would converse with Heckle and Jeckle, Gandy Goose and other barnyard creatures.

The Fleischer's *Out of the Inkwell* series created a surreal havoc with the animated Koko. Max Fleischer teased, fought, chased and pulled pranks on his rotoscoped clown. Max 'breathes the breath of life' into a pool of ink in his palm to bring forth Koko, much like the Genesis account of Adam. In 'Koko's Earth Control' (1927), creator Max draws the world and places Koko and his sidekick Bimbo on top of the globe. Walking its circumference, they stumble upon the Control of Earth headquarters. They play topsy-turvy with the world, throwing switches that manipulate rain, snow, day and night. One switch in the centre of the room is forbidden. It warns: 'Danger. Beware. Do Not Touch Earth Control. If this Handle is Pulled, the World will Come to an End.' Of course, Bimbo pulls it and all hell breaks loose, in the real world as well as in the cartoonland. Max Fleischer gave his creatures the keys to their own destruction and they used them.

Another animator created a creature that sought the animator's destruction. The starving artist, Kartoono, in Hy Gage's *Kartoono* (c. 1922) practices his lightning sketches on an easel, drawing a hungry dragon that eats his meat and drinks his beer. Here Gage could be crying his own woes about the poverty that his chosen profession has driven him. In fact, the artist talks to his creation and confesses: 'I'm Busted, Starving, Got Cold Feets. Now to get Busy. No Work. No Eats!' The giant winged dragon, drawn by the miserable artist, shows no empathy and chases Kartoono throughout the cartoon. Ultimately, an intertitle asks: 'What's This, Kartoono, Stumped Again? No, Just Watch My Trusty Fountain Pen.' The cartoon artist is able to draw an escape vehicle and bomb the monster. The triumph over the beast is followed by a hand signing the name of Hy Gage and then, in lightning-sketch fashion, a drawing of a caricature of the real animator out of the signature. As if such a graphic representation were insufficient evidence for the artist's work, Kartoono ends with a live action shot of Gage tipping his straw hat to his audience.

In Jack King's *A Cartoonist's Nightmare* (1935), a portrait of what animators feel about their craft is clearly drawn as the early scenes show a bunch of crazies leaving the asylum. A wife pulls her husband away from his magnificent obsession, but he resists, claiming: 'I gotta finish tonight.' Falling asleep at his drawing board, one of his wicked characters pulls the sleeping cartoonist into the cartoon, much like the actors in the Joe Dante episode in *Twilight Zone: The Movie* being caught and incarcerated in a cartoon television program. The hairy monster drags him down the corridors through the gag department, the story and music departments, down to the dungeons of 'cartoon villains', such as Spike the Spider. Each is assigned a number such as #130 for Dirty Dan and #20 for Battling Barney. (These characters prefigure Jessica Rabbit who confides to Eddie Valiant in *Roger Rabbit* that she really isn't bad; she is 'just drawn that way'. Her explanation resonates with Dudley Andrew's synopsis of Stephen Heath's argument that the 'movies draw us, have learned to draw us . . . they have taught us how to be drawn'. One of the ironic curiosities of this construction of an attractive female character is the contrast of Jessica with the archetypal sexist cartoon character of the pre-Hays Betty Boop, who pales in comparison to her modern counterpart.) These wayward characters, creations fallen from his own imagination, sing to him: 'It's our turn. Now you are in our clutches! We are creations from your pen, it's in your hands we lie; you always manage to have us sin, now by your own hand you die.'

The animator's rescue comes by way of one of his good characters, Beans, an early compatriot of Porky Pig, who throws him a pencil by which he is able to vanquish his evil creations by first drawing and then using an eraser, a symbol of apocalyptic judgement in the cartoon world. The live action Jack King never appears in this cartoon like the earlier Max Fleischer or Walter Lantz; rather he is incarnated or incartooned, into the animation world. The actual animator sends his cartoon image into the cartoon world to suffer at the hands of his creation and to straighten out or correct that world, judging the wicked and blessing the faithful. The final scene shows the cartoon 'King' drawing and bestowing a large bowl of ice-cream upon his good and faithful servant Beans.

Another relation of a text's character to its author is portrayed in Otto Mesmer's *Comicalamities* (1928), in which Felix engages in an on-going argument with his master. When a cut-out hand outlines a white Felix, the cat orders a tail to be drawn and then that he be blackened. When he meets an ugly female cat, who pines that she wishes she were beautiful, Felix takes up eraser and pen and, like Galathea with Pygmalion, he creates the female in his own image. At one point, the animator's hand picks up a far-off movie star and brings her into proximity for Felix. She arrogantly rebukes the cat for daring to make love to her. 'Oh well', sighs a rejected Felix as he tears her off, 'She is only a paper lover anyway'.

Felix continually calls in the hand of his creator to redress problems or difficulties, even praying that he save him from the threat of underwater monsters. When the author decides to 'end' the film with an iris out, Felix resists, claiming: 'This picture isn't finished by a long shot.' The paper cat shakes its puny fist at the universe as though it could by a matter of fictional will postpone its own demise. Ironically, the animator actually gives his creature a sense of causality and extends the life of the cartoon.

The opening title sequence signalling the inauguration of the 1986 Hamilton International Animation Festival transforms the festival's character logos, a Canadian owl into a known (in the sense of *connaître* rather than *savoir*) personality. A golden egg bounces onto the screen. It first hatches into a fluffy, downy, Disneyian white baby owl. Suddenly, a pencil appears and erases the figure in the egg shell and draws another. This time a wild, raucous, punk version of the owl appears. Immediately, the pencil rushes in, erases and gives birth to the genuine representative of the festival to the cheers of the audience. This clever introduction worked to make one aware (and appreciative) of the artistry behind the film. We become cognisant of the labours and frustrations of the artists in conceiving and giving birth to this familiar feathered character.

L'invité (1984) by Guy Jacques poignantly reveals both the lonely, tedious work of the animator and the curious personal relationship between the artist and his or her work A clay animator shapes, frames, moves and shoots a life-sized clay human character one click of the camera at a time, slowly filming a sequence in which his character-man walks into his (the animator's) home. Through stop-motion, the animator brings his inanimate guest into his life, including himself in each shot, so that it appears that they sit, sup and chat together. After his devoted labours are completed, he projects the film. It shows host and guest eating, drinking and communing. The solitary artist has not only brought his lifeless sculpture to life, but has laboured to give birth to friendship and fellowship. A step toward transcendence occurs, in what David O. Thomas has termed a 'communion' between a work of art and the viewer/reader. In *L'invité*, the author of the cartoon within the cartoon is the primary reader, drawn out of himself to experience a transcendent moment of communion through art. The audience of secondary readers become sympathetic communicants with this lonely old animator, identifying with him and his art in the way that Thierry Kuntzel says we identify with the hand knocking on the door in *The Most Dangerous Game*. We also become the suffering animator who creates a world and incarnates himself into it.

The union of creator and creature in a single story contrasts with the rebellion of other creatures in Mesmer's *Trials of a Movie Cartoonist* (1916). Crafton says that the:

> . . . first half of this film shows the trials and tribulations of a movie cartoonist at work. The figures that he draws become rebellious and refuse to act as he wants them to, so he has a terrible time to make them do his bidding. They answer back and say that he has no right to make slaves of them even if he is their creator.[24]

'If you want to make a good cartoon, you have to be in one first', one of the characters in Kathy Rose's *Pencil Booklings* (1978) tells her. Rose has directed a dreamy and fluid cartoon in which she appears in two cartoon forms: in her own rotoscoped cartoon incarnation and in the redrawn image of her cartoon characters. The film begins with her sitting at her drawing table and her tiny cast of bubbling characters emerging from a bottle complaining about their voices. One whines that its voice is too squeaky. Others chime in; for example, 'I don't like my voice either' and 'We don't want to be in your film'. The characters incessantly give advice to their creator, often ordering her where and when to insert a 'nice cycle'.

Eventually Rose reproves them: 'I can't make a film if everyone here is fighting.' She makes a brief exit and when she is gone, the characters decide to remake their own world. 'Hello, I'm Kathy's pencil', one says and joins the others to 'make our own film, just like Kathy'. Exhilarated by freedom from Kathy's control, they reconstruct their universe with a goofier, cartoonier image of their maker. They want to make their distorted image of Kathy talk like they do. However, no one will participate unless they can have their own way, so they float without direction or order until communication with their creator is re-established and life begins anew. Through identification with her doodled characters as a doodle herself, Kathy is able to communicate with them and gain their obedience. The author recognises how her text can take on a life of its own and add to the original text. John Canemaker praised Rose's ability to draw us into this original, fascinating world and make:

> . . . us believe in its special reality . . . In one breathtaking scene Ms. Rose 'becomes' one of her characters . . . Later, Ms. Rose oozes and bleeds her cartoon cast from her body, as strong a visual statement of an artist's identification with her art as you're liable to find in animation.[25]

Rose and her fellow artists are in the same tradition as those who, at some time in their careers, sought to represent themselves in their work. Painters like Dürer, Rembrandt, Van Gogh and Norman Rockwell handed down a habit of famous self-portraits mirroring their own variegated souls. They signed their work with an image rather than a signature. For artists like Camus, 'art detached from its creator is unthinkable'.[26]

If any genre can subvert recent materialist theory that banishes the personal voice in the film's relation to its audience, it is the animated cartoon. Of particular relevance are those discursive cartoons outside the studio system, including the Warner Bros. material. Their work and that of a diverse body of independent and irrepressible animators can be submitted as evidence of personal speakers in the artistic process. Chuck Jones, Tex Avery, Friz Freleng and Bob Clampett *et al.* merely addressed their films to themselves, aiming to entertain themselves. These animators were both authors and readers. Jones confessed that they didn't design their pictures for kids or adults. 'My cartoons', he said, 'weren't made for children. They were made for me'.[27]

Independent animators like Kathy Rose are also true *auteurs*, incarnating themselves, or at least their voices, into texts. Their sovereignty over all aspects of production allows them to claim the camera as Astruc's *stylo*. Caroline Leaf (*The Street* interview) acknowledged: 'I like to control everything within my frame . . . I like to make things move. It is like making them alive.'[28] Eliot Noyes Jr in *Clay: Origin of the Species* also testified to the appeal of personal authorship, of creating animation:

> the way a painter would use paints and a canvas. The reason I am in animation is that it is a form of self-expression; what I want to get across is mostly a very personal view of the world.[29]

The personal attention of the author can lead to her or his involvement in the cartoon, leaving traces (and even faces) of the self as playful signals of transcendence. Hints of a supernatural cosmos, of a world outside the celluloid, are laid about like nets to catch the reader unawares and draw attention beyond the text to the author and his/her world.

The artists whisper the answers to the questions of who framed and drew Roger Rabbit or Daffy Duck.

One of the most exhilarating moments for my graduate students was when we placed Mike Jittlov's pixilated *Wizard of Speed and Time* on the Steenbeck to ascertain whether or not we were 'seeing' something subliminal tucked away in the frame. His secret signatures were unveiled clearly in the frame-by-frame analysis. In his frames, Jittlov spelled his name out in lights, hid messages against the Hollywood industry and even listed his home phone number on a clapboard, inviting any detective who discovered this message to call him. We immediately dialled the number and had a live, direct line back to a very live and friendly author. Attending to the dynamic force of the textual discourse and probing into its secrets led us to a dialogue beyond the text.

Conclusions

With its potentially heuristic and pragmatic values, the animated film serves as a site for exploring certain aspects of post-modernism, particularly the realms of double-coding, intertextuality and carnival comedy. Its use of pastiche and parody, of extended quotation and of multiple perspectives – of heteroglossia within one small discourse – situate it as prime property for post-modern analysis.

The mere cartoon offers a vital sample for lively discourse and for the discovery of the carnival spirit in cinema. As a pervasive source of pleasure and consumption, it merits critical attention as an ideological product. As a phenomenological text, it invites consideration of a 'theological' encounter, a meeting with the quiddity of the text and even with the author of the text.

Reflexive cartoons are also blatantly disruptive of Jean Baudrillard's diabolical seduction of images. Strategically, images seem to refer to 'the real world, real objects and to reproduce something which is logically and chronologically anterior to themselves'.[30] Cartoons do not even pretend to have a referent; in fact, they function as referents for a legion of simulacra that have become consumer products; those large, cuddly products that walk around theme parks and malls selling their stuff and seducing innocents into a reading of reality that is only cartoon illusion.

The cartoons presented here are exemplary of the intertextual practice of alluding to, plagiarising, absorbing, imitating, quoting and playing with ironic self-reflexive references to the entire cinematic apparatus, from its plastic raw material to its spectatorship. But certain of these cartoons extend beyond their textuality. They are transcended by authorship and signs of a super-celluloid existence. As post-modern texts they can eschew and even mock classic narrative paradigms, but they do affirm personal narrators.

Animated films are the deconstructing agents that have subjects who created them; they do have authors. And it is the company of authors who communicate not only with themselves but with spectators who play along with them in their inter-textual games.

A much shorter version of this paper was given by T. Lindvall at the 1989 SAS Conference; another longer and extensively revised version, co-authored with J. Matthew Melton, was first published in the *Animation Journal* (Fall 1994), vol. 3 no. 1.

Notes

1. Mikhail M. Bakhtin, *Rabelais and His World*, trans. Helene Iswolsky (Cambridge: MIT Press, 1965). Comic ambivalence can be defined as a perpetual dynamic relationship between opposites such as life and death; the grotesque involves the 'funny monster' wherein horror has been infused with comedy; and the universal demands that the comedy laugh at everyone and everything, including itself and its forms. Such playfulness in light of the terrible is a characteristic of post-modernism. Susan Ohmer suggested that *Who Framed Roger Rabbit?* might be considered the first post-modernist cartoon, 'for the way it appropriates narrative and visual elements from other sources and juxtaposes them to create new relationships with the past'. 'Who Framed Roger Rabbit?: The Presence of the Past', in *Storytelling in Animation*, John Canemaker, ed. (Los Angeles: AFI, 1988), 102. This paper argues that such practice occurred since the genesis of the animated film.

2. Vladimir Propp, *Morphology of the Folktale*, trans. Laurence Scott (Austin, Texas: University of Texas Press, 1968).

3. Siegfried Kracauer, *Theory of Film* (New York: Oxford UP, 1960), 90.

4   Jean Mitry, *Le Cinema experimental* (Paris: Editions Seghers, 1974), 204.

5. Erwin Panofsky, 'Style and Medium in the Motion Pictures', *Film Theory and Criticism*, eds Gerald Mast and Marshall Cohen (New York: Oxford UP, 1979), 252n.

6. Dana Polan, 'A Brechtian Cinema? Towards a Politics of Self-Reflexive Film', in *Movies and Methods*, vol. II, ed. Bill Nichols (Los Angeles: UC Press, 1985), 667. In contrast to the self-referential quality of the Hollywood musical, insightfully demonstrated by Jane Feuer, the animated film is better equipped to bring about 'distanciation', the effect 'whereby the spectator is lifted out of her transparent identification with the story and forced to concentrate instead on the artifice through which the play or film has been made' (Jane Feuer, 'The Self-Reflective Musical and the Myth of Entertainment', *Quarterly Review of Film Studies* (August, 1977): 313–326), for the animated film can make visible its own invisible frame and plasticity as well as its artistic conventions.

7. As cited in Dudley Andrew, *Concepts in Film Theory* (New York: Oxford UP, 1984), 181–182.

8. C.S. Lewis, *Experiment in Criticism* (Cambridge: Cambridge UP, 1960), 139.

9. Polan, 'A Brechtian Cinema?', ibid., 662.

10. Steve Schneider, *That's All Folks: The Art of Warner Bros. Animation* (New York: Henry Holt and Co., 1988), 30.

11. Steve Seidman, *Comedian Comedy* (Ann Arbor: UMI Research Press, 1981).

12. Lewis, ibid., 85.

13. Andre Bazin, *What is Cinema?*, vol. I, trans. Hugh Gray (Berkeley: University of California Press, 1967), 78.

14. Leonard Maltin, *Of Mice and Magic* (New York: New American Library, 1980), 259.

15. Ibid., 258.

16. Richard Corliss, 'Warnervana', *Film Comment*, 21, 6 (November–December 1985): 18.

17. Roland Barthes, 'The Death of the Author', *Image-Music-Text*, trans. Stephen Heath (New York: Hill and Wang, 1977), 148.

18. G.K. Chesterton, *As I Was Saying*, ed. Robert Knille (Grand Rapids: Eerdmans, 1985), 264.

19. J.R.R. Tolkien, 'On Fairy Stories', *Essays Presented to Charles Williams*, ed. C.S. Lewis (New York: Oxford UP, 1947), 67.

20. Woody Allen, 'The Kugelmass Episode', *Side Effects* (New York: Ballantine, 1980), 67.

21. Donald Crafton, *Before Mickey: The Animated Film, 1898–1928* (Cambridge: MIT Press, 1982), 11.

22. Ibid., 338.

23. See Crafton, *Emile Cohl, Caricature and Film* (Princeton: Princeton UP, 1990).

24. Crafton, *Before Mickey*, 187.

27. John Canemaker, 'Animation for Adults', *Take One* (November 1978): 37, 40–41.

28. Marie-Helene Davies, *Laughter in a Genevan Gown* (Grand Rapids: Eerdmans, 1983), 133.

27. Robert Russett and Cecile Starr, *Experimental Animation* (New York: Van Nostrand Reinhold Co., 1976), 14.

30. Jean Baudrillard, *The Evil Demon of Images* (Sydney: Power Institute Publications, 1984), 13. As

cartoon characters are the quintessential simulacra of an image industry, their texts are ontologically related to themselves and to their evolved *oeuvre*. As their identities become encrusted and reified, they are realised in shopping malls, on tee-shirts, coffee mugs and a plethora of trivial consumer objects. Among the post-modernists, one might even find an isomorphic correspondence of characters to theorists. Lyotard would be Bugs Bunny, of course; Baudrillard would most appropriately be identified with an apocalyptic Eyore (Disney's not Milne's) or a nihilistic Puddleglum (not C.S. Lewis's Christian pessimist), but within Hollywood's animated zoo, Daffy Duck would suffice, especially in his incoherent frustration of trying to pin down a referent. Habermaas might be an optimistic proletariat Porky Pig, looking for the completion of the project of modernity.

Bibliography

Adamson, J., 'Suspended Animation', *Film Theory and Criticism*, ed. Gerald Mast and Marshall Cohen (New York: Oxford UP, 1979), 606–16.

Allen, W., 'The Kugelmass Episode', *Side Effects* (New York: Ballantine, 1980).

Andrew, D., *Concepts in Film Theory* (New York: Oxford UP, 1984).

Barthes, R., 'The Death of the Author', *Image-Music-Text*, trans. Stephen Heath (New York: Hill and Wang, 1977), 142–148.

Bazin, A., *What is Cinema?*, vol. I, trans. Hugh Gray (Berkeley: University of California Press, 1967).

Benayoun, R., 'Animation: The Phoenix and the Road Runner', *Film Quarterly*, 17, 3 (Spring 1964): 16–25.

Berger, P., *A Rumor of Angels: Modern Society and the Rediscovery of the Supernatural* (Garden City, NY: Anchor Books, 1970).

Canemaker, J., 'Animation for Adults', *Take One* (November 1978): 37, 40–41.

Chesterton, G.K., *As I Was Saying*, ed. Robert Knille (Grand Rapids: Eerdmans, 1985).

Chute, D., 'Keeping up with The Jones' ', *Film Comment*, 21, 6 (November–December 1985): 14–15.

Corliss, R., 'Warnervana', *Film Comment*, 21, 6 (November–December 1985): 11–13, 16–19.

Crafton, D., *Before Mickey* (Cambridge: Cambridge UP, 1982).

Feuer, J., *The Hollywood Musical* (Bloomington: Indiana UP, 1982).

Friedwald, W., & J. Beck, *The Warner Brothers Cartoons* (Metuchen, NJ: Scarecrow, 1981).

Halas, J., *Masters of Animation* (London: BBC Books, 1987).

Hoffer, T.W., *Animation: A Reference Guide* (Westport, Connecticut: Greenwood Press, 1981).

Johnston, C., & P. Willemen, (eds), *Frank Tashlin* (Colchester, England: Vineyard Press, 1973).

Kracauer, S., *Theory of Film* (New York: Oxford UP, 1960).

Lewis, C.S., *Experiment in Criticism* (Cambridge: Cambridge UP, 1960).

MacDonald, S., 'Avant-Garde Film: Cinema as Discourse', *Journal of Film and Video*, 40, 2 (Spring 1988): 33–42.

Maltin, L., *Of Mice and Magic* (New York: New American Library, 1980).

Mast, G., *The Comic Mind* (Chicago: University of Chicago Press, 1979).

Mitry, J., *Le Cinema experimental*, (Paris: Editions Seghers, 1974).

Mundy, Rick. 'Letting the Cat Out of the Bag'. *Film Witness 3*: 3 (March 1987). 2–4.

Palmer, J., *The Logic of the Absurd: On Film and Television Comedy* (London: BFI, 1987).

Panofsky, E., 'Style and Medium in the Motion Pictures', *Film Theory and Criticism*, eds Gerald Mast and Marshall Cohen (New York: Oxford UP, 1979), 243–263.

Polan, D., 'A Brechtian Cinema? Towards a Politics of Self-Reflexive Film', *Movies and Methods*, vol. II, ed. Bill Nichols (Los Angeles: UC Press, 1985), 661–671.

Propp, V., *Morphology of the Folktale*, trans. Laurence Scott (Austin, Texas: University of Texas Press, 1968).

Russett, R., & C. Starr, *Experimental Animation* (New York: Van Nostrand Reinhold Co., 1976).

Schneider, S., *That's All Folks: The Art of Warner Bros. Animation* (New York: Henry Holt and Co., 1988).

Seidman, S., *Comedian Comedy* (Ann Arbor: UMI Research Press, 1981).

Seldes, G., 'The Lovely Art: Magic', *Film Theory and Criticism*, eds Gerald Mast and Marshall Cohen (New York: Oxford UP, 1979), 594–605.

Thomas, D.O., 'Moments, Experiential Density and Immediacy: The Screenplay As Blueprint For Communion', *Journal of Film and Video*, 36, 3 (Summer 1984): 43–50.

'The Self-Reflective Musical and the Myth of Entertainment', *Quarterly Review of Film Studies* (August, 1977): 313–326.

Thompson, R., 'Meep Meep', *Film Comment*, 12, 3 (May–June 1976): 37–9.

Tolkien, J.R.R., 'On Fairy Stories', *Essays Presented to Charles Williams*, ed. C.S.Lewis (New York: Oxford UP, 1947).

Tomasulo, F. P., 'The Text-in-the-Spectator', *Journal of Film and Video*, 40, 2 (Spring, 1988): 20–32.

Tzvetan, T., *The Fantastic* (Ithaca, New York: Cornell UP, 1975).

Williams, S.H., 'Cartoons: From Folklore to Fairy Tales'. Athens, Ohio: Paper at UFVA Conference (1986).

Woolery, G.W., *Children's Television: The First Thirty-Five Years* (Orange: George W. Woolery, 1982).

18

Restoring the aesthetics of early abstract films

William Moritz

Critical writing about the abstract films of the 1920s is generally 'bogged down' with the question of primacy. Hans Richter, who supplied information to most early film historians, stressed the point that his own films were the *first* abstract, experimental films ever made – along with Viking Eggeling's *Diagonal Symphony* – which Richter dated 1919 or 1921, even in film titles that he had made during the 1950s and 1960s. He consistently suggested that Walther Ruttmann and Oskar Fischinger began filmmaking later, that Fischinger was a pupil and assistant of Ruttmann's, and furthermore insisted that Ruttmann was an artistic fraud whose films lacked a true sense of rhythm or harmony. Following the publication of Louise O'Konor's superb biographical study of Eggeling[1] and Wulf Herzogenrath's collected research for the 1977 *Film als Film* exhibit at the Kölnischer Kunstverein, it became clear that Richter was lying.

In late 1920 or early 1921, Richter and Eggeling had UFA studio technicians animate (or perhaps just shoot) some tests of their scroll drawings. Richter's test strip, about 30 seconds long (at silent speed), he named *Film is Rhythm* and showed it publicly, and by his own account[2] this test strip was so short that one critic in Paris missed the whole thing because he took off his glasses to clean them and the film ended before he had put them back on. Werner Graeff[3] recalls how Richter, in 1922, had still not realised that the film-frame format was basically horizontal instead of the vertical imagery in Richter's drawings – and how he helped Richter to shoot some additional seconds of footage (also disappointing and unsatisfactory) which Richter added to *Film is Rhythm* and showed this now one-minute-long 'film' at the famous May 1925 Absolute Film Show in Berlin. By October 1927, after his marriage to Erna Niemeyer (who had been Eggeling's animator for *Diagonal Symphony*), Richter had acquired another 30 seconds of film, now titled simply *Rhythm*, for a London Film Society program. This approximately 90-second fragment by Richter's own admission corresponds to the middle section of the erroneously titled *Rhythm 23*, while the rest of *Rhythm 23* and the so-called *Rhythm 21* were shot in late 1927 and early 1928 by Erna Niemeyer while preparing the *Film Study* (which Richter habitually dates 1926, despite the Film Society's

21 October 1928 program notes indicating that this new film was completed after his 'less finished work' shown the previous year).

To further correct Richter's misinformation, Eggeling's first UFA animation tests, circa 1920–21 from his *Horizontal–Vertical Orchestra*, seemed totally unsatisfactory to him and he appears not to have shown this film in public. Eggeling tried several more *Horizontal–Vertical Orchestra* tests during 1922 and 1923, but they also proved inadequate compared to his vision of how they should proceed in time – his complex imagery on the scrolls still constituted a storyboard rather than viable animation drawings. When the young Bauhaus student Erna Niemeyer began to animate his *Diagonal Symphony* scrolls in 1923, he appears to have abandoned the *Horizontal–Vertical Orchestra* entirely. Erna Niemeyer finished animating *Diagonal Symphony* in the fall of 1924 and the film was shown publicly only in May 1925 at the Absolute Film Show, just days before Eggeling's death.

With the discovery in the early 1980s of a partial print of Ruttmann's *Light-Play, Opus No. 1*, it became clear why Richter was lying. Unlike both Eggeling and Richter, Ruttmann had actually mastered filmmaking and animation techniques – something, by the way, which Richter would never master because he had to rely on camera operators, editors and even projectionists all his life since he found mechanical details too complex to deal with. Ruttmann's *Opus No. 1* proves to be vivid, cogent, dynamic and rhythmic – all qualities lacking aesthetically in Richter's own films, which consequently needed the special pleading of 'first, early, primitive' to make them worth considering. Furthermore, Ruttmann had undeniably[4] mastered film technique (not just scroll painting) by 1919, shot and tinted his *Opus No. 1* in 1920 and turned the film over to composer Max Butting to prepare the closely timed musical score that was rehearsed and performed in public before a paying audience at a regular cinema in April 1921. With his pioneer status impugned, Richter's artistic stature as a filmmaker has also crumbled – and we will hear little more of him in this paper. The integrity of Eggeling's and Ruttmann's films, however, remains irreproachable. Yet, during the past 20 years, little is written to suggest what aesthetic qualities or issues might be inherent in their styles of animation. I propose to scrutinise these two film texts, Ruttmann's *Opus No. 1* and Eggeling's *Diagonal Symphony*, for that very purpose here.

Both of these animators were initially painters. Ruttmann began studying architecture at age nineteen in Zurich in 1906, but switched to painting and music in 1909, moving to Munich where he became friends with Klee, Feininger and Corinth, among others. He supported himself as an artist before World War I, when he was drafted and sent to the Russian front where he, as a pacifist and a gentle man, suffered great emotional distress before his release from service as unfit early in 1917. He continued to make expressionistic graphics, which grew gradually more simplified and refined as he strove to capture the essence of things without the ephemera. Although the military service left him a broken man physically, his spiritual energy seemed renewed and concentrated and by the end of 1917 he was painting wholly abstract canvases of great power. By late 1918, he renounced the painting of still images in favour of animating abstract imagery that could develop in space as well as time, which he saw as the art form of the future.

His first animations for *Opus No. 1* were painted with oil paints on glass plates beneath an animation camera, shooting a frame after each brush stroke or each alteration because the wet paint could be wiped away or modified quite easily. He later combined this with geometric cut-outs on a separate layer of glass. Ruttmann had met the composer

Max Butting during their school days in Munich and Ruttmann himself played the cello in the string quintet that Butting wrote for the premiere of *Opus No. 1*.

I mentioned that a partial print of *Opus No. 1* had been discovered. In 1976, Enno Patalas of the Filmmuseum in Munich requested Lang and Murnau footage from the Moscow archives for his superb restorations of *Metropolis* and *Nosferatu*. One reel they sent coincidentally contained extensive fragments of Ruttmann's *Opus No. 1*, along with pieces of other Ruttmann *Opus* films and some advertising or special effects footage. The Moscow fragments of *Opus No. 1* were from a positive-print release that had been tinted; the colours seemed faded in some cases and particularly scenes that ought to be yellow were in bad condition or missing. It seems possible to me that this one positive print of *Light-Play Opus No. 1* could represent, actually, the only copy that ever existed. This print is not only tinted but also toned and then certain figures are hand-tinted frame by frame, so that there are three and four colours in some sequences. This means that there would never have been one simple, consistent negative. Those scenes that would have been toned blue and tinted red, for example, would have to be printed separately in the laboratory from a sequence that was toned red and tinted yellow. And, if a given movement (like a musical phrase) was to appear once tinted blue, once tinted violet and once tinted orange (as indeed some are), the same black-and-white negative original would simply be printed three times at the lab with a different tint or tone for each pass. This means that Ruttmann would have had 50 or more small fragments of negative from which the original 1921 print of *Opus No. 1* was printed, and each individual projection print, however many there were, would have been spliced together from those fragments by hand, by Ruttmann, who would have done the hand-tinting on certain shapes at the same time.

Opus No. 1 was not shown much after 1921 and was not included in the Absolute Film Show of May 1925, although his *Opus No. 2*, *Opus No. 3* and *Opus No. 4*, which use only general 'mood' tinting and have no specific soundtrack, were. Thus, some commentators have assumed that because the style of the film was too primitive and outmoded compared with the more painterly subtlety of *Opus No. 2* and *Opus No. 3*, Ruttmann himself had withdrawn it. I suspect that quite the opposite might have been true; rather, *Opus No. 1* was too complex, too difficult to 'perform', since the colours and music are aesthetically integral to the experience of Ruttmann's first film. Although the images are beautiful and dynamic without the music, the sound counterpoint adds a significant perspective to the imagery which, after seeing *Opus No. 1* several times with the original music in 'editions' by Lothar Prox, Berndt Heller and myself, should not really be lost. In the musical score of Butting's string quintet (now in the Film Museum in Stockholm), Ruttmann has not only drawn many colour illustrations for the musicians to synchronise with, but he has also provided exacting metronome and timing indications for each musical phrase, so we know how precise and how important the music was to the filmmaker. The difficulty, however, of arranging a projection of a thirteen-minute film with a live string quintet (with considerable rehearsal time, during which the precious hand-made print might be damaged) must have proved so daunting that Ruttmann quickly resigned himself to the fact that it could not soon be performed again in its integral form.

The Russian copy, although it is shorter by about three minutes from the original running time, does not seem to lack any specific *type* of imagery; rather, it is merely missing repetitions (often in alternate colours) of an image that exists at least once. Therefore, thanks to the exacting instructions of Ruttmann in the Butting sheet-music (colour indication, numbers of repetitions and timings) I was able to reconstruct *Opus No. 1* fairly accurately. The missing pieces might have decomposed due to chemicals in particular dyes, or they could even have been cut out by Ruttmann himself to use them in two commercials he made in 1922, *The Winner* (Der Sieger) for Excelsior automobile tires and *The Miracle* (Das Wunder) for Kantorowicz liqueur. In those two films, we see not only examples of Ruttmann's style of tinting and toning, but also specific images 'borrowed' from *Opus No. 1* – possibly reprinted from the negative, but also possibly cut from a positive print, if Ruttmann faced a tight deadline.

As we watch Ruttmann's *Opus No. 1* in its restored colour version with the original music, several aesthetic principles emerge. Ruttmann consciously refuses the illusion of depth: his abstract film is non-representational in this sense, just as John Whitney and other later non-objective animators would reject the representational illusion of perspective. *Opus No. 1* is overtly a painting, but a painting that moves, a painting in time as well as space. Like a classical piece of concert music, the film falls into three movements with black 'visual silences' between them. Colour also plays an important role in structuring the film, sometimes to differentiate certain shapes, movements or repetitions, but sometimes to establish general mood or atmosphere, as in the long all-blue 'nocturne' section of the second movement that yields suddenly to a yellow-based 'scherzo'. Ruttmann denies any colour/tone correspondence (which fascinated such people as the Russian composer Scriabin or the Swiss animator Charles Blanc-Gatti); rather, he uses the colour as an element in choreography, almost like stage lighting, which reinforces another central aesthetic analogy: for practical purposes, *Opus No. 1* is an expressionistic drama. The film frame, like the theatrical proscenium, encloses entrances and exits, creates conflicts between round shapes and pointed shapes and effects counterpoised balances of rhythmic gestures – all of which is emphasised by *scale* (even as it is in Fischinger's black-and-white *Studies)* when we remember that this 35 mm film was designed to be seen on a 50-foot square screen, with figures streaking across 20-foot trajectories that cause the viewer to turn his or her head, instead of the six-inch micro-movements we see on video monitors or the two-foot action on many 16 mm projections.

Music and colour both provide essential elements in this expressionistic drama. Sometimes the contrast between two differently coloured shapes heightens their tension, while at other times a confrontation between shapes of the same colour can make us concentrate on their formal action. Sometimes the music shrouds the simple geometric shapes in portentous or pensive moods (as in the opening movement), while other times it undercuts the piercing and crushing of the seemingly aggressive shapes with a sensuous waltz (as in the second movement). And lest, by the way, you doubt the 'aggressive' or 'sensuous' intentions of the pointed shapes and the softly curved shapes, remember the two advertising films *The Winner* and *The Miracle* in which evil triangles puncture round tires and the amorous overtures of the lovers find expression in the caresses of two soft crescents.

Eggeling also came to filmmaking with a strong influence of music (he maintained a vital friendship with composer Busoni) as well as painting. He was a key member of the Dada group, one of the creators of the new art, the new universal language of the future which would be needed when the Dadaists had destroyed conventional bourgeois responses to traditional art. Eggeling took this role as an art-prophet very seriously and hoped to establish a Theory and Counterpoint of Visual Elements, which would provide a firm theoretical basis for the composition of non-objective imagery in movement, development and time frame. He meant to annex the wisdom of auditory music (which had accumulated over thousands of years of experimentation and accretion) by applying, through analogy, its basic principles of parallel and antithetical arrangements to geometric elements. Eggeling requested that his film be seen in silence (probably the first filmmaker to do so) so that the visual harmonies might be appreciated in their own right and not thought to be 'illustrations' of the accompanying auditory music.

The results of some seven or eight years of concentrated research, experimentation and composition that we see in his *Diagonal Symphony* might at first seem simple, but grow more fascinating the closer we study the film. Eggeling also treats the film screen as an overt field for painting, not for representation or illusion. For Eggeling, the musical analogy is all important and the screen area remains self-contained, with no 'entrances' or 'exits' implying a reality outside this frame. Eschewing the notion, as good music theoreticians do, that there are 'high' and 'low' notes (the intensity of vibration has no direction), Eggeling balances his forms around the centre of the screen. Given that the film frame was the space of a concert hall, available to be filled with sound, Eggeling posits a master shape, which nearly fills the film frame and contains dozens of intricate details (interlocking curves and sharp angles, parallel comb-like repetitive forms and solid surfaces), which seems to correspond to the 'ensemble' of an orchestra, with all the instruments playing together, each with its distinct timbre, tone, texture or melodic line that blends into the whole sound of the music. All of the imagery and action in the film is derived from this composite master-shape by extracting various figurative elements (like 'solos') that perform motions commensurate with their form, sometimes in combinations (like 'inversions', 'variations', 'fugues') with one another, or with the master itself. Figures sometimes grow larger and bolder (as if 'louder' in volume) and occasionally develop complex interlocking patterns; for example, the pairs of diagonal 'combs', rounded and triangulated, of which the strands in graduated lengths seem like notes in a chord, that, facing each other, alternate in antithesis, one growing larger while the other grows smaller, one sliding in one direction while the other slides in the opposite, and so on.

Primarily, however, the figures appear and disappear (like the attack and decay of musical sounds). This might be, of course, also a manifestation of the animation process – Eggeling drew some hundred basic variations on the master shape (mostly on scrolls of ten to twenty images), which Erna Niemeyer traced onto tin foil, delicately cut them out from the foil, then animated them under the camera by carefully slicing away minute strips, shooting a frame after each slice; and, planning to shoot in reverse order (possibly with the orientation of the artwork-to-camera turned upside down so that the resulting filmstrip could be simply spliced heads to tails, thus reversing the direction of movement) for a shape to 'grow' or 'appear'. This cut tin foil might be considered a limitation, since its use did not really constitute a 'full' animation in the sense of Fischinger's layered cels for *Allegretto* and *Radio Dynamics*. But, Eggeling knew Ruttmann and Fischinger, he visited the UFA animation studio and knew that Erna Niemeyer could have done a more complex, fuller type of animation. I believe that Eggeling's limited animation was not a technological failing but a conscious choice of aesthetics, just as his choice not to use sound or colour was an aesthetic decision. For Ruttmann, the string quintet was something he could manage, making a visual parallel to the delicate balance of five instruments using colour and fluid painted motions. For Eggeling, the symphony was the greater challenge, even a necessary challenge, since the orchestration of 50 timbres in complex layers represents the pinnacle achievement of Western music

– but a challenge that could not be easily or wholly conquered immediately. While the title *Diagonal Symphony* suggests an indication of key or theme, like César Franck's *D Minor Symphony*, it also, perhaps, suggests something of the 'limitation' of 'mood' titles like Franz Berwald's *Capricious Symphony*, Beethoven's *Heroic Symphony* or Tchaikovsky's *Emotional* [pathétique] *Symphony*. Just as those composers seemed to be saying: 'This piece presents just my light-hearted whims', or 'You're not getting everything here, just Heroism', or 'If you want something else besides a touching, moving experience, you'll be disappointed', so too does Eggeling warn us that he is primarily exploring one particular aspect, diagonal tension, and not 'everything'. And what Eggeling chose to do, he does very well indeed.

The final result of restoring these two films, both physically and within their historical context, should be to allow them to be understood and appreciated more fruitfully and to connect them with a larger continuum of experimental film and animation. What can we say about that now? At first glance, it is very easy to like the Ruttmann film for its colourful, dynamic energy, its passionate exuberance and witty dexterity. Conversely, to many people, Eggeling's film might seem rather dull and repetitive at first, a 'primitive' film lacking music, colour and 'full animation'. But, we can now recognise how the two films differ in purpose. Ruttmann's expressionism led him to exploit movement and colour as tools for communicating moods, sensations and abstracted confrontations or interactions. He used a few simple geometric shapes to perform elaborate choreographies, where entrances and exits, collisions and complementary trajectories establish a linear, cumulative scenario or development in which new configurations, colours and shapes appear right up to the last moments of the film. Eggeling, by contrast, establishes a complex form that immediately constitutes the totality of available resources and then develops variations on this given material in conscious and conscientious patterns of analogy and antithesis. Both of these approaches are valid and successful and both survive as viable modes of animation today. To use a standard critical topos, Ruttmann is more of a romantic and Eggeling more of a classicist. Ruttmann demands and inspires the participation and emotion of his spectator, while Eggeling requests contemplation, the fixed stare and an analytic/synthetic appreciation by his audience.

Ruttmann's simple forms in complex choreography found further development in Oskar Fischinger's black-and-white *Studies* – which, by the way, date from the late 1920s and early 1930s, after Ruttmann had abandoned animation for live action; Fischinger's earlier films (e.g. *Wax, R-1, A Form-play*), contemporary with Ruttmann's *Opus* films, carefully eschewed the Ruttmann style and developed full-screen grids of complex imagery. James Whitney's *Yantra* (1955), which consciously limits the building block to the dot or pure point of light, also carries on this tradition while at the same time exploits new and different perceptual aspects of intermittence (flickers) and dynamic choreography into complex patterns. And, Larry Cuba's computer graphics of the 1970s in *3/78* and *Two Space*, also with pure points of light in dynamic choreography, further explore motion as pattern and afterimage.

One might expect that Eggeling's simple film would engender few progeny; yet, ironically, advanced technology has enabled a number of Eggeling-like 'classists' to appear in the 1980s. Jules Engel turned the clumsiness of computer-graphics programs into the overt subject of his architectonic painting in *Times Square*. One of Engel's students, John Adamczyk, also artfully used cycles of colour-mapping to make virtually static fractals come alive in formal variations in his *Recurrents*. Videographics/computer artist Michael Scroggins (also a teacher of Adamczyk) created more than a dozen of a series of *Studies* composed of serene cycles of geometric balances that develop out of given complex material with delicate alterations. But, to pigeon-hole Scroggins, for example, also detracts from a broader perspective on his work in some sense. In the hands of great artists, artists conscious of their aesthetic tradition, as Scroggins is, both the Ruttmann and Eggeling methods can be evoked simultaneously. While James Whitney's early 1940s *Variations* might be 'perfect Eggeling' in their appearances and disappearances, analogies and antitheses, his 1963 *Lapis* magnificently transmutes the Ruttmann-based movement-of-simple-forms style into an Eggeling-like whole pattern, and manages to maintain the tension between the two over a breathtaking ten minutes. Another example is Oskar Fischinger who, in his masterpieces the 1943 *Radio Dynamics* and the 1947 *Motion Painting No. 1*, creates a similar tension between Ruttmann and Eggeling styles: in *Radio Dynamics* Fischinger evokes the fixed stare on the complex imagery but gradually (in the flicker sequence) creates such dynamic variations that everything seems to move and change; and in *Motion Painting*, beginning with a fixed-field canvas, slow increments of change in complex patterns are used, which, only after nine minutes, gradually become larger and larger gestures of simpler forms. So, both Ruttmann's *Opus No. 1* and Eggeling's *Diagonal Symphony* are successful films and viable strategies for continued animation, just as both the string quartet and the symphony (and opera and song, for that matter) remain viable formats for music.

Notes

1. Louise O'Konor, *Viking Eggeling 1880–1925, Artist and Filmmaker – Life and Work* (Stockholm: Almqvist & Wiksell, 1971).
2. Roger Manvell, *Experiment in the Film* (London: Grey Walls Press, 1949), 223.
3. Catalogue for *Film als Film* (Kölnischer Kunstverein, 1977): 58.
4. Jeanpaul Goergen, *Walter Ruttmann, eine Dokumentation* (Berlin: Freunde der Deutschen Kinemathek, 1988).

Resistance and subversion in animated films of the Nazi era

The case of Hans Fischerkoesen

William Moritz

The average person today might not know much about German film during the Nazi era and even animation scholars might not know what German animation existed between 1933 and 1945. Such a gap in cinema studies reflects a larger problem present in the United States' perception of this crucial period. Forty years after the World War II, many Americans still naively accept simplistic stereotypes of the Nazis such as the demonic fiend whose appetite for sadistic cruelty is matched only by his ravenous, perverse sexual appetite (who inhabits such dramatic works as Visconti's *The Damned*, and is the bumbling fool, somehow quaintly charming, popularised by such comedies as *Hogan's Heroes*). A similar simplistic notion of the era itself – i.e. everything from 1933 to 1945 was Nazi, everything before or after wasn't – clouds and weakens our perception of one of the most tragic and dangerous episodes in human history. Distancing the Nazis by making them into the stereotypes of demons and fools means we can comfortably say that 'they weren't like us', and by containing them so solidly in a particular time slot, we can assure ourselves that 'such horror can't happen here and now'. Yet, the complex truth about the Nazi era is considerably more menacing.

While undoubtedly some Nazi demons and some Nazi fools did flourish, many Nazis were average German citizens who were bought into an existing fascist scheme – many German citizens were never supporters of Nazism and actively attempted to resist the government's fascist rule. Germany, after all, had a brilliant intellectual, scientific and artistic community for two centuries before the Nazi era and, during the 1920s in particular, Germany had played a leading role in intellectual and artistic avant-garde developments as well as producing many of the finest, most respected films of the era. Not every creative, intellectual person who rejected fascism could leave the country.

Similarly, while the Nazi party legally ruled Germany for only twelve years, between

March 1933 until May 1945, the Nazi party existed as a minority party throughout the 1920s: Hitler was jailed in the early 1920s for terrorist activities. When the Nazis seized power over the German government through a virtual *coup d'état* in 1933 (they were not elected by a majority vote, remember; Hitler was appointed by the senile Hindenberg and the burning of the parliament building gave the leaders an excuse for martial law), many Germans believed that the party could never pull it off and that they would fall from power very quickly. With the disastrous inflation of the 1920s and the Great Depression of the 1930s, Germany had not really recovered from World War I and unemployment hovered over six million – the same figure, ironically, that is usually given as the total number of people executed in the concentration camps. If the Nazis were to stay in power, they had to perform an economic miracle, which many thought such a radical fringe group (rather like the Ku Klux Klan) could never do. But, the Nazis did remain in power and it was precisely their economic success that lured many average citizens to lend them increasing support.

The first few years, however, were still tenuous. The mass arrests of gypsies, homosexuals and 'political dissidents' (socialists, communists and fringe religious fanatics like Jehovah's Witnesses) went unchallenged by many 'nice, normal' German citizens who rather thought 'those people' probably deserved to be disposed of.[1] New jobs created by the absence of those minorities and by the flight of many people needing refuge in other countries helped to cure unemployment, as did the beginning of the massive public works projects such as the building of a freeway system and the new 'People's Auto' (Volkswagen) factories. And, the 1936 Olympics brought a windfall influx of hard currency from millions of tourists. It was only after 1937 – after four years of propaganda indoctrination and four years of increasing economic growth – that the Nazis could launch major anti-Semitic campaigns or ignite the harassment against Catholics and Protestants who resisted Nazi policies.

The German film industry during the Nazi era

The Nazis intended the German film industry to play a key role in their economic recovery. The international success of German films had brought in enormous amounts of foreign exchange into the country during the pre-Nazi days. Although quality productions could also cost millions of marks, the risk was worth it if some resulted in great box-office profits. Therefore, the film industry was placed under special surveillance, to make sure that all vital talent was kept and used to the maximum. In the first days after the Nazi takeover, everyone had to register with an appropriate 'union' (remember, Nazi means 'National Socialist German Workers Party'), so that each person could be monitored through weekly and monthly reports to local and regional offices. For the film industry personnel, this meant that you had to continue doing whatever you were doing – script writing, editing, costume making and so on – or explain why you were falling behind in your work. This vigilant guard duty was necessary: as in the bohemian milieu of the stage for centuries, many of the film world people were eccentrics and liberals, leftists and radicals, homosexuals and free lovers, lavish in the use of liquor and drugs, fond of parties and extravagance. Very few were Nazi sympathisers: even in the 1937 'Degenerate Film' catalogue *Film 'Art', Film Cohen, Film-Corruption*, the desperate authors could list only a handful of minor names as 'good Nazis'.[2] Key talent had to be pampered and coerced. As some industry-related people fled, others were forcibly promoted to fill their jobs.

Despite the fact that about 1500 people from the German film industry did manage to flee the country over an eight-year period – and the presence of many of these exiles in Hollywood would leave a lasting mark on American film style – it was never easy to leave Nazi Germany.[3] No one was allowed to take money out of Germany, and unless you had connections in a host country or foreign bank accounts (as some film people who had been involved in co-productions had), you might not be able to leave. If you had a large family, you probably could not leave, since a complete family leaving at once would be too obvious. Although Fritz Lang was fond of saying that he fled Germany the very day that Propaganda Minister Goebbels offered him the job of production head at Universum Film AG (UFA) Studios, his passport reveals that it took 25 different official stamps and a whole year's time before he could finally leave for America.[4] Nor was it unusual that the Jewish Lang should be courted for a major film industry job at the very time anti-Semitic employment policies were being announced; so hypocritical were the Nazis about money, that they would, for example, force a Jewish director like Reinhold Schünzel to make film after film – including the devastatingly subversive *Victor and Victoria* (Viktor und Viktoria, 1933) – just because every one of his films was a money-making hit. Schünzel and his family were not able to escape until 1937.[5]

The question of animation in the Nazi era has been largely ignored or even falsified. In many texts and film rental catalogues, the dates for films such as Oskar Fischinger's *Composition in Blue* (Komposition im Blau, 1935) or Reiniger's *The Stolen Heart* (Das gestohlene Herz, 1934) are given as 1932 or 1933, as if to suggest that they had not been made in Nazi Germany. Similarly, sound films by the Diehl brothers (Ferdinand, Hermann and Paul), Ladislas Starevitch, Paul Peroff and others are available in silent prints that can discreetly be listed as from the 1920s, even though they were actually produced in 1937 or 1941 in Germany. In fact, Starevitch's *Reynard the Fox* (Reinicke Fuchs, 1937 and Le Roman de Renard), although it was largely shot in Paris around 1930, has been completely ignored in discussions of 'the first feature-length animation film' because it finally received its finishing funds from German sources (since Goethe had written a classic version of the Reynard legend) and had its world premiere in Berlin in April 1937, still eight months before Disney's *Snow White* (December 1937).[6]

In fact, dozens of animators worked in Germany before and during the Nazi era, including such relatively forgotten names as Kurt Wiese, Otto Hermann, Hans Zoozmann, Lore Bierling, Toni Raboll, Harry Jaeger, Kurt Wolfe, Kurt Kiesslich, Curt Schumann, Kurt Stordel, Richard Felgenauer, Bernhard Klein, Paul Peroff, the team of Hedwig and Gerda Otto, the team of G. Wölz & G. Kruger and the team of Schwab and Gerhardt, as well as such slightly better-known figures as Louis Seel, the Diehl brothers (who made more than 50 puppet films), Rudolf Pfenninger, Wolfgang Kaskeline, Lotte Reiniger and the Fischinger brothers, Hans and Oskar.[7]

Only one of these people seems to have been able to leave the country. Oskar Fischinger emigrated in February 1936, but he made three of his best films in Germany during the Nazi era: *Circles* (Kreise, 1933), *Muratti Gets in the Act* (Muratti Greift Ein, 1934) and *Composition in Blue*. He also made several other films and was denied the right to make a colour abstract film *Squares* (Quadrate, 1934). *Circles* and *Composition in Blue* were made in defiance of the Nazi policy on 'degenerate art' and only released with some danger and some difficulty that involved the heroic co-operation of a number of sympathetic anti-Nazi critics, especially those centred around Dr Anschutz's *Colour–Music Congress* in Hamburg (there were four: 1927, 1930, 1933 and 1936) and the Waterloo Theatre in Hamburg, which managed to keep an 'alternate' film club open until they hosted the 1939 premiere of Hans Fischinger's abstract animation *Dance of the Colours* (Tanz der Farben).[8]

Lotte Reiniger and her socialist husband Carl Koch made seven films in Germany between 1933 and 1935. These films continue Reiniger's previous style, using opera and fairy tales in general, but it is also easy to see in a film like *The Stolen Heart* how the filmmaker has carefully tuned the allegory so that it reads as an anti-Nazi resistance fable: When the wicked miser robs the village of its joy in music, the instruments of joy themselves fight back by creating even more musical enjoyment. Under the ruse of going on a vacation to Greece in 1936, Koch and Reiniger attempted to emigrate to France or England. They were denied any permanent status in either country, so they travelled back and forth between the two every few months from 1936 until the outbreak of the war in 1939, when they were declared 'enemy aliens' and refused refuge in either France or England. They then chose a job (arranged by Jean Renoir) in Italy rather than return to Germany, but a few years later, when the Allied troops first landed in Italy, the retreating Nazi occupation army forcibly evacuated Reiniger and Koch back to Germany, where Reiniger was forced to work on an animation film even as bombs fell and troops invaded Berlin.

Other animators could have managed to flee Germany but, in any case, emigration was not necessarily a panacea.[9] Before 1933, Bertold Bartosch had fled to Paris, but in 1940, the invading Nazis destroyed *Saint Francis*, a pacifist film he had been working on for nearly a decade, along with other original negatives of his, including that of his masterpiece *The Idea* (L'idée, 1932), which fortunately survived through one release print in England.

Almost all the animators who worked in Germany between 1933 and 1945 had been making films before this period and most continued to make them after. Germany managed to maintain an economically sound animation industry largely because of advertising films. Before World War I in 1911, Polish-born Julius Pinschewer had pioneered the use of animated films as advertising in regular movie theatres, where the projection of graphic slides had been used previously. Pinschewer believed that if a film were entertaining, the audience would pay attention and respond positively to the product. Therefore, he commissioned films from the best animators (including eventually Guido Seebcr, Walther Ruttmann and Lotte Reiniger) and allowed them a leisurely three or five minutes in which to develop some charming story or graphic idea. So successful was Pinschewer that his films were sold and re-sold in countries all over the world, usually adapted to other products by simply changing the wording of the advertising slogan. The Jewish Pinschewer fled to Switzerland in 1933 and took with him several of his favourite animators, including Rudi Klemm, but he also left many behind.[10]

German animation during World War II

Until 1937, Germany had been well supplied with popular American-made cartoons. American productions had reigned supreme since the *Felix the Cat* and *Out of the Inkwell* series had appeared in the 1920s and had impaired the expansion of the German cartoon industry.[11] Propaganda Minister Goebbels had paid Disney good money for 'Mickey Mouse' shorts, *Silly Symphonies* and the *Three Little Pigs* (1933), but he balked at the high price Disney asked for *Snow White* and refused to pay it. Goebbels predicted that *Snow White* would be a flop, and when it turned out to be a sensational hit, he set about trashing it in a series of well-planned critical attacks in the German press. The criticisms stressed how the pure German tale had been polluted by the addition of Hollywood kitsch and were quick to point out (and re-point out frequently) that the British censors had banned *Snow White* for younger children because it was too violent and frightening.[12] In addition, Goebbels issued a general call to German animators to step up their production of colour animated films for children and specifically commissioned a live action feature film of *Snow White* (Schneeweisschen, 1939) to be made by the nature-documentarian Hubert Schonger, with 'documentary' fidelity to the original Grimm fairytale version (ironically, since most of the German *märchen* originals contain far more violent and frightening details than any American version – text or film). This 'genuine German' *Snow White* turned out to be an awful bore (and awkwardly made), but never one to admit a mistake, Goebbels commissioned seven other live action fairytales (three of them feature length) from Schonger, along with three short combined live-action and animation films, and four drawn-colour fairytale cartoons – all, apparently, of a decidedly second-rate quality both in imagination and execution.[13]

The Diehl brothers, who had been making a variety of romantic and lyrical puppet films earlier, were encouraged to turn their attention to folkloric subjects, which they did with such charming fables as *The Town Mouse and the Country Mouse* (Die Stadtmaus und die Feldmaus, 1939), *Puss in Boots* (Der gestiefelte Kater, I 940), and *Sleeping Beauty* (Dornroschen). They also managed to break out of the cycle with a rather chilling *Max and Moritz* (Max und Moritz, 1941), based on Wilhelm Busch's original nineteenth-century comic strip, from which the later *Katzenjammer Kids* was derived. The Diehls render the disgusting pranks of these two evil children in such grotesque detail that it is difficult not to read the film as a protest against the wilful and petulant carnage of the Nazi overlords.

Thirty-five-year-old Hans Held, who had come from the theatre to being an assistant director for live action movies at the Bavaria Studios (he specialised in design and colour consultation), was pressed into the production of animated films and produced a rather nasty thirteen-minute film *The Troublemaker* (Der Storenfried, 1940). The film demonstrates, in good mock-Disney style, how the weaker animals of the forest can band together to drive out the fox – all in specific militaristic imagery (such as formations of birds which dive-bomb the fox).[14] Some sources list a second Held film *Unity Makes Strength* (Einigkeit macht Stark, 1941), but this might well be an alternate title for *The Troublemaker*.[15]

There were other productions as well: Kurt Stordel, for example, produced two very popular cartoons about Purzel the Dwarf.[16] But, the trickle of cartoons produced by German studios was not enough to cover for the loss of Disney and other American product. To rectify the situation, an official ministry plan of May 1941 called for the establishment of a strong German animation industry capable of producing not only a continuous flow of colour-cartoon shorts, but also feature-length animated films. At the behest of this goal, all able animators were commanded to step up their production and focus on theatrically viable entertainment cartoons.[17] Among the animators called into action at this time was Hans Fischerkoesen, who was among the most distinguished animators remaining in Germany between 1933 and 1945.

The case of Hans Fischerkoesen

Hans Fischer was born 18 May 1896 in Bad Koesen near Naumbürg (with its famous cathedral) on the road between Leipzig and Weimar. Because Fischer was such a common name in the film world, he would later add on the name of his birthplace in order to distinguish himself from the others. He was a delicate child, plagued by asthma, so his parents allowed him and his sister Leni to indulge their taste for fantasy and spectacle by creating puppet shows and home entertainments. After basic schooling, Leni and Hans attended the Leipzig Art Academy together. Leni stayed with Hans and worked with him on many films.

Because of his asthma, Hans could not serve as a soldier during World War I, but he did work in army hospitals near the front lines where he experienced the grotesque inanity of trench warfare. He dreamed about making an animated film *The Hole in the West* (Das Loch im Westen, 1919), which would expose the War Profiteer as the real cause of war and the real manipulator of victory and defeat. When the war ended, Fischerkoesen returned to his family home and spent months drawing about 1600 sequential images that made concrete the dream (or rather nightmare) vision he had experienced in the trenches. He took the drawings to a Leipzig movie company and paid them (a borrowed) 700 marks to shoot them onto film; but, as it turned out, the company was near bankruptcy and had never shot single-frame material before. Hans lost that money, but he persevered to build his own animation stand out of a wooden margarine crate and shot the film himself. Fischerkoesen himself described the film as a political cartoon brought to life and it certainly suggests something of Bartosch's *The Idea*, made a decade later. Fortunately, a Leipzig film distributor bought *The Hole in the West* cartoon from Fischerkoesen for 3000 marks, so he was able to continue making animation films.

He made a successful advertising film *Strolling Peter* (Bummel-Petrus, 1921) for the Leipzig shoe factory Nordheimer, which led to a two-year contract with Julius Pin-schewer, after which he established his own Fischerkoesen Studio in Leipzig to specialise in advertising films. Fischerkoesen was perfectly suited to the advertising industry; he had an irrepressible sense of humour, a good sense of musical rhythm and a charming, flexible cartoon style, as well as the obsessive concentration necessary to work exhaustingly until an animation production was perfected in every detail. He also had a knack for seeing a pun or twist in some old saying, common situation or popular song which would fit right in with a product. He philosophised about advertising, proposing that the 'if/then' formula (if you use this product, then this will happen; if you have this problem, then this product will help) was the best format for a succinct, cogent ad.[18]

In 1931, a Leipzig newspaper celebrated Fischerkoesen, 'the darling of audiences', with a full-page article entitled 'Watch out, Mickey Mouse, Felix the Cat and Co.!' which contains delightful images of a cow with a lyre built into her horns, a bull in a tuxedo and an enchanting art-deco-style kangaroo ballet – all popular cartoon figures from his ads.[19] By 1937, when he won both first and second prize at a Dutch-sponsored international competition for advertising films (the runners-up included such luminaries as George Pal and Alexander Alexeieff), Fischerkoesen had made around 1000 publicity films. Unfortunately, all but a few of his pre-war films seem to be lost or languish unidentified in collections that do not consider advertising films important.

For many years, Hans Fischerkoesen managed to keep his production confined to the kind of commercial work he did so well. But after the ministry plan of May 1941 was enacted, the Propaganda Minister, through the UFA studios, had demanded that he move his staff and studio from Leipzig to Potsdam, where he would be near UFA's 'Neubabelsberg' studios, to be available for consultations and special effects work for UFA features and documentaries. When the 45-year-old Fischerkoesen, loathe to become any more closely involved with Goebbels than necessary, protested that he did not really have the talent to invent ideas for story films, he was assigned to work with 35-year-old Horst von Möllendorff, a popular Berlin newspaper cartoonist who had just been 'drafted' to work as a gag man for the new German cartoon industry.

An aside: Möllendorff's 'authorship'?

Möllendorff received the 'story' credit of three films I have seen: Fischerkoesen's *Weather-Beaten Melody* (Verwitterte Melodie, 1942) and *The Snowman* (Der Schnee-mann, 1943) and a film called *Wedding in the Coral Sea* (Hochzeit im Korallenmeer, 1945), which was animated by Jiri Brdecka during the last year of the war in Prague. How much Möllendorff actually contributed to these films seems a moot point to me. Fischerkoesen's two films are sheer masterpieces, thoroughly witty and inventive (in exactly the same ways his many advertising films are), and often the weight of the story is carried by graphic brilliance and astonishing small details; the bare bones of the story ideas (a bee finds an abandoned phonograph in a meadow or a snowman hides in a refrigerator in order to experience Spring) hardly tell why they are such wonderful films.

The Brdecka *Coral Sea* is regarded by the Czechs as a Czech film, since not only Brdecka, but also Eduard Hofman, Stanislav Latal, Josef Kandl and Jilis Kalas worked on it (all of whom would continue in Czech animation production after the war). The film is a nice, pleasant piece, well animated, but overall neither terribly clever or witty – the story, in fact, is painfully simple: a pair of fish are about to get married when an octopus steals the bride, so the fish co-operate to get her back. Nor is it very original, in that Friz Freleng's 1935 cartoon *Mr and Mrs is the Name* has basically the same story and style (replete with sunken ship), except that the Warner Bros. 'star', Buddy, is the hero instead of a boy-fish.[20] Fischerkoesen also made a third cartoon *The Silly Goose* (Das dumme Gänslein, 1944) based on his own story, which is again humorous, vivid and touching.[21] The fact that the Fischerkoesen films (and remember that Hans's sister Leni was an omnipresent collaborator) demonstrate a consistent wit and inventiveness, while the Möllendorff film made in Czechoslovakia lacks those very qualities, suggests to me that Möllendorff might have been merely a functionary and his contribution to the Fischerkoesen films was negligible. The credit for these masterpieces rests with Hans and Leni Fischerkoesen.

A closer look at the films

Among the specific things that Goebbels mandated for the new German cartoon industry was the development of 'three-dimensional' effects that could compete with Max and Dave Fleischer's stereo-optical process (which combined model sets with cel animation), or Disney's multiplane camera (which filmed several layers of cels), both of which had been lauded in the American and European press. Fischerkoesen had already been using, in his advertising films, a simple multiplane type of effect derived from the multi-layered glass animations that Reiniger had used in the 1926 animated feature *The Adventures of Prince Achmed* (Die Abenteuer des Prinz Achmed) (and that Bertold

Bartosch, who had worked on special effects for that feature, continued to use in his exquisite half-hour tragic allegory *The Idea*). Fischerkoesen had also been working with puppet and model animation and could hardly have been ignorant of Oskar Fischinger's brilliant simulation of a deep-space-travelling boom shot around the Muratti cigarettes parading towards the Olympic stadium in his classic ad film *Muratti Gets in the Act*.

The opening sequence of *Weather-Beaten Melody* demonstrates a bravura mastery of both the multiplane and stereo-optical processes, and a meaningful use of depth, following the flight of a bee down from the sky, flying through twelve layers of grass and flowers in a meadow and circling around an abandoned phonograph which lies, puzzlingly for the bee, in the middle of the meadow. Behind this long-travelling point-of-view sequence is also the assumption that the bee is a personage worthy of following and in fact she turns out to be adventurous, resourceful, perceptive, talented, witty and friendly, among other admirable, even noble 'human' characteristics. Fischerkoesen demonstrates these personality traits in little episodes that are characteristic of his style: she uses dandelion seeds as parachutes for a joyous free ride, and when her game of tossing a blueberry ends in disaster (the overripe fruit bursts over her head), she meticulously wipes herself clean on a daisy petal. Fischerkoesen also delineates her personality with unexpected complexities. For example, is she jealous of the hedgehog who takes over her place as 'phonograph needle' while she is away sharpening her stinger, or is she merely exasperated at the confusing quality of his multi-needle pickup? The very idea of ambiguity was anathema for the Nazis, who could only hope to maintain their fascist program by enforcing strict, unbending codes of behaviour and absolute, inviolable 'ideals and truths'. Precisely because of its technical brilliance, *Weather-Beaten Melody* could contain quite a bit of forbidden material. Ironically, inherent in the 'stereo' animation techniques, as Fischerkoesen uses them, lies the most subversive metaphor: A sense of freedom of movement, an affirmation of the multi-layered nature of reality – of ambiguity and change – which demands (even subconsciously) that the viewer think for herself or himself and consider other things as valid as the subjective self – something truly forbidden by Nazi doctrine as the most dangerous action of all.

To fully appreciate Fischerkoesen's daring, one must remember that the Nazis had forbidden jazz and swing music as an Afro-Judaic plot to undermine traditional German culture. The 1937 'Degenerate Film' catalogue contained an anti-jazz spread entitled 'Africa Speaks . . . ?', which stigmatised 'Al JolsonRosenblatt' among other black and black-face jazz musicians, and the 1938 'Degenerate Music' exhibition had on its cover the image of a black saxophone player wearing a Star of David. Detlev Peukert chronicles how the swing movement became a key symbolic rebellion, while the British film *Swing Under the Swastika* documents the sad and ironic fates of jazz musicians during this period.[22]

In this context, the discovery of an abandoned phonograph takes on new meaning, especially when the record left on the turntable is a swing number with lyrics that say 'The week wouldn't be worthwhile without a weekend when we can get away to enjoy nature'. Near the phonograph lies an 'abandoned' clasp from a woman's garter belt (with a 'lucky' four-leafed clover growing out of it!), which suggests that the interrupted picnic that left behind the musical instrument had also involved erotic play – something also strictly forbidden by the puritanical Nazi codes. So, from beneath the charming surface of this cartoon emerges a subversive message: women, far from filling the unnatural Nazi-designated stereotype of revolving around 'children, church and kitchen', can escape into Nature to be self-reliant and adventurous, erotic and free –

they can rediscover or revitalise a suppressed world of forbidden joy that is found in music and friendship between diverse creatures; creatures who could be brown or white, a frog or a caterpillar, or even a pair of ladybug beetles who might be a same-sex couple. Especially compared with many American cartoons of this same period (profligate with gratuitous violence and racist/sexist stereotype victims), the entire community of animals depicted in *Weather-Beaten Melody* are peaceful, friendly, fun-loving, imaginative and altruistic – quite the opposite of the Nazi requirements for a dedicated Aryan citizen.

The same spirit of ambiguity and subversive sub-text pervades Fischerkoesen's next film *The Snowman*. The opening sequence, as in *Weather-Beaten Melody*, establishes the filmmaker's mastery of creating the illusion of three-dimensional space. Behind the credits are layers of snowflakes, with their elaborate abstract patterns (including pure geometrical circles – all of which justify 'degenerate' abstract art as a natural phenomenon!) – falling down through the frame. As the credits finish, the viewer flies down over a snow-covered twilight village, around the steeple of a church (a stereo-optical-type model), down to a snowman that stands in an open space – just as if we were seeing the world from the point of view of a snowflake. This point of view is confirmed when snowflakes alight on the snowman in the pattern of a heart, suggesting that he is a creature of feelings, rather than a military/political figure (who would wear medals or insignia) or an ostracised victim (such as the Jewish and gay people who wore yellow stars or pink triangles). Unlike the opening of *Weather-Beaten Melody*, which establishes the point of view as that of the protagonist bee, *The Snowman*'s opening sets the audience up as a visitor/observer of the snowman protagonist.

The character of the snowman is more complex and 'humanly' equivocal than that of the bee and thereby makes us question more critically the meanings behind the actions he is involved in and, ultimately, the social context from which he comes. In his seminal 1927 lecture series about narrative theory *Aspects of the Novel*, E.M. Forster discusses two principles of narrative organisation that are particularly relevant to *The Snowman*.[23] Forster points out that Pattern, the audience's slow perception of an overall shape or direction to the story, can heighten our awareness. Or, the inexorable conditions that produce the narrative 'destiny', whether or not they are, for example, the traits of personality that cause one protagonist to succeed while another fails, or the nexus of social conditions that bring together a diverse group or people to a particular time, place and incident. Forster also observes that Rhythm, the recurrence of certain details, events or persons at several intervals in a story, can cause us to re-evaluate the meaning of both the repeating item and the narrative as a whole. Fischerkoesen employs both Pattern and Rhythm to make us consider seriously the plight and destiny of his protagonist snowman.

In the first episode, the snowman begins to play, by juggling snowballs – a curiously appropriate pastime since he himself is composed of snowballs. His game angers a watchdog, who rushes in barking at him. In his attempts to get away from the watchdog, he squashes the dog into the snow and then laughs at the dog's distress. When, in retaliation, the dog bites a chunk out of his rump, the snowman pelts the dog with snowballs, which finally hurts the dog and gets rid of it. The snowman tries to have fun again by skating on an icy pond (using icicles as his skates), but finds the three snowballs of his body begin to bounce apart. Soon the ice breaks and the snowman is melted down to a thin skeleton of his former self. He is able to restore himself by rolling down hill until he accumulates his former bulk of snow and, when his torso and head get mixed (just as they did while skating), a crow helps to find and assemble his body parts into proper order. A tree laughs at him, as he had laughed at the watchdog, so the crow shakes its coat of snow away as revenge. While the snowman tries to nap, a rabbit attempts to steal his carrot-nose, so he decides to go inside to sleep where it will be safer.

As he walks into a nearby cottage, the viewer is treated to a spectacular 180-degree stroll around the stereo-optical building, which recalls the brilliant opening shot with snow falling over the city square. Once inside, he disturbs a grumpy cat in order to sleep on its couch and the cat's huffy hiss reminds us of the petulant, territorial dog's snappy barks. Increasingly, we become aware that (as the scoffing tree had recalled the scoffing snowman) events are beginning to parallel former incidents – in fact, a Pattern that contrasts the events in Winterland with the events in Summerland and several Rhythmic recurrences that will heighten our perception of the differences between these alternate worlds.

The snowman notices his own picture on the winter portion of a calendar, but also sees (on later months) some lovely flowers that he has never experienced. He decides to hide in the refrigerator so that he can re-emerge when the flowers are in bloom. When he attempts to leave the refrigerator in July, however, his rump has stuck to the its shelf and he loses a chunk (as he had lost a chunk to the watchdog), which he regains by turning down the temperature in the icebox (an intelligent, ecological choice, also recalling his earlier ruse of throwing snowballs at the dog until the dog retaliated by tossing back his lost rump-chunk as a weapon). He plays pranks on the chicken and cows, just as he had teased the dog in Winterland (yet when he finds that he is freezing a ladybug, he kindly becomes a ski run for her by turning somersaults across a meadow – another dazzling animation feat). After he melts, singing 'How lovely summer is/My heart breaks from happiness', a rabbit eats his carrot-nose (and her bunnies frolic in his hat, as if he had been a magician).

Parallel incidents reveal the complexities of the snowman's character and highlight the ambiguities of the action as a parable: The snowman, an average person with some good and some bad qualities, is trapped in a given environment, Winterland. Although it is functional, it is cold and in some ways inhospitable. He reads that there is another place, sunny and free and arranges to escape to this Summerland for some thrilling moments of warmth and freedom, even at the cost of his life, as we hear him gurgle in the death throes of song, twisting and melting in the hot sun. The dog, crow, cat, ladybug, rabbit and others are characterised as parallel human-like creatures, which supports an open, thoughtful humanitarian world view that was anathema to the Nazis. *The Snowman* is also full of beautiful, touching, affirmative and spectacular scenes, such as the long pan across unfolding Spring.

Fischerkoesen's third wartime film *The Silly Goose* provides another thought-provoking parable. Through the bars of a wooden cage on a cart driving across town, a young goose glimpses the seemingly glamorous allures of city life: among them an exotic parrot silhouetted in a dance hall and an elegant fox (stole) with feathers. Back at the farm, while her brothers and sisters receive their schooling in swimming, marching, laying eggs and such, she dreams narcissistically by a pond, swings on the gate like a parrot, uses the plough as a mirror and creates for herself a pseudo-sophisticated costume by thieving and exploiting her neighbours. She acquires a caterpillar stole, a straw bottlecover hat, pollen powder, a spider-web veil, cork high-heels and pig-bristle eyelashes. Her sashay through the barnyard creates mixed anger and astonishment from the other animals. The gander, however, chooses to woo her instead of her more modest sisters, though she rejects him and wanders off into the woods where she is seduced by a fox. The fox's sinister lair is run by slave labour – a weasel cranks a spit, a cat on a treadmill makes xylophonic music with dangling bones, and a cage full of geese await slaughter. She manages to escape and the barnyard animals co-operate to drive the fox away and free his victims. While, on the surface, this film could satisfy Goebbels's dictum for 'blood and soil' films that glorify the German peasant life, Fischerkoesen creates a complex and ambiguous narrative that confuses and contradicts Nazi policy.[24] The city *is* glamorous, especially as seen in a long stereo-optical, multiplane sequence from the goose's point of view, while the barnyard activities are quaint and confining. At the same time, however, the silly goose's exploitation of the barnyard for her costume is mean and thoughtless. When the goose is seduced by the fox, we momentarily hear a crypto version of the old (Yiddish) popular song 'Bei mir bist Du scheen' and could think that the villain is being identified as a Jew. Quickly, however, we see that just the opposite is true: the goose herself is being exploited. The fox is using her as he does various other animals, which seems to allude to the Nazis' exploitation of the Jews as slave labour and prisoners doomed to execution. This sub-text becomes even more obvious by comparison with two other German films of the period: Held's 1940 *The Troublemaker* (in which the fox is a simplistic villain and the farm animals drive him away in specifically militaristic fashion) and Frank Leberecht's 1943 *Poor Hansi* (Armer Hansi), in which the gratuitous violence that drives Hansi the canary back home rivals the worst of Warner Bros., truly supporting a 'blood and soil' ideal. Very much to the contrary, *The Silly Goose* warns against being seduced by the glamour of fascism and encourages the viewer to think carefully about home and the city and responsibility, to realise what happens to victims and to do something about it.

So, in these three wartime cartoon masterpieces, we see how Hans Fischerkoesen demonstrated that even at the darkest, most menacing hours of human depravity, men of principle can resist by subverting, with subtlety, the rules and prejudices of the tyrant.

Conclusion

At the end of World War II, the invading Russian troops arrested Fischerkoesen (along with all other film personnel) as possible Nazi collaborators. Although he could prove that he was not only never a Nazi sympathiser but actually a member of an underground resistance group of artists during the war years, he was kept in Sachsenhausen concentration camp for three years before his case was tried and he was exonerated. During that time, he worked in the kitchen and painted on the walls ironic allegorical murals of vegetable caricatures, which are now preserved as a national historical monument. As in great animal fables, these kitchen murals play out the daily trials and terrors of prison living, yet provide an ironical perspective by enacting these traumas through vegetables that we humans would calmly eat without a second thought. A parsnip inspects a carrot for 'vermin' (in this case, a worm), while another parsnip stands by, sharpening his knife (surgical or punitive?): Is it not absurd that parsnips should be in control of carrots, when they're clearly relatives? In other paintings, a carrot gratefully showers under a plain faucet spigot, while potatoes, eager for a swim, peel off their own skins and dive into the soup. A procession of happy cucumbers carry a pumpkin on a palanquin, yet they also help one another to slice themselves away on a kitchen 'guillotine'. These (and other) paintings provide a glimpse of humanitarian warmth in the grim camp where so many suffered and lost their lives.[25]

By the time Fischerkoesen was finally exonerated and released from prison in 1948, he had shown that he was not a Nazi, and also that he wasn't a communist, so he was not allowed to work privately on his own films, but only as a functionary on assignments in the state-controlled DEFA studios. Later that year, he and his family made one of those daring night-time escapes from East Germany carrying only a camera, and he re-established an animation studio for advertising films near Bonn in West Germany. I have viewed thirty or so of his post-war ads and have found most to be witty, lively, graphically interesting and memorably clever. Certainly, he received critical acclaim: by 1956, he had won major prizes at commercial film festivals in Rome, Milan (three times), Venice, Monte Carlo and Cannes. He also appeared on the cover of the 26 August issue of the prestigious *Der Spiegel*, which is Germany's equivalent of the American *Time* magazine.[26] Fischerkoesen continued to make advertising films until 1969 and died in 1973.

This is a revised version of a paper given at the 1991 SAS Conference, Rochester, which was first published in the *Animation Journal* (Fall 1992) vol. 1 issue 1.

Notes

In addition to the various written sources cited in these notes, I have also used throughout information from interviews with the following people: Alexandre Alexieff, Maria Bartosch, Ali Benitz, Thorold Dickenson, Dr Hans Curlis, Dr Hans Fischerkoesen, Elfriede Fischinger, Dr. Leonhard Furst, Henri Langlois, Gerd Opfermann, Claire Parker, Lotte Reiniger, Paul Sauerlander and Hedwig Traub. After this article was written, I corroborated many details by reference to a term paper written in 1985 by Hans Fischerkoesen's granddaughter, Stephanie McMillan, which is now in the John Canemaker Animation Collection at the Bobst Library of New York University.

1. Details and documents appear in the exhibition catalogue *Eldorado* (Berlin: Berlin Museum, 1984) and James Steakley, *The Homosexual Emancipation Movement in Germany* (New York: Arno, 1975), among other sources.
2. Carl Neumann, Curt Belling and Hans-Walther Betz, *Film-'Kunst', Film-Kohn, Film-Korruption* (Berlin: Hermann Scherping, 1937). The list of thirteen names, none important stars or directors, appears on page 153.
3. A list of names appears in Ronny Loewy, *Von Babelsberg nach Hollywood: Filmemigranten aus Nazideutschland* (Frankfurt am Main: Deutsches Filmmuseum, 1987), 8–22.
4. The claim is quoted in Lotte Eisner's biography *Fritz Lang* 1976 (New York: Da Capo, 1986), 14–15. The passport is reproduced in Loewy's *Von Babelsberg nach Hollywood*, 27–31. Gosta Werner has written up the incident: 'Fritz Lang and Goebbels, Myths and Facts', *Film Quarterly*, 43 (Spring 1990): 24–27.
5. William Moritz, 'Film Censorship during the Nazi era', *'Degenerate Art': The Fate of the Avant-Garde in Nazi Germany* (New York: Abrams/Los Angeles County Museum of Art, 1991), 184–91.
6. Leona and Francois Martin, *Ladislas Starewitch* (Annecy Festival, 1991), 42–43. See also Hans Schumacher, 'Starewitch in Berlin', *Film Kurier*, 30 (27 April 1937): n.p.
7. Peter Hagemann and Herbert Schulz, *Deutsches Trickfilm Kaleidoskop* (Berlin: Stiftung Deutsche Kinemathek/Annecy Festival, 1979). Reinhol Johann Holtz, 'Die Phanomenologie und Psychologie des Trickfilms', PhD diss., Hansischen Universitat, 1940.
8. After the screening, the theatre's permit was withdrawn.
9. Paul Peroff, for example, was working in New York during the 1950s, but I have been unable to determine when he left Germany.
10. Roland Cosandey, *Julius Pinschewer: cinquante ans de cinema d'animation* (Annecy: Annecy Festival, 1989). Martin Loiperdinger and Harald Pulch, in their article 'History of the Advertising Film in Germany' point out that film ads really began in the nineteenth century with the Lumière brothers and their German parallels, although most of these earlier films have been lost.

Pinschewer, as probably the first film-ad agent, was certainly the first to make film ads an important, lucrative movie phenomena, which could sustain careers and an industry. *Symposium Werbefilm: Gesichte und Gegenwart*, 38 (Internationale Kurzfilmtage Oberhausen, 1992): 3–9.

11. The cartoon industry was affected in terms of growth, as opposed to the 'art animation' of Fischinger or Reiniger or the adverting films of Pinschewer and Fischerkoesen, which were not.

12. Items on Disney's *Snow White* appear in the trade paper *Licht-Bild-Buhne*: 'Even Protests in US about Disney's Unreasonable Fees for *Snow White*' (26 January 1938); 'Who cares if *Snow White* is Too Expensive, Since It's so Violent' (15 February 1938); '*Snow White* Banned in London for Under Age 14!' (31 May 1938); 'Is *Snow White* Even an Appropriate Subject for a Kids' Film?' (9 July 1938). The Schonger film was already being promoted as 'the real German *Snow White*' on 9 June 1939, although it did not open until October 1939.

13. A.U. Sander, *Jugend und Film* (Berlin: NSDAP, 1944), 26–29. This first live action film appears to be based on the Grimms' fairytale *Snow White and Rose Red* since a second Schongar *Schneewittchen* appeared in October 1942. Perhaps Goebbels wanted to avoid immediate comparison with Disney or wanted to avoid pointing out how gruesome and violent the Grimms' *märchen* really are.

14. 'Storenfried', troublemaker, had special connotations for the Nazi era children: one of the most pervasive *Hitlerjugend* posters declared 'Drive Out All Troublemakers!'. Reproduced on the dust-jacket of H.W. Koch's *The Hitler Youth* (New York: Dorset, 1975).

15. Reinhold E. Thiel, *Puppen-und-Zeichen-Film* (Berlin:Rembrandt, 1960), 10.

16. The films: *Purzel* (1939) and *Purzel der Zwerg* (1942).

17. Boguslaw Drewniak, *Der Deutscher Film 1938–45* (Dusseldorf: Droste, 1987), 33.

18. Erich Boyer, 'Auf jeder Leinwand – ein Fischerkoesen-Film', *Hobby* (September 1955). Arne Andersen, 'Hans Fischerkoesen – der Walt Disney des deutschen Werbefilms', *Technikum*, 9 (November 1958): 396–398.

19. S. Ceha, 'Achtung! Mickey Maus, Felix der Kater & Co.', *Leipziger Abendpost* (5 August 1931): 5.

20. Even if this particular Warner cartoon was not distributed in Germany, it is likely that a print was captured during the conquest of other European countries and Goebbels showed it to his filmmakers in order for them to make a rival German version. Thus the Disney *Snow White* was screened in 1939 for the students at the Film Academy and various Fleischer cartoons were in fact shown to general audiences with the names 'Kurt Fleischer' and 'Carl Fleischer' substituted for the 'Jewish' names Max and David. *Film Kurier* 21 (28 October 1939): 2.

21. Ingrid Westbrock in her study *Der Werbefilm* suggests that Silly Goose was not finished until after the war ('. . . begun 1945, finished 1947 . . .' she says), but that cannot be true, since the film was begun immediately after the successful *Snowman* in 1943 and Fischerkoesen was still in a concentration camp in 1947. Her mistake probably arises from censorship notices, since the three Fischerkoesen cartoons were cleared and re-released in Germany in 1947. Ingrid Westbrock, *Der Werbefilm* (Hildesheim: Olms, 1983), 45.

22. Detlev Peukert, *Inside Nazi Germany: Conformity, Opposition and Racism in Everyday Life* (CT: Yale UP, 1987). John Jeremy's 1987 *Swing Under the Swastika* (BBC) was accompanied by a BBC documentation book in both English and German editions.

23. Edward Morgan Forster, *Aspects of the Novel* (San Diego: Harcourt Brace, 1985), 149–169.

24. Blood and soil films were just one category in Goebbels's programme to commemorate German culture in film.

25. The great actor Heinrichz George, for example, died there in September, 1946.

26. 'Minnesand auf Markenartikel', *Der Spiegel*, 10 (29 August 1956): cover, 34–40.

European influences on early Disney feature films

Robin Allan

The Disney company today has become one of the most powerful entertainment conglomerates in the world. As the years go by it seems more than ever important to identify some of the cultural and aesthetic forces that influenced the founder of this empire, Walt Disney. The empire is based on film and still relies upon succeeding generations being familiar with the situations, stories and characters made popular through Walt Disney's films, and the films themselves were indebted to an older cultural heritage which Disney absorbed and recreated for a new mass audience as part of the popular culture of his period. This essay[1] examines the early period of Disney's film career, in particular the European influences on his early films, and then goes on to examine in detail one section of *Fantasia*, the animation of Beethoven's *Pastoral Symphony*. This period was a critical moment in the history of Walt Disney the man and Disney the company, when confidence in the Disney films led to expansion and extension between 1937 and 1941, before the company's near collapse in 1941.

Before *Snow White*

Animation had enjoyed, along with live action film, a vigorous period in Europe before the first world war. Hollywood came to dominate the industry and Disney allied himself to the centre of American popular film culture by basing himself in Hollywood rather than in New York where most of the animation studios were established. As Donald Crafton has shown, Disney's was one of many studios in the animation business; his early films were not very different from the output of his rivals but they quickly became technically and stylistically superior.[2] He produced his first *Laugh-o-Gram* films in Kansas City with the help of his friend Ub Iwerks who was the son of a Dutch émigré and like Disney did not complete his secondary school education. Kansas City was famous for its European immigrants and the other young men Disney employed were also the sons of émigrés.[3]

The importance of Europe and Germany in particular as a cultural heritage for the new

Max und Moritz, gar nicht träge,
Sägen heimlich mit der Säge,
Ritzeratze! voller Tücke,
In die Brücke eine Lücke.

Als nun diese Tat vorbei,
Hört man plötzlich ein Geschrei:

Und schon ist er auf der Brücke,
Kracks! Die Brücke bricht in Stücke;

Americans of the Midwest cannot be over-emphasised. At the turn of the century more than 27 per cent of Americans were of German descent, with at least one parent born in the 'old country'. They came from all parts of Germany and settled in the Midwest. The majority were from humble farming, artisan and later on, proletarian backgrounds. Many were illiterate. The process of emigration was largely complete by 1917, though another influx took place in the late 1920s and throughout the 1930s which in turn affected Disney's work in the late 1930s and 1940s.[4]

Seven out of Disney's first eight films are based on European fairytales or folktales. In 1922, he used the well-known German folktale *The Four Musicians of Bremen* for the second film in his early *Laugh-o-Gram* series. The subtitle is 'a modernised version of that old fairytale' by 'cartoonist Walt Disney'. The 'that' expresses a discourse which invites a sense of identification with the filmmaker; the implication is of a new working and a superior one, of an original which in some way is old fashioned or inferior. The taking over and making afresh of material from the 'old world' is demonstrated. The end is signalled by what was to become a standard conclusion to all Disney's films: 'and they lived happily ever after'. Although it has little in common with its original, the film reveals fluid animation and a series of meticulously plotted gags culminating in a chase and a battle; the Felix-like cat shows how animators then, as now, borrowed from one another. The graphic line is vigorous, reminiscent of the comic strip; the situations rely on surprise and metamorphosis, staple ingredients of the animated films of that time. The running gag was constantly used; short climaxes with much repetition saved money and helped to divide labour so that animators could work on their own sections without the need to know what lay on either side of their sequences.

The graphic style of these films indicates the influence of newspaper cartoons and indeed many of the animators worked on newspaper comic strips. At Hearst International, the animators shared floor space with the comic strip cartoonists, one of whom was George McManus of *Bringing up Father* fame. (As early as 1913, the great

European pioneer of animation Emile Cohl worked with McManus on a cartoon film series, now almost completely lost, of *The Newlyweds* [5]). Another of Hearst's animated cartoon series was *The Katzenjammer Kids* produced by Gregory la Cava and based on the comic strip drawn by Rudolph Dirks, a young artist of German descent. This had started in 1897 after Hearst, on a visit to Europe, had seen picture stories of the naughty boys Max and Moritz by the German artist Wilhelm Busch (1832–1908). The comic pictures and verses of this gifted artist were popular both in Germany and in the United States. Working at Hearst's on *The Katzenjammer Kids* were George Stallings and I. Klein, who both later worked for Disney.

Bold outlines characterise the animated films of the early Disney, using the period's tradition of the comic strip with a graphic fluidity of storyline laced with gags exemplified by Busch. Like Disney's, Busch's world is a rural one, his characters and situations rooted in a popular tradition of peasant and lower bourgeois culture. The cruelty in Busch (Max and Moritz are ground up as corn and eaten for their naughtiness) is reflected in the ruthless *Schadenfreude* of the early Disney. (Mickey makes a violin out of a cat in *Steamboat Willie* and hangs on to Claribel Cow's udder when the latter becomes airborne in *Plane Crazy*, both from 1928). The early Mickey Mouse and Donald Duck parallel Busch's harsh conflict between safe and repressive authority and the yearning for self-assertion. Before the mid-1930s, these characters are like Busch's 'mar-peace or troublemaker . . . the dangerously vital, untrained, "unaccultivated" child, animal or rebel who challenges and ridicules the established order and the morality precariously constructed to sanctify it and uphold it'.[6]

Disney's concern for a continuous narrative set him apart from his rivals. In this he reflected Busch's narrative drive and editorial flair which had led to the development of the comic strip. There is another link with Busch, in that Disney's characters also inhabit a folktale world. Just as Disney looked back to a rural past in his films – and this applies throughout his work – so Busch looked back to a sentimentalised golden age of pre-industrial rural Germany, exemplified in romantic period painting and decoration. This nostalgic movement, known as the Biedermeier tradition, is translated by *The Oxford German Dictionary* as a 'simple style of German interior decoration of about 1830', but the term includes realistic painting of the romantic period, admired by the bourgeoisie at the turn of the century. Bourgeois *Gemutlichkeit* came to be seen as its keynote.[7] The word *gemutlich* is difficult to translate; cosy, pleasant, snug, warm, genial – adjectives applicable to much of Disney. Indeed, Disney was a Biedermeier artist *par excellence*, since he used realism to promote nostalgia for a past that had never existed.

There is a strong graphic line in the early films which recalls that of Busch and this extends to the grotesque. In Busch this can be seen in the corkscrew legs of the listener and multiple arms and fingers of the performer in the story 'A New Year's Concert'.[8] So Pegleg Pete pulls Mickey's body till it collapses in a coil onto the ground and Mickey has to pick it up in folds to tuck it back into his trousers (*Steamboat Willie* 1928). Disney's early work was not afraid of the grotesque or cruel, but quickly became more Biedermeier than Busch. Just as in post-romantic Germany, naughty children were exorcised and transformed by the little angels of the children's magazines and journals, so Disney came to sanitise and sentimentalise his mouse in the post-Hays Code environment of Hollywood.

Another influence that derives from Europe is the use of anthropomorphised animals

Opposite page
Wilhelm Busch's illustration Max und Moritz *(1865). Busch was popular in Germany and the United States*

(Still courtesy of Edith Wilson)

Three illustrations from artists following the Biedermeier tradition of the German romantic period:

Top   *Retzsch's illustration for* Schiller *(1834)*

(Author's collection)

Bottom   *Ludwig Richter's* Deutsche Art und Sitte *(1872)*

(Author's collection)

Opposite page *Wilhelm Busch's* Ein Neujahrskonzert *(1865)*

(Still courtesy of Edith Wilson)

for comic purposes, noticeable in most of the short cartoons of the period and in all of Disney's early work. The *Alice* comedies began in 1923 with the live action protagonist surrounded by cartoon animals but, by the end of the series in 1927, she is swamped by the animals who dominate the screen area. The debt to Carroll and Tenniel is slight, but the animals are, like many of their contemporaries, direct descendants of the European anthropomorphised creatures from stories, magazines and popular journals flourishing in the late nineteenth and early twentieth centuries. Anthropomorphism is perhaps as old as storytelling itself and from Aesop onwards has been used for many purposes, including social and political satire. As humanity has become less dependent on animals for its day-to-day life, this century has seen an increase in the anthropomorphic impulse, from Beatrix Potter in the 1900s to Kermit the Frog in the 1980s. The impulse was, however, flourishing earlier; Honore Daumier (1808–1879) was acknowledged by the Disney artists as one of the painters they most admired.[9] Daumier's ability to caricature society and to exaggerate with line and mass, appealed to the caricaturist in the Disney artists. His dancing line and visual commentary upon human behaviour was noted especially by the artists who were to work on the feature films.

In addition, the work of Gustave Doré (1832–83) was immensely popular and particularly accessible through popular editions of his illustrations for Dante, Coleridge, Cervantes and the Bible.[10] The other striking examples of anthropomorphic and grotesque illustration lay in the work of Grandville (1803–47) in France with his fantastic drawings of animals and insects engaged in human activities.[11] As Lionel Lambourne points out, the anthropomorphic impulse is 'part of the recurrent mystery by which man, by his artistry, achieves the status of God and remakes creation to his own fancy'.[12] Disney achieved this with his films and then three-dimensionally in the Magic Kingdoms. His first cartoon star was an animal, Oswald the Rabbit, a softer and more flexible Felix; his first international success with another animal, Mickey Mouse, reveals this impulse even more clearly; Mickey mirrors man.

At first Mickey is the pioneer, pushing westwards and tackling the unknown by riverboat (*Steamboat Willie* 1928), triumphant in love over his feline rival, Pegleg Pete, (*Cactus Kid* 1930), rescuing Minnie from a fate worse than death or from a calamity (*The Fire Fighters* 1930). Though his playground is the world and Disney offers a universal background to Mickey's adventures, the environment is predominantly rural, small-

*Two illustrations show-
ing European-style
anthropomorphised
animals from the
nineteenth century:*

Top *Honore
Daumier's*
Emigration *(1856)*

(Author's collection)

Bottom *Gustave
Doré's 'Fables' from* La
Fontaine *(1867)*

(Author's collection)

town, the Midwest countryside close to Disney's heart. Foreign lands and exotic locations may be the ostensible backdrops, but the rural atmosphere of the Midwest remains central. This is a world recreated in comprehensible terms and defined comfortably within the theatrical framework of the drama of the mouse and his friends.

If Busch is the European father of the comic strip and a reference for the early animation of the Walt Disney Studio, then illustrative art and in particular the popular picture books and magazines of nineteenth- and early twentieth-century engravings become increasingly a visual source – one of many – for the *Silly Symphonies*. These films followed closely on the success of *Mickey Mouse*, because Disney saw the need to expand his animation in a fiercely competitive field. Paul Terry, Walter Lantz and the Fleischer brothers were all bringing out cartoons with sound; Disney's able musical director Carl Stalling, who had also come from Kansas City, felt that the medium could be used purely to express music, without specific comic characters. Stalling said, 'I suggested not using the word "music" or "musical" . . . but to use the word "symphony" together with a humorous word. Walt asked me,

An example of Grandville's fantastic drawings of animals and insects engaged in human activities, entitled the Public and Private Life of Animals *(1877)*

(Author's collection)

"How would *Silly Symphony* sound to you?" I said, "Perfect!".'[13] The attitude towards high art is demonstrated by coupling the word 'symphony' with 'silly'; we are reminded of the 'that' in *That Old Fairy Tale*.

The first *Silly Symphony* was *Skeleton Dance*, released in 1929, a few months after *Steamboat Willie*. Ub Iwerks animated almost the entire film; like Disney he was an instinctive artist without a conventional cultured background. The imagery of *Skeleton Dance* is taken from nineteenth-century gothic melodrama. A howling dog, cats, bats and dancing skeletons are in a graveyard with a chapel, tombstones, the moon and waving branches. The film uses imagery of the ghost train of the fairground, the thrill of the 'haunted mansion', skeletons rising from tombs, cobwebs brushing the visitor. Stalling also recalled a vaudeville act of skeleton dancers that he had seen as a boy. Here is a making over into film of various forms of popular art and culture. The Disney 'Imagineers' were to exploit the same genre in the 'Haunted Mansion' ride at Disneyland many years later. What gives the film its distinction is not only the comic effrontery with which it treats death and the convention of horror (one skeleton makes a xylophone of his fellow's ribs) but the graphic fluidity and conviction of its animation.

The fairytale and European folktale had been used in some of the *Mickey Mouse* shorts;

(*Mickey's Nightmare* (1932) and *Ye Olden Days* (1933) are examples), but the exploitation of European sources developed with the *Sillies*. In *The Clock Store* (1931) for example, the ticking clocks and dancing figures are antecedents for those in *Snow White* and more particularly in Geppetto's workshop in *Pinocchio*; another variation on the same theme is *The China Shop* (1934). The references to European popular illustration and entertainment are numerous; the wicked behaviour of the villain gloating over the lady shepherdess is out of Victorian melodrama via the Hollywood silent film. *Three Little Pigs* (1933) develops individual character and uses both music hall and melodrama in a comic mixture of both.

As Disney's studio developed and as more staff were employed from universities and art schools, the films became more sophisticated, the style more realistic. In 1932, art classes were begun by Don Graham, art teacher at the Chouinard Art Institute in Los Angeles. The Disney veterans found him an inspiring teacher with his 'action analysis' classes and insistence on the close observation of the movement and repose of the living model, following the European tradition of art training and life painting. As well as using live action film footage and the artists' own animation, Graham conducted classes at the nearby Griffith Park Zoo where the artists could observe and sketch living animals. There was some resistance to Graham at first, particularly from the older artists and animators from New York, but both sides learnt from each other.

The inspiration of the Swiss born Albert Hurter is acknowledged by the Disney artists. He joined Disney in 1931 after working in animation on the East Coast and he was given complete freedom to offer his own idiosyncratic sketches as ideas for film; he humanised inanimate objects in bizarre and surreal ways; flowers, plants, objects took on strange and sometimes alarming life under his pen. He introduced the studio to the work of Busch, Hermann Vogel and Heinrich Kley. (The two latter German artists influenced the early feature films.) Hurter had a great knowledge of European art and a photographic memory. Bill Cottrell remembered that he could identify errors of architectural design or a period costume detail without recourse to reference books or photographs. 'He could look at a cartoon character, say a military man and he'd say, "That uniform needs six buttons, not five". "How do you know?", we asked. "Because I saw it in a museum in Zurich", he said.'[14] Walt Disney, who rarely praised and who ruthlessly suppressed the individuality of those who worked for him,[15] said in a tribute to Hurter after the latter's death:

> Albert Hurter was a master creator of fantasy. In his whimsical imagination all things were possible. The sketches in this book testify not only to his rare sense of humour but also to his genuine ability as an artist.[16]

Hurter had a profound influence on the work of the studio; of the 74 *Sillies* produced between 1929 and 1939 when they ceased, 52 are based on European stories or ideas. *Babes in the Woods* and *Santa's Workshop* (both 1932) show the influence of Hurter's gothic fantasy and love of the droll. His influence pervades *Lullaby Land*, *Pied Piper* and *The Night Before Christmas* of 1933 and *The Flying Mouse*, *Goddess of Spring* and *Peculiar Penguins* of 1934. The list continues in 1935 but by 1936 he was working on *Snow White* and his inspiration was felt into the 1940s. In the catalogue for the last major exhibition of Disney art in Britain in 1976, John Russell Taylor wrote:

> His influence is visible in many of Disney's shorts and features up to (his) death at the time of *Pinocchio*, particularly those aspects of the gothic and the grotesque which relate most closely to European book illustration of the period and look back

An illustration by Hermann Vogel for Grimm's Fairy Tales *(1894)*

(Author's collection)

towards art nouveau and symbolism. Hurter indeed seems to have been responsible almost single handed for grafting this strain on to Disney's original home-grown American.[17]

Increasing strain and the fear of another breakdown (he had suffered from nervous exhaustion in 1931) led Disney to take an extended holiday with his brother Roy in the summer of 1935. With their wives, the brothers visited England, France, Belgium, Holland, Luxembourg, Italy and Switzerland. Disney discovered sources in Europe for model making, picking up feathers and fabrics which could be used later in the model department. 'He brought back automata, he admired a mechanical man that whistled and model birds that sang', recalled Bill Cottrell who had accompanied Disney on his European tour.[18] The seeds for Disney's obsession with the mechanical simulation of reality can be traced to this European visit. The European forests of *Snow White* and the little town of *Pinocchio* led on to the miniature Europe of Disneyland. The mechanical man who whistled led him on the audio-animatronic figures that populate his fantasy worlds of the theme parks.

After eleven weeks, he returned refreshed and full of new ideas. While in Europe he had ordered a large quantity of books. Some he brought with him and the studio's library received a further consignment from 5 July to 24 September 1935 with 90 titles from France, 81 from England, 149 from Germany and 15 from Italy.[19] They included many standard illustrated classics. In a memorandum dated 23 December 1935, Disney outlined his ideas to Ted Sears and the story department:

> Some of these little books which I brought back with me from Europe have very fascinating illustrations of little peoples, bees and small insects who live in mush-rooms, pumpkins, etc. This quaint atmosphere fascinates me and I was trying to think how we could build some little story that would incorporate all of these cute little characters . . .[20]

Disney's enthusiasm is captured in the dictated memorandum as he went on to suggest ideas incorporating Mickey and the gang into the world of European nursery rhyme and fable:

> ... Maybe to make these things more individual so they would stand out from the mob type of cartoons, we could incorporate Mickey or Minnie or the Duck into the fantastic settings they suggest. Mickey and Minnie might take a ride on a magic carpet and arrive in a weird land or forest, meet little elves of the forest or be captured by an old witch or giants and ogres. They could eat some fruit that makes them grow very tall or small – or get into a forest of wild trees and flowers and grotesque mirror pools with reflections and images. They might be trapped by three enormous spiders. Might get into a land of shadows ...

He also mentions *The Big Frog and the Little Frog* and *The Frog Who Would A Wooing Go*: 'We might use something on this order where we could bring in frogs, crickets, bugs and insects around ponds and marshes, etc.' This idea was used in *The Old Mill* (1937) which opens at dusk in a long shot. We see a pond with reeds and a cobweb in the foreground and an old mill in the distance. Cows move slowly home across the landscape. The colours are muted, the outlines soft, a sense of dampness, mist and impending darkness is obtained through light and shade, a chiaroscuro which reminds us of Dutch landscape paintings. Frogs, crickets and fireflies begin a twilight chorus. This is a late, complex example of a *Silly Symphony* (Academy Award winner, 1937) and it shows how the studio was able to present a short subject with great subtlety, even when its resources were being fully stretched on the first feature film. The staff number had grown from a handful to over 100 in the early 1930s and to 750 by the time Disney was making *Snow White*. His artists had a cultural background and an understanding of European influences which he utilised and developed in the popular American form of cinema. The energy of the technician and the perfectionist were not the only qualities that he added, however. He brought a gift of storytelling, a restating in visual terms of an old popular form. This quality began to show itself in the shorts and was developed, along with complex associations, resonances and tensions in *Snow White*. It was a period of intense creativity, which is summed up by a comment of Joe Grant, one of Disney's closest associates:

> I was enthusiastic as hell about that business. I thought it was the greatest thing; I couldn't think of anything beyond it ... I had fallen in love with the *idea*, particularly the idea and then him later because, God, he was – he *was* the idea.[21]

Beethoven's sixth symphony – *The Pastoral Symphony*

By the time Disney had conceived the idea for his ambitious *Fantasia* in 1937, the studio had nearly completed *Snow White* and was continuing to absorb and recreate European sources for an essentially American mass audience. *Fantasia* was in production, like *Pinocchio*, throughout the expansive and self-confident period that followed *Snow White* in 1938 and 1939. Recent releases of the film, with a decision by the company today to produce a new version entitled *Fantasia 2*, which will incorporate some of the original sections along with new material, prompts a continuing reappraisal. Its uneven quality and its themes can be traced aesthetically and ideologically in part to its sources, which are largely European.[22] We have seen how these sources were adapted in the early years before *Snow White*; an examination in some detail of the animation of Beethoven's *Pastoral Symphony* especially, with its reliance on the format of *Silly Symphonies*, might help us to move towards an understanding of its uneven tone and uncertain style, its lurches from art to artiness, its mixture of 'kunst und kitsch' as one German reviewer put it.

Indeed, the uneven quality of *The Pastoral Symphony*, both aesthetically and technically, still perplexes people today. It is a complex piece; at least twice as many people have worked on it than for the other sections. The piece also elicits a complex response from audiences ranging from admiration to outrage. There are two historical reasons for its uneven quality – its pictures were inspired not by the music of Beethoven but by that of Pierné – and it harks back more than any other section to the *Silly Symphonies.*

It is really an extended *Silly Symphony* because it has many of the qualities that characterise the later films in that series: naivety, archness, self-consciousness and a straining for effect, coupled with technical accomplishment and delicacy in the rendering. These are all present in the Beethoven film. Characters and gags, too, are carried over from the shorts. *Wynken, Blynken & Nod* (1938) is a miniature *Pastoral*; the babies are forerunners of the cupids and fauns and they float through an art deco sky similar to that in *The Pastoral.* In *Little Hiawatha* (1937), there is a similar child/baby and there are many babies in *Merbabies* (1938). This section of *Fantasia* is not, therefore, breaking new ground with regard to some of its characterisation, situations and backgrounds. Once again, it draws upon the known in an appeal to a mass audience and a female audience too, which will recognise the signification of its imagery.

This section was first designed for Pierné's short ballet *Cydalise* and the aesthetic problem lies in the fact that imagery for a light, brief piece of music composed for the stage was transposed to Beethoven's much more complex work, and pictures conceived to accompany lightweight music suitable for *The Silly Symphonies* cannot match the kind of imagery required, if any is required, to accompany *The Pastoral Symphony*. Here seems to be the heart of the difficulty, the origin of the rottenness at the core of the 'Disney Pastoral'.

(Henri Constant) Gabriel Pierné (1863–1937) was a French composer of serious organ music – and also of sensual, popular music. His light and pretty *Cydalise* (1923) clearly comes under this latter heading,[23] and it was chosen as one of the items for inclusion for *The Concert Feature* (a working title given to the film before its final name was decided upon) in September 1938. Work began immediately. The first outline stressed that, 'We play for comedy . . . Improving on the Greek, we show the winged horse Pegasus, nesting in a tree and in the nest are winged colts . . .'.[24] On October 13, George Stallings presented a story outline which developed these ideas and still contained some of the ballet's narrative, although it emphasised the identifiably burlesque: 'The Fauns come upon a herd of grazing Unicorns which they mount and ride them [sic] like cowboys and pursue the Girls.'[25] The outline ends with the centaurs returning from the hunt, spanking and routing the Fauns. Unlike the ballet, there is no link between the mythological and real worlds and the romantic love between a Faun and a mortal is not suggested.

The reference to flying horses is, however, taken up and developed: 'They finally light on the lake, fold their wings back and swim like swans.'[26] This enchanting image is preserved in the film, a lyricism taken over from the original Pierné interpretation and emphasised by Disney in his discussions: 'Don't get too complicated with story, George, because the music . . .' The inference is clear and so is Disney's inability to articulate. In these early discussions he emphasised a comic strip element: 'The old man is hunting for them (the Fauns). Show him chasing . . . He has a club there don't you think? Like calling the Katzenjammer boys.'

By 2 November, however, Disney felt that Pierné's music was 'wrong for the story. We should find music to fit the things we have in mind here – but good music'. The discussion then turned to *Petrouchka* ('*Patricia*'in the transcript) which Disney rejected and the meeting closed with his comment:

> Let's do some exploring first. Let's see if we can't put together the right stuff . . . if the music hasn't the right class, we will have to hold it up – we can always come back. Of course, Pierné doesn't mean anything.

Disney's final comment is significant; it represents his concern for the value of the music as product for mass consumption since Pierné was not a 'known' name with popular appeal. The quality of the artwork that was being produced also caused him to shift focus:

> We've taken good music and bastardised it and it's served our purpose and nobody kicked. This is something different we're selling the public, though, and we've got to stay in line. I know it's not right yet . . . It could be done a little differently. I hate this *Katzenjammer Kid* angle entirely. You feel there's something good in all this stuff and we don't seem to get it.

Beethoven was mentioned in early November, though no specific work was cited. The decision to use the *Pastoral* was taken after story, design and continuity had been worked on for several months and had been clearly approved by Disney. The quality of his artists' work was impressive. Not a man to praise often, he said: 'The material is so damn good here!'

By the middle of 1939, work was being done to accompany the Beethoven music and at a meeting in August, Disney was explaining to Stokowski that he did not want 'to get too serious'. He was also aware of the quality of the music and the discussion shows the tensions between the cartoon filmmaker and the conductor:

> **Walt:** We're not going to be slapstick. We'll go for the beautiful, rather than the slapstick . . . I thought maybe you felt we were going overboard and make a Donald Duck of it.
> **Stokowski:** The thing I want is to be loyal to you and the picture and to be sure that we don't offend the kind of worship there is all over the world for Beethoven.
> **Walt:** I think this thing will make Beethoven.
> **Stokowski:** That's true. In a certain sense it will. Some who have never heard his name will see this.
> **Walt:** It creates a whole new feeling, a whole new sympathy for this music . . .[27]

These extracts emphasise the struggle Disney had in encompassing material that was not immediately identifiable to him as popular. His artists were providing an extended comic strip version with gags appealing to his penchant for anal-erotic jokes and at the same time they were offering the lyrical quality of the flying horses that so touched his aesthetic sense that he wanted this to be matched by appropriate music. Such ambiguities emphasise the difficulty that Disney had in both claiming classical music as his provenance for reinterpretation and denying at the same time any claim to artistic pretension or status. These ambiguities are demonstrated by the studio's difficulty in selling *Fantasia* to the American public after its premiere and limited release. The difficulty is still evident today.[28]

Another telling phrase in these discussions is Disney's defensive remark: 'We've taken good music and bastardised it and it's served our purpose and nobody kicked. This is something different we're selling the public . . .' The struggle to deal with art from the old world, European art that has a certain 'class' – another of Disney's phrases – is central to an understanding of the work and of its complexity of content and of the continuing complexity of audience response.

The narrative was handled by Dick Huemer and Joe Grant who worked with four different units, until they were ready for Disney's comments. Beethoven's music was slightly shortened but otherwise presented in the right order. The 'nymphs' of the original outline of 29 September 1938 have become centaurettes in Stallings's outline of 13 October:

> Luxuriating, primping by a pool, are Centaurettes . . . beautiful faces and voluptuous breasts atop the body of a horse, come-hither eyes and the seductively switching rump of a truck horse. You've seen the type . . . In short, the Golden Age of Greece reborn.[29]

The centaurs of Greek mythology possessed both wisdom and sexual licence. They were depicted as mature, robust, bearded and 'were not differentiated from satyrs in early Greek vase paintings'.[30] The Disney centaurs lack age, wisdom or sexual prowess; they are emasculated idealisations of the contemporary all-American clean-cut college boy, Nordic rather than Latin. The idealisation of the purely Germanic in Nazi art is a parallel that is worth making historically; the war with Germany was still three years away and the influence of nineteenth-century academic art, in particular from Germany, is, as was the case with *Snow White*, demonstrable.

Albert Hurter inspired the early studies of centaurs and centaurettes. He looked at both academic and illustrative sources, searching for the comic and the bizarre. His doodles show that he had seen the work of Franz von Stuck (1863–1928), who was one of the few artists to depict female centaurs. Symbolist qualities appear in the film in moments of voluptuousness, such as the parade of the centaurettes before the centaurs, but the dangerous eroticism that informed von Stuck (and Arnold Böcklin) is missing in Disney. Instead, the studio's uncertainty led it to appeal to the contemporary audience's taste, and the robust humour which Hurter picked up from Böcklin is missing, replaced by a nervous prurience. The Staff Bulletin devoted to *Fantasia* stated:

> If you scan mythology books from Gayley to Fraser, you'll find no saucily stepping Centaurettes. The word and character originated in story meetings, stepped down off Fred Moore's walls onto 6 field. They put brassieres and garlands on the gals, but aside from that, they're much the same as when they hung photostated

The use of centaurs and centaurettes in the art of Franz von Stuck (here a book-plate from the turn of the century) might have inspired other artists such as Albert Hurter

(Author's collection)

EX LIBRIS

FRANZ VON STVCK

in scattered rooms throughout the Studio.[31]

The mention of brassieres and garlands refers to the problem of what should be done about the nipples on the centaurettes. Fear of the Hays Code led to the decision outlined here, although nipples were painted in on women depicted as witches and evil spirits in the Moussorgsky piece, and Hays blushed not. The sexism of the scenes that feature the centaurettes is blatant, as was the racism which has now been removed.[32]

Another artist who depicted female centaurs was the German Heinrich Kley, an important influence on *The Dance of the Hours*. His female centaurs are women of determination in a world of ribald licence. Centaurs and centaurettes had also appeared in earlier animated films by Winsor McCay and the Swedish animator Viktor Bergdahl.[33] Early model sheets for the centaurettes show hair styles that date to the early part of the century and look anachronistic; they are based on either McCay or Bergdahl. Disney usually avoided direct appeals to the contemporary by eschewing localising historiographical references. Here, the appeal is overt, linking the film to marketing and merchandise. The centaurettes' hair is deliberately dressed in late 1930s fashion and contemporary hats are styled for them by the cupids. This was a point taken up by the Disney Merchandising Department and the House Bulletin noted that 'Hat designers and manufacturers eyed with interest the flower hats from the centaurette fashion show in the *Pastoral* sequence'.[34] John Culhane quotes Bill Tytla, the Disney animator, who regretted that he did not work on the *Pastoral* sequence. He thought the centaurs in both the McCay and Bergdahl films were superior in design, draughtsmanship and animation to those in the *Pastoral*: 'They should have been big stallions with dark Mediterranean faces on them. Instead they were castrated horsies [sic] with a type of Anglo-Saxon head . . .'[35]

A scene from Heinrich Kley's Skizzenbuch *(1909), which shows his use of centaurs and centaurettes*

(Courtesy William Moritz)

Nobody was willing to take the blame for the centaurs and centaurettes. Joe Grant, widely read and with a large library of his own, was familiar with Böcklin and Kley and his model department developed the models; he gave his signature of approval to the model sheets. Dick Huemer, also well read, was Grant's co-story director for *Fantasia*. On being asked if *The Pastoral Symphony* was his idea, replied: 'No, you can't blame me.' Later in the same interview he added that he and Grant had presented the Beethoven to Disney who agreed to use the music. 'But Stokowski didn't like it at all. Not a damn bit!'[36] Stokowski's dislike for the mythological approach is confirmed in the transcript for a story conference at which Disney was not present: 'I don't want to come out of my own field', he said. 'I'm only a musician, but think what you have there, the idea of great mythology, is not quite my idea of what this symphony is about. This is a nature symphony.'[37] The late Eric Larson, recalled not only his contribution to the sequence, but also his distress at the result:

> It was such an asinine approach . . . This is a block on my life. We didn't do proper research. It was my *job* and I did it [animating the centaurs and centaurettes] the easy way, like humans do it, consequently they were not humans *or* animals.[38]

Herb Ryman (1908–89), one of the six art directors for this item commented: 'Nobody knew what the hell to do with it.'[39] The error was to attempt to copy human movement. The staff's Bulletin also mentions the rotoscoping of 'chubby Erwin Verity, who served with distinction in the matter of acting as hind-quarters of a dainty Centaurette'.[40] The first movement invites us to enter a mythological world, which is enchantingly fantastic (Stokowski had urged Disney to create 'the more fantasy the better').[41] By the second movement we are invited to laugh at this world, because Disney has relied on the burlesque element of the *Silly Symphonies* in his attempt to make the Beethoven music more acceptable to American audiences. The high seriousness of art, the cultural heritage of Europe expressed in Beethoven's music has to be made over, in a consciously popular form, through comedy and burlesque. Rick Altman has also pointed out the romance and courtship element of Hollywood feature films during this period[42] and the coupling of the centaurs and centaurettes is another example of the appeal to a mass audience. The reduction of the centaurettes to stereotypical objects of desire by cardboard cavaliers adds to the destruction of any suspension of disbelief. Another source is the comic strip, expressed in the character of Bacchus on his diminutive and dim-witted steed, the unicorn/donkey Jacchus. Ward Kimball's animation has the assurance lacking in the rendering of the centaurs and centaurettes. This is a comic-strip god; the antecedents are Hurter and Wilhelm Busch. Also, Böcklin's leering mermen are close cousins to the figures in Busch's drawings and there is Dickie Doyle's Punch/Bacchus figure which was on the cover of *Punch* from 1849 to 1956. Illustrative sources imbue the Disney Bacchus with an energy that sits unhappily with the contemporary account of the centaurs and centaurettes. The same ambivalence applies to the greater deities which are seen in close association with the backgrounds.

Early inspirational paintings show a symbolist influence,[43] but this changed to art deco. The backgrounds are a blending of the old world and the new. High academic Victorian art is borrowed for the sylvan settings; John Waterhouse (1849–1917) painted classical scenes with romantic overtones. His *Hylas and the Water Nymphs* (1896) was adapted for an early inspirational painting of the centaurettes in the water. The fondness of nineteenth-century academic painting for children frolicking in the countryside is reflected in Disney; fauns, baby unicorns and cherubs cavort in a landscape of bright stylisation. Philipp Otto Runge (1777–1810) painted allegorical landscapes with chil-

Top   *Wilhelm Busch's*
Silenus *(1878)*

(Courtesy Edith Wilson)

Bottom   *Richard
Doyle's Punch/
Bacchus figure
appeared on the cover
of* Punch *between
1849 and 1956*

(Author's collection)

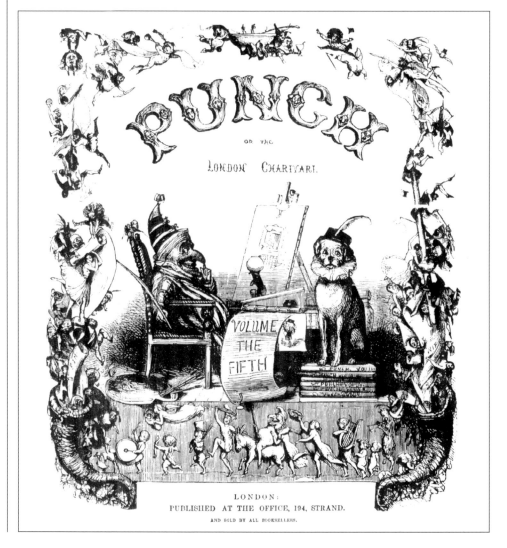

dren; one German reviewer commented that *Fantasia* 'was as natural as a Department Store or Petrol Station. Disney's artists were collaborators of Dali, Grandville and Runge'.[44]

The Beethoven piece is an example of Victorian ideals set in an art deco landscape. The old world meets the new; women are seen as alternately desirable and seductive objects (centaurettes) or deified (Diana, Iris). In this respect, the centaurettes are like the soft pornographic delineations of women in sculpture and painting that adorned the wealthy Victorian home.

Edward Poynter's (1836–1919) girls in *A Visit to Aesculapius* (1880) stand before the physician in the same way as the Disney centaurettes parade before their beaux. The high academic art of England is as emasculated as the worst of Disney; but the coarsely exuberant imagery of the film comes not from England but from Germany, with a mixture of rudeness and reverence demonstrated in the work of Arnold Böcklin (1827–1901).

Böcklin was well known to the Disney artists. Joe Grant and Albert Hurter were familiar with his work and the model department based studies of the centaurs on his paintings. Ken Anderson (b. 1909), an art director for the sequence and John Hench (b. 1908) who painted some of the backgrounds also knew his work.[45] Disney's attention was drawn by Dick Huemer and Joe Grant to Böcklin's combination of mysticism and vulgarity which was attractive to the artists working on this sequence. Böcklin's Teutonic kitsch and dark eroticism also disturbed contemporary reviewers. Claude Phillips's comment in 1885 might apply to Disney:

> [Böcklin] succeeds so thoroughly in giving form and life to the mythical beings in a sense created anew for him, that the effect produced is often a startling one – so strong is the contrast between the theme and its treatment; nay, the boundaries which separate art from the purely grotesque are often reached and well-nigh transgressed.[46]

Ken Anderson used Böcklin as reference for the backgrounds that he designed for the *Pastoral*: 'I was inspired by Böcklin's *Isle of the Dead*', he said, 'and also by The Isola Bella in Italy. Walt said, "Read up on Beethoven and get some style". So I read up on the ribald and the classical.'[47] The result is the only consistent element in the item for which Anderson and his colleagues Gordon Legg, Herb Ryman and others were responsible. The rounded art deco landscapes and stylisation in the backgrounds can be partly attributed to another art director for the sequence, Gordon Legg:

> They wanted Classical backgrounds ... and they didn't care too much how accurate it was. I kind of followed Grant Wood and Rockwell Kent – you know, cleaned up the trees, so that everything was neat and clean and precise. It was like Forest Lawn. I wanted to keep the colours rich and subtle – olive greens and maroons – played down colours like you see in the backgrounds of portraits that were painted in the Italian School ... I worked with Ken Anderson; he was the final layout director (for the *Pastoral*) and a very talented artist. But I guess Disney got in there someplace and said 'Let's brighten this thing up'. That's where we got into the peppermint candy. It bothered me; I didn't want it that way. It was too sticky, too sweet.[48]

Many of Legg's inspirational sketches are reproduced in the first book on *Fantasia*.[49] The beauty of the opening landscape survives on film, though the work was painted over by another artist.[50]

Throughout this section there is a tension between reverence for and misunderstanding of sources. There is a confidence of expression and draughtsmanship in the rendering of the flying horses in the first movement and there is crassness in the account of the centaurs, centaurettes and *putti* in the second. This reflects the inability to distinguish between the calibre of Pierné's music and that of Beethoven; the studio struggled to accommodate Beethoven by a mixture of reliance on the graphic signification of *The Silly Symphonies* and by an appeal to a mass audience that would identify the contemporary references to fashion and to sexual stereotyping in the centaurs and centaurettes, while at the same time attempting to match the lyricism of the music in the landscapes. These moments give this section its mixture of 'Kunst und kitsch',[51] and are expressed in the closing scene of the film: Apollo and Diana are animated with great beauty and based on the inspirational paintings of Gordon Legg; and Iris and Morpheus are unconvincing deities, larger versions of Snow White. The viewer is lurched from beauty to bathos within the same frame and at the same time in a complicated, layered struggle to present visually, 'to create a whole new feeling' for the audience, one of the most sublime pieces of music in the Western world.

This is a revised and amalgamated version of two papers given at SAS Conferences in 1989 and 1991 and represents sections of the author's forthcoming book *Walt Disney and Europe: European Influences on the Animated Feature Films of Walt Disney*, published in 1998 by John Libbey & Company, Sydney.

Notes

1. A condensation of papers for two SAS conferences.
2. Donald Crafton, *Before Mickey* (Cambridge: MIT Press, 1982). See Russell Merritt and J.B. Kaufman, *Nel Paese delle Meraviglie: Walt Disney in Wonderland* (Pordenone: Edizione Biblioteca dell'Immagine, 1992) for an excellent account of Disney's early creative years. This, like Crafton's book, is one of the few scholarly works on Disney relying on primary source material.
3. H.W. Gatzke, *Germany and the United States* (Cambridge: Harvard University Press, 1980), 30. The young men were Hugh Harman, Rudolf Ising, Carman Maxwell, Lorey Tague and Otto Waldman. Some made distinguished names for themselves in animation.
4. German expressionism would have an effect on the first three feature films; Oskar Fischinger was to work briefly for Disney on *Fantasia*.
5. Crafton, *Before Mickey*, 83. One film of the series has recently been discovered. See Donald Crafton, *Emile Cohl, Caricature and Film* (Princeton: University Press, 1990), 164.
6. Walter Arndt, *The Genius of Wilhelm Busch* (Berkeley: University of California Press, 1982), 16.
7. Geraldine Norman, *Biedermeyer Painting* (London: Thames & Hudson, 1987), 8.
8. William Vaughan, *German Romantic Painting* (New Haven: Yale University Press, 1980), 203.
9. Interviews by the author with Disney artists in 1985, 1986 and 1989.
10. Dore's illustrations to famous books derived from a romantic Germanic background. Though French, he was brought up in Strasbourg, close to the Black Forest. His interest in the dramatic and menacing expressed itself in over a hundred illustrated books and in literally thousands of drawings. His technically brilliant, often vulgar and melodramatic work appealed to Disney and his artists. He used a comic strip technique in his *Histoire Pittoresque, Dramatique et Caricaturale de la Sainte Russie*, 1854.
11. There is also an American tradition of graphic anthropomorphism in cartoons and illustrations. Three of the most famous artists are A.B. Frost, the illustrator of *Uncle Remus*; Harrison Cady, who invented a world of insects for his Beetleburgh; and the brilliant T.S. Sullivant whose hippos, in particular, continue to endear.
12. Lionel Lambourne, *Ernest Griset* (London: Thames & Hudson, 1979), 4.
13. Quoted in Richard Holliss and Brian Sibley, *The Disney Studio Story* (London: Octopus 1988), 18.
14. Bill Cottrell, interviews with author, Toluka Lake, California (31 May 1985 and 12 June 1985).
15. 'When I first joined the Studio, Walt took me on one side and said, "If you have any idea about

making a name for yourself, get out. I'm the only star here".' Ken Anderson, interview with author, 10 May 1985.

16.   Albert Hurter, *He Drew as He Pleased*, intr. by Ted Sears (New York: Simon & Schuster, 1948).

17.   *The Artists of Disney*, intr. by John Russell Taylor (London: Victoria & Albert Museum, 1976).

18.   Bill Cottrell, interviews with author.

19.   Records of Walt Disney Studio Library, disbanded in 1986.

20.   Memorandum by Walt Disney, 23 December 1935.

21.   Joe Grant, interview with author, Glendale, California, 30 May 1985.

22.   Apart from the fact that all the music for *Fantasia* is by European composers, direct European artistic influences can be traced in a number of sections; Oskar Fischinger's work on Bach's *Toccata and Fuge* is well known, thanks to his biographer William Moritz and to the indefatigability of Fischinger's widow, Elfriede. Sylvia Holland, an English artist, worked on *The Nutcracker Suite* by Tchaikovsky and German expressionism can be noted in Dukas's *The Sorcerer's Apprentice*. The satiric art of Heinrich Kley is evident in Ponchielli's *The Dance of the Hours* and the Danish artist Kay Nielsen contributed to *The Night on Bald Mountain* by Moussorgsky and to Schubert's *Ave Maria*.

23.   Information on Pierné is taken from *The New Grove Dictionary of Music and Musicians*, vol. 14, ed. Stanley Sadie (London: Macmillan, 1980), 736; and from Cyril W. Beaumont, *Complete Book of Ballets* (New York: Grosset & Dunlap, 1938), 546–550.

24.   Outline of Proposals for *Concert Feature*, 29 September 1938.

25.   George Stallings, Story Outline for *Cydalise*, 13 October 1938.

26.   Quotations in this and the following paragraph are taken from Transcript of Story Conferences on 17 October, 2 November and 23 December 1938.

27.   Transcript of Meeting on Sound Stage, 8 August 1939.

28.   The difficulty that the Disney Company has experienced in distributing the film is examined by the author in 'The Real *Fantasia* at Length, at Last', *The Times Saturday Review*, 25 August 1990.

29.   Outline of Proposals for *Concert Feature* 29 September 1938 and Story Outline for *Cydelise* 13 October 1938.

30.   Robert Graves, *The Greek Myths*, vol. 1 (Harmondsworth: Penguin, 1955), 361.

31.   Disney Studio, *House Bulletin: Fantasia*, vol. 3, no. 5 (15 November 1940).

32.   David Williams, Lecture on the subject on 5 January 1991. This was in connection with his exhibition on *Fantasia* at the Durham Light Infantry Museum, 19 December 1990 to 7 January 91. (See also his 'Whatever Happened to Sunflower?', *Animator*, 28 (1991): 13).

    In the carefully restored print for release in 1990, references to Sunflower, the black centaurette who preens the tail of a green centaurette and who polishes her hooves like a boot black, have been skilfully omitted. The image has been enlarged to exclude Sunflower from the frame; an earlier release of the film in the 1980s reorchestrated these sections to cover the cuts. These are examples of the conventional ideology of the period and present the current appeal to contemporary audiences.

33.   John Canemaker, *Winsor McCay: His Life and Art* (New York: Abbeville, 1987), 157; and Crafton, *Before Mickey*, 250. *The Centaurs* (1916) by Winsor McCay (the creator of *Little Nemo* and *Gertie the Dinosaur*) only survives as a fragment and has never been issued commercially. The Swedish animator Victor Bergdahl saw McCay's *Little Nemo* in Sweden, however, and made his own animated films as a result, directly influenced by McCay. In Bergdahl's Kapten Grogg bland andra konstiga kroppa (*Captain Grogg Among Strange Creatures* 1920), the Captain gets into trouble with a centaur when he is found making amorous advances to the centaur's wife. The animation is fluid and confident and appears to be based on some form of rotoscoping; the centaurs and lady centaurs have considerable conviction and vigour. The *Captain Grogg* series was widely distributed and we can assume was seen by the Disney artists.

34.   Disney Studio House Bulletin, 10.

35.   Bill Tytla, quoted in John Culhane, *Walt Disney's Fantasia* (New York: Abrams, 1983), 138.

36.   Dick Huemer, 'With Disney on Olympus: an Interview with Dick Huemer', *Funnyworld*, vol. 17 (Fall 1977): 40.

37.   Transcript of Story Conference, 14 July 1939.

38.   Eric Larson, interview, 19 June 1985. It should be noted that on page 138 in Culhane it states that Larson 'did not work on them [the centaurettes]'.

39.   Herbert Ryman, interview with author, Van Nuys, California, 7 July 1985.

40.   Disney Studio House Bulletin, 10. Bob Jones had the task of finding props and costumes for the live action filming that was used for rotoscope. He recalled one of Disney's sudden whims:

> Three o'clock on a Thursday Walt called me: 'What if Deems (Taylor) comes up to the mike after the *Pastoral* and he was half a man and half a horse? Get me a costume.' I called Western Costume and I said I would be over in an hour. They had nothing. I was frantic. We went to United and found a pony costume which I could *just* get into. Went home, put up mirrors and tried it on with my brother. I knew it wouldn't work. So next morning I took it to the sound stage. Walt said, 'Let's see it', so I put on the back part and Taylor took the front. 'Bob', said Walt, 'You know, if someone told me that you'd end up being Deems Taylor's ass . . .'
> – *Bob Jones, interview with author, Fullerton, California, 1 November 1989.*

41.   Meeting on Sound Stage, 8 August 1939.

42.   Rick Altman, *The American Film Musical* (Bloomington & Indianapolis: Indiana University Press, 1987), 105–106.

43.   Charles Solomon, *Enchanted Drawings: The History of Animation* (New York: Alfred Knopf, 1989) 69.

44.   Helmut Farber, '*Fantasia* – Neuester orbis pictus', trans. author, *Suddeutsche Zeitung*, 14 April 1971.

45.   Interviews with Ken Anderson, La Canada, 10 May 1985; and with John Hench, Glendale, California, 29 June 1989.

46.   Claude Phillips, *Magazine of Art* (London: Cassell, 1885), quoted in Bernice Phillpotts, *Mermaids* (New York: Ballantine, 1980), 72.

47.   Ken Anderson, interview, 10 May 1985.

48.   Gordon Legg, interview with Milton Gray, South Pasadena, California, 13 March 1976, 1.

49.   Deems Taylor, *Fantasia* (New York: Simon & Schuster, 1940).

50.   Gordon Legg, interview with author, South Pasadena, California, 21 June 1989. Legg's original paintings, which formed part of an exhibition of Disney art in Manchester in 1990, included Pegasus at night on his tree, Apollo in his sun chariot and Diana shooting the stars out with the crescent moon. They are reproduced in Robin Allan, *Picture Books and Disney Pictures* (Manchester: Portico Gallery & Library, 1990).

51.   Helmut Farber, '*Fantasia* – Neuester orbis pictus'.

Norm Ferguson and the Latin American films of Walt Disney

J.B. Kaufman

One of the most unusual chapters in the history of the Walt Disney studio began in 1941, when Disney was approached by the United States government to make a goodwill tour of South America. The United States had not officially entered World War II at that time, but the government noted with some concern a growing Nazi influence in South America and was seeking to counter that influence by promoting friendly ties between the Americas. Disney did make the trip, along with a group of his artists, and thus began a chain of events which eventually produced two feature-length pictures, *Saludos Amigos* (1943) and *The Three Caballeros* (1945), along with a variety of Latin American-influenced short subjects. (These dates represent the United States releases of the films, but it should be noted that they were both released in other countries first. *Saludos Amigos* opened in Brazil and Argentina in, respectively, August and December 1942; *The Three Caballeros* had its world premiere in Mexico City in December 1944.) In selecting the artists who were to make the South American trip, Disney appointed the distinguished animator Norm Ferguson as unit producer. Fortunately for anyone interested in documenting the story of that tour and the films that later emerged from it, Ferguson took literally hundreds of photographs along the way – and kept the photographs, along with other mementoes of the occasion. Today, these materials survive in the collection of the artist's daughter Bonnie Ferguson Brown. By combining them with other papers in the Disney Archives and with the memories of other participants in the project, we can reconstruct a fascinating and quite complete account of the tour and of subsequent production.

Norm Ferguson's stature as an animator is of course legendary and it was recognised as such at the time. In the industry at large he was known for his creation and development of the character Pluto; within the studio he was recognised for his refinements of style, which had virtually reshaped the whole process of Disney animation. But the qualities that make a great animator are not necessarily those of an efficient administrator and Ferguson, after directing a single short (*Pluto's Playmate*, 1941) and one sequence apiece in *Fantasia* and *Dumbo*, was abruptly placed in charge of the entire South American project, second in command only to Walt Disney himself. Why?

'Because people would follow Fergy', Jack Kinney answered promptly. 'I mean, they admired him as a person and for his abilities, you see. First off, he was a fine gentleman and secondly, he taught anyone that wanted to ask him a question. He was never high-hat; he was strictly a down-to-earth nice person.'[1] Kinney, who directed important segments in both *Saludos Amigos* and *The Three Caballeros*, felt that Ferguson became an effective supervisor through the sheer inspiration of his example.

Bill Cottrell, a member of the group that made the tour, concurred: 'Norm was liked by everyone', he explained, 'and there was no resentment, if that's the right word to use, that he was given that position. Someone else who might have been given that position, if they didn't have the talent or if they weren't liked, they would be resented. You couldn't go wrong with appointing Norm Ferguson as producer of that thing, because everyone liked him and he had the talent besides'.[2]

'But again', added veteran story and character-design artist Joe Grant, 'it was a great loss, in a way, to lose him as an animator. It's pulling something out and not replacing it, you know, his uniqueness is so obvious in everything he does'. Still, Grant agreed with the general assessment of Ferguson's approach as a producer: 'He was, as I remember, very easy-going. He was not a stern taskmaster with the animators, but his vision and what he wanted was clear because they knew his method and they knew what he would expect to see on the screen.'[3]

The Disney group left California in early August of 1941 and flew first to Miami, Florida. Their tour had been well publicised, as had the fact that they were undertaking it at the request of the United States government, in order to cement friendly relations with South America. From Miami, the group flew to San Juan, Puerto Rico, and on 18 August[4] arrived at their first major South American destination, Rio de Janeiro. Here they stayed at the Copacabana Hotel, enjoyed the hospitality of the Brazilian government and most importantly, scattered to soak up their various impressions of the city and its culture. These ranged from characteristic customs, costumes and music of the area to details of the city's architecture, all of which emerged in both of the South American features. Before leaving Rio, the group's musical director Charles Wolcott arranged for a recording session at which optical–sound recordings were made of some of the area's musicians performing a variety of numbers. Some of these recordings would later be used in the finished Disney films. For example, two takes were made of the popular song 'Tico Tico' and one of them was later heard on the soundtrack of the *Aquarela do Brasil* segment of *Saludos Amigos*. The trip was also scheduled so that the Disney group could attend the Brazilian premiere of *Fantasia* on 23 August 1941. This became a pattern which continued throughout the trip: as the group travelled around South America, their arrival in each major city coincided with that city's opening of *Fantasia*, at which they were honoured guests.

Along the way, several of the group shot 16 mm home movies of the trip – among them Walt Disney himself, using a Bell & Howell Filmo 141-A camera, which is preserved today in the Disney Archives. More 16 mm material was shot by Larry Lansburgh and Lee Blair and this live action footage later proved far more significant than anyone realised at the time.

From Rio the group moved on to Buenos Aires, arriving on 8 September[5] and remaining there for most of the month. Here the group's activities became still more concentrated; a makeshift studio was even established on the top floor of the Alvear Palace Hotel. This was not a studio in the sense of a full production facility, but rather a large 'music

room' like those at the Disney studio in Burbank, a sort of headquarters where the artists could meet and develop stories, music and sketches of all kinds. Bill Cottrell recalled it:

> We had this large glassed-in area on the roof of the Alvear Palace Hotel that served as an office for us, where we could pin up the sketches. There was a grand piano up there, where Chuck Wolcott followed through on the music of the various countries. In this large room that we had, we were able to have occasional story meetings as to what we were accomplishing and to meet people who would come to see us with ideas and so forth, people from libraries and museums, people who were interested in the type of thing that we were doing.[6]

Norm Ferguson's photographs show the artists working in a spacious, sunny room, well equipped with drawing boards and accessories and also sketching outdoors on the roof of the hotel.

In Buenos Aires, the tour assumed a more public aspect. Disney's visits with government dignitaries and prominent local filmmakers became more frequent and he and the artists gave public drawing exhibitions. Buenos Aires also served as a home base for several side trips, the most important of which was to the studio of F. Molina Campos. Campos was a tremendously popular South American painter who had become known as an artistic spokesman for the gauchos and an authority on their lifestyles and clothing. The scenes of his studio which appear in *Saludos Amigos* were shot during a visit there on Friday, 19 September 1941. Campos later came to the United States and visited the Disney studio while the films were in production; his influence can be most clearly seen in *El Gaucho Goofy*.

After Buenos Aires, the Disney group briefly split up into smaller units which visited various South American regions. One group went to northern Argentina to gather more

gaucho material, while another headed for La Paz, Bolivia. Norm Ferguson travelled to Mendoza, Argentina, with a group that also included Walt Disney, Bill Cottrell and Ted Sears. After a few days, most of the group converged in Valparaiso, Chile, and boarded the Grace Lines ship *Santa Clara*, sailing on 4 October for a voyage that would take them up the west coast of South America and eventually back to New York.

The voyage of the *Santa Clara* was memorable in itself. The captain of the ship was Bligh Parker USNR who was, the artists were told, a descendant of the notorious Captain Bligh of HMS Bounty fame. The gathering clouds of World War II, which had been indirectly responsible for Disney's trip to South America in the first place, were felt once again during the voyage. The *Santa Clara* had large American flags emblazoned on its prow and, although it was in technically neutral waters, there was constant apprehension over the threat of German submarines. One night, Bill Cottrell recalled:

> Captain Parker was talking to a group of us around the piano in the lounge and was suddenly interrupted by a series of blasts from the ship's horn, which is a loud, frightening sound. And he said, 'Excuse me', and ran out the door to the deck and on up to the bridge and we didn't see any more of him that night. So we never did find out what it was, but there was a lot of speculation on our part – was it a submarine that they sighted from the bridge or was it a small boat in distress or what? We never knew, but of course, because of the war and so forth – you imagine a lot of things, you know.[7]

The *Santa Clara* did complete its voyage without incident and sailed from Cristobal on 15 October, arriving in New York on the 20th.[8] From there the team flew back to Burbank and began the long, arduous process of putting on film the wealth of material they had gathered. It was here that Norm Ferguson's job as production supervisor began in earnest. The original agreement with the government had called for a series of twelve separate short cartoons to be released in three groups of four each. Ferguson's unenviable task was to marshal a vast array of visual and musical impressions, some of them quite abstract and fleeting, into more or less uniform packages of one reel apiece. Some of his memos to Disney at this time suggest both the rich variety of ideas that had been spawned by the trip and Ferguson's own insight. As early as 14 November 1941, a few short weeks after returning to the studio, he suggested combining animation with some of the 16 mm live action footage the group had brought back from the trip, thus establishing one of the most notable characteristics of *The Three Caballeros*, a feature which was not to be released until three years later.

In retrospect, one of the most interesting things about the creative explosion that took place at this point is the way the separate, often unrelated ideas were ultimately combined into a single subject. The group that had visited Mendoza had been impressed by the comic possibilities of the Avestruz, the Argentine ostrich, and had considered building an entire short around him. In the end, the character was absorbed into *El Gaucho Goofy*. Mary Blair's watercolours from Rio were so striking that an attempt was made to work them into a film, but because of the difficulty of building a solid story on something so abstract, it was suggested that Donald Duck be brought into the subject somehow. At the same time, another story crew was trying to fashion a short around the Papagayo, the Brazilian parrot. In Rio, some of the artists had been taken to see a trained parrot named Sonia which, in Ferguson's words, 'sings, dances and talks Portuguese'.[9] (She can be glimpsed briefly in *Saludos Amigos* but is not identified by name.) Of course, Sonia evolved into a new character named Joe Carioca and eventually all three elements – the watercolours, the duck and the parrot – were combined in the finished version of *Aquarela do Brasil*.

Still more fascinating are the surviving fragments of stories which, in the end, were not produced. While in Brazil, the team had picked up a song called 'The Match Box Song', which for a time served as the tentative basis for a short titled *Caxanga*. The project survived as late as April 1942, when it went into production under Wilfred Jackson's direction, but it was never completed. Similarly, the story that reached the screen as the *Flying Gauchito* segment of *The Three Caballeros* was originally projected as one of a series of shorts featuring the same little-boy character. Jim Bodrero submitted a number of story ideas for this character including *The Laughing Gaucho*, in which the gauchito was found to have a laugh so shrill that it shattered glass. This story, too, went into actual production but was never finished. (*The Flying Gauchito* – or as it was originally known, *The Remarkable Donkey* – was actually one of the first shorts to be completed, but was held out of the first package of films because Argentina was already represented in that package by *El Gaucho Goofy*.)

In at least two cases, material was incorporated that originally had nothing to do with the South American project. When the tour group returned to the studio in October 1941, Jack Kinney and Ralph Wright had been working on a cowboy story for Goofy. When *El Gaucho Goofy* was framed as a contrast between the North American cowboy and the Argentine gaucho, ideas from that story were worked into the opening of the segment. A more substantial transformation involved a story idea that Joe Grant and Dick Huemer had developed around a humanised little aeroplane named 'Petey O'Toole' – the name derived from his identification number: P-T-O-2-L. This idea coincided neatly with the experience of some of the tour group, flying from Mendoza to Santiago in a Pan-American Airways DC-3. Bill Cottrell recalled the experience:

On that flight we passed very close to Aconcagua, which is the largest mountain in the Western Hemisphere. It's over 22 500 feet high; a very impressive, rugged thing and it seemed like we flew so close to it you could almost reach out and touch it. Of course, we weren't that close, but it seemed like it. At the border between Argentina and Chile, high up in the mountains, there's a big statue of the Christus and this is supposed to bring eternal peace between the two countries. When we flew over, the snow was very deep and there was a weather station built on the side of a mountain, opposite Aconcagua. In the winter they received their food from an aeroplane, a small two-passenger plane that would fly over and parachute food down to them. We saw a plane that had crashed, nose down, in the snow; apparently it had been caught in a down-draft and the pilot and co-pilot were killed in the crash. This was rather an ominous-looking thing to see! Altogether it was a very impressive, exciting flight.[10]

The story of 'Petey' and the experience of the South American group made a fortuitous combination and Petey became Pedro, the mail plane. In later years Joe Grant shrugged off his part in the adaptation process: 'It just fit, because from the Rockies to the Andes was a short jump as far as we were concerned.'[11]

In spring 1942, the decision was made to incorporate the first four shorts (*Donald at Lake Titicaca*, *Pedro*, *El Gaucho Goofy* and *Aquarela do Brasil*) into a single feature: *Saludos Amigos*. For the sake of unity, some of the 16 mm live action footage – originally shot only as vacation pictures or reference material – was brought into the film to serve as a linking device. This involved many hours of screening, selecting and editing the shots and writing narration to fit them. (At the same time, more of the same material was assembled in a promotional short called *South of the Border with Disney*.) Meanwhile, work was going forward on the next package of films which, it had now been determined, would include some sequences on Mexico. This turned out to be more difficult than the original South American project, for various reasons. Disney artists made not one but three trips to Mexico, and at least one of these, the second in March 1943, was beset with problems. In a memo to Disney, Ferguson detailed some of them: hotel reservations were not honoured, an attempted recording session was delayed and impaired by a dispute between the radio musicians' union and the studio musicians' union, and requests for raw film stock were delayed by administrative processing.[12] Perhaps because of such difficulties, the studio's Mexican material came from a variety of sources. In addition to the Disney artists' trips to Mexico, a number of Mexican performers visited California to appear in scenes that would eventually be used in the finished films. Research material also came from diverse sources. In September 1943, on the eve of the third Mexican trip, the staff even screened eight recent 'FitzPatrick TravelTalks', borrowed from MGM, which dealt with various aspects of Mexico.

While this was happening, some miscellaneous shorts that had originated with the South American trip were being completed and released as separate films. Interestingly, when such films were divorced from the package features and absorbed into Disney's regular schedule of shorts, they tended to lose much of their South American identification and become more generic. Perhaps the best example is a film that went into production in February 1942 with the working title *Down Uruguay Way*, 'using the River Plata as the locale'.[13] Eventually it was released in January 1944 as *The Pelican and the Snipe* and the finished film reveals little obvious connection with South America except that the leading characters are named Monte and Video! Similarly, *Pluto and the Armadillo* was conceived in 1941 as a Brazilian story, possibly making use of Mary Blair's watercolours. By the time of its release in February 1943, this short – the only one of the Latin American films to include either Pluto or the studio's figurehead, Mickey Mouse – was so vague in its setting that it could easily have been made without going on the tour at all.

The second Latin American feature evolved into the film that we know today as *The Three Caballeros*. Of course, the finished film shows no signs of the difficulties involved in its production, nor – save for its eye-popping variety of tone and content – the widely diverse sources of the material that appears in it. Jack Kinney later recalled that the scenes ostensibly showing bathing beauties on the beach at Acapulco were actually shot in the parking lot of the Disney studio: 'They brought in the sand and laid it out, but it had been raining and the sand was wet. And it was cold; this took place in January or February and the poor girls had goose flesh all over.'[14] Here again, a great deal of material that had been created for the film was eventually discarded. Kinney mourned, in particular, the loss of two segments that had already been completed. *Xochimilco* was a little romance, set in the famous 'floating gardens' of the same name outside Mexico City. *Paricutín* would have been an extremely topical story. In early 1943, in the midst of the Disney group's visits to Mexico, a series of major eruptions there created a new volcano. It was given the name Paricutín and continued to erupt at sporadic intervals throughout the year. Kinney's story depicted a farmer who unwittingly finds himself with a crop planted on the side of the volcano. Like *Xochimilco*, *The Laughing Gaucho*, *Caxanga* and numerous other films, it was never released.

The Latin American project came full circle, in a sense, with the production of *Blame It On the Samba*. One of Ferguson's first memos to Disney, upon returning to the studio in 1941, suggested that a Brazilian musical short be built around the samba[15] and now, more than five years later, the idea was carried out. The live action footage of Ethel Smith was photographed under the direction of Ken Anderson in February 1947, while Clyde Geronimi directed animation featuring Donald Duck, Joe Carioca and the Aracuan from *Three Caballeros*. *Blame It On the Samba* was eventually used as a segment in the package feature *Melody Time*, which was released in the late summer of 1948, ending the Disney studio's Latin American venture – a venture whose tremendous scope can only be suggested in a paper of this length. It had produced a wide variety of popular motion pictures, but the story behind their production was quite as fascinating as anything that appeared on the screen.

This is a slightly revised version of a paper presented at the 1989 SAS Conference.

Acknowledgement

Grateful acknowledgement is hereby made to the interviewees who spoke with me, to Bonnie Ferguson Brown for the generous use of materials in her collection and to the staff of the Disney Archives for access to their resources.

Further reading

Because of space restrictions in the writing of this paper, I tried to omit material which was readily available from other sources. Since writing this paper I have embarked on further research, with the intent of producing a book-length account of the Disney studio's Latin American project.

In the meantime, an elaborate laserdisc set has been released by Disney Home Video, not only featuring *Saludos Amigos* and *The Three Caballeros* in the CAV format, but also offering such exciting rarities as an Argentine newsreel of the 1941 South American tour, and reconstructions of *Caxanga* and *The Laughing Gaucho*.

In addition, to readers who are unfamiliar with the subject and who desire further information, I recommend Richard Shale, *Donald Duck Joins Up: The Walt Disney Studio During World War II* (Ann Arbor, Michigan: UMI Research Press, 1982), chapters 4 and 9. Both chapters are abridged in *Funnyworld*, 17 (Fall 1977): 15–18 and 29–32.

Notes

1. Jack Kinney to author, 14 September 1989.
2. Bill Cottrell to author, 24 September 1989.
3. Joe Grant to author, 18 September 1989.
4. Date taken from a telegram from Norm Ferguson to his wife.
5. Date taken from a telegram from Norm Ferguson to his wife.
6. Bill Cottrell to author.
7. Bill Cottrell to author.
8. All sailing dates from ship's schedule, annotated by Norm Ferguson.
9. Norm Ferguson's handwritten comment in the margin of an unidentified newspaper clipping, sent to his family.
10. Bill Cottrell to author.
11. Joe Grant to author.
12. Memo, Norm Ferguson to Walt Disney, 23 July 1943.
13. Memo, Norm Ferguson to Walt Disney, 12 January 1942.
14. Jack Kinney to author.
15. Memo, Norm Ferguson to Walt Disney, 14 November 1941.

Notes on the contributors

ROBIN ALLAN began his career as a typographical designer before working overseas writing, producing and presenting English programmes on TV for The British Council. He is now a freelance lecturer in English, Drama and Film and lectures for the University of Manchester and Keele, as well as for his own theatre-going bus service, *InterTheatre*. He has made a special study of the work of Walt Disney over a number of years and has lectured on this subject in England, Scotland and the United States, where he has been invited to lecture at the Disney Studio to its new generation of artists. He was awarded his PhD on *Walt Disney and Europe* by the University of Exeter in 1993.

SHARON COUZIN is an experimental filmmaker who has won numerous awards at international festivals and screenings. Since 1978, she has taught at the School of the Art Institute of Chicago where she has been the Chair of the Film Department for the last ten years and teaches film production and film history. In 1992, she received a Fulbright Fellowship to research and film a project on Ritual Space and Practice in Japan.

ANDREW DARLEY is senior lecturer in Animation Studies at The Surrey Institute of Art & Design. He recently completed a doctoral degree at the University of Sussex on the role of the computer in contemporary visual culture.

HARVEY DENEROFF founded the Society for Animation Studies and then went on to be the first editor of *Animation World Magazine*, Animation World Network's on-line journal, from which he recently stepped down to concentrate on his own projects, including an industry news report. He frequently works as a consultant (most recently to Microsoft's Softimage division) and is currently finishing his first book on a new Don Bluth animated feature, *The Art of Anastasia*.

PHILIP KELLY DENSLOW is an animator, writer and multimedia designer living in the Atlanta, Georgia (USA) area. A graduate of the UCLA Animation Workshop and former technical supervisor of that program, he has written articles for several animation publications and served as the editor of the *Society for Animation Studies Newsletter*. His short film *Madcap* (1991) was awarded First Prizes at the L.A. Animation Celebration and Ann Arbor Film Festival and he was the Interactive Designer on the award-winning CD-ROM, *Forrest Gump: Music, Artists, and Times* (1995). You can find out even more about Phil at the Internet web site www.webcom.com/kellyd/

LESLIE FELPERIN is Deputy Editor of Sight and Sound and an Associate Lecturer in Film Studies at Middlesex University.

MICHAEL FRIERSON is an associate professor at the University of North Carolina at Greensboro. He received his PhD from the University of Michigan in 1986 and teaches film production and theory in the Department of Broadcasting/Cinema and Theatre. He has served as an associate producer for Mardi Gras 1992, a high-definition television program for NHK in Japan. With his wife Martha Garrett he has produced short clay animations for Children's Television Workshop and Nickelodeon. His book, *Clay Animation: American Highlights 1908 to the Present* won the 1995 McLaren–Lambart Book Award for Animation Scholarship. Currently, he is completing an hour-long film documentary on the life and work of New Orleans photographer Clarence John Laughlin.

J.B. KAUFMAN is a film historian with a strong interest in early Disney animation. Since presenting the enclosed paper on Disney's Latin American films, he has written the historical text for the collectors' edition laserdisc of *Saludos Amigos* and *The Three Caballeros*. He is co-author with Russell Merritt of *Walt in Wonderland: The Silent Films of Walt Disney*, and the two are currently completing a second book on the Silly Symphonies.

SANDRA LAW lives in Calgary, Alberta, Canada where her interest in animation has been fostered through workshops and courses offered by a local film co-operative. She has completed one film, *Eve-olve!*, a clay-animated film that is a critique of social Darwinism, and has begun work on a second film entitled, *RamJane*. Her background in the biological sciences and anthropology receives expression in her films.

MARK LANGER is an Associate Professor of Film Studies in the School for Studies in Art and Culture at Carleton University in Ottawa, Canada. He has been a contributor to such scholarly journals as *Cinema Journal*, *Screen*, *Animation Journal*, *Film History*, *Wide Angle*, and *The Velvet Light Trap*. Langer is an Associate Editor of *Film History* and serves on the Editorial Board of *Animation Journal*. He has programmed animation retrospectives for the Museum of Modern Art in New York, the Ottowa International Animation Festival, La Cinémathèque française and other archives, museums and festivals internationally. In addition to his work on animation, Mark Langer publishes on topics concerning American cinema, the work of Robert Flaherty and issues of historiography.

TERRY LINDVALL received his doctorate from the University of Southern California (USC). Terry has taught film for fifteen years. He is currently president of Regent University in Virginia Beach, Virginia, USA and has published *Surprised By Laughter: The Comic Spirit of C.S. Lewis* and numerous scholarly and popular articles on animation, film and religion.

MATTHEW MELTON graduated with a PhD from Regent University and is currently Chair of the Communications Deparment at Lee University in Cleveland, Tennessee, USA.

LEV MANOVICH was born in Moscow in 1960 and is a theorist and critic of new media. He has lectured widely at major international festivals and symposiums on electronic art, including Siggraph, ISEA, Ars Electronica and Multimediale. He holds an MA in experimental psychology and a PhD in Visual and Cultural Studies. Since

1993 he has been an Assistant Professor at the University of Maryland where he teaches the theory and history of media, computer graphics and computer animation. In 1995, he was awarded a Mellon Fellowship in Art Criticism by California Institute of the Arts to work on a book on realism in digital media.

WILLIAM MORITZ received his doctorate from the University of Southern California. His 34 films (experimental, documentary and animation) have been screened internationally. His publications include work on Oskar Fischinger and James Whitney, as well as the Fleischer Brothers, Bruce Conner, Experimental Film Before 1950, The Aesthetics of Computer Graphics and The History of Visual Music. He contributed to the new *Oxford History of Cinema*. He has lectured at film festivals and conferences (including Siggraph) around the world and was guest curator for several Art exhibitions including *The Spiritual in Art* and *'Degenerate' Art* at Los Angeles County Museum of Art. In 1993, the Royal Academy of the Netherlands awarded him a lifetime achievement trophy for service to Visual Music, and he was recently awarded the Anthology Film Archive Award for his work on restoring early animation films. He is currently working on an half-hour animated film, *All My Lost Lovers*, on a grant from the American Film Institute. He is also a poet and playwright. At the California Institute of the Arts he teaches the Histories of Experimental and Animation film, as well as Creative Writing and filmmaking courses.

MICHAEL O'PRAY is Reader in Visual Theory at the School of Art and Design, University of East London and a contributing editor of *Sight and Sound*. He edited *Andy Warhol: Film Factory* (1989), *The British Avant-Garde Film 1926–1995: An Anthology of Writings* (1966) and co-edited *Inside the Pleasure Dome: The Films of Kenneth Anger* (1989). His book *Derek Jarman: Dreams of England* was published in 1996. He has also written extensively on the Czech animator Jan Svankmajer.

JAYNE PILLING is a freelance film programmer, sometimes journalist and translator, who also writes and teaches on film and animation, currently at the Royal College of Art in London. As an editor and contributor, her publications include *Ladislas Starewicz* (1984); *That's Not All Folks, A Primer in Cartoonal Knowledge* (1984); *Comedy – Italian style* (1987); *Women & Animation: A Compendium* (1992); *Cartoons and the Movies* (bilingual edition, 1997), and co-edited *Into the Pleasure Dome: The Films of Kenneth Anger* (1989). Before going freelance, she worked for several years at the British Film Institute in film programming and distribution, and initiated the animation series for BFI's Connoisseur video label. She was Director of the International Animation Festival, Cardiff 1994; and contributes programmes to a number of international festivals as well as cinemas in the United Kingdom. She recently made a six-part television series on European animation for UK television. Currently director of the British Animation Awards, she can be contacted at jsp@easynet.co.uk

SIMON PUMMELL has made many short films, in various combinations of live action and animation for a variety of British television and film funders. They include *Surface Tension, Secret Joy, Stain, Temptation of Sainthood, Rose Red* and *Butcher's Hook*. The films have won numerous awards at major film festivals and have been broadcast internationally as well as in the United Kingdom. Retrospectives of his work have been screened at a number of international film festivals. He is currently developing his first feature film *Dogfight* based on a short story by William Gibson.

LUCA RAFFAELLI is an Italian writer living in Rome. He has written articles for magazines and newspapers about animated films and three books: 'Pesce Pinolo e

Albero Armando', a novel published by Stampa Alternativa; 'Le anime disegnate', 'Les Ames Dessinées', 1996) and 'Il Fumetto', about comics, published by Il saggiatore/Flammarion. He writes screenplays for animated series, and songs and television programs for children. He is Artistic Director of Cartoombria, the International Festival of Animated Films in Italy.

STEVE WEINER was born in Wisconsin, the United States, in 1947. He graduated the University of California, Berkeley, with a degree in literature and writing. He received a master's degree in animation production at the University of Southern California. He has previously written on Jan Lenica, and has published a novel *The Museum of Love* (1993). He has taught the history of animation at Emily Carr Institute of Art and Design in Vancouver, Canada, where he lives with his wife. He is currently working on a novel.

PAUL WELLS is Principal Lecturer in Film and Media Studies and Course Leader at the School of Arts and Humanities, De Montfort University. He has written extensively on animation and on film and media, with particular reference to comedy, horror and popular culture and has made a large number of radio programmes across this range of topics. He recently edited a special issue dedicated to animation of the art journal *Art & Design*. He developed the first course module on Critical Approaches for the Media Studies degree programme, on which is based his forthcoming book, *Understanding Animation*. He is currently writing a book on British animation.

List of SAS Conference papers

The following information derives from the SAS newsletters.

FIRST ANNUAL SAS CONFERENCE (1989)

University of California, Los Angeles, October 26–29

Aesthetic problems

Leskosky, Richard J. (University of Illinois – Urbana-Campaign), **Repetition in Animated Films**.

McNamara, Martin (San Francisco State University), **Shot Duration in Animation**.

Disney

Allan, Robin (InterTheatre, Stockport, England), **European Influences on Disney: The Formative Years Before** *Snow White*.

Jarvik, Laurence (UCLA), **The Photographic Ecstacy:** *The Three Caballeros* **– The Baia Sequence: A Close Analysis**.

Mayerson, Mark (Toronto), **Right and Wrong – Morality and the Story Structure of** *Pinocchio*.

Furniss, Maureen Ruth (University of Southern California), **An Analysis of live action/Animation in Disney's** *The Three Caballeros* **and** *Mary Poppins*.

Kaufman, J.B. (Wichita), **Norm Ferguson and the Latin American Films of Walt Disney**.

Merritt, Karen (University of California), **Falling and Flying: Dopey Meets Horatio Alger in** *Dumbo*.

Merritt, Russell (Oakland, CA), **Analysis of** *Pinocchio*.

Towards a theory of animation

Cholodenko, Alan (University of Sydney), **Framing the Framing of Animation**.

Mays, Peter (Second Wave Software, Topanga, California), **Towards a Theory of Animation: Real-time Computer Animation as a New Art Form**.

Yoresh, Y. (Bezalel Academy of Arts & Design), **Animation – Ethics and Esthetics**.

Early television

DelGaudio, Sybil (Hofstra University), **The Cel Meets the Sell: Early Television Commercial**

Animation.

Frierson, Michael (University of North Carolina, Greensboro), **Art Clokey and the Rebirth of Clay Animation**.

European independents

Gizicki, Marcin (Rhode Island School of Design/Polish Filmmakers Union), **Metaphorical Meanings of Piotr Kamler's** *Chronopolis* **and Jan Lenica's** *Labyrinth*.

Silberman, Robert (University of Minnesota, Minneapolis), **The Brothers Quay, Bruno Schulz and the Middle Europe of the Mind**.

Weiner, Steve (Davis, California), **Jan Lenica's** *Landscape*.

The world upside down: The poetics of the animated cartoons

Jones, Chuck (Chuck Jones Productions, Costa Mesa, CA), **The Joy of Animation**.

Kenner, Hugh (Johns Hopkins University), **Modernism in Animation**.

Aspects of independent and institutional filmmaking

Dobson, Terence (University of Cantebury, New Zealand), **Confluence and Conflict in Norman McLaren's** *Synchromy*.

Moritz, William (California Institute of the Arts), **Walter Ruttmann, Viking Eggeling – Restoring the Esthetics of Early Experimental Animation**.

Walz, Gene (University of Manitoba), **Animation at the National Film Board of Canada on the Eve of its Fiftieth Birthday**.

Labour-management problems

Deneroff, Harvey (Los Angeles), **The Terrytoons Strike**.

Langer, Mark (Carlton University), **Standardisation of Production Practices in the 1930s**.

Smoodin, Eric (American University), **Whistling While They Work: Labour, Cartoons and Popular Journalism During the 1940s**.

Aspects of independent animation

McLaughlin, Dan (UCLA), **Independent Animation in the Magic Kingdom: Between a Rock and Hollywood**.

Pitt, Suzan (Harvard University), **Animation and the Creative Process**.

Priestley, Joanna (Oregon Art Institute), **Themes in Contemporary Women's Animation**.

Narrative structure and animation: Influences

Curtis, Scott (University of Iowa), **Defining the Frame of the Figural: Comic Strips and American Silent Animation**.

Hoxter, Julian (University of East Anglia, England), **Garbage Bags for the American Dream? Post-Modern Narratives at the End of Cinema and Animation**.

Lyons, Jonothan (Los Angeles), **Comedy, Clowns and Cartoons**.

Schenkel, Talia (Baruch College), **Yiddish Folklore in Animation**.

SECOND ANNUAL SAS CONFERENCE (1990)

Carleton University, Ottawa, Canada, October 5–7

Modes of production

Attallah, Paul (Carleton), **Animation and Canadian Television**.

Furness, Maureen (University of Southern California), **Life in Post-Modernism: It's Prime Time for the Simpsons.**

Lorenzo, William (Brooklyn), **Foreign-Toons: An Examination of Foreign Theatrical Animation on Early US Television.**

Canon formation

Joubert-Laurencin, Herve (Université Lumière Lyon II), **La canonisation du film d'animation.**

Wassenaar, Michael (Madison, Wisconsin), **A Canon Without a Discipline?**

Ehrlich, David (Vermont & New Hampshire Arts Councils), **Experimental Animation as Formal Narrative and Its Proper Role Within the Traditional American Festival.**

Studies of filmmakers

Gizycki, Marcin (Rhode Island School of Design), **Stefan and Franciszka Themerson: Unknown Masters of Experimental Animation.**

Mayerson, Mark (Toronto), **Jim Tyer: The Animator Who Broke the Rules.**

Walz, Gene (University of Manitoba), **The Animated Richard Condie.**

Moritz, William (California Institute of the Arts), **Norman McLaren in Context.**

Modes of production: Flipbook, multiplane and puppet

Leskosky, Richard (University of Illinois at Urbana-Campaign), **Flip-books: History and Use.**

Hayes, Ruth (California Institute of the Arts), **Flip-books: Animation in the Free Zone.**

McNamara, Martin (San Francisco State), **The Quest for Depth: Classic and Contemporary Multiplane Animation.**

Azerad, Michael (National Film Board of Canada), **The Brain – a Multi-Axis, Location/Studio Camera/Subject, Robotic Motion Control System.**

Ethnicity and gender

Page, Judy (University of Wisconsin, Madison), **Feminine Gender as Animated Reality in an Irrational World: Why Inspector Clouseau's Panther Is Pink.**

Lawling, John (Regent University), **Hollywood Shuffle: Images of African-Americans in the Animated Film.**

Wallace, Donald (Carleton), **Fleischer Animation and Representations of Black Music.**

Fleischer Studios, Inc.

Deneroff, Harvey (Los Angeles), **The Fleischer Studios Go To Miami.**

Frierson, Michael (University of North Carolina, Greensboro), **Analysis of *Modeling*.**

Langer, Mark (Carleton University), **From Fleischer to Famous: A Study in Institutional Failure and Reorganisation.**

Modes of production: The computer

McLaughlin, Dan (University California, Los Angeles), **The Retooling of Animation: Is the Tool Now the Message?**

Dutrisac, Julie (National Film Board of Canada), **Animaster.**

Tafler, David (Philadelphia College of Art & Design), **Moving Backward Into the Future: The Legacy of Computer Animation.**

Manovich, Lev (University of Rochester), **Grids, Stars and Glows: Toward an Analysis of Style of Computer Animation in Television.**

Theories and aesthetic questions

Prochorov, Anatoly (Pilot Animation Studio), **On Animation Technologies Metaphysics.**

Macmillan, Robert (Ottowa), **Einstein, Levy-Bruhl and Disney: Totemism in the Disney Cartoon**.

Sifianos, George (Paris), **La représentation due mouvement aux peintures des grottes préhistoriques et les origines du cinéma d'animation**.

Herbert, Pierre (National Film Board of Canada), **Présence et représentation du corps en cinéma d'animation**.

National cinemas

Carrière, Louise (CEGEP Vieux Montréal), **L'animation à l'Office National du film du Canada** *et al.* **protestation (1941–89)**.

Gercheva, Krassimira (Bulgarian Institute of Cinema, Theatre and Television), **Bulgarian Animation Before and After Glasnost**.

Mackássy, Kati (Pannonia Film), **Animation and Politics in Hungary**.

Marinchevska, Nadezhda (Institute of Art Studies, Bulgarian Academy of Sciences), **The Bulgarian Way of Animation and the Alternative Destination of Henri Koulev's** *Tale of the Road*.

Narrative strategies and mechanisms

Bouse, Derek (University of Pensylvania), **True-Life Fantasies: Animated Features and the Development of Live Action Wildlife Films**.

Lindvall, Terry (Regent University), **Lively and Animated Discourse: Self-Reflexivity and the Mere Cartoon**.

Straw, William (Carleton), **Decorative Entrances: The Animated Credit Sequence in American live action Comedies of the Early 1960s**.

George, Russell (University of Kent), **Narrative Repetition in the Classical Cartoon: Poe, Lacan and** *Rabbit Seasoning*.

Modes of production: Advertising films

Strøm, Gunnar (Møre og Romsdal College), **Norwegian Animated Cinema Commercials From the 1920s and 1930s**.

Cohen, Karl (San Francisco), **Development of the Animated TV Commercial, 1944–49**.

DelGaudio, Sybil (Hofstra University), **Marketing Marky: The Maypo Campaign and Other Storyboard Stories**.

THIRD ANNUAL SAS CONFERENCE (1991)

Rochester Institute of Technology, New York, 4–6 October

Allan, Robin (InterTheatre, Stockport, England)), *Fantasia* **revisited**.

Bishko, Leslie (Ohio State University), **The Use of Labian Analysis for the Discussion of Computer Animation**.

Carr, Steve (University of Texas at Austin), **Coon or Cohen? Animation and the Transmutable Ethnic Stereotype**.

Cartwright, Lisa (University of Rochester/Brown University), **'The Ultimate Force Multiplier': Army Aviation Training Flight Simulation Missions and the Decline of the Referential in Mass Media**.

Chisholm, Brad (University of Nevada, Las Vegas), **Stooping** *The Simpsons* **(and Looking at them Again)**.

Cholodenko, Alan (University of Sydney), **Speculations on the Animatic Automation**.

Clancy, Keith W. (University of Sydney), **In the Blink of an Eye: Animation and the Division of the Present**.

Cohen, Karl (San Francisco), **The Investigation of Alleged Communists in the Animation Industry**.

Couzin, Sharon (School of the Art Institute of Chicago), **The Woman's Voice in Contemporary American Animation**.

De Cordova, Richard (DePaul University), **The Mickey in Macy's Window: Childhood, Consumerism and Disney Animation**.

DelGaudio, Sybil (Hofstra University), **Acts of Faith: The Works of Faith Hubley**.

Deneroff, Harvey (Los Angeles), **Are We Mice or Men?: The 1941 Disney Strike**.

Frierson, Michael (University of North Carolina, Greensboro), **Will Vinton and Clay Animation**.

Furniss, Maureen (University of Southern California), **American Independant Animation, 1945–1965**.

Gentile, Phillip (University of Southern Mississippi), **Line, Metamorphosis and the Modernist Impulse in the Films of Eggeling, McLaren and Breer**.

George, Russell (University of Kent at Canterbury), **Primitivity in the Cartoon Text: The Language of Puns**.

Heil, R. Douglas (University of Wisconsin, Oshkosh), **Visualising Subversion: Shaping Form to Content at the Walter Lantz Studio**.

Kennedy, Gary (Carleton University), *Cartoon All Stars To The Rescue*: **The New Recruits in the Drug War and the Animated World of Consumerism**.

Langer, Mark (Carleton University), **Innovation and Industrial Competition: The Stereotypical and Multiplane Processes**.

Leskosky, Richard J. (University of Illinois, Urbana), **Two-State Animation: The Thaumatrope and Its Spin-Offs**.

McLaughlin, Dan (University of California, Los Angeles), **The Visual in Disney's** *Peter Pan*.

McLaughlin, Mary Serbia (California State University, Los Angeles), **The World Reviewed: A Phenomenological Reading of Pat O'Neil's** *Water and Power*.

McMillan, Robert (Ottawa), **Transformations and Totemism: Bugs Bunny/Levi Strauss and Bateson**.

Manovich, Lev (University of Rochester), **Effects of the Real in Computer Animation**.

Ohmer, Susan (New York University), **Plenty of Action and Just Enough Romance': Debates Around Disney's Adaptation of** *Peter Pan*.

Prokhorov, Anatoly (Pilot Animation Studio, Moscow), **Structure of Emil Cohl's Films: Variational Forms on Screen**.

Roger, Andrew (National Archives of Canada, Ottawa), **John Grierson Meets Donald Duck: The National Film Board of Canada and the Disney Studios**.

Rubin, Martin (Dallas), **Rise and Fall of the Spot-Gag Cartoon**.

Smoodin, Eric (American University), **A Night at the Movies: Ideology, the Film Bill and Audience Construction**.

Staven, Karl (Ithaca College), **Collaborative Animated Films: Less Than the Sum of Their Parts?**

Vartanian, Carolyn Reed (University of Southern California), **Animated Characters and Commercials**.

Wallace, Anne D. (University of Southern Mississippi), **Legibility, Literacy and Authority: Bakshi's Reality Codes in** *The Lord of the Rings*.

Walz, Gene (University of Manitoba), **Character Design in Animation: The Case of Charlie Thorson**.

Williams, J.P. (Georgia Southern University), **Lois Lane and the War Effort: Narrative and Gender Construction in** *Superman*.

FOURTH ANNUAL SAS CONFERENCE (1992)

California Institute of the Arts, Valencia, California, 23–25 October

Teaching animation

Grush, Byron, **Digital Technology and Teaching Animation.**
Mones-Hattal, Barbara, **Figure to Field – Computer Animation.**
Schwartz, Gary, **Teaching Animation to Prisoners.**

Animation theory

Denslow, Phil (Atlanta, Georgia), **What is Animation and Who Needs to Know?**
Wright, Prescott, **The ASIFA Definition of Animation.**
Van Baerle, Susan, **An Expanded Definition for Animation for the Virtual Reality Era.**
Williams, Suzanne, **Toward Establishing Assumptions and Theoretical Framework for Value Analysis of Animated Texts.**
Klein, Norman, **Animation in Real Space.**

Applied methodology

Ohmer, Susan, **Towards an Industrial History of American Animation: 1940s Economic and Structural Changes.**
McNamara, Marty, **Script Evolution and Story Adaptation.**
Kennedy, Gary, *Young Sherlock Holmes*: **Popular Hero and the Technological Imagination.**
Langer, Mark (Carleton University), *Ren & Stimpy,* **Animatophilia and the Trash Aesthetic.**
Deneroff, Harvey (Los Angeles), **John Matthews' Children's Animation.**
Gurevich, Michael, **Animopolis or Urbanimation?**

Historical perspectives

McLaughlin, Dan, **Animation Before Film.**
Leskosky, Richard, **Phenakistoscopes.**
Frierson, Michael (University of North Carolina), **Early Pioneers in Clay Animation.**
Ferriter, Christine, *Joie de Vivre,* **Art Historical Context.**
Dill, Jane, **Jules Engel: Film Artist.**
Furniss, Maureen, **Abstraction in Film: Techniques and Relationships.**
Gene Walz (University of Manitoba), **Frédéric Back.**
DelGaudio, Sybil (Hofstra University, NY), **Blues, Breaks, Lines and Shapes: Jazz and Animation at the Hubley Studio.**

Animation propaganda

Carr, Steve, **Stereotypes in 1930s Cartoons.**
Mastronardi, Michael, **Bugs Bunny and FDR Go To War.**
Penkoff, Diane, **Slipping 'em a Mickey? The Enchantment of Alcohol in Disney Animated Films.**
Knapp, Trischa, **Popular Political Culture: Rocky & Bullwinkle and the Cold War.**
Cohen, Karl, **Methods of Censorship for Animated Features and TV.**

Women and animation

Beams, Mary, **Subverting Time: A Woman's Perspective.**
Moritz, William (California Institute of the Arts), **The Genius of Lotte Reiniger.**
Allan, Robin (InterTheatre, Stockport, England), **Sylvia Holland, Disney Artist.**

Vartanian, Carolyn, **We're Not Bad, We're Just Drawn That Way – Animated Women:** *Cool World* **and** *Roger Rabbit*.

Priestley Joanna, **Faith Hubley: Creating a Healing Mythology**.

FIFTH ANNUAL SAS CONFERENCE (1993)

Surrey Institute of Art and Design, Surrey, England, 26–28 November

History and culture

Bendazzi, Giannalberto (Italy), *La Rosa Di Bagdad*: **The first full length Italian animated feature film**.

Orientalism

Sharman, Leslie (United Kingdom), **The Thief of Buena Vista: Disney's** *Aladdin* **and the Orientalism Debate**.

White, Timothy, & Winn, Emmett (Singapore), **Allah versus Disney in the South China Sea**.

The body

McLaughlin, Dan (United States), **Beauty and Beastiality**.

Pummell, Simon (London), **Francis Bacon and Walt Disney Revisited**.

Wells, Paul (De Montfort University), **Body Consciousness in the Films of Jan Svankmajer**.

Technology

Carles, Edwin (Belgium), **Old Techniques in New Technologies**.

Guldin, Jere (United States), **Processed by Cinecolor: The Use of the Color Process in Animation**.

Leskosky, Richard (United States), **Zoetrope: History and Uses**.

History

Williams, Suzanne H. (United States), **The Many Incarnations of Two American Superheroes**.

O'Brien, Kevin (United States), **Chuck Jones/MGM**.

Russ, Paul (United States), **Felix the Cat as Chaplin's Cartoon Persona**.

Wagner, Hart (United States), **Tom Death and Jerry Saviour: Chuck Jones Haunted Mouse and the Harrowing of Hell**.

Williams, David (United Kingdom), **Sniffles – The Mouse that Chuck Built**.

Technology and computers

Darley, Andy (Surrey Institute of Art & Design), **Computer Animation: Second Order Realism & Post-Modern Aesthetics**.

Wright, Richard (United Kingdom), **Visual Technology and the Poetics of Knowledge**.

Aesthetics

Kirkham, Pat (United Kingdom), **Science, Technology, History and Philosophy Made Easy and Accessible**.

Noake, Roger (United Kingdom), **The End in Sight: Historical Narrative in Animation and Posthistoire**.

O'Connell, Kenneth (United States), **The Missing UPA Films: Cartoons and Modern Art**.

O'Pray, Mike (University East London), **Eisenstein, Stokes and Disney: Animation and the Omnipotence of Thought**.

Culture and identity

Allan, Robin (InterTheatre, Stockport, England), **Gustav Tenggren and European Influences on Early Disney Feature Animation.**

Egbert Barten (Netherlands), **Animating for the Enemy: Animation Films in Holland 1940–45.**

Knapp, Trischa (United States), *The New Spirit* **Income Taxes: Donald Duck, Persuasion and World War II.**

Moritz, William (California Institute of the Arts), *The Idea* : **Bartosch & Masereel.**

SIXTH ANNUAL SAS CONFERENCE (1994)

San Francisco State University, 6–9 October

International abstracts

Noake, Roger (Surrey Institute of Art & Design), **The Witchetty Grub – Len Lye's Model of Communication.**

Darley, Andrew (Surrey Institute of Art & Design), **The British Documentary Tradition and New Animated Non-Fiction.**

Bendazzi, Giannalberto (Italy), **Osvaldo Cavandoli: A Life on the Line.**

Langer, Mark (Carleton University, Canada), **Why the Atom is Our Friend: Disney and State Interests.**

Hu, Gigi (Singapore), **Adaption of Traditional Ethnic Narratives into Half-English.**

Williams, David (England), **The** *Fantasia* **That Wasn't Quite.**

Law, Sandra (University of Calgary), **Putting Themselves in the Picture – Female Images in the Work of Selected Women Amimators in the UK.**

Walz, Gene (University of Manitoba), **Charlie Thorson and the Fleischer Brothers Studio at Twilight.**

Knight, Laura (Jackdaw Media, Liverpool, England), **New British Documentary: Zoetrope Artists.**

Pilling, Jayne (British Film Institute), **Genre Redefinition: Redocumenting the Real.**

Palmer, Roger (LaTrobe University, Australia), **Cultural Difference in Reading American Animation Down Under.**

Gurevich, Mikhail (Russia/United States), **Literary Poetics and Animation Stylistics.**

Barten, Egbert, & Peters, Mette (Netherlands), **Joseph Goebbels' Efforts to Create an 'Anti-Disney Animation Umbrella' in Occupied Europe.**

American abstracts

Engel, Jules (Cal Arts), **Experimental Animation: Art in Motion.**

Mikulak, William (University of Pensylvania), **Bugs and Oscar: A History of Animation Exhibition Practices at the Museum of Modern Art, NY.**

DelGaudio, Sybil (Hofstra University, NY), **Journey to the Mystery Place: Indigenous Forms in Faith Hubley's** *Cloudland* **and** *Tall-Time Tales.*

Cohen, Karl (San Francisco), **Importance of the FBI's Walt Disney File to Animation Scholars.**

Rubin, Jon (Brooklyn), **Preview of 'Cartoon Chronicles' CD-ROM.**

McLaughlin, Dan (UCLA), **Animating Interactive Multimedia.**

Gorringe, Carrie (Seattle), **Blues in the Night(club): The Characterisation of Female Sexuality and Wartime Tensions in** *Coal Black an de Sebben Dwarfs* **and** *Red Hot Riding Hood.*

Griffin, Sean (Los Angeles), **I'll Give You Such a Pinch: The 'Queerness' of Animation.**

Sandler, Kevin (New York University), **Gendered Evasion: Bugs Bunny in Drag.**

Blonder, Roger (UCLA), **Mosquitoes, Dinosaurs and the Image-ination.**

Frierson, Michael (University of North Carolina, Greensboro), **A Close Reading of** *A Nightmare Before Christmas*.

Leskosky, Richard (University of Illinois), **Animation by the Side of the Road: Fixed Art/Moving Spectators**.

Williams, Suzanne (Trinity University), **Business, Regulatory and Social Structures Leading to Narrative Forms in Contemporary American Animation**.

Moritz, William (California Institute of the Arts), **Narrative Strategies in Borowczyk/Lenica's** *Home*, **Priit Pärn's** *Le Déjeuner sur l'Herbe* **and Yori Norstein's** *Tale of Tales*.

Staven, Karl (New York), **Anijamming: Thematic Devices of a Burgeoning Sub-genre**.

Morse, Deanne (Grand Valley State University), **Evolution in Computer Animation Art and Design in Siggraph 1994**.

McNamara, Martin (San Francisco), **Animated John Henry: Race and Gender Subtexts in Heroic Legend**.

Deneroff, Harvey (Los Angeles), **Structural Changes in American Animation Relating to Employment Patterns, 1937–1994**.

Ohmer, Susan (CUNY/College of Staten Island), **Myth and Marketing: Disney Production Documentaries**.

SEVENTH SAS CONFERENCE 1995

University of North Carolina, 29 September to 1 October

Disney

Sweeney, Gael (Syracuse University), **'What Do You Want Me to Do, Dress in Drag and Do the Hula?': Pumbea and Timon's Alternative Life Style Dilemma in Disney's** *The Lion King*.

Griffin, Sean (UCLA), **I'll Give You Such A Pinch: 'Queerying' Animation**.

Muwzea, Adwoa X. (Wayne State), **Discourse on Disney and the Legend of Sundiata**.

O'Brien, Pamela C. (Indiana University), **Everybody's Busy Bringing You a Disney Afternoon: The Creation of a Consumption Community**.

Ohmer, Suzan (CUNY), **On the Edge: Economic and Industrial Restraints on Animation in the 1940s**.

Williams, David (United Kingdom), **The Dope on Dopey: The Development of Character Personality in Disney's** *Snow White and the Seven Dwarfs*.

International movements

Darley, Andrew (Surrey Institute of Art & Design), **Recent Experimental, Nonfiction Animation in the UK**.

Lent, John A., **The Status of Animation in Asia Based on Interviews with Animators in China, Taiwan, Hong Kong, Thailand and India**.

Herron, Alastair (University of Ulster), **Practical Animation Yield in a Time of Restraint: An Irish Experience**.

McNamara, Martin, **Manipulation of Line in E. European Animation: Jankovics and Drajic**.

Authorship

Springfield, Susan (SMU), **Animation and German Expressionist Film: The Silhouette Films of Lotte Reiniger**.

Frierson, Michael (University of North Carolina), **Tim Burton's Early Works:** *Vincent* **and** *Frankenweenie*.

Noake, Roger (Surrey Inst.), **A World Enough and Time: George Dunning**.

Technology and animation

Crafton, Donald (UWM), **Mickey Mouse on Broadway**.

Furniss, Maureen (Chapman University), **The Effects of New Technologies on Made-for-Television Animation**.

Langer, Mark (Carleton University), **Ko-Ko in Context: A Study in Early Technology and Organisation**.

Leskosky, Richard (University of Illinois), **The Animation Inventions of Willis O'Brien**.

Bosworth, Leah M. (RIT), **An Analysis of Four Direct-On-Film Animators**.

Lindvall, Terry (Regent University), **Darker Shades of Animation History: Cartoon Images of African Americans**.

Cohen, Karl (San Francisco), **How Criticism Helped Bring About the End of Black Stereotypes in Animation**.

Animation and culture

DelGaudio, Sybil (Hofstra University), **If 'Truth' Be Told, Can 'Toons Tell It?: Animation and Documentary**.

Sandler, Kevin (NYU), **Gender-Mania: Anthropomorphization in Animaniacs**.

Raffaelli, Luca, **Conflicts Between Generations in the Animated Series**.

Animation and sponsorship

Saks, Ron (Columbus College), **The Making of Ted D. Bear: The Pitfalls of Client/Student/Classroom Relationship**.

Rapf, Maurice (Dartmouth College), **Animation in the Sponsored Film**.

EIGHTH ANNUAL SAS CONFERENCE (1996)

University of Wisconsin, Madison, September 25–29

Animation technology

Leskosky, Richard (University of Illinois, Urbana-Champaign), **The History and Technical Development of the Mutoscope**.

Shaffer, Carolyn (University of Wisconsin, Madison), **The Technology of Stop-Motion Animation**.

McLaughlin, Dan (UCLA), **The Role of Animation in the New Digital Media**.

Rubin, Jon (Cooper Union), **Animation and New Technology**.

Animation and other forms

Gurevich, Mikhail (University of Wisconsin, Madison), **Literary Animation: Problem/Image of the Text**.

Bishko, Leslie (Simon Fraser University), **Laban Analysis of Squash and Stretch**.

Furniss, Maureen, & Beal, Anthony (Chapman University), **The Adaptation of Japanese Animation Series for Use on American Television**.

Japanese animation

Desser, David (University of Illinois, Urbana-Champaign), **Why Anime?**

Bordwell, David (University of Wisconin, Madison), **Stylistic Transformations Between Live-Action and Animation in Japanese Cinema**.

Animation and 'live' cinema

Becker, Christine (University of Wisconsin, Madison), **Cross-Over Aesthetics: Frank Tashlin's Cartoons and Live Action Films**.

Sartin, Hank (Notre Dame University), **Anything For My Public: Bugs Bunny and the Problems of Cartoon Stardom**.

Representing the 'Other'

Mittell, Jason (University of Wisconsin, Madison), **I'm Not Black, I'm Just Drawn that Way**.

Frierson, Michael (University of North Carolina, Greensboro), **The Image of the Hillbilly in Warner Bros. Cartoons of the 1930s**.

Sieving, Christopher (University of Wisconsin, Madison), **Mouse Trouble: A Social Analysis of MGM's *Tom and Jerry* Cartoons**.

Animation and World War II

Okamoto, Rei (Temple University), **Ideological Representations and Cultural Myths in a Japanese Wartime Animated Film, Momotaro – Divine Troops of the Ocean**.

DelGaudio, Sybil (Hofstra University), **What Did You Do in the War, Daddy? Animation and WWII Training Films**.

Social constructions of cartoon stardom

Desilets, Michael, **International Migration of Cartoon Stars**.

Sartin, Hank, **Anything for My Public: Bugs Bunny and the Problem of Cartoon Stardom**.

International media

Lent, John A. (Temple University), **Korean Animation: The Boom Years**.

Camp, Brian (NYU/CUNY-TV), **The Evolution of Street Fighter: From Video Game to Spiritual Quest**.

Historical observations

Moritz, William (California Institute of the Arts), **Abstract Dreams**.

Williams, David R., **Animating the Inanimate**.

Codes of realism

Kreul, James (University of Wisconsin, Madison), **Why Composite Roger Rabbit?**

Fay, Jennifer (University of Wisconsin, Madison), **The Cameraman's Revenge: The Reality Status of the Image**.

Textual evolutions

Langer, Mark (Carleton University), **Northern Silhouettes: The Work of Bryant Fryer**.

Allan, Robin (InterTheatre, Stockport, England), **Alice in Disneyland: The Gestation and Creation of the Animated Feature Film**.